Doppelgänger Dilemmas

DOPPELGÄNGER DILEMMAS

Anglo-Dutch Relations
in Early Modern English
Literature and Culture

MARJORIE RUBRIGHT

PENN

UNIVERSITY OF PENNSYLVANIA PRESS

PHILADELPHIA

Published by
University of Pennsylvania Press
Philadelphia, Pennsylvania 19104-4112
www.upenn.edu/pennpress

Printed in the United States of America on acid-free paper
1 3 5 7 9 10 8 6 4 2

Library of Congress Cataloging-in-Publication Data
Rubright, Marjorie.
Doppelgänger dilemmas : Anglo-Dutch relations in early
modern English literature and culture / Marjorie
Rubright.—1st ed.
     p.   cm.
Includes bibliographical references and index.
ISBN 978-0-8122-4623-0 (hardcover : alk. paper)
    1. English literature—Early modern, 1500–1700—History
and criticism.   2. Great Britain—Relations—Netherlands.
3. Netherlands—Relations—Great Britain.   4. Cultural
relations in literature.   5. Ethnicity in literature.
6. National characteristics, English, in literature.   I. Title.
    PR408.I59R83   2014
    820.9′358492—dc23
                                                    2014011453

To Valerie with gratitude, for always inspiring

CONTENTS

Introduction

Double Dutch

Antipholus of Syracuse: And where stood Belgia, the Netherlands?
Dromio of Syracuse: Oh, sir, I did not look so low.
   —William Shakespeare, *The Comedy of Errors*, 4.1.136–37

In early modern England, the category "Dutch" worked like a pun on the English imagination. Nowhere is this more vividly displayed than when the real and imagined cultural proximities between England and the Low Countries emerge in the form of a double entendre. In Thomas Dekker and Thomas Middleton's theatrical comedy *The Roaring Girl* (1611), for instance, the extramarital promiscuity of the play's citizen sempster is figured through a series of double entendres that render the Low Countries and London's suburbs as overlapping sites of illicit sexual commerce:

> *Mistress Openwork:* Have I found out one of your haunts? I send you
>   for hollands, and you're i' the low countries with a mischief. . . .
> *Master Openwork:* She rails upon me for foreign wenching, that I,
>   being a freeman, must needs keep a whore i'th' suburbs, and seek
>   to impoverish the liberties.[1]

Beyond the legal jurisdiction of the city's mayor but buttressing its borders, the liberties of London were notorious spaces for all kinds of illicit activity, particularly the running of houses of prostitution. Master Openwork bemoans being driven beyond the liberties, just outside the city walls, and into the suburbs for his extramarital delights. Earlier in the play, Mistress Openwork similarly puns on a nearby province of the Low Countries when she castigates her husband for his whoring: "keep you your yard to measure shepherd's holland!—," she admonishes (2.1.170). The "yard," an instrument of measurement necessary in the cloth trade to which the Openworks owe their livelihood, is also a bawdy double entendre for male genitalia. Within the framework of Mistress Openwork's pun, "holland" is a product that she sent her husband out of their shop to procure—a fabric whose origin of production is in the Low Countries—and a double entendre for the region of the female body that she suspects he has procured instead. That Mistress Openwork modifies holland as *shepherd's* holland underscores the range of meaning within the signifier on which her punning admonishment turns. In her attempt to delimit the meaning to a kind of textile, Mistress Openwork unintentionally reveals the multiplicity of its spatial as well as sexual connotations. Mistress and Master Openwork's exchange opens onto the multivalent signification of the Netherlands, the Low Countries, and Holland in the English imagination of the early seventeenth century. Referencing a geographical territory, a material commodity, even the body's parts, these signifiers were especially productive in comedy precisely for how they oscillated from one meaning to the other. Indeed, to speak of things "Dutch" in early modern English was almost always to traffic in double meaning.

More than a sequence of bawdy puns interlinking the sexual geographies of London with the Low Countries, the Openworks' dialogue opens onto the real and symbolic ways in which imagining England entailed imagining a range of identifications with people, products, and spaces that were "Dutch." To tease apart the various double entendres that imbricate London and the Low Countries in the bawdy conversation above is to discover how the spatial proximity of England and the Netherlands structures the trope by which a paradoxical geography emerges. The Low Countries is at once represented as an extension of London's sexual and commercial geographies and as a space beyond home and homeland. Historically speaking, Anglo-Dutch relations had long been animated by paradoxes of proximity. In London, the Dutch were socially and culturally ubiquitous, constituting the city's largest alien immigrant population from the mid-sixteenth century through the early seventeenth century.[2] The mid-sixteenth century saw an unprecedented immigration of Dutch refugees to London, when the Low Countries' battles with Spain made England sanctuary to thousands of Dutch immigrants. In the population survey of 1568, for instance, 77 percent—over seven thousand of the nine thousand plus aliens recorded residing in and around London— were "Dutch."[3] By 1593, over seven thousand aliens from beyond England, Scotland, Ireland, and Wales resided in the capital; among these by far the most represented place of origin was the Spanish Netherlands (today's Belgium and parts of France) and those provinces that later became known collectively as Holland (today's Netherlands).[4] In *The Roaring Girl*, the doubly situated nature of the Netherlands emerges in the implicit fantasy of England's spatial proximity to the Low Countries; so close are they that the Englishman Openwork can get there and back in the time it takes to travel to and from the suburbs. In turn, the suburbs of London are rendered all the more foreign, as they are figured not as part of London's sexual and commercial economy per se but as a surrogate of the Low Countries. To travel beyond the liberties and into the suburbs was to find oneself both at home and abroad, just beyond London and into the Netherlands. Historically speaking, this exchange reveals that imagining and representing London involved imagining and representing the Low Countries (as place, material culture, and economy). More importantly, it suggests that representing the Anglo-Dutch relation in theatrical comedy did not necessarily entail the appearance of Dutch characters on stage, a point that has implications not only for how we understand the genre of city comedy, as I argue in Chapter 1, but also for how and where we focus our critical inquiry when reading for representations of cross-cultural relations in the period.

Doppelgänger Dilemmas argues that English representations of Anglo-Dutch relations engender and entail the kind of double vision embedded in the Openworks' punning exchange—one that holds similitude and difference together within its scope. Puns, like the paradoxes they often generate, frustrate reductive resolution, requiring instead that the auditor fix attention on the presence of contradiction or an irresolvable doubleness. A pun "is a process" that animates simultaneous levels of comprehension.[5] The double entendre is thus aptly named not only for the doubling it enacts but also for the double consciousness it effects in its listeners.[6] This doubling of English consciousness—what I characterize as a "double vision analytic"—animates the dynamic tensions that emerge in English representations of Dutchness. In briefly exploring Dutch puns in *The Roaring Girl*, for instance, we discover how discursive operations structured Anglo-Dutch relations as a relation of similarities and differences held in tension by tropes of proximity. The punning banter imagines two things at once: within the framework of the pun, the Low Countries is a different place insofar as it is just beyond, bordering but outside, "foreign" and abroad; the Low Countries is a similar place—even the same space—insofar as it is familiar, intimately known, and situated nearby. If puns draw differences, even oppositions, into proximity (here/

there; licit/illicit; English/Dutch), so too they can work alchemically, forging correspondences and paradoxical approximations by means of the interplay they enact (here *is* there, England *is* the Low Countries, insofar as the possibility of the pun itself tells us so). The paradox that animates this pun reveals that "Dutchness" is at once alien and immanent in early modern London life, and that to take up the invitation that Dromio of Syracuse declines—to "look so low" as to explore the workings of Dutchness in early modern English culture—is simultaneously to explore the problems and pleasures to which proximate cultural relations gave rise.

When English authors sought to represent England's affiliations with the Dutch they were deeply engaged in a process that produced ideas of ethnic approximation. For the English to be or seem approximately like the neighboring Dutch was not simply to be situated next to them but to be understood, characterized, and classified in relation to them. The etymological connection between "proximity" and "approximation" suggests why this might be so. "Proximity" comes from the Latin *proximitās*, which literally means the state of being nearest, "nextness." In early modern English, "proximity" was used both to describe a spatial relation and to describe relations of affiliation, such as kinship. "Approximate" comes from the Latin *approximare* (ap- + *proximus*), which means to draw near to. Approximation raises anxieties about interchangeability and sparks sometimes-desperate efforts to exaggerate minor differences. In the cultural sphere, to be rendered approximately alike is to be made to seem just about the same, nearly similar, but not fully identical. In English representations of Anglo-Dutch relations, English people, places, material culture, and linguistic history are often wittingly and unwittingly approximated to Dutch counterparts, raising pressing concerns about ethnic identity and interchangeability that I explore throughout this book.

The following chapters analyze a wide range of cultural productions, including stage plays, playbooks, political discourse, philological tracts, vocabularies, dictionaries and grammars, atlases, accounts of civic pageantry, travel writing, and popular news. These varied sources reveal not only that "Dutch" was a category that the English liked to think with but that when it was raised so too were many of the central paradoxes of English identity. On the one hand, this book begins to redress the fact that, despite the tremendous Dutch presence in early modern English culture, the Dutch have remained relatively absent in scholarship on the formation of English ethnic identity.[7] On the other hand, and relatedly, it aims to recalibrate how we read the self-other dynamics at play in the forging of ethnic identity in this period. Exploring the semiotics of Dutchness as a critical intervention in literary scholarship on the construction of English ethnic identity sheds new light on how proximate relations and representations of those relations put particular pressures on the process of that evolving self-definition. I analyze how proximate relations are imagined, forged, represented, and contested and ask in what ways real and imagined proximity to one's neighbors—those who live just beyond and within England—shaped constructions of ethnic, and sometimes racial, self-definition. In so doing, I am calling for a renewed attention to how multiple and overlapping notions of proximity—geographic, spatial, religious, commercial, political, linguistic, ethnic, and racial—play out as part of related processes of self-definition and cross-cultural identification. Throughout, I consider the hyphen within Anglo-Dutch relations as a flexible and tensile field of relation rather than a mark of separation. To explore the semiotics of Dutchness thus requires an analytic that attempts to preserve the paradoxes and maintain the double vision that structures representations of Anglo-Dutch proximate relations.

Taking my methodological cue from the heuristic process entailed in deciphering the double entendre, I explore both correspondences and differences between the English and the Dutch—Englishness and Dutchness—in representation, and attend closely to the chiastic interplay that held this relation in tension. As I will discuss at more length below, on the one hand, the Dutch were partly characterized by fashions, appetites, habits, and a geography that set them apart from the English. On the other hand, the Dutch and English shared similarities and correspondences: religiously, both underwent Protestant reformations; politically, both faced the military and political aggression of Spain; economically, their woolen industries had long been interdependent, and with the turn of the seventeenth century, they engaged in parallel colonial endeavors; ethnologically, the English and Dutch were both northerners. Throughout the Elizabethan and Jacobean periods, the English regularly characterized the Dutch as "neere neighbours," "friends," "allies," even kin, whose bonds were thought to tie them in "perpetual union."[8] So too Dutchness was negatively characterized as inherently slippery. Sometimes the Dutch were represented as "dissemblers" whose ability to be one thing and seem another infused Dutchness itself with a troubling doubleness in the English imagination.[9] Across the Anglo-Dutch relation, geographic, religious, linguistic, commercial, and cultural borders were represented more like intersections, sites of cultural overlap, than parameters marking difference. Correspondences between Englishness and Dutchness often undercut, even destabilized, many of the oppositional frameworks (race, religion, monarchy, cultural habits) that so often helped to define distinctions between people and places in the early modern period. Both analytically and historically, the category "Dutch" deconstructs the oppositions that might have sharpened English self-definition. It also challenges scholars of the period to reconstruct how the English understood and represented cultural similitude, approximation, and resemblance.

This Introduction grounds my project historically, lexically, and methodologically. First, I offer a brief sketch of Anglo-Dutch social and political relations in London, touching on moments of the greatest influx of the Dutch into London in order to give a frame to the more detailed portrait of Anglo-Dutch relations that emerges in the following chapters. Second, I consider the semantic complexity of the category "Dutch," pinpointing some of the social as well as representational confusions it engendered in England. Third, I introduce the interlinking arguments and methodology of *Doppelgänger Dilemmas,* exploring how and why our critical access to English representations of Anglo-Dutch proximate relations requires a reorientation of some of our most naturalized critical ideas regarding the processes by which English identity was taking shape. Finally, I turn to the texts, sites, and contexts that I address in each of the book's six chapters, outlining the various arguments that braid together throughout the book.

Anglo-Dutch Relations: A Historical Sketch

In recent years, historians and literary critics have suggested that the relationship between English subjects, particularly freemen in the trades, and strangers or denizen residents living in and around the city of London was largely antagonistic.[10] Some social historians have emphasized the xenophobia underpinning English attitudes toward foreigners in their midst,[11] while others have begun to ask whether xenophobia is "an epithet [gone] too far?"[12] As Londoners moved through their urban landscape, a long history of cultural exchange with the Dutch informed their engagements. The social history of Anglo-Dutch relations was shaped throughout the late medieval and early modern periods by geographic, religious, commercial, and political proximities that open onto the complexities of the intermingled diversity of northern European urban life. Attending to these complexities, I propose, ventilates critical debate by challenging both literary critics and historians to reconsider the heuristic value of thinking in terms of xenophobia.

Geographically, the Thames estuary faces those of the Scheldt, the Maas, and the Rhine across the North Sea. Historian Kenneth Haley reminds us that "in the age of the sailing ship the Dutch were in practice less distant from London and the south-east than were the French . . . until the age of the turnpike, indeed, except in prolonged stormy weather, the Netherlands were less remote from London than the more distant parts of England."[13] Throughout the sixteenth century, the Dutch were a doubly situated people, the majority living just beyond England in the various provinces of the Low Countries, with a significant minority living within and around the city of London itself. While many Dutch aliens sought temporary refuge from Spanish oppression in the southern Low Countries, others became part of a Dutch diaspora, developing their spiritual, commercial, and domestic lives in London.[14] The majority of immigrants who entered England during Elizabeth Tudor's reign came from the southern and maritime provinces of the Netherlands. Many were religious refugees, fellow Protestants who were forced to flee Spanish oppression. Though the Low Countries were under Hapsburg control and officially Catholic, Protestantism grew in popularity from the 1550s onward, particularly in the southern provinces. In 1566 reformers in the northern and southern Netherlands attacked Catholic altars in an iconoclastic fury known as the *beeldenstorm*. Margaret of Parma, then the Spanish regent of the Low Countries, attempted to reach a compromise with the Protestant movement in the officially Catholic territories of the Spanish Netherlands by allowing Protestant worship in places where it was already practiced. This policy, riven by contradictions, ultimately proved "untenable," according to Jonathan Israel, thus resulting in the Protestants positioning their cause in terms of armed revolt or submission.[15] In 1567, Don Fernando Alvarez de Toledo, third Duke of Alva, arrived in the Netherlands with ten thousand troops and the intention of suppressing the Protestant action. Alva imposed military rule, and fashioned himself simultaneously as leader of the Spanish army and governor-general of the Netherlands. Under his regime, almost sixty thousand Protestants fled the Netherlands in what was, at the time, the largest emigration movement of the early modern period.[16] This heralded the beginning of a Protestant emigration that would occur in waves over the course of the second half of the sixteenth century, resulting in what Nigel Goose characterizes as "the largest uprooting experienced in early modern Europe."[17]

Religious affiliation and cultural identity were complexly intertwined in this period, constantly under the pressures of negotiation from within confessional entities and alternately imperiled or bolstered by Europe's swiftly changing geopolitical landscapes. As Jonathan Israel and Benjamin Kaplan have demonstrated, the politics of confessionalization played out province by province, even town by town, within the Low Countries, where—in the wake of the Dutch Revolt—rival traditions of orthodox Calvinists clashed with the more libertine regents of the public church. For London's Dutch émigrés, matters of confessionalism spilled across linguistic and political borders, creating a circuit of spiritual and ideological exchange between England and the Low Countries.[18] The movement of Protestants throughout northern Europe and their relocation, temporary and permanent, in England would shape much of Anglo-Dutch political, military, and social policy in the last half of the sixteenth century.[19]

England's relations with the Dutch were informed by different historical factors than those shaping French or Spanish relations with the English, and the representations of Anglo-French and Anglo-Spanish relations are charged with different political, religious, and cultural valences. The Elizabethan period was marked by the waning of dynastic struggles between England and France and the increasing threat of Spain to England's political and commercial health. Both France and Spain were governed by monarchs against whom England had fought over territory. France and Spain were officially Catholic monarchies when England began its Protestant Reformations. In vilifying these Continental others, English authors called up anti-Catholic rhetoric and pilloried Spanish and French royalty in satirical prints and broadsides.[20] The Dutch, like the English, underwent waves of Protestant Reformations and struggled to understand what might unify the Seventeen Provinces in the face of the diversified religious ideologies and practices that divided their lands.[21] Many in England considered the Dutch their Protestant coreligionists. Therefore, drawing sharp religious distinctions between the English and Dutch was less effective in forging clear ideas of cultural difference. Moreover, until the mid-seventeenth century, the English did not fight wars against the Dutch over issues of territory, and when they did, the territory at stake was the sea. Their proximity was thus not informed by the same dynastic tensions that underwrote England's histories with France and Spain.

The history of Anglo-Dutch relations reaches even further back.[22] So connected were their religious and commercial relations that J. F. Bense has argued that the English and Dutch were "almost inseparable" throughout the sixteenth century.[23] The English had ample opportunity to reflect on their relations with the Dutch because the Dutch were *everywhere* in early modern English culture. In terms of Dutch immigration into England, from 1521 to 1560, the majority of aliens who sought letters of denization and acts of naturalization in England were "Netherlanders."[24] Among the immigrants whose places of origin are recorded in the historical record, Brabant (including the city of Antwerp), is the "most frequently mentioned."[25] Immigrants from Antwerp would go on to play an important role in the management of the Dutch, French, and Italian Churches in London during the second half of the sixteenth century.[26]

During the first half of the sixteenth century, two-thirds of the Netherlanders who sought denization or naturalization lived in London, Southwark, and Westminster; the other one-third lived elsewhere in England.[27] Professionally, these immigrants were "mostly occupied with clothing the English."[28] They were shoemakers, cordwainers, weavers, and tailors, but also metal workers and printing tradesmen. Marriage between Dutch men and English women was not uncommon during this period.[29] The traffic between England and the Low Countries ran both ways. From 1483, when Flemish printers began issuing books for the English market, English printers and publishers ventured to the Netherlands to learn the trade.[30] English ideas were shipped into the Netherlands for printing when printers determined it would be safer to publish their English books there than in England.[31] Ideas, material culture, and people crossed back and forth between England and the Low Countries throughout the sixteenth century, creating networks of both personal and professional affiliation. The result of all of this shuttling was apparent even on London's commercial landscape. Sir Thomas Gresham, an English merchant and agent of the English Crown in Antwerp, spent years of his life working and residing near Antwerp's mercantile exchange, the "Nieuwe Beurs." His experiences watching the world's merchants trade under covered walkways at Antwerp's Beurs inspired him to build a copy in London. For English merchants, particularly those involved in the cloth trade, it would not have been unusual to split some of their time between England and the Netherlands. The close commercial relations between England and the Netherlands, particularly relating to the cloth trade, made spotting "English merchants in Bruges, later in Antwerp, and Dutch clothiers in London . . . a common sight. . . . Even when in the late Middle Ages the exportation of wool from England stagnated because it began to process its own wool," rather than exporting it to the Netherlands for finishing, "the

Netherlands remained important for the export of English cloth. And so the commercial route quite naturally became the escape route."[32]

Dutch diasporic networks created by the exodus of Protestants from the southern and maritime provinces of the Low Countries in the later half of the sixteenth century worked to knit England and the Netherlands ever more tightly in a bond of Protestant alliance—if not always at the affective, local level, then often at the level of state-sanctioned policy and military action. Twice, Queen Elizabeth I was offered and rejected what were effectively offers of sovereignty: first over the provinces of Holland and Zeeland in 1571 in exchange for joining an alliance with France and the German Protestants in expelling Spain from the Netherlands; and again in 1585 when she agreed to send six thousand troops into the Netherlands at a cost of 126,000 pounds, which, Kenneth Haley calculates, "amounted to about half of the Queen's ordinary revenue in peacetime."[33] In *A Declaration of the Causes Mooving the Queene of England to Give Aid to the Defence of the People Afflicted and Oppressed in the Lowe Countries* (1585), England's military engagement in the Low Countries is justified, in part, because of the proximity of England to the Netherlands: "and joyning thereunto our owne danger at hand, by the overthrow & destruction of our neighbours, and access & planting of the great forces of the *Spanyards* so neere to our countries, with precedent arguments of many troublesome attempts against our Realme: we did therefore . . . determine, to sende certaine companies of souldiers to ayde the naturall people of those countries."[34] Spanish aggression in the Low Countries presented a "common danger" for both England and her neighbor: "we have found the general disposition of al our own faithful people very ready in this case, & earnest in offring to us, both in Parliaments & otherwise, their services with their bodies & blood, & their aides with their lands & goods, to withstand & prevent this present common danger to our Realm & themselves, evidently seene & feared by the subverting & rooting up of the ancient nation of these low countries, & by planting the *Spanish* nation & men of warre, enemies to our counyries, there so nere unto us."[35] Indeed, England and the Netherlands rarely enjoyed a distanced view onto one another's political landscapes. These were near neighbors whose mutual struggle against Spanish domination, whose geographic propinquity and shared Protestant affiliations, intertwined their fates. Following a botched military campaign in the Netherlands, Robert Devereux, Earl of Essex, would thoroughly naturalize the intimate political proximities of England and the Low Countries in terms that echoed his sovereign: "Is not the Lowe Countries the Rise, by which shee [Spain] may leape into England?"[36] The Low Countries were often imagined to be less a buffer zone than a bridge to England, so when troubles erupted there the English, though often slow to take action, were always on guard.[37]

As Elizabeth extended the finances and military powers of her realm into the Netherlands, the presence of Dutch strangers in England's southern and eastern towns and cities sparked an array of pressing political questions for the English, who found themselves living, working, and worshiping alongside a people who were broadly classified as "Dutch." Prime among the issues raised by the large presence of Dutch refugees was that of enfranchisement. How would the strangers living and working in England earn a living, maintain their religious affiliation, and secure a right to appeal to legal authorities for wrongs committed against them? What was the language of belonging and alienation by which the Dutch were either enfranchised or disenfranchised in their host city? Legally speaking, those immigrants with the financial means, motivation, and appropriate institutional connections could apply for denizenship, a powerfully flexible category of belonging. "Denizenship" emerges as one of the central terms by which English authors explored the neither-here-nor-there (yet both of here-and-there) reality of the Dutch in early modern London. The rights conferred by each letter varied, case by case. A letter patent of denization, granted by the Crown, extended to the stranger the right to hold but not inherit real estate in England and it could also grant the stranger rights to bequeath it to children who were born after the patent of denization was granted. After securing denizenship, however, strangers were still required to pay alien custom rates that amounted to twice the lay subsidy taxes paid by natural-born English men and women. The cost involved in seeking denization, together with what was a complicated and cumbersome process, discouraged many alien residents from seeking denizen status.[38] Aliens could also become naturalized subjects by means of an Act of Parliament, which conferred on the subject the right to both inherit and pass on property to children.[39] Strangers could also seek enfranchisement by appealing to the City. The "freedom" was a status granted by the City to strangers as a result of marriage or, most commonly, through "redemption," a fee paid to the City.[40] The strangers living and working within England thus existed in a range of both legal and extralegal relationships to the English state.

Immigrants from the Low Countries who sought refuge in London following Alva's military campaign emigrated primarily, but not exclusively, from the provinces of Flanders and Zeeland.[41] Once in London, those Dutch- and French-speaking Netherlanders found churches established by and for their particular communities.[42] Their members met, worshiped, and socialized within London city walls in Broadstreet Ward, where their services were held in Dutch and in French.[43] Founded in 1550 by Edward VI, the Dutch Church of Austin Friars and French Church of St. Anthony provided refugees with a social, economic, and religious infrastructure of safe harbor.[44] The institution of stranger churches provided much of the necessary social support for London's growing stranger population, which would have turned to their churches in cases that required petitioning of English authority.[45] The sanctioned integration of Dutch coreligionists into London helped to produce an atmosphere that Jean Howard has aptly characterized as "forced cosmopolitanism," driven, in this instance, less by the expansion of overseas trade than by the ongoing politics of proximate Protestant relations at home.[46]

By the turn of the seventeenth century, London might well have been characterized as Europe's little Netherlands. Precisely how many Dutch aliens resided in London is a question vexed by both historical and semantic issues. Historically speaking, it was not unusual for people to shuttle back and forth across the North Sea over the course of a lifetime as the politics and religious landscapes of England and the Low Countries changed and as new mercantile opportunities arose. No census can capture that mobility, but my sense is that it was significant.[47] In addition, as I detail in the following section, semantic confusion surrounding the category "Dutch" poses a significant challenge to recovering the origins of those people entering London. The population data collected in the period, nonetheless, tells the story of a robust Dutch presence in London. A survey of the City of London, its liberties, and suburbs in 1562 counted 4,534 alien men, women, and children residing therein.[48] Following the 1567 troubles in the Netherlands, 6,704 aliens were counted in London and the liberties, another 2,598 in Westminster. Of the 9,302 aliens residing in and around London at this time, 77 percent were "Dutch" (approximately 7,162 men, women, and children).[49] Although the population surveys of the sixteenth century "frequently convey an impression of careful preparation," Nigel Goose emphasizes that "all of these enumerations are likely to underestimate the number of aliens. . . . An Elizabethan 'norm' in the region of 8,000 would therefore be a sensible estimate, this figure rising periodically (but also repeatedly) as high as 10,000."[50] A historian of London's Protestant communities, Andrew Pettegree, estimates that by 1568 the French Church of London (which many "Dutch" attended) had a community 1,800 strong and the Dutch Church nearly 2,000.[51] As members of sanctioned houses of religion, this minority was made visible by its religious enfranchisement. The first compiler of an Anglo-Dutch grammar, for instance, advises his English readers to go to London's Dutch Church to practice Dutch with the strangers there.[52] Even so, just what it meant to be "Dutch" in early modern London was not always transparent, as the stranger population surveys themselves make clear.

On the Category "Dutch"

In 1593 a London city official knocked on the door of Judith Strete, widow and seamster, to inquire about her status as a stranger in London. Widow Strete resided in St. Olave in Bridge Ward Without on the Southbank of the river Thames, where she was householder and nondenizen.[53] Her son, age twenty four, was "English-born," she told the city official, and she was "of the Dutch Church." The record reflects that Judith Strete had dwelt in England twenty-seven years, which, if accurate, suggests she left her homeland in 1566, the year of the beeldenstorm. Having noted her name and if any English or stranger servants were set to work by widow Strete, the city official had but one more question: where was Judith Strete from? Nothing in the 1593 record suggests that Judith had reason to obfuscate her place of origin. Indeed, hundreds of strangers ostensibly reported precisely where they were born or where they had resided before coming to London. The widow Catharine Payne, silk weaver and resident of England for twenty years, reportedly specified that she was from "Andwerpe (Antwerp) in the Province of Brabande (Brabant)," for instance.[54] However, as Judith looked into the face of London's city official what she is reported to have said was that she was "a Dutchwoman."[55] As Judith closed the door behind her and returned to her work, the London official jotted down Judith's response, which apparently sufficed. Indeed, Judith's answer was not unusual. Ninety-one other strangers, when asked that year where they were from, said they too were Dutch, from Dutch, or "of the Dutch nation."[56] As both a category of identity and a general name indicating a geographic territory, Judith's response was not a misuse of the term. Instead, her identification as "a Dutchwoman" was useful in translating her sense of belonging in London. Together with her affiliation with the Dutch Church, by identifying herself as "Dutch,"

Judith asserted her Protestant affiliation and thus her status as a coreligionist and "friend" of the officially Protestant English state. Although Judith likely would have identified more regionally among her Netherlandish and Germanic peers, for the immigrant in the English civic and legal contexts, "Dutch" sufficed as a response to questions of origins.[57] In London, "Dutch" was a broad and elastic classificatory term for geographic, cultural, and linguistic identity.

The lack of clarity around the category was due, in part, to the fact that the meaning of the word was in transition in the English language during this period. In Old High German, *diota* or *diot* originally meant people or nation. As early as the ninth century, the word was used "to distinguish the vulgar tongue from the Latin of the church and the learned; hence it gradually came to be the current denomination of the vernacular" applied to dialect and "the people" alike.[58] By the twelfth and thirteenth centuries, *Diutisklant* (*Deutschland*) came to indicate the country of the German people in English usage. In the fifteenth and sixteenth centuries, however, the geographic and ethnic attribution indexed by the word "Dutch" expanded to include not only the people and regions we now call "German" but also the "language and people of the Netherlands as part of the 'low Dutch' or low German domain." With the declaration of the independence of the United Provinces from Spain (1581), "the term Dutch was gradually restricted in England to the Netherlanders."[59] Only in the seventeenth century did the English begin to employ "Dutch" more exclusively to refer to the people of the Seventeen Provinces and the word "German" to refer to people of Germany, as we do in English today.

This brief etymology obscures two important realities of sixteenth-and seventeenth-century usage. First, it does not address the potential differences between how English authors and native speakers of Dutch used the words "Dutch" and *duitsch* respectively. As the *Oxford English Dictionary* explains, "in Holland itself *duitsch*, and in Germany *deutsch*, are, in their ordinary use, restricted to the language and dialects of Germany and of adjacent regions, *exclusive of the Netherlands and Friesland*; though in a wider sense 'deutsch' includes these also, and may even be used as widely as 'Germanic' or 'Teutonic.'" Grammarians William Z. Shetter and Inge van der Cruysse-van Antwerpen argue that the terminological distinction between "Dutch" and "German" was settled only in the past two centuries: "Until two centuries or so ago the covering term for the languages of the Low Countries was *Duits* or *Nederduits*, which at the same time meant 'German.' The Dutch word *Duits* now means only 'German,' and corresponds to the German word *deutsch*. The English word 'Dutch,' which originally did not distinguish 'Dutch' from 'German,' has simply been restricted in a different direction."[60] Thus, a second qualification to the etymology above emerges. While it has been argued that by the seventeenth century, "Dutch [had] come to be exclusively associated with the northern Netherlands,"[61] in the Netherlands, in London's population returns, in English theatrical comedy and political discourse, "Dutch" continued to refer broadly to the people, geography, and Germanic languages of the northern and southern provinces of the Low Countries along with Germany. Historian Alastair Duke rightly contends that for the English, as well as for the "Dutch," a "semantic haze" hung over the Low Countries: "by the 1560s anyone wishing to refer to the Low Countries was spoilt for choice. . . . Perhaps only Switzerland, whose identity posed comparable problems for contemporaries, was so well endowed."[62] Even as a linguistic category, "Dutch" was a term more perplexing than clarifying. Duke relays the muddiness of the problem by way of comparison to England and France: "while language provided a plausible basis for the construction of nationality in late medieval England, as it did likewise in France, it was singularly unhelpful in the case of the Low Countries, which sat astride the Romano-Germanic linguistic fault line."[63] If "Dutch" referred to a community of people, the language of that community was not necessarily "Dutch" (or "Nether-Dutch" or Low-Dutch or Flemish), for it might as likely be French or German (High-Dutch). In attempting to identify the salient terms of identity of those who resided in the Low Countries and Germany, Europeans produced, instead, a perplexing abundance of options, an *"embarras de choix."*[64]

In English usage, "Dutch" was a category that obfuscated the array of meaningful differences that structured social life in the Low Countries. Simply put, the term lacked a sharp edge. The geography it evoked referred generally to the Low Countries but could bleed east into Germany and southwest to include the Walloon (French-speaking) population living on the border of France. This lack of clear definition is evident in the plethora of terms circulating in the world atlases of the period, to which English readers might have turned for some clarification. Abraham Ortelius, creator of the influential *Theatrum Orbis Terrarum*, was so bothered that strangers from beyond the Low Countries regularly referred to the whole of the Seventeen Provinces as "Flanders," a single province within the seventeen, that he provided his readers with a list, like no other in the entire atlas, of "common synonymas or sundry names of certaine particular places" in the Low Countries and Germany that are used interchangeably but inaccurately, in Ortelius's estimation, and so cause confusion even among the geographers of the day.[65] A glance at the table of contents in the English translation, *Theatre of the Whole World*, reveals the ways in which the interchangeability of place names, particularly in relation to Germany and the Low Countries, may have perplexed the armchair traveler and seasoned cartographer alike. In Ortelius's table of contents, the reader finds "Dutchland" listed, but inside the atlas itself the pages indexed under "Dutchland" are entitled "Germanie." The "Low-Countreys" listed in the table directs the reader's attention to pages with the heading "Germanie on this side Rhene, commonly called the Netherlands or the Low Countries." In these two instances, readers encounter a potentially confusing series of correspondences: Dutchland is Germanie and the Low Countries is Germany, commonly called the Low Countries.

Complicating matters further, the English had a multiplicity of terms by which they referred to their neighbors' language(s).[66] In the seventeenth century, "Netherlandish," "Nether-dutch," "Netherland language,"[67] and "Low German" were all "convertible terms" in English that meant Dutch language.[68] English-Dutch dictionaries of the seventeenth century employ a range of words for the Dutch language, including "Dutch,"[69] "Duyts,"[70] "Neder-duytsche" and "Neder-duitsche,"[71] "Ne'erduitschen" and "Low-dutch,"[72] and "Nederduits."[73] So too English was replete with names for people considered "Dutch," including "Netherlander," "Hollander," "Fleming," "Brabanter," "Walloon," "Dutchman," and—to mention only one of many satirical labels—"low lander." Latinisms only vexed matters further.[74] On the English stage a "Dutchman" or "Dutchwoman" may be associated with Antwerp or Amsterdam, but may also hail from Augsburg; a "Fleming" may be a person from Flanders or, in the more general sense, a Dutch person. "Walloon," a less frequently occurring word in the drama, was more geographically and linguistically restricted, referring in most instances to French-speaking people of Flanders and Brabant.[75] On the whole, however, these words were used interchangeably—especially in drama, often in political discourse, and sometimes in philological tracts, grammars and dictionaries. This interchangeability tended to smooth over regional linguistic and cultural differences that a French-speaking Calvinist from Antwerp, for example, would have registered as profoundly salient when she immigrated to a Dutch-speaking community in Holland following the sack of Antwerp.

In London, immigrants from the Low Countries were evidently aware of the classificatory multiplicity available to them. When asked in 1593 by surveyors where they were from, some strangers reported that they were from Antwerpen or Brugges, answers that still register as meaningfully delimited geographic areas today; others responded that they were from "Dutch," "Walloon," and "Lo Countrie."[76] Still others simply declared that they were a "Dutchwoman" or "Dutchman." That these answers made sense enough to the immigrants and to the surveyors to make their way into the official records suggests that understanding what "Dutch" meant in the early modern period entails grappling with the multivalence of the category Dutch in early modern English.

Double Vision: Ethnicity in the Making

In representation, as in life, Dutchness was a slippery yet capacious category, hard to capture but easy to be caught up in. In literary representation, it raised both anxieties and pleasures because of the way in which the doubleness of all things Dutch bifurcated English perspective on Dutchness, and then on Englishness too. Owen Felltham, a Commonwealth polemicist, illuminates the messy multivalence of Dutchness in his satirical work *A Brief Character of the Low-Countries* (1652), wherein "the Dutchman anatomized and truly dissected" emerges in the form of a diptych portrait of England's Netherlandish neighbor. Figures of both virtue and vice, the Dutch are represented as holding the very oppositions that define them in an unresolved tension. "They are a general sea-land," Felltham begins, initiating a series of paradoxical characterizations that renders paradox itself as central to the character of the Low Countries, its people, institutions, and geography. Prime among these paradoxes was the Netherlands' lack of clearly defined geographical borders. It is described as the "great bog of Europe," an "Aequilibrium of mud and water," the soil itself "the buttock of the World, full of veines and bloud, but no bones in't."[77] Echoing and extending the implications of Felltham's characterization of the Low Countries, Andrew Marvell's poem *The Character of Holland* (1665) similarly characterizes Holland as a place always half-steeped in the sea: "Holland, that scarce deserves the name of Land, / As but th' off-scouring of the British Sand."[78] Not merely ill defined because of its doubly situated geography in land and water, the Low Countries emerges in Marvell's poetic imagery as detritus that has been scoured off or exfoliated from British land. The Netherlands is at once claimed and discharged by Britain, a part of and apart from British land, a geographic denizen. As with the Openworks' pun, explored at the beginning of this Introduction, here too the imagined doubleness of the Netherlands' geographic location together with its paradoxically constituted environmental nature brings a portrait of Anglo-Dutch proximity into focus.[79] For both authors, the Nether*lands* is a misnomer for a geography characterized as a slurry of land and sea, a place neither fully land nor sea.

In *A Brief Character* and *The Character of Holland*, the people too are similarly represented as doubly situated. Felltham satirically represents the Dutch as amphibians: they are "like frogs" for they "live both on land and water," an idea crystallized by Marvell who characterizes the people as "half-anders, half-wet, half-dry."[80] Halfness, in this instance, is another way of expressing ideas of doubleness—to be half one thing and half another is to be imperfectly or incompletely two things at once. At the same time, to be characterized as a people and a land that are half land–half sea is to challenge the fixity of nature's peripheries and borders themselves. Just as the Low Countries was frequently figured as doubled, with its amphibious mixing of land and sea, so too was its relation to England figured in terms of linguistic, cultural, and geographical doublings. "Half-anders" proves a fitting pun, Richard Todd observes, since *anders* in Dutch means "other[wise]," "different," suggesting that the Dutch are "only *in part*" different from the English, or *half* others.[81] Michael C. Schoenfeldt glimpses a part anagram whereby "half-anders" registers visually and aurally as "half Flanders," turning England itself into a half Flanders, a paradox that the English no doubt experienced when living alongside the significant Dutch population in Norwich and London.[82] This clever English joke, which at first aims at the Dutch, boomerangs to the English when it is understood in Dutch. As the following chapters reveal, on the stage a laugh at the Dutch often cut the English off at the knees. What is more, when the English were representing Anglo-Dutch relations they were calibrating degrees of sameness and difference from their nearest Continental neighbors, reflecting on their own variously constituted identity and exploring a complex range of identifications that both buttressed and unsettled English identity. Indeed, Marvell's imagery raises pressing questions about England and Englishness: if Holland is the "off-scouring of the British Sand," then just where are the borders that distinguish England from the Netherlands? If nature's borders are so porous as to fail to inscribe a difference between land and sea, what cultural difference can hold in distinguishing the Dutch—those experts in half (other)ness—from their English neighbors?

The study of Dutchness that emerges in the following chapters opens onto a world wherein paradox abounds, where tropes of doubleness depend on images of halfness, where that which is proximate begins to look approximately alike, and where minor difference—like that between half-*anders* and half-Flanders—makes all the difference as to whether or not Englishness might find its footing on unshifting ground. As the puns that animate the works of Felltham, Marvell, Dekker and Middleton powerfully suggest, exploring the expansiveness and depth of "Dutchness" in English culture requires more than tracing representations of the Dutch, a people from the Low Countries. For reasons that I explore more fully below, this book does not focus on representations of *the Dutch*.[83] The following chapters emphasize instead the ways in which ideas about Dutchness in the English cultural imagination far exceeded any real or imagined presence of Dutch people on the streets or characters on the stage. In so doing, this book reanimates the semiotics of Dutchness in early modern English culture by recovering literary and cultural operations whereby identifications with one's proximate other emerge in the form of vexed identifications as approximated kinds. This relational process, which I characterize as *ethnicity in the making*, is rarely so neat as to reveal itself through straightforward representations of types. Instead, I focus our critical attention on the ways in which English representations of Dutchness were meditations on the elasticity of the self-other divide, revealing a picture of English culture as far more alive to variations by degree than has generally been appreciated.

Over the course of the past thirty years we have better come to understand how epistemologies of racial, ethnic, and national difference were instrumental in forging constructions of English (and later British) identity. *Doppelgänger Dilemmas* directs attention to the ways in which desirable and disquieting similarities to one's neighbors shaped that definition as well. In attending to approximations, I argue that imagining Anglo-Dutch relations produced different effects and incited different tensions within the emergence of English identity than did imagining Anglo-French relations, for instance.

Linda Colley argues that in the eighteenth century "Britons defined themselves in terms of their common Protestantism as contrasted with the Catholicism of Continental Europe. They defined themselves against France
throughout a succession of major wars with that power . . . not just through
an internal and domestic dialogue but in conscious opposition to the Other
beyond their shores."[84] Colley's argument that England's national self-
definition emerges "in conscious opposition to the Other" became axiomatic
in literary and historical scholarship of the 1990s. Indeed, with the rise of
New Historicism in the late 1980s, "difference," "alterity," and "otherness"
became key terms in the critical lexicon and the primary analytic framework
for exploring the impact of cultural diversity within the "British" archipelago
and beyond.[85] In particular, literary critics sought to define the processes
whereby nation thinking emerged and explored with renewed sensitivity the
roles gender, religion, race, and cultural geography played in bringing ideas
of Englishness to bear on the shaping of an English nation. Michael Neill, in
an influential essay on representations of Anglo-Irish relations in the period,
crystalizes the point: "England is always discovered elsewhere, defined by the
encounter with the Other."[86] Janette Dillon concurs, arguing that after the
defeat of the Spanish Armada in 1588, "the construction of 'England'
remained firmly entrenched in the definition and exclusion of otherness,
whether racial, religious or political."[87] In his comprehensive study of representations of national types in drama from the period, A. J. Hoenselaars
explores "examples of the binary relationship between the dramatists' presentation of the Englishman's auto-image and his hetero-image" in plays that
present Englishmen and foreigners together on stage: "The juxtaposition of
these groups of characters in the drama crystallizes differences and facilitates a
comparison between them. . . . Once the foreigner is presented in an English
environment, contrastive stress procedures tend to foreground him since he
is the 'odd one out.' Conversely, when the Englishman is presented in a
nonnative environment, his nationality in turn is emphasized."[88]

    In ranging beyond dramatic representation, Michael Duffy surveys
English satirical prints to find "what a marketable commodity this patriotic
xenophobia was for English printmakers," whose art ascribed varied characteristics to different national kinds.[89] During the first half of the seventeenth
century, Duffy argues, it was not the French but the Spanish who were the
"foremost" foreigners and Others in English minds.[90] In a reading of the
figure of the Spaniard in Thomas Heywood's *The Fair Maid of the West, Part
I*, Jean Howard finds that "the difference between Spanish and English is

figured as a series of binary oppositions, and the relations between the two powers are straightforwardly antagonistic. The Spanish are Catholic, cruel, and rapacious; the English are Protestant, merciful, and generous."[91] Howard nuances this insight by underscoring that the Spanish were "also constructed *in relation* to the English in a way that suggests a subterranean fraternal bond between the two nations, a bond defined precisely by rivalrous antipathy. . . . These two European powers are national rivals and enemies, but necessary to one another's self definitions."[92] By configuring Anglo-Spanish national antipathy as religious difference, English dramatists cast Catholicism abroad, giving it a distinctly Spanish hue. James Shapiro has argued that Englishness was forged against the ethnic, racial, and religious alterity of Jews, whose "differences were greatly exaggerated and at times simply invented"; they were a people deemed "un-English in the way that they looked, prayed, ate, smelled, dressed, walked, and talked," and increasingly racially marked during this period.[93] Even so, one of the most perplexing problems of the era was how to understand "what happened to their racial otherness when [Jews] converted and entered, or tried to enter, a Christian commonwealth."[94] The Jew raised conversion confusion for an England still struggling to make sense of its Reformation and Counter-Reformation experience: what about the self (blood, belief, custom, nation) can be radically altered and electively renounced in a process of willful dis-identification, and what of the former self remains? Conversion set in motion "anxieties about sameness and difference, about nature and nations" that expose the uneasy and often unpredictable interplay of nation, race, ethnicity, gender, sexuality, and religion in this period, and the Jew proved a loaded signifier for these confusions. Also, England's cultural encounters and commercial traffic with Muslim powers "exacerbated prevalent tensions and anxieties about religious and cultural differences," Ania Loomba has argued.[95] Yet these differences were not absolute: "if on the one hand references were made to the shared Protestant and Muslim hatred of Spain and 'idolatry,' then, on the other, English anti-Catholicism was often articulated by suggesting a continuum rather than a difference between Muslim infidels and Catholics."[96] For Emily Bartels, the theater could demonstrate its own role in the process of estrangement across kinds; in granting the alien center stage, Christopher Marlowe's plays "expose the demonization of an other as a strategy for self-authorization and self-empowerment."[97]

Even those proximate relations closer to home, like that between England and Ireland, have been understood primarily in terms of difference.

Michael Neill writes that Ireland functioned "as the indispensable anvil upon which the notion of Englishness was violently hammered out"; it was "Irish 'barbarity' that defined English civility, Irish papistry and 'superstition' that warranted English religion; it was Irish 'lawlessness' that demonstrated the superiority of English law, and Irish 'wandering' that defined the settled and centered nature of English society." Even so, Neill continues, "while the ideology of national difference required that the Irish be kept at a distance and stigmatized as a barbaric Other, the practicalities of English policy more and more pressingly required that Ireland be absorbed within the boundaries of the nation-state," a process that entailed conceiving of Ireland as "an errant province to be 'subdued' rather than a foreign land to be subjugated."[98] Even Italy, so omnipresent in early modern English drama, provided a "field of fantasy" for "irresistible evil" that the English often "located elsewhere: across the Channel, west of the border, below the equator," argues Ann Rosalind Jones.[99] These critical explorations of the forging of English identity have thus largely affirmed, even as they have nuanced, the postmodern insight that "to exist is to be called into being in relation to an otherness."[100]

Considerably less scholarly attention has been paid to how correspondences and likenesses between the English and their near neighbors might also have threatened, disrupted, ruptured, or coalesced ideas of Englishness. In a 1994 essay published in the collection *Women, "Race," and Writing in the Early Modern Period*, Lynda Boose, writing on racial discourse in early modern England, contends that "to chart early modern England's discourse of racial difference, we clearly need a more detailed cartography of what the English assumed within notions of the same."[101] Compared with scholarly inquiry that focuses on epistemologies of difference, this is a project that remains in its infancy. Despite an asymmetry of critical attention paid to constructions of difference over that given to sameness, important studies focusing on proximate relations have shaped the critical conversation. Frances Dolan, Jonathan Dollimore, Jean Feerick, Kathryn Schwarz, Laurie Shannon, and Valerie Traub, among others, have revealed the work of proximity, similitude, and likeness in representations of religion, race, sexuality, gender, and friendship, shedding light on the ways various kinds of proximity were instrumental in forging and challenging self-definition.[102] Dollimore argues that "terror of the other may be premised on a terror of the proximate; not only does the excluded remain adjacent, but the adjacent becomes threatening in a way that the excluded never quite does."[103] Studies of England's relations with the Irish, in particular, have emphasized this "terror of the proximate."

Andrew Murphy argues compellingly for how representations of Anglo-Irish proximity reveal the English confronting their own self-fragmentation: the images of the Irish "are at one and the same time images of the Other invoked by the English and images of the Self evoked by Irish proximity. It is that process of fragmentation that English writing on Ireland seeks—and finally fails—to contain."[104] The terror of the proximate need not depend on a literal geographic propinquity, as Emily Bartels has recently demonstrated in her discussion of how English representations of the Moor were concerned less with exoticism than with the Moor's proximity to European culture and its geopolitics.[105] Two decades after the publication of *Sexual Dissidence,* Dollimore's insight nonetheless still resonates: "within metaphysical constructions of the Other what is typically occluded is the significance of the *proximate*—i.e., that which is (1) adjacent and *there-by* related temporally or spatially, or (2) that which is approaching (again either temporally or spatially), hence the verb 'to approach or draw neere' (1623, *OED*), and thus (3) the opposite of *remote* or *ultimate.*"[106]

A recent noteworthy venture in redressing the asymmetry of scholarly focus on difference is Lloyd Edward Kermode's *Aliens and Englishness in Elizabethan Drama.* Kermode significantly qualifies the idea that difference is what most matters in the forging of English identity by demonstrating how depictions of aliens on the English stage underwent an important shift from Marian drama, which "set up Englishness *against* otherness by homogenizing the varieties of alien identity," to Elizabethan drama, in which aliens are more often "con-fused" with their English counterparts, that is they are both ideologically destabilizing and "absorbed" within Englishness.[107] Central to this diachronic argument is the idea that Englishness itself "constitutes an absent presence. . . . [Thus] to play at being other, to be alien, to incorporate the foreign, and to confuse the actor and the 'other' part being played is to show Englishness itself in action."[108] The point Kermode persuasively underscores is not—or not only—that Englishness fails to signify on its own, but that this very process of being "in action, always in a position of relativity" is *how* Englishness improvises itself into being time and again, and differently each time.[109] In his historically wide-ranging survey *The Idea of English Ethnicity,* Robert Young concurs that "from the Normans onward, to be English was, literally, to be eccentric. . . . The Norman invasion showed that being English is something that you can 'put on': it is a perpetual process of becoming, a pursuit of authenticity in which the copy is allowed to be as authentic as any original."[110] It is precisely this process of improvisation, this position and condition of relativity, with which the study of English *ethnicity in the making* must contend.

To do so, I believe we will need to reconsider the limitations of framing our critical inquiry in terms of a study of "types."[111] *Aliens and Englishness* offers a significant reconsideration of the process of self-alienation that inheres in representations of encounters between Englishmen and aliens in Elizabethan drama. While Kermode anticipates some of the discoveries of my book, the trope of "absorption," which he uses to characterize English-alien "con-fusion," carries with it the implication that players—and the historical counterparts they represent (Englishman/alien)—were once, and may once again be made into, distinct and different types. While I am sympathetic to the challenges our current critical vocabulary (so infused with tropes of hybridity and mixing) poses to the process of identifying the deconstructive processes involved in the forging of Englishness in this period, I suspect, in the case of Kermode's fine book, that its methodology complicates this already difficult task. *Aliens and Englishness* focuses on "physical representations of contemporary and recognizable *aliens* [that] appear on the *stage*," thus advancing the critical presumption that the most powerful signifiers of alienness inhere in representations of aliens themselves.[112] By attending to the semiotic field of Dutchness, rather than limiting inquiry to the "physical representation" of Dutch characters on stage, I aim to expand the canon of what Kermode characterizes as London's "alien stages" by exploring both aliens *and* the discourses of alienation, representations of Others and the processes of othering, the forging of difference *and* similitudes across and within kinds.[113]

While important contributions have begun to dismantle an exclusive focus on difference, broadly speaking, if there is a single concept around which humanities scholars interested in questions of identity turn our collective energies it is *difference*. Race, class, caste, ethnicity, gender, sexuality, religion, place, and language are among the categories now regularly explored as those that have and continue to make differences that matter. Among literary critics of early modern English literature, "difference" long has been a keyword as scholars have demonstrated the ways in which the sixteenth and seventeenth centuries saw the emergence of ideologies and epistemologies that have informed the development of modern notions of race;[114] gender, sexuality, and embodiment;[115] and rank and status.[116] What could be more intuitively correct or theoretically reiterated than the idea that difference is central to how social identities are constructed, represented, articulated, affiliated, and contested? Social identity, we have learned, "lies in difference."[117] Without it, various social groups lack the edge against which to sharpen and define themselves, affirm or disavow distinctions. In comparison to our collective critical effort toward mapping, historicizing, theorizing, and just generally *reading* for difference, we have developed a far less expansive expertise for discussing and understanding how similitude between people and across groups and notions of cultural correspondence have also been historically constructed, represented, articulated, and contested. This is a striking blind spot not least because our analytic investments in difference are in fact also investments in sameness. In reading for how difference has been historically constructed are we not asking how it is that notions of sameness have been imagined, cast over, or wittingly and unwittingly adopted by particular groups, including races, ethnicities, genders, sexualities, classes, and nations? This book interrogates ethnic difference in the making, but in imagining Dutchness with the early moderns it also takes up Lynda Boose's call to attend to early modern constructions of "the same"; indeed, understanding the category "Dutch" requires this, given that its cultural valence so often had the English thinking in terms of similitude. *Doppelgänger Dilemmas* thus intervenes in debates on early modern English ethnic identity by reading with a double vision—a heuristic that attempts to trace and *to keep in play* the movement between differentiation and similitude in the construction of English ethnicity.

According to current literary and historical scholarship on early modern English ethnicity, then as now, ethnicity was a fluid framework within which to structure identity. Recent literary scholarship on ethnology has argued that "in sixteenth century England humoralism is ethnology."[118] Rooted in classically derived ancient philosophy, which posited a tripartite division of the world's *oikumene* ("inhabitable world"), "geohumoralism" (a "regionally-framed humoralism" that applied to "people of all climates") rendered England's northern clime marginal and intemperate.[119] Mary Floyd-Wilson has demonstrated how the English grappled with their northern and intemperate bodies by infusing positive value in their marginalized northern status even as such valuation paradoxically involved manipulations that aimed to remedy that status.[120] *English Ethnicity and Race in Early Modern Drama* conveys a global story of how the early modern English imagined ethnicity and also race and, in so doing, tends to accentuate the divisions between north, middle (temperate), and south, as those that were most distinctive in the formation and conceptualization of ethnic identity. Less clear are the ways in which ethnicity was shaped, constructed, and understood *within* each of these geohumoral zones. In the context of geohumoralism, for instance, the northern homelands of the Dutch and the English might seem to imply that English and Dutch peoples thought of themselves as sharing a common ethnological self-definition. Even so, Floyd-Wilson cautions that ethnicity in the early modern period was not overly determined by geohumoralism:

> What constituted ethnological identity was exceedingly fluid and malleable—shaped not only by the environment but also by other horizontal, synchronic, and "civilizing" forces, such as government, law, travel, diet, fashion and education. . . . These shaping influences played a particularly significant role in the conception and formation of English ethnicity because "Englishness" itself was understood primarily as a collection of markedly fluid qualities. . . .[121]
>
> Ethnic distinctions in the early modern period were necessarily plastic. Given the sheer number of variables in the external world (diet, environment, clothing) and the multiple cultural agents (government, travel, custom, performance, education, for example), people could intentionally or accidentally estrange themselves from their native kind.[122]

Taking its cue from Floyd-Wilson's discussion of ethnic distinction, my study affirms this sense of the plasticity and fluidity of ethnic distinctions in the period. It begins with the premise that, while important, geohumoralism alone did not define ethnicity in the period. While Floyd-Wilson's work emphasizes the distinctions between the world's tripartite zones and the early modern epistemologies that reorganized those distinctions, I show how Anglo-Dutch proximate relations, and English attempts to represent those relations, encouraged attention both to the plastic variables of ethnic distinction and to the *plasticity of* those variables. Even while the English and the Dutch shared a northern location, representations of Anglo-Dutch relations open a perspective on Englishness that exposes unsettled tensions within English ethnic identity. Clothing, foodstuffs, language, and other cultural habits could, with minor alterations, shift from signifying Englishness or Dutchness. In the chapters that follow I explore how very minor the meaningful signs of ethnic distinction between Englishness and Dutchness could be—the phonetic difference, for instance, between the pronunciation of the English word "will" and stage Dutch "vill"—and direct attention to the fungibility that is characteristic of these proximate ethnic categories.

"Ethnic identity" would have been a baffling locution for the early moderns. The fact that characterizations of early modern English ethnicity (as "plastic" and "fluid") resonate so closely with poststructuralist discourse about identity has raised considerable scholarly skepticism regarding its conceptual purchase on the study of the past. "Ethnic identity" is indeed an anachronism on two scores but, if understood in relationship to current scholarship on identity and ethnicity, this anachronistic concept can be strategically mobilized to reorient and revitalize our methodological approach to the study of identity formation in the early modern past. For the early moderns, "ethnic" meant "heathen" or "pagan," not—as it would come to mean only in the early 1950s—racial or cultural characteristics of a group.[123] The word "identity" has also undergone a striking semantic shift. Colin Kidd proposes that there has been a "total reversal" between the historical meaning of "identity" in early modern English and our current understanding of the word today: "Whereas now identity has come to signify that which divides humanity into nations, ethnicities, and other minorities of one sort or another, it once stood for the underlying unity of human kind."[124] While the modern English noun derives from the Latin *idem*, meaning the same, "identity has come to mean not only sameness, but the sameness of a person or thing at all times and in all circumstances. By extension, this has become the condition whereby that person or thing is itself and not someone or something else. This has led to a total reversal of the original meaning of identity as sameness, as now identity has come to mean 'individuality,' 'personality,' something distinctive."[125] Put differently, in the early modern period, "identity" pointed to similitude and correspondences across kinds (or within the selfsame)—"identity" signified an *indivisible* bond; but it has come to signify the distinction and difference that guarantees the uniqueness of the individual self—one's *divisibility from* all others.[126] Early modern scholarship would be well served, Kidd contends, by attending to the changing meanings of "identity," which have sometimes been obscured, even distorted, by anachronistic evocation. My study aims to urge on a critical turn toward studies of likeness, resemblance, and "identity" (in the early modern sense) with the aim of exploring cultural constructions of similitude with the analytic pressure with which we have long engaged difference. Observing that "identity" and the kind of sameness it expresses changes over time is a meaningful first step in that direction.

Kidd's study of the term "identity" reveals the counterintuitive insight that sameness changes, insofar as the conceptions of sameness that underpin the idea of identity have shifted radically. However, what the linguistically sensitive historian interprets as a "total reversal" at the level of semantics, psychoanalytically informed scholarship since poststructuralism casts instead as a tension inherent to the play of identity formation. In particular, Kidd's astute historical engagement with the concept of identity partly obscures the process of *identification,* which Diana Fuss contends both "aids and abets" as well as "embarrass[es]" and deconstructs identity:[127]

> Identification, understood . . . as the play of differences and similitude in self-other relations, does not, strictly speaking, stand against identity but structurally aids and abets it. . . . Identification is a process that keeps identity at a distance, that prevents identity from ever approximating the status of an ontological given, even as it makes possible the formation of an *illusion* of identity as immediate, secure, and totalizable. . . . [Identity] becomes problematic in and through the work of identification. . . . Any politics of identity needs to come to terms with the complicated and meaningful ways that identity is continually compromised, imperiled, one might even say *embarrassed* by identification.[128]

Attending to the process of *identification* (the "play of differences and similitude in self-other relations") across the Anglo-Dutch relation—as well as to the relation between identification and identity—reframes the object of analysis, shifting analytic pressure from the "what" (groups, identities, ethnic distinctiveness) to the "how" (the dynamic processes wherein questions of identity and ethnicity emerge). In reading for identifications as evidence of ethnicity in the making, I also have in mind Judith Butler's articulation of the work of identification: "Identifications belong to the imaginary; they are phantasmatic efforts of alignment, loyalty, ambiguous and cross-corporeal cohabitations, they unsettle the I; they are the sedimentation of the 'we' in the constitution of any I, the structuring presence of alterity in the very formulation of the I. Identifications are never fully and finally made; they are incessantly reconstituted . . . , constantly marshalled, consolidated, retrenched, contested and, on occasion, compelled to give way."[129] In emphasizing the provisional ("incessantly reconstituted"), situational ("compelled to give way"), even strategic ("constantly marshalled") nature of identifications, Butler captures the ongoing ("never fully and finally made") process identifications entail.

Scholars working on premodern Europe have found that ethnicity was similarly "strategic and situational,"[130] "fluid," "plastic,"[131] provisional, and contestable. This analytic shift toward the processual corresponds with recent scholarship in the fields of sociology and anthropology on the topic of ethnicity, as has been articulated in the work of Rogers Brubaker, who advances the case for the study of "ethnicity without groups."[132] Whereas social anthropologists once studied ethnic groups as bounded units with decisive features whose cultural distinctiveness (identity understood as selfsameness) was thought to be observable independent of interactions with others, today social anthropologists contend that "ethnicity is essentially an aspect of a relationship, not a property of a group," something that is *between* and not *inside*"—a process, in other words, that entails the sometimes uncanny and never wholly predictable work of identification.[133] Ethnicity, as understood throughout this book, thus describes "both a set of relations and a mode of consciousness."[134] For the early modern English that mode of consciousness was a double vision that held open a perspective on Englishness and Dutchness that revealed ambiguities about Englishness itself. Understood in this way, ethnicity pressures the self-evidence of our widely held conviction that social identity "lies in difference" by calling attention to a correlative logic that reveals that identity formation requires identifications *with*—a process that is as likely to slide toward identification *as* as it is to backtrack in the form of a disavowal of the "Other."[135]

Ethnicity, I contend, is a process that happens when identifications are made or disavowed in the cultural sphere. What I am tracing, then, is not a thing in the world (an ethnic group and its self-representation) but the identifications that put identity in question.[136] The critical reorientation that I propose—from what to how, from groups to processes, from identity to identifications—reanimates the minor differences as well as the uncanny correspondences that are so often obscured or dismissed when our analytic framework is digitally rather than analogically calibrated. That is, if we think in terms of categories whose boundaries are always being negotiated, rather than groups whose membership depends on a tipping point equation for inclusion, we begin to think analogically about ethnicity. Representations of Anglo-Dutch relations reveal that differences of degree can and did prove just as culturally salient as differences of kind.[137] The various literary and cultural works that I explore provide traces of both desired and disavowed identifications within representations of Anglo-Dutch relations, and in so doing, provide us with a rich archive for the study of ethnicity in the making.

The topic of ethnicity in the early modern period has long been tethered to discussions of nationhood. The question "how readily did ethnicity translate into nationhood?" ignites a "semantic and methodological minefield" among scholars sensitively engaged with the plurality of ethnic identifications by which people staked a claim to belonging within the "English archipelago."[138] In the brief discussion that follows, I do not aim to clear this minefield. I want instead to direct attention to the way in which scholarship on early modern England often too narrowly limits the concept of ethnicity to groups, particularly in the context of discussions of nationhood.

Scholarship on nationhood has tended to grant an imbalance of attention to the construction of differences, thereby limiting our understanding of the ways in which Englishness was shaped also by the identifications that draw the desirable and disquieting effects of resemblance to the fore. This critical emphasis has been undergirded by an unexplored assumption that ethnicity is best understood in terms of groups. In both historical and literary scholarship, the relation of ethnic to national identity is often implicitly framed as a relation of the cluster to the whole (ethnic groups *within* nations) or as a relation of evolution (ethnic groups *then* nations). Yet in the early modern period the relation of ethnicity to national identification is not this straightforward.[139] Richard Helgerson's now classic *Forms of Nationhood* has advanced widely influential arguments regarding the formation of early modern English nationhood. I draw attention to this well-known study because of how lucidly it illustrates the critical emphasis on difference that has underpinned subsequent arguments relating to the emergence of English nationhood, and how it crystallizes the way in which the case made for English national self-definition has smuggled into critical discourse on English identity a too-limited notion of ethnicity understood as a group. Helgerson argues:

> The rhetoric of nationhood is a rhetoric of uniformity and wholeness. The unified self of the Englishman or Frenchman, the Italian

or German, is founded on the political and cultural unity of the
nation to which each belongs. . . . Put most abstractly, to be is to
mean, and meaning depends on difference. Writing of ethnicity in
general, Emily Benveniste has remarked that "every name of an ethnic character, in ancient times, was differentiating and oppositional.
There was present in the name which a people assumed the intention, manifest or not, of distinguishing itself from the neighboring
peoples. . . . Hence the ethnic group often constituted an antithetical
duality with the opposed ethnic group." Even here one finds an
element of self-alienation. Meaning arises not from some central
core of identity but rather at a margin of difference. Self-definition
comes from the not-self, from the alien other.[140]

What interests me here is the way Helgerson's swerve from nation to ethnicity restricts ethnicity to a matter of and between groups. The analogy between
national consciousness and ethnicity, which Helgerson adopts from Benveniste, suggests that the behavior of ethnic groups anticipates or underpins the
early modern project of national consolidation and differentiation. The analogy raises a number of questions: Is the difference between ethnicity and
nationhood a matter of scale (ethnicity is a phenomenon of groupism that is
smaller than that of nationalism) or a matter of historical circumstance (some
ethnic groups become nations, while others do not)? Might this analogy be
reversed? If so, is nationhood an expression of the (larger, previous, more
essential, more pervasive) dynamics of ethnicity? In Helgerson's formulation,
ethnic groups are reified (groups already self-defined) whose identities are
clarified in "antithetical duality" with other groups. Analogously, national
consciousness "arises" from encounter with the "not-self," the "alien other."
　　Helgerson's analysis of the formation of English nationhood does not
end there, however. As his argument develops, he deftly attends to the doubleness (what he characterizes as the "divided legacy") of England's ancient
and medieval pasts by drawing attention to the ways in which English
national consciousness entailed the absorption of alien (ancient colonizing
Roman) cultural legacies as models for English self-definition. This emulative
remedy directs attention not to the work of "difference" but to the importance of "likeness" to Englishness, a point Helgerson highlights in a later
article: "Contrary to what we might expect, there is no thought here of
expressing a specifically national experience or of giving voice to a uniquely
national self. Their ambition is rather to do what others have done, to be

what others have been. The models of civility are elsewhere. A truly national literature must therefore strive to emulate those foreign models. Likeness, not difference, will be the measure of success."[141] If we were to revise Helgerson's earlier formulation in light of this later insight, then, we would assert that "to be is to mean, and meaning depends on difference [and likeness]." Taking our revision a further step requires that we recognize that ethnicity transpires in the process whereby those differences and likenesses are vested with cultural authenticity, even as they are fictive, provisional, and situational.[142]

My book does not argue for the place of the Dutch in the formation of English national consciousness, nor does it posit ethnicity as a phenomenon that presages nationhood. As I demonstrate in Chapter 2, at the beginning of the seventeenth century, ideas about the relation of English and Dutch ethnicity posed significant challenges to the period's emergent nation thinking because ethnicity, as it was understood in the period, exceeded the geopolitical parameters of kingdoms, United Provinces, and nations. Representations of Anglo-Dutch relations often rattled those notions of Englishness that existed eccentric to concepts of national self-definition. In attending to them, I am also anticipating that our next critical venture in early modern literary studies will entail exploring the question of what lies *beyond* national literary history.[143]

An Anglo-Dutch Archive

The following chapters engage with the drama of many of the period's most popular playwrights, including Thomas Dekker, Thomas Heywood, Ben Jonson, William Haughton, John Marston, Thomas Middleton, and John Webster, exploring their works as part of a broader exploration into representation of proximate relations under way in English political discourse, philological tracts, dictionaries and grammars, world atlases, accounts of civic and royal pageantry, travel writing about England and the Netherlands' early ventures to the East Indies Spice Islands, and popular pamphlets. Threaded throughout the chapters is a focus on various cultural and literary operations by which Anglo-Dutch identifications are made or disavowed. Prime among these is wordplay, in the form of double entendre, homophones, malapropisms, and false cognates that open onto what Patricia Parker characterizes as "a network whose linkages expose (even as the plays themselves may appear simply to iterate or rehearse) the orthodoxies and ideologies of the texts they evoke."[144] Wordplay provides an archive of culture in action and studying its nuances draws us ever closer to the paradoxes that animated early modern English life. The printed page is not only a site for semantic study, it is also a rich graphic field that I analyze for how visual puns emerge by means of the typographic arrangements of the mise en page of playbooks and dictionaries. The final two chapters expand beyond ethnolinguistic concerns to analyze how the English and Dutch turned to performances, staged in London and the East Indies, to negotiate their cultural and ethnic proximities. The book's geographical scope thus expands from London to England as a whole and the Netherlands, to the East Indies. While the texts I consider range from mid-sixteenth to late seventeenth century, I focus primarily on the late sixteenth and early seventeenth centuries, the initial period when Dutch cultural and demographic influx into England was greatest.

Chapter 1 initiates the model of close reading for the semiotics of Dutchness that I practice throughout the book. In John Marston's representative city comedy *The Dutch Courtesan* (1605), English and Dutch characters pose a particular interpretive challenge because their representation resists binary distinctions predicated on national, linguistic, or even distinct geographic difference. Northern European ethnicities are represented instead through performances of approximation in which distinctions between Englishness and Dutchness cannot be easily parsed. Against a critical trend of reading city comedy for its production of "types," I contend that by examining only those characters overtly designated as Dutch in a list of dramatic personae or those identified as Dutch within a play, we risk reifying rather than exploring the category of Dutchness that the early seventeenth-century theater and its audience were actively producing. Instead, I explore processes of approximation by examining the ways in which the plasticity of ethnic distinction and fluidity of ethnic identity played out across comic representations of Englishness and Dutchness, sharpening the double vision of English audiences in the process. In particular, the chapter attends to the robust wordplay by which English and Dutch ethnicities were distinguished and interlaced, and foregrounds the power of the proximate as central to representation of Anglo-Dutch religion, language, and culinary appetite on the London stage.

The following three chapters offer different and wide-ranging considerations of the role of language in representations of Anglo-Dutch proximate relations. In the period's language debates, in representations of Anglo-Dutch linguistic exchange on the stage, and through the typographic arrangements of printed pages of playbooks and dictionaries, sophisticated language lessons emerge that showcase how ideas about cross-cultural similarities and shared heritage were forged. Chapter 2 explores the period's debates about the origins and value of the English vernacular to discover how historical philology transformed that which was most near, geographically and linguistically, into a correspondence of racial kind. In the year 1622, polemicist Thomas Scott asserted that the Dutch "come of the same race originally that wee [English] do, as our speech witnesseth."[145] I analyze how the English and Dutch languages came to be understood as witnessing this racial homology by exploring the interrelation of the linguistic, cultural, and historical arguments made by turn-of-the-seventeenth-century English antiquarians Richard Verstegan and William Camden. Their seminal works emphasize Anglo-Dutch shared linguistic history and blur the geopolitical boundaries between England and the Low Countries in surprising and politically risky ways. Contemporary visual representations and descriptions of the propinquity between England and the Low Countries, featured in the popular world atlases of Abraham Ortelius and Gerhard Mercator, dovetail with Verstegan's historical philology, shoring up the story of English and Dutch shared heritage and racial kinship.

The theater offered Londoners language lessons that thematized antiquarian emphasis on Anglo-Dutch kinship by displaying the shared syntax and phonetic correspondences between English and stage Dutch. Chapter 3 outlines a historical survey of representations of Dutch speech on the London stage, tracing an increase in the staged intelligibility of stage Dutch from Marian drama to that of late Elizabethan and early Jacobean drama, and details the range of linguistic encounters English speakers were likely to have had with Dutch-speaking residents of London. Moving on to a close reading of the *lingua matrix* of Thomas Middleton's *No Wit [No] Help like a Woman* (ca. 1611), I show how this play complicates prevailing critical understanding of foreign speech and broken English as marginalizing dramatic devices, as Middleton's Dutch and Dutch-speaking characters prove other than "funny foreigners who do not know how to speak."[146] I analyze the triangulated interplay among English, authentic stage Dutch, and inauthentic stage Dutch, tracing how similarities between English and Dutch emerge in contrast to the amplified differences between inauthentic and authentic stage Dutch. The difference that matters in shoring up one's identity as an honest Englishman does not hinge on the distinction between Englishmen and foreigners, as Janette Dillon has suggested, or on the absorption of the alien within, as Lloyd Kermode has recently argued, but instead depends on the

Englishman's ability to decipher the difference between authentic and inauthentic representations of Dutch speech.[147] The play offers its audience a paradoxical insight into English identity: those who most identify as honest Englishmen might best secure that Englishness by identifying with speakers of authentic Dutch.

Moving beyond ideas about linguistic heritage and representations of those ideas in the theater's language lessons, Chapter 4 takes up the question of the relation of language to ethnicity from the vantage point of the printed page. I analyze the semiotics of typography across the mise en page of seventeen dramatic works ranging from the mid-sixteenth through mid-seventeenth century in which stage Dutch is spoken (or Dutch characters or English characters pretending to be Dutch appear); all of the period's bilingual Anglo-Dutch vocabularies, grammars, and dictionaries; and some of the most influential multilingual parallel word lists. The first section of the chapter explores the unusual appearance of black letter stage Dutch in early seventeenth-century playbooks and a masque in order to consider how an English reader might have interpreted this unusual typographic choice. I contend that the typographic arrangements that appear to distinguish Dutch from English in these dramatic texts are an expression of what Sigmund Freud characterized as the "narcissism of small difference." While black letter appears to stand in as the minor difference that might secure a distinction between English (printed in roman) and Dutch (printed in black letter) on the page, when read together with the semantic content of the play, it reveals instead their uncanny relatedness. In addition to playbooks, bilingual grammars, dictionaries, and vocabularies offered England's reading public a rich panoply of Anglo-Dutch language lessons whose graphic expression conveyed subtle messages about linguistic and cultural relations. Recent scholarship on early modern lexicography has argued for its instrumentality in forging ideas of cultural heritage.[148] Paying particular attention to the graphic representation of English and Dutch, I show how the mise en page of early modern wordbooks also shaped ideas about the relatedness of languages and the cultural heritage they signify. The period's wordbooks were organized by means of a flexible typographic arrangement that I characterize as "typographic relativism": a dynamic system of typographic and linguistic organization that is both relative, in the sense of being content specific, and a system that forges and underscores relations between languages across the mise en page. I demonstrate how polyglot vocabularies, in particular, impressed on readers an implicit message that English antiquarians and playwrights of the period were thematizing more explicitly, the similarity—even relatedness—of the English and Dutch languages.

Chapter 5 moves off the page and into the streets of London to argue that London's commercial marketplace, the Royal Exchange, registered on the English imagination like a material pun for the overlapping of English and Dutch material culture, as well as English and Dutch cultural identities. An architectural copy of Antwerp's Nieuwe Beurs, the Royal Exchange ignited significant concern about the building's representative Englishness, the status of the Dutch community living and working in London, and the Anglo-Dutch cultural identifications it signified. Like London's Dutch residents, who were often represented as of London but not from London, the Exchange was also understood as doubly situated—both within London and beyond it. I explore the contested civic vocabularies of Dutch belonging and estrangement that emerge in three performances featuring the Royal Exchange: Queen Elizabeth's visit to and renaming of the Exchange in 1571, King James's royal progress by the Exchange as recorded in Thomas Dekker's *The Magnificent Entertainment of King James* (1604), and the mayoral pageant of 1605, which begins with the fictional arrival into London of a ship named the *Royall Exchange*. I explore how the Dutch of London engaged the semiology of their host city by strategically mobilizing the double vision that structured English representations of Dutchness. These performances reveal the Dutch as integrated into the economic, social, material, and semiotic fabric of London life and render London a city and mercantile economy palimpsested with Dutchness.

The final chapter tests the limits of the double vision analytic by expanding beyond the northern European context to analyze representations of Anglo-Dutch relations in the early years of England's engagement in the East Indies spice trade. In the first two decades of competition for dominance in the spice trade, English and Dutch rivalry was catalyzed by a doppelgänger dilemma: the problem of the English and Dutch being mistaken for one another, both by indigenous people and other European traders in the region. Literary and historical scholarship regarding the English and Dutch ventures in the Indonesian archipelago has emphasized the economic rivalry between the corporate bodies of the Dutch Vereenigde Oost-Indische Compagnie and the English East India Company, obfuscating the powerful ways in which ideas about proximate ethnic relations back home informed English and Dutch relations abroad. In Dutch and English epistolary correspondence, as well as in English-authored travel accounts, the crisis of Anglo-Dutch inter-changeability not only threatens the ability of East India Company factors to trade on behalf of England in the region, it catalyzes concerns about the very legitimacy of ethnic and national identity. I analyze English attempts to redress this dilemma of self-representation through performance, on the one hand, in the context of English lived experience in the Indonesian archipel-ago, through what I characterize as "ceremonies of distinction," and, on the other hand, in London theaters after the Restoration, particularly in John Dryden's tragedy *Amboyna* (1673), which stages a notorious instance of Anglo-Dutch agon dating back to the first half of the seventeenth century. In reading travel accounts from the early seventeenth century together with a late seventeenth-century stage tragedy that recalls the violence of Anglo-Dutch relations in the Spice Islands in the earlier part of the century, I reveal the difficulties the English faced as they attempted to jettison the double vision that had long held the English and Dutch, Englishness and Dutchness, in tandem. While the English turn to performance to make a difference between themselves and the Dutch, these performances ultimately imper-fectly suppress the similarities that rendered the English and Dutch inter-changeable in the East and approximated kinds at home.

In reading for the semiotics of Dutchness across a range of English sources, the following chapters analyze the ways in which Dutchness was constituted, revised, and contested throughout the period and how that pro-cess entailed a cultural double vision that was simultaneously shaping ideas of Englishness too. Approaching early modern English culture with an analytic engendered by this double vision, we discover that how identities were approximated has as complex a representational history, and as important a place in the history of English ethnicity in the making, as did ascriptions of cultural difference.

CHAPTER I

Going Dutch in London City Comedy

To be Dutch on the early Jacobean stage was to be a jumbler of kinds. More than butter-loving, slop-adorned, herring eaters whose gibble-gabble speech and penchant for drink induced laughter, the Dutch of London city comedy were actively producing and revealing English anxieties about potential interchangeability with their nearest European neighbors. At the turn of the seventeenth century, city comedies, whose events transpire in London, were offering audiences ways to reflect on the proximate relations that shaped their daily lives.[1] From the mid-sixteenth century through the early seventeenth century, Dutch immigrants constituted London's largest alien population. While many sought temporary refuge from Spanish oppression in the Low Countries, others became part of a Dutch diaspora, developing their spiritual, commercial, and domestic lives in London. As Londoners walked to their theaters they passed through a city that was home not only to English men and women but to a significant presence of Dutch residents, with whom the English traded and apprenticed, alongside whom the English worshiped, and with whom some English married.[2] Arriving at the theater, Londoners paid admission for plays entitled *The Dutch Courtesan, The Hollander,* and *Holland's Leaguer,* to name but a few whose billings promised the fictive presence of the "Dutch" on London stages.[3]

While in literary analysis the Dutch of London city comedy often are folded into the larger category of Continental "others," historically they were unlike their French, Spanish, and Italian counterparts insofar as they lived for decades in significant numbers in and around London. Anglo-Dutch proximity in early modern London has prompted social historians to comb dramatic literature "for what [it] could reveal about popular attitudes" toward England's Dutch neighbors, living both within and beyond its borders. For example, Laura Hunt Yungblut argues that there is "no evidence of an overwhelming preoccupation with the Continental immigrants" in early modern literature and that "depictions of foreigners . . . fall into two basic, stereotypical categories: contemptuously comical or darkly threatening and subversive."[4] Yungblut's search for a cultural preoccupation with Continental immigrants imagines that where there is cultural anxiety about the Dutch, for instance, we should expect to find literary representations of a Dutchman. Conventional literary interpretation of city comedy has focused on the genre's characterization of "city types," such as the merchant, citizen, gentleman, widow, and whore.[5] As Theodore Leinwand has demonstrated, such scholarship has revealed how the "comic staging of social roles permits audiences to question their adequacy."[6] City comedies offer powerful social commentary insofar as they "call attention to the stereotypes that constitute 'a merchant' or 'a wife' outside the theater."[7] A troubling critical slip occurs, however, if in literary and historical analysis the exploration of a stereotype begins by assuming the self-evidence of a category such as "Dutch." Dutch characters have been understood largely either as stereotypes that evince English xenophobia or as another Continental "other," interchangeable with French, Italian, or Spanish counterparts.[8] Less attention has been paid to how "Dutchness" as a category is constituted in particular ways by the English stage.

John Marston's *The Dutch Courtesan* (1605) reveals how wordplay, to borrow from the dramatist's own lexicon, "jumbles" Englishness and Dutchness and thus vivifies the subtle and unstable characterizations of English and Dutch ethnicities in London city comedy. "Jumbling" is an apt term for the process traced throughout this chapter since in early modern English it meant not only to mix up or muddle but also to make up. Analyzing the fluidity of signifiers of ethnic difference, particularly language, diet, and religious belief, I reveal how ethnicity emerges less as a property of a group—or an aspect of a "type"—than as part of a relational process that catalyzes a double vision analytic. In so doing, I revise our now-conventional understanding of city comedy as a genre that primarily depends on and mobilizes stereotypes of foreigners and Englishmen to make sense of the diversity of London city life. Marston's play challenges the claim that "city comedies depend less on verbal traces than on exaggerated characterizations" by employing verbal puns and wordplay to vivify subtle and unstable characterizations of northern European, in particular, English and Dutch, ethnicities.[9] The chapter analyzes

how this representative comedy forged minor differences as essential to the
maintaining of English ethnicity, a process that required English audiences
to sharpen their double vision, and foregrounds the difficulty of this task
given the proximate relations between English and Dutch geographies, faith,
culinary appetite, and language.

How did the stage "Dutch" its characters and how were Londoners
imaginatively refigured in the process? *The Dutch Courtesan* offers a compelling response to these questions by figuring English characters who are alternately overwritten with Dutch influence and who imperfectly suppress the
trace of the stranger within. Three "shaping influences" of ethnicity—
specifically, language, religion, and culinary appetite—are the means by
which Dutchness and Englishness are represented as problematically proximate ethnicities.[10] In Marston's *Dutch Courtesan*, lustful women—prostitutes
and wayward wives—play central roles in affiliating English with Dutch
appetite and belief. Teasing out the operations that make such representation
possible demands a close and textured reading of the wordplay, double entendres and bawdy puns that interlace English and Dutch belief and appetite.
Often, in order to get the joke or register double entendres in city comedy,
the listener must hear both the English and the Dutch reference. I underscore
the doubleness and simultaneity of this perception because this double vision
was an important part of what city comedies produced as they performed
northern European ethnicities as troublingly proximate.

English Love of the Low Countries

In the opening scene of *The Dutch Courtesan*, Freevill, whose cooling
affection for the play's Dutch courtesan sets the plot in motion, proffers a
defense of prostitution intended to persuade his reluctant friend Malheureux
to join him in his visit to a brothel. On the face of it, the defense Freevill
recites is familiar, even formulaic: prostitutes, being consumed with lust
themselves, provide married and unmarried men an outlet for desires that
would otherwise be turned toward other men's wives.[11] What is curious about
Freevill's speech is the way in which his argument is subtended by a claim of
England's spatial proximity to the Low Countries:

> *Malheureux:* I dare not give you up to your own company; I fear the
> warmth of wine and youth will draw you to some common house
> of lascivious entertainment.

Freevill: Most necessary buildings, Malheureux. Ever since my
   intention of marriage, I do pray for their continuance.
Malheureux: . . . sir, your reason?
Freevill: . . . lest my house should be made one. I would have
   married men love the stews as Englishmen love the Low Countries: wish war should be maintained there lest it should come
   home to their own doors. (1.1.58–68)

In Freevill's imagination, the geographic proximity of the Low Countries to
England allows England's Continental neighbor to function as a "buffer
zone" that absorbs the Low Countries' war with Spain, which would otherwise spill into English cities and the domestic space of the home.[12] Similarly,
by harboring male lust, the brothels of London buffer the patriarchal household from sexual transgression. The brothel, just beyond the city wall, and
the Low Countries, across the North Sea, are each figured as neighbors whose
difference and traversable distance from London facilitate peace within it.

The fiction of this tidy geographical fantasy was writ large in post–
Spanish Armada London. The war with Spain had come home in 1588, entering even London's Thames. Moreover, for the audience of 1605, it was the
porosity, rather than the imperviousness, of geographic borders that was
everywhere evidenced in Londoner's daily lives.[13] The Low Countries' battles
with Spain had made England sanctuary to thousands of Dutch immigrants,
many of whom remained in England to raise families and to practice their
trade. Strangers from the Low Countries had "come home" to London's
"own doors." The generation of Londoners attending Marston's play had
never known their city without a significant presence of Dutch strangers.

Although the play opens with a vision of distinct and "maintain[able]"
borders, as the play unfolds Dutch influence on English religious belief and
culinary appetite reveals the Low Countries as a space less securely beyond
the pale than is suggested by Freevill's speech. The lynchpin of Freevill's
analogy is the house. The house is imagined as a private, domestic, patriarchal, and chaste enclosure guarded by its "own doors"; yet houses can be
commercialized, made public, bawdy, and "common."[14] In the play both of
these houses are sites of family. Freevill's fantasy of a patriarchal, lawful family rooted in the wife's marital fidelity is ensured by the labor of another
family, an affiliation of women in the sex trade whose commercial home in
the play is called the "Family of Love."

Curiously, Freevill's idealized, patriarchal household never materializes on stage. Instead the play invests the audience in a domestic portrait of life with the Mulligrubs, an English family of vintners whose religious affiliation is with none other than the banned religious sect the Family of Love, thought to have originated in the Low Countries.[15] The play thus introduces four concepts of "family": idealized patriarchal household, common bawdy house, banned religious sect, and the commercialized home-tavern.[16] By multiplying the sites of family, the play exposes the fault line of Freevill's binary logic (patriarchal household versus bawdy house equals England versus the Low Countries) to expose the instability of the ground on which his two houses and two geographies rest. In *The Dutch Courtesan*, the home-tavern, local brothel, and religious sect ultimately become symbolically overlapping communities constituted by a cross fire of double entendre that depends on a more subtle negotiation between foreign and domestic than Freevill imagines.

Dutching the Courtesan

With Franceschina's first appearance, the Dutch courtesan ignites a controversy of classification. The difficulty other characters in the play have in naming her underscores the uneasy nexus of affiliations that the courtesan draws together. Though Freevill euphemistically glosses over her occupation by lending her the capacious title "mistress," by the play's conclusion she will have served as an index for early modern terms for whore. Upon first sight of Franceschina, Malheureux wonders if he is seeing "[a] courtesan?" and then moments later he pronounces, somewhat more confidently, "Ha, she is a whore, is she not?" (1.2.99). Freevill responds, "Whore? Fie, whore! You may call her a courtesan, a cockatrice, or (as that worthy spirit of an eternal happiness said) a suppository. But whore, fie! 'Tis not in fashion to call things by their right names. . . . Come, she's your mistress, or so" (1.2.100–107). Throughout the play the professional appellations used to describe Franceschina proliferate. She is: "a creature of a public use," "courtesan," "strumpet," "punk," "polecat," "rampant cockatrice grown mad," "wench," "fair devil," "cacafuego," "fair whore," "common up-tail."[17] A Dutch courtesan with an Italianate name who is called a plethora of slang words for an English whore, her ethnically inflected differences, projected by those around her, resist a stable national and ethnic categorization.[18] The range of affiliations the naming of Franceschina engenders is suggestive of her openness to business with all European men. Mary Faugh, the bawd who governs the brothel where Franceschina works, boasts, "I have made you acquainted with the Spaniard, Don Skirtoll; with the Italian, Master Beieroane; with the Irish lord, Sir Patrick; with the Dutch merchant, Haunce Herkin Glukin Skellam Flapdragon; and specially with the greatest French; and now lastly with this English" (2.2.13–18). Franceschina prospers by indifference to the geographical origin of the men she serves; and those men who multiply her common epithets demonstrate an indifference to her geographical origins.

As the play's "Dutch courtesan," however, Franceschina recalls the historical presence of Dutch sex workers in London. Dutch courtesans and bawds were known elements in the sexual economy of early modern London. Among English writers from the medieval period through the early modern period, there was a recurring charge that "Froes of Flanders" were in the business of London sex work. In England's late fourteenth-century wars of rebellion, for example, the stews of Southwark were transformed into a sanctuary for rebels. The *Anonimalle Chronicle* reports, "that same day being Corpus Christi in the morning these comons of Kent despoyled a house near London Bridge which was in the hands of Froes of Flaunders who farmed out the sayd house from the Mayor of London."[19] The association of women from Flanders with prostitution reemerges a decade later in an ordinance entitled Concerning Street Walkers by Nyght and Women of Ill-Repute, which set curfews in London in an attempt to curtail the "broils and affrays" sparked by evening traffic among "common harlots, at taverns, brewhouses of huksters and other places of ill-fame"; the ordinance specifically addresses "Flemish women who profess and follow such shameful and dolorous life," requiring that all prostitutes were "to keep themselves to the places thereunto assigned . . . the stews on the other side of the Thames and Cokkeslane."[20] Ruth Mazo Karras notes that "Flemish, Dutch, and Low German women are particularly prominent in the records as prostitutes and bawds. . . . 'Dutch' brothelkeepers appear to have been particularly common. . . . Court rolls from the London suburbs of Southwark (outside the Winchester liberty), Lambeth, and East Smithfield name several Dutch women as brothelkeepers."[21] The imputation of prostitution directed toward Flemish women living in London and its suburbs carries through to the late sixteenth century. Karras has discovered in John Stow's late sixteenth-century account of the 1381 rebellion "an editor's marginal heading" that reads, "English people disdained to be bawds. Froes of Flanders were women for that purpose."[22]

Finally, those English who regularly sailed across the North Sea to the ports of Amsterdam and Haarlem were likely to have encountered Dutch prostitutes upon their arrival. According to Sir William Brereton, in his *Travels to Holland . . . 1634–1635*, Dutch prostitutes aggressively marketed their wares to strangers arriving at port: "About nine hour we passed Harleimer Port and came into a fair street, wherein of late swarmed the most impudent whores I have heard of, who would if they saw a stranger, come into the middle of the street unto him, pull him by the coat, and invite him into their house."[23] Both abroad and at home, the Dutch prostitute was a familiar and long-standing figure in the English sexual economy and cultural landscape.

In Marston's play, Franceschina's part-Dutch and part-English lexicon enters her into this cultural association of Dutch women with sex work. Though her speech has been characterized as "a helter-skelter of Germanic, French, [and] Italian," making her something of a "linguistic monster," it is everywhere inflected with what the play's title and its list of dramatis personae indicate should register as a *Dutch* accent and lexicon.[24] Franceschina rails, "Ick sall be revenged! Do ten tousand hell damn me, ick sall have the rouge troat cut" (2.2.43). Cheek by jowl, Dutch pronouns ("Ick") mix with imperfectly translated English phonology ("tousand"; "troat"), English loan words ("revenged"), and Anglo-Dutch cognates ("sall"—for English "shall"/"zal" [from Dutch *zullen*: shall]).[25] Franceschina may indeed speak something of a "Babylonian dialect" but that dialect is heavily laden with the sounds of English and "stage Dutch." A flexible formula for representing Dutch speech on stage, stage Dutch is partially or mostly intelligible to English characters on stage and to the theater audience. Often a mix of German, Flemish, and Dutch sounds, it consists of Dutch-accented English interlarded with a relatively limited, well-worn theatrical lexicon of Dutch words and phrases. Words such as *Ick* (I), *vro* or *frow* (woman, maid, or girl), *bedanck* (thanks), *vader* (father), *vater* (water), *heb* (have), *niet* (not), and *met* (with) would not need to be glossed explicitly in order to be rendered intelligible in the context of performance.[26] The English-speaking theater audience may have known but a few words and phrases in Dutch; they were, however, likely familiar with the sound of Dutch merchants speaking English with Dutch accents as they transacted business in London's commercial centers, such as the Royal Exchange.

More importantly, the London theater-going audience was growing familiar with the theater's production of Dutch speech on the English stage. In Thomas Dekker's popular *The Shoemaker's Holiday* (1599), Lacy, having taken on a disguise as a Dutchman named Hans, speaks a macaronic twist of a predominately English lexicon inflected everywhere with his adopted Dutch accent. The Skipper of the same play is represented as a "real" Dutch sailor. His Dutch and Lacy's are nonetheless markedly similar. They understand one another because the Dutch they speak is tailor-made for the *English* ear and for the London stage:

> *Skipper: Ik sal yow wat seggen Hans: dis skip dat comen from Candy is*
> *al fol, by Got's sacrament, van sugar, civet, almonds, cambric end*
> *alle dingen, towsand, towsand ding. Nempt it, Hans, nempt it vor*
> *your meester. Daer be de bills van laden. Your meester Simon Eyre*
> *sal ha'good copen, wat seggen yow, Hans?*
> *Firk: Wat seggen de reggen de copen, slopen.* Laugh, Hodge, laugh.
> *Lacy: Mine liever broder Firk, bringt Meester Eyre tot den signe van*
> *swannekin. Daer sal yow find dis skipper end me. Wat seggen yow,*
> *broder Firk? Doot it, Hodge.* (7.1–9)[27]

This exchange is comical not merely because of the garbled approximation of a part-English, part-Dutch lexicon, or English words made to sound Dutch, but because of Firk's response to the Skipper. Firk is neither Dutch nor playing a Dutchman in this scene. His nonsensical mockery of the cadence of the Skipper's language reveals a familiarity with the sounds made by Dutch tradesmen in action. Firk's satirical performance of Dutchness underscores the representational quality of both the Skipper's and Hans's stage Dutch. Every word is self-consciously theatrical. A similar instance of Englishmen satirizing the sound of Dutch occurs in William Haughton's *Englishmen for My Money* (1598) when Frisco, the play's clown, declares he can speak Dutch:

> *Frisco:* I can speak perfect *Dutch* when I list.
> *Pisa:* Can you, I pray let's heare some?
> *Frisco:* Nay I must have my mouth full of Meate first, and then you
> shall heare me grumble it foorth full mouth, as *Haunce Butterkin*
> *slowpin frokin.* (1.1.179–84)[28]

The clown's "slowpin frokin" recalls Firk's "copen slopen," suggesting that the aural cues of stage Dutch had settled into a somewhat consistent emphasis on long open vowels, followed by sharp consonants, and occasional rhyme.

Finally, two years after the *Dutch Courtesan* was published, Thomas Dekker's and John Webster's *Northward Hoe* offered up Hans van Belch, whose consonantal confusions make him a memorable satirical character. As was the case in *The Shoemaker's Holiday*, English speakers (in this case, Doll) respond to the characters speaking stage Dutch with a similar mix of English words delivered with a stage Dutch accent:

> *Hans:* How ist met you, how ist vro? vrolick?
> *Doll:* Ick vare well God danke you: Nay Ime an apt scholler and can take.
> *Hans:* Datt is good, dott is good: Ick can neet stay long: for Ick heb en skip come now upon de vater: O mine schoonen vro, wee sall dance lanteera, teera, and sing Ick drincks to you mine here[.]
> (2.1.63–67)[29]

Like Marston, Dekker and Webster portray stage Dutch as at once comic and comprehensible by emphasizing the ways in which stage Dutch approximates English speech. In the case of stage Dutch, minor linguistic differences stand in as salient but slippery codes of ethnic difference.

Playwrights were not alone in exploring the sounds of Dutch and English. To one well-tuned English ear the cacophony of consonants evident in this stage Dutch was a feature that made the Dutch language unfit for poetry. Sir Philip Sidney remarked in his *Defence of Poesy,* "the Dutch . . . [is] so [full] with consonants, that they cannot yield the sweet sliding, fit for a verse."[30] Late sixteenth- and early seventeenth-century city comedy produced characters whose stage Dutch gives life to Sidney's thesis in the playhouse. In order to be rendered alien, Franceschina need not appear to be a "real" Dutch speaker; she instead must merely evoke the conventions of cacophonous sounds that the theater was constructing as "Dutch" in performance.

Not only does Franceschina's speech mingle the phonologies of English and stage Dutch, Dutch words also slip into her expressions of emotion: "Oh mine aderliver love, vat sall me do to requit dis your mush affection," she inquires of Freevill when she first sets eyes on him. Her attempt to translate a specifically Dutch term of endearment, "alderliefest" ("dearest") into the lexicon of amorous parlance within the bawdy house results in her making "mush" of her affection for Freevill.[31] In this way, Franceschina's attempt to translate her love for Freevill from her native tongue to the language of love in the Family of Love renders her heart-felt affections comic. Franceschina's stage Dutch is a performance of imperfect phonological approximations to English and failed translations of Dutch. This specifically linguistic incapacity is rendered, not surprisingly, in erotic terms. By the play's end Franceschina will be condemned "as false, as prostituted, and adulterate, as some translated manuscript" (4.3.6–7).

What emerges from this play is anything but Franceschina's inherent Dutchness. The very capaciousness of this category—the ways in which stage Dutch is constituted by a jumbling of Dutch- and English-sounding words—introduces a particularly problematic set of linguistic codes by which ethnic difference might be instantiated. In the minor difference between "what" and "wat"—or "much" and "mush"—English and Dutch dally on each other's fringes.

Just as Franceschina's speech unsettles linguistic boundaries, so too her exchanges with Freevill demonstrate that she cuts across his opposing sexual geographies: London and the Low Countries. Franceschina is the neighbor whose presence threatens to depreciate the value of the home(land) precisely because she challenges the cultural fantasy of fixed, impermeable geographic and linguistic borders. In the final scenes of the play, the Dutch courtesan is silenced. But the lingering echo of her stage Dutch combined with her affiliation with "the Family of Love" leaves in place a challenge to Freevill's neatly structured worldview. This challenge plays itself out in the *The Dutch Courtesan*'s subplot to which Franceschina and Freevill's story lends coordinates by establishing a chiastic structure that crosses England with the Low Countries as well as domestic with commercial sexual economies.

The Family of Love

The brothel where Franceschina resides is given a name, the "Family of Love," by Freevill (1.1.146–47). Later in act 1, the brothel's bawd, Mary Faugh, declares, "though I am one of the Family of Love and, as they say, a bawd that covers the multitude of sins . . . I am none of the wicked that eat fish o' Fridays" (1.2.17–20). By claiming affiliation with the Family of Love, Mary Faugh ranks herself above Catholics and so reshuffles her social position along the cultural register of belief over trade. Her statement, along with Freevill's remark, links the religious sect, an import from the Low Countries, with the sexual commercial space of the bawdy house.

Critics have observed that early seventeenth-century theater yoked representations of the Family of Love together with inherent sexual licentiousness,
a charge that plagued the community throughout its life in England.[32] For
example, in John Day's *The Isle of Gulls* (1606) we learn that "the Familie of
Love hold it lawful to lie with [a woman] though she be another mans
wife."[33] *Any Thing for a Quiet Life* (written c. 1621, published 1662), by
Thomas Middleton and John Webster, makes explicit the sexual impropriety
of Familists, members of the Family of Love, while also underlining the sect's
link to the Low Countries: "Let's divorce our selves so long, or think I am
gone to'th'Indies, or lie with him when I am asleep, for some Familists of
Amsterdam will tell you [it] may be done with a safe conscience."[34] On the
veracity of the theater's charge of sexual immorality, historian Jean Dietz
Moss argues: "There are grounds . . . for terming Familists dissemblers, but
the more dramatic accusations of licentious behavior appear to have little, if
any, foundation. Chronicles, state records, annals, and reports of clerical
officials mention Familists imprisoned for their religious opinions and Familists who publicly recanted of their errors, but no accounts are included of
Familists discovered in immoral circumstances."[35] While Moss finds that
silence pervades state records and reports, on the early seventeenth-century
stage there nonetheless is no dearth of imputation of the sexual licentiousness
of Familists. Both Marston's play and the anonymously authored *The Family
of Love* (1608) make visible the sect by transferring the unknowable geography
of Familist faith onto the sexual landscape of London's bawdy houses.[36]

These plays are penned and performed at a significant historical moment
for the Familists. Historians have emphasized the radical nature of Familist
doctrine and the troubling inscrutability of Familist identity. J. A. van Dorsten in *The Radical Arts: First Decade of an Elizabethan Renaissance* argues that
"among London's unofficial churches the most controversial and probably
the most influential was the 'Domus Charitatis' or Family of Love."[37] The
Family of Love or Familism was a religious fellowship founded around 1540
by Hendrik Niclaes, who was born in Munster but resided throughout his
adult life primarily in Amsterdam. Christopher Vittels, a joiner residing in
Southwark, is credited with spreading the ideas of Familism to England in
the 1570s when he translated Niclaes's treatises.[38] In its first decades of influence in England, the faith was disparaged by Englishmen who emphasized
its foreign origins. Disseminators of the faith risked being impugned as foreigners, as evidenced by the attempt of one of Vittels's contemporaries to
defame Vittels by charging that his translation of Hendrik Niclaes was "not

done like a godly Christian nor a true English hearted man. For indeed, as I am informed, you are of the Dutch race yourself."[39] Prior even to Vittels's translation of the Familist doctrine, the Dutch Stranger Church in London found itself implicated in affiliation with Familists when in the 1550s a minister of the Dutch congregation, Andrian van Haemstede, was "suspected of harboring Familists sympathies" because he publicly defended an Anabaptist. Van Haemstede's stance resulted in his eventual excommunication.[40] This kind of conflation regarding dissenting Protestant sects was by no means unusual; James VI of Scotland would inscribe the same conflation of Familists with Anabaptists in his *Basilikon Doron*.[41] Van Haemstede's story reveals not an actual link between Familism and the Low Countries or ties between Dutch stranger communities in London and Familism, but rather that a cultural fantasy of affiliation between Familism and the Dutch community in London was forged on English soil.[42] This was an affiliation that the Dutch Church itself was eager to disavow.

The sect flourished during the second half of the sixteenth century through the mid-seventeenth century, when it was absorbed into Quakerism.[43] The core ideas of the English manifestation of this sect were "the denial of the divinity of Christ, the belief that baptism should not be taken before the age of thirty, and the idea that once 'Godded with God' the regenerate had been perfected and could not sin."[44] The practice of such a late baptism followed from the belief that full union with God was only achieved by "a progressive growth in the service of love in which the individual developed from a child to an adult in his understanding and practice of *caritas* or Christian Love. This spiritual growth culminated in an elaborate ritual of baptism at the age of thirty."[45] At that moment the follower was recognized by the community as "Godded with God," a complete union of the perfected self with God.[46] The Familist's view that Christ was the Son of God, not God himself, aligned the sect, in popular imagination, with other anti-Trinitarians such as the Anabaptists and the Mennonites.[47]

In 1580 Elizabeth banned the sect by means of a royal proclamation, which officially declared Familism heretical.[48] The proclamation links the sect with its "Dutch" roots, laments the spreading of it into the English realm, and warns that these believers are "dangerous" because, when asked to declare their belief, they deny their affiliation with the Family of Love.[49] During an era when popular reading included martyrology (stories that remembered those who died declaring rather than recanting their faith), the Familists struck a particularly heretical note in the ears of those who aimed to tune the English state to an Anglican harmony. From an Anglican perspective, the Family of Love was a spiritually promiscuous sect untroubled by making claims of allegiance to more than one religion. They were, in other words, dissemblers because they willfully doubled their vows of allegiance, rather than seeing themselves as divided against Anglicanism because of their faith.

The perception of spiritual promiscuity slides into accusations of sexual promiscuity in a 1606 publication entitled the *Supplication of the Family of Love*.[50] First submitted to King James I in 1604, the text, an appeal to overturn Queen Elizabeth's proclamation, was published along with an examiner's editorial commentary in 1606.[51] The 1606 publication suggests that the 1604 petition had garnered attention enough at court that an anonymous examiner, someone likely "involved in the earlier campaign against the fellowship," felt pressed to respond.[52] The 1606 *Supplication* is interrupted throughout by the examiner's commentary. Ironically, the *Supplication* is so embedded with this commentary that the 1606 text reads as a successful polemic *against* the Familists, including the examiner's insinuation of sexual as well as religious transgression. Early in the *Supplication* the Familists are characterized as exhibiting "always a lust to themselves, and cleave unto the covetouesnesse, the voluptuousnesse of the flesh" (12). This, of course, is a familiar Anglican trope applied to Catholics, Muslims, Jews, and "radical" Protestant sects.[53] Yet the examiner's subsequent suggestion that the Familists make a common house of their meeting houses goes further: "they build diverse common houses, which they name Gods houses. And they occupie there manie-manner of foolishnesse" (15). The phrase "common house," deployed in the context of the examiner's condemnation of Familists as lustful, carries with it clear implication: either the Familists meet not to worship God but to engage in the "lust" of the flesh or their worship of God involves performance of such lust. What might seem a passing remark in a catalogue of condemnation becomes, on the contemporary London stage, the central trope for imagining the Family of Love.

The Great Jumbling

The common house had long been a troubling space of domestic and foreign mixing because, as Jean Howard has argued, the prostitute's activities "threaten to erase differences between man and man, nation and nation, as her clients are rendered interchangeable"; so too, Valerie Traub has demonstrated, the brothel was associated with the culturally and sexually disordering potential of disease.[54] In Marston's play, the symbolic resonance of the common house crosses commercial with religious affiliation, lust with *caritas*, catching more in its semantic network than the bawds and clients of the bawdy house. As the play progresses, characters who are members of the religious sect become charged with signifying the sexual excess of the London bawdy house. This happens both through commonplace accusations of the sexual availability of a tavern wife and through her reflections on her own culinary labor.

The play's subplot serves up an English family of vintners, who happen to be members of the Family of Love, as the target of the knavish Cocledemoy's devices. Characterized as a "capricious rascal" (1.2.67), Cocledemoy targets the Mulligrubs "for wit's sake" (5.3.137). We learn of the Mulligrubs' religious affiliation with the Family of Love as Mistress Mulligrub prepares her tavern for guests. "Perfume!" she cries out, "this parlour does so smell of profane tobacco. I could never endure this ungodly tobacco since one of our elders assured me, upon his knowledge, tobacco was not used in the congregation of the Family of Love" (3.3.48–51). She prepares her table and scents her tavern to no avail. Mistress Mulligrub has been gulled by Cocledemoy.[55] She has traded a "great goblet" for a jowl of rotten salmon upon the promise that Cocledemoy's master and wife should return for dinner that evening (3.3.30–56).

Adulterated or poor quality foodstuffs are at the heart of what aggravates Cocledemoy about the Mulligrubs, thus making his gift of rotting fish a fitting jibe. In one of the only motivations he offers for his antipathy and thieving, Cocledemoy imaginatively metamorphosizes Master Mulligrub from a vintner into wine itself: "I'll gargalize my throat with this vintner, and when I have done with him, spit him out . . . to wring the withers of my gouty, barmed, spigot-friging, jumbler of elements, Mulligrub" (3.2.31–42). Cocledemoy is not alone in his characterization of the Mulligrubs as "jumbler[s] of elements." Mistress Mulligrub expresses an anxiety about her vocation in similar terms: "Truth, husband, surely heaven is not pleased with our vocation. We do wink at the sins of our people, our wines are Protestants and,—I speak it to my grief and to the burden of my conscience—we fry our fish with salt butter" (2.3.7–10). What resonates theatrically as a comically overblown crisis of conscience reveals, characterologically, Mistress Mulligrub's concern that the culinary products of her home-tavern break the rules of her "congregation." The concatenation of "our people, our wines" suggests that religious affiliation and culinary appetite are homologous in her mind. By serving Protestant wines, the Mulligrubs rupture the neat metonymic logic that makes diet an extension and expression of faith. The air, a mix of perfume and tobacco, like fish fried in salt butter, registers the difficult negotiation of religion residing in the home when the home is also a commercialized terrain.

The jumbling of dietary elements, central to the characterization of the Mulligrubs, springs forth even from the patronymic itself. In early modern parlance, to be "sick of the Mulligrubs" was a way of indicating one had an acute stomachache, colic, or diarrhea induced by humoral imbalance. Contemporary texts reveal that devils, dogs, and university students alike are struck with the Mulligrubs. Samuel Rowley in *The Noble Souldier* (1634) writes, "The Divell lyes sicke of the Mulligrubs," thus suggesting the shared fallibility of the stomach of both man and the devil.[56] The *Oxford English Dictionary* cites the use of the word in John Fletcher's *Monsieur Thomas* (1639): "Whither goe all these men-menders, these Physitians? Whose dog lyes sicke o'th mulligrubs?"[57] Earlier in the century and just a year prior to the publication of *The Dutch Courtesan*, Thomas Middleton employed the term in *Father Hubburds Tales; or, The Ant and Nightingale* (1604), in which university students are derided for their dependence on their mothers: "Some Londoners Sonne . . . that must heare twice a weeke from his mother, or else he will be sick . . . of a university Mullygrub."[58] The term was of common parlance. In Marston's play, the Mulligrubs' own name implicates the vintner and his tavern-keeping wife in digestive distress, itself a sign of humoral imbalance.

In *Staging Domesticity*, Wendy Wall shows how national identity for the "middling sort" was, in part, constituted by "reflections on the material realities of household work," above all the foodstuffs, health remedies, and products that women prepared in the domestic sphere.[59] Domesticity stands in as the staple of Englishness and "template for political order," even as it is fraught with the violence of food preparation and the mixedness of alien ingredients.[60] Patricia Fumerton likewise emphasizes the ways in which everyday practices of domestic life in the early modern period could "be charged with strangeness even to its practitioners."[61] Mistress Mulligrub's reflection on her culinary concoctions reveals the way a tavern hearth could register both religious and state conflict. In serving Protestant wines, her tavern reflects the religion of the Anglican English state and, so she fears, conflicts with her own religious affiliation. The salt butter registers as further evidence of the mingling of foreign and domestic ingredients that characterizes Mistress Mulligrub's tavern menu.

Throughout the seventeenth century the English link butter consumption to the Dutch, going so far as to create an origin myth for Belgium in which the land itself springs from a butter-box (*The Dutch-mens Pedigree* [1653]).[62] The Dutch are commonly referred to as "butter-boxes" in dramatic as well as in satirical texts. In Henry Glapthorne's *The Hollander* (1635), for instance, the play's Dutchman reflects on the weakness of his bodily constitution as "guilty of Bacon grease, and potted Butter."[63] David Crane has argued that Mistress Mulligrub "laments the use of cheap Dutch (i.e. salted) butter instead of the good English sort."[64] By using preserved butter that tastes "Dutch" to fry her customers' fish, Mistress Mulligrub brokers a product associated with the geography from which her faith was thought to have been imported. This minor difference—the added ingredient of salt in butter—give the Mulligrubs' menu a distinctively Dutch flavor. So too, its inextricability, the way it homogenizes the domestic foodstuff, makes it a particularly fitting signifier of Dutch presence in London life. Mistress Mulligrub, however, does not identify her faith as foreign; rather, it is the *Protestant* faith of her customers, evidenced by their palate for fried fish and Protestant wines, that generates her ambivalence about a commercial livelihood earned by serving a menu whose ingredients fall outside the dietary guidelines of her faith. Living and working in a space rife with culinary adulterations, her consequent epicurean anxieties lay the groundwork for the play's suggestion that she is vulnerable to being lured into a sexually adulterous relationship with her husband's antagonist, Cocledemoy.[65] In other words, Mistress Mulligrub's willingness—however reluctant—to adulterate foodstuffs in her tavern puts at issue a supposed predilection for marital adultery. The play has prepared the groundwork for this insinuation not merely with commonplace innuendos about the sexual availability of tavern women but by linking the Mulligrubs to the Family of Love and the Family of Love with the bawdy house.

Cocledemoy maliciously stages Mulligrub's arrest on the grounds that the vintner's "house has been suspected for a bawdy tavern a great while" (4.5.106–8). Mistress Mulligrub's exchanges with her husband's enemy do little to put suspicions of her sexual availability to rest. Her oft-repeated self-characterization as a woman of commerce, the keeper of a public house, unwittingly implicates her in adultery: "Squires, gentlemen, and knights diet at my table. . . . [They] give me very good words, and a piece of flesh when time of year serves. . . . My silly husband, alas, he knows nothing of it" (3.3.19–27). Audiences no doubt registered the sexual innuendo in "the piece of flesh" that tavern guests give to Mistress Mulligrub without her husband's knowledge. Here Mistress Mulligrub sports with adultery with language evocative not of the bedchamber but of her kitchen.

By the play's conclusion, Mistress Mulligrub's religious affiliation has joined with her professional role as public house keeper to set in motion an imputation of sexual transgression articulated in terms of *culinary* mixedness. So too her culinary transgressions are depicted as a religious sin. As her husband's accuser, now also her suitor, declares the charges brought against Master Mulligrub, it turns out that it is precisely this mixing that Cocledemoy's prank attempts to police:

> *Cocledemoy:* But brother, brother, you must think of your sins and
> iniquities. You have been a broacher of profane vessels; you have
> made us drink of the juice of the whore of Babylon. For whereas
> good ale, perries, braggets, ciders, and metheglins was the true
> ancient British and Troyan drinks, you ha' brought in Popish
> wines, Spanish wines, French wines . . . to the subversion, stag-
> gering, and sometimes overthrow of many a good Christian. You
> ha' been a great jumbler. (5.3.102–11)[66]

Having confessed to Cocledemoy's charges of being "a great jumbler," Mulligrub is released into a city whose sexual economies have been reworked from inside his own home. This reworking is part of what the genre of city comedy itself is working out. Jean Howard has argued that city comedy "often specifies the danger to the household . . . as the penetration of domestic space by foreign bodies—foreign people, foreign goods, or class enemies who function as strangers or aliens—and by the subsequent weakening of the boundaries of the household as a container for the people, especially the women, who dwell within it."[67] One might argue that Marston's play extends Howard's generic definition by adding faith and foodstuffs to the list of what "penetrates" and endangers domestic space; but this would fall short of the challenge Marston's Mulligrubs pose to the idea of the London home as a metonym for Englishness itself. Mistress Mulligrub's menu brings in through the tavern door and circulates within domestic space ingredients that ensure her commercial livelihood while alienating her from her chosen faith. Her religious identity reaches out beyond her commercial household to couple with that other commercial space run by women, Mary Faugh's bawdy house, the "Family of Love." In contrast to Freevill's neatly articulated dichotomies with which the play began, the Mulligrubs reveal that distinctions between household and common house, England and the Low Countries, are not easily "maintained." By the play's end each space is refigured *in terms of the other.* The effect of this mutual construction in Marston's play cannot be reduced to an act of penetration, evinced in the failure of boundaries to contain, forefend, and defend, for to conclude thus would be unwittingly to reproduce Freevill's logic.

The Dutching of the English Mulligrubs suggests that one critical challenge for understanding the theater's role in constructing northern European ethnic proximity lies in reanimating early modern lexicons. The comedy's wordplay, which sets in motion an affiliation between wives and sex workers, religions of England and the Low Countries, depends on the audience's ability to decipher puns on the "Family of Love" and to register certain culinary references as charged with Dutch strangeness, even as this strangeness is embodied by English characters. What is more, Marston's *The Dutch Courtesan* demonstrates that recovering how the Mulligrubs become the play's "great jumblers" demands recognition that the historical particulars of what they set into circulation matter to how they imbricate Dutch and English ethnic identities. The play demonstrates that part of what was under way in city comedy was more than an exploration of the metropolis and its types. The theater's attempts to differentiate English from Dutch characters result throughout in operations that expose the overlap between them. While there can be little doubt that London playwrights trafficked in and produced border-generating logics of self and other, these same authors and their audiences were also exploring the ways in which English people, products, and places were reshaped by their proximate—even intimate—relations with Dutch people, products, and places. *The Dutch Courtesan* traffics in discursive operations that open up a palimpsestic perception: one that sees Dutchness within, beneath, and overlayed onto Englishness. In this way, the play produces a cultural double vision, one that envisions the signifiers of Englishness and Dutchness as emerging always in relation to one another. The pressing question that *The Dutch Courtesan* leaves its London audience pondering is this: who among us *isn't* going Dutch?

CHAPTER 2

"By Common Language Resembled"

Anglo-Dutch Kinship in the Language Debates

Writing from Holland, the Englishman Thomas Scott begins his polemic in support of the resumption of the United Provinces' war for independence against Spain with a curious remark: "Let us now [go to] . . . the United Provinces, and considering her wayes, learn to be wise. Neither need wee be ashamed of such Tutors, who come of the same race originally that wee do, as our speech witnesseth."[1] Scott's *The Belgicke Pismire* (1622) positions the United Provinces as a tutor to the English people, their state, and its seafaring corporations.[2] As the text's titular pismires, the Hollanders' diligent management of the domestic sphere, organization of their provinces, and navigational prowess are qualities that Scott extols as he implores his countrymen, "let us weave our selves more closely together [with the United Provinces], and tye our selves inseparably in a true-loves knot" (99). For Scott, this lover's knot is not only a strategic political alliance. It is also an expression of a forgotten kinship between the English and Dutch, a kinship characterized both by the minor differences that animate theatrical representations of Anglo-Dutch ethnic approximation and by resemblances across the English and Dutch "race." For Scott's polemical purposes, resemblances matter most to the Anglo-Dutch relation. Customs, manners, and habits, what in the previous chapter I explored as plastic variables of ethnic distinction, are "small differences which will be betwixt Nation and Nation, even by the different temperature of the soyle and ayre, or other naturall accidents, as betwixt brother and brother in a house." But for these minor differences, Scott declares, "wee agree well, and seeme as if wee were one people" (97).

On its face, the political motivation for Scott's claim is clear: by asserting an "original" alliance rooted in "race," he naturalizes Anglo-Dutch political alliance as an outgrowth of kinship ties. Yet beneath the surface of Scott's polemic lies a more complex story of Anglo-Dutch ancient kinship and racial similitude and a history of their proximate relations. This history, as Scott inherited it, begins to unfold when we consider how the seventeenth-century reader might have made sense of Scott's unqualified assertion that the English and Dutch "come of the same race . . . as our speech witnesseth." Clearly, for Scott the "true-loves knot" between England and the United Provinces has been loosened by false suspicions between the neighboring states. Less clear, however, is the logic governing the idea that the Dutch and English peoples *were* the "same race," and how Dutch and English languages were thought to "witness" this racial homology. This chapter aims to untie the "true-loves knot" that Scott imagines binds his English countrymen to their Dutch neighbors by exploring the prehistory of Scott's racial assertion.

Decades before Scott's essay, another polemic regarding England's intervention in the Low Countries' efforts to throw off the Spanish yoke also naturalized Anglo-Dutch political alliance by means of a reference to linguistic kinship. *A Declaration of the Causes Mooving the Queene of England to Give Aid to the Defence of the People Afflicted and Oppressed in the Lowe Countries* (1585) declares: "in respect that they were otherwise more straightly knitte in auncient friendship to this realm then to any other countrie, we are sure that they could bee pitied of none for this long time with more cause and grief generally, then of our subjects of this realme of *England*, being their most ancient allies and familiar neighbours, and that in such maner, as this our realm of *England* and those countries have bene by common language of long time resembled and termed as man and wife."[3] Queen Elizabeth's *Declaration* traffics in a number of tropes of proximity by which Anglo-Dutch relations were regularly represented. As was the case with the puns circulating in the drama, Anglo-Dutch proximity is here figured as intimate (familiar), gendered (male and female), and ultimately familial (man and wife). Schematically speaking, the *Declaration* positions the Dutch along a continuum of proximate relations as they are figured first as ancient friends, then as neighbors, and finally as selfsame (kin). As in the drama, explored in the previous chapter, here too the geographical proximity of Anglo-Dutch relations is expressed in terms of cultural approximations. In ever more closely approximating the English, the Dutch of the *Declaration* express the tension between difference and sameness characteristic of the English double vision of their nearest neighbors. In moving from the political (shared anti-Spanish politics) to the domestic—from a discussion of the union of states (with Protestant religious sympathies) to that of the union of marriage—the *Declaration* figuratively expresses Anglo-Dutch relations as family. The alchemy of this figurative language transforms neighbors into kin and makes resemblance emerge in the sign of a family's shared language. And a family's language, being among its members common, is likewise a figure of racial kinship.

At the turn of the seventeenth century, the idea that England and the Low Countries share a common language emerges not only as a metaphor for political alliance but as its own philological argument. This chapter traces the philological arguments governing the idea that the Dutch and English people were the "same race," and explores how the Dutch and English languages were thought to "witness" this racial thesis. On both sides of the North Sea, Dutch and English authors involved in the antiquarian movement, which "developed out of the convergence of Renaissance historical scholarship with Reformation concerns about national identity and religious ancestry," advanced a thesis emphasizing the propinquity of English and Dutch language, English and Dutch peoples.[4] Their arguments had the effect of diminishing geopolitical boundaries and distinctions, emphasizing instead a shared cultural, linguistic, and racial heritage among the Germanic peoples of northern Europe. In advancing the Teutonic origins of English, antiquarians linked the linguistic and cultural histories of the English and Dutch in surprising, even politically risky, ways.

The figurative language of the queen's *Declaration* proves more than a harbinger of notions of Anglo-Dutch kinship to come. It demonstrates the role of figurative language in forging resemblance across kinds. This chapter recovers the prehistory of Scott's assertion of a racial kinship between the English and Dutch by attending closely to the tropes and metaphors within the language debates as instrumental to the expression of new ideas about language, linguistic history, and ethnicity. Far from a secondary mode of expression, figurative language about language forged ideas about cultural similitude, resemblance, and approximation. By tracing the prehistory of Scott's assertion through the intersections of language, ethnicity, and race, I reveal the making of ethnic and racial correspondences between the English and the Dutch.[5]

Our Two-Headed English Tongue: The Stranger and the Inkhorn

> All the words which we do use in our tung be either naturall English,
> and most of one syllab, or borowed of the foren, and most of manie
> syllabs. Whereby our tung semeth to have two heds, the one
> homeborn, the other a stranger[.]
> —Richard Mulcaster, *The First Part of the Elementarie,* 1582[6]

Historians of the English language agree that an important shift in perceptions about the English vernacular took place over the course of the last
third of the sixteenth century when English—once considered rude, bereft
of expressiveness, even barbarous—was endowed with positive qualities of
eloquence.[7] The late sixteenth-century debates regarding the value of English,
in relation especially to Latin and French, have been coined the "inkhorn
controversy," a phrase that recalls the instrument into which authors dipped
their quills for writing. The inkhorn became the central image of debates
regarding the aesthetic value of English for humanist pursuits. These debates
were divisive, as Richard Bailey notes: "The argument about English . . .
resolved itself into two distinct and opposing views. One side sought to
enhance the 'purity' of English and to foster simplicity and uniformity. . . .
The other celebrated 'copiousness' and 'eloquence.'"[8] As the purity of
English was opposed to ideas about its copious mixedness, the inkhorn
became a symbolic instrument for this opposition. The inkhorn revealed the
impurity of an English text—the more ink drawn from the horn in the process of writing, the lengthier and therefore more foreign the words and text.
George Gascoigne summed up the case in *Certayne Notes of Instruction Concerning the Making of Verse and Ryme in English* (1575): "The most auncient
English wordes are of one sillable, so that the more monasyllables that you
use the truer Englishman you shall seeme, and the less you shall smell of the
Inkehorne."[9] The more ink conserved, the shorter the words used, the purer,
more "naturall" the English text. The inkhorn was a reservoir whose dwin-
dling or preserved resource indicated the respective dissolution or preserva-
tion of a pure English. From the position of both the purists (who rejected
foreign borrowings) and archaizers (who advocated the discovery and rede-
ployment of Old English vocabulary instead of borrowing from classical and
Continental lexicons), inkhorn terms diluted the value of English.

To be charged with smelling of the inkhorn, then, implicated one in
excessive consumption of foreign languages, as well as linguistic and cultural

miscegenation. From the perspective of purists and archaizers, an important part of what was at stake in the inkhorn controversy was stabilizing English-ness itself, a problem that manifests itself in almost all expressions of English identity throughout the early modern period. Thomas Wilson in *The Arte of Rhetorique* (1553) warned that the use of inkhorn terms estranges English peoples from one another, one generation from the next: "Among all other lessons this should first be learned, that wee never affect any straunge ynke-horne termes, but so speak as is commonly received. . . . Some seeke so far for outlandish English, that thei forget altogether their mothers language. And I dare swere this, if some of their mothers were alive, thei were not able to tell what thei say."[10] Here the changeableness of English undermines any fantasy of consolidating identity—familial, local, ethnic, or national—around claims of linguistic unity. Wilson's narrative of linguistic mixing imagines a local, intergenerational myth of Babel taking place across the king-dom, where mothers and children no longer share a "mother tongue," where the language of the homeland becomes literally outlandish. Similar images of linguistic mingling abound in the drama of the period wherein, for instance, the English suitors in William Haughton's *Englishmen for My Money* (1598) worry that should they lose their suit in marriage to the Dutch, Italian, and French strangers, "a litter of Languages" would "spring up amongst us."[11] In John Webster and Thomas Dekker's *Westward Hoe* (1607), a later city comedy that also thematizes intra-European marriage in terms of linguistic mixedness, characters attempt to redress the impurity of their English in terms familiar to the language debates: "No more *Plurimums* if you love me, lattin whole-meates are now minc'd, and servde in for English Gallimafries: Let us there-fore cut out our uplandish Neates tongues, and talk like regenerate Brittains" (2.1.24–29).[12] Not only words but even the instruments of writing should be abandoned according to Justiniano, the play's English-Italian businessman: "Why then clap up coppy-bookes: down with pens, hang up inckhornes" (2.1.140).

Like these examples from the drama of the period, one commonplace of the language debates was to identify the mixedness of English, particularly the trend in seeking neologisms that would enrich the English tongue, as a sign of a characteristically English disposition toward other kinds of cultural jumbling, from fashion to diet. Further along in the passage cited above, Thomas Wilson bemoans: "Some farre jorneid jentlemen at their returne home, like as thei love to go in forrein apparel, so thei will pouder their talke with oversea language. He that cometh lately out of France, wil talke Frenche English, and never blushe at the matter."[13] Here the adoption of linguistic material is akin to the English taste for foreign fashion. Similarly, in the Epistle to *The Shepheardes Calendar* (1579), EK bemoans that authors make a "hodgepodge" and "gallimaufray," a dish made up of odds and ends, of other languages: "they patched up the holes with peces and rags of other languages, borrowing here of the french, there of the Italian, every where of the Latine, not weighing how il, those tongues accord with themselves, but much worse with ours: So now they have made our English tongue, a gallimaufray or hodgepodge of al other speches."[14] By evoking a "gallimaufray," this passage imagines the English mouth as consumer and producer of cultural "hodge-podge." Like Richard Mulcaster's imagined English tongue—which "semeth to have two heds, the one homeborn, the other a stranger"—here the English tongue is imagined as fractured, patched up with "rags of other languages." In *The Arte of English Poesie* (1589), George Puttenham chafes against the mixedness of English speech, a vice he characterizes as linguistic "mingle mangle": "Another of your intollerable vi[c]es is that which . . . we may call the (*mingle mangle)* as whe[n] we make our speach or writinges of sundry languages using some Italian word, or French, or Spanish, or Dutch, or Scottish, not for the nonce or for any purpose (which were in part excusable) but ignorantly and affectedly."[15] Puttenham's characterization of English as mingle-mangled captures the double consequence of the infiltration of foreign speech into the English lexicon. While mingling denotes combining, the act of mangling entails cutting, hacking, lacerating, or tearing. Linguistic mingling is more difficult to redress once English has been "mangled" by the process. In the philological debates and in the drama of the period, threats to English identity are regularly thematized as the dissolution and mangling of English word stock.

Enfranchized Speech: The Stranger-Made-Denizen

> The alteration and innovation in our tongue as in all others, hath beene brought in by entrance of Strangers . . . by enfranchising and endenizing strange words.
>
> —William Camden, *Remaines of a greater worke, concerning Britaine*, 1605[16]

The inkhorn proved a difficult symbol to co-opt from language purists by
those who celebrated instead the copiousness and eloquence of English.
Authors who took a less revisionist stance in relation to the mixedness of
English strategically deployed the figure of the denizen to describe the integration of other languages into English in more positive terms. To conjure
the denizen within the context of the language debates was to deny the binary
opposition that subtended the symbolic economy of the inkhorn. The denizen, a once stranger who, through an appeal to the City, an act of Parliament,
or a royal proclamation, becomes recognized as having some of the legal
rights of a natural-born English subject, is a subject who has been "made."[17]
Once a stranger, the denizen is translated, through the mechanisms of the
state, into a subject less strange. As neither a natural-born subject nor an alien
stranger, the denizen expresses what the inkhorn disallows: the possibility of
thinking in terms of transitions along a continuum, rather than tipping
points. To draw the denizen into the language debate, then, is to recharacter-
ize the nature of its stakes. If the inkhorn implies that English's native and
foreign parts are quantifiable, the denizen underscores instead English's qualities of flexibility and accommodation.

As a figure of alterity *in process of transition*, the denizen became especially powerful in the language debates. For Richard Mulcaster, first headmas-
ter of the Merchant Taylors' School in London, the denizen stood for the
positive value of English's mixedness. In *The First Part of the Elementarie
Which Entreateth Chefelie of the Right Writing of our English Tung* (1582), an
analysis of the education of his time, Mulcaster argued that it was precisely
the willingness to incorporate foreign terms that rendered English a venerable
"tongue of account":

> If the spreading sea, and the spacious land could use anie spech,
> theie would both shew you, where, and in how manie strange places,
> theie have sene our peple, and also give you to wit, that theie deall
> in as much, and as great varietie of matters, as anie other peple do,
> whether at home or abrode. Which is the reason why our tung doth
> serve so manie uses, because it is conversant with so manie peple,
> and so well acquainted with so manie matters, in so sundrie kindes
> of dealing. Now all this varietie of matter, and diversitie of trade,
> make both matter for our speche, & mean to enlarge it. For he that
> is so practiced, will utter that, which he practiseth in his naturall
> tung, and if the strangenesse of the matter do so require, he that is

to utter, rather then he will stik in his utterance, will use the foren term, by waie of premunition, that the cuntrie peple do call it so, and by that mean make a foren word, an English denison.[18]

Trade, commerce, and traffic with strangers "require" that a "tongue of account" incorporate foreign words.[19] Mulcaster's imagined English trader elects to use foreign terms in order to navigate "sundry kinds of dealing." This positive affirmation of the mixedness of English depends on reference to a broader logic of the state and its laws, by which the immigration of foreign and alien subjects might be classified and regulated. In Mulcaster's text, the process of linguistic denization controls foreign and domestic interplay. Foreign words immigrate into English and exist in a relation of forced assimilation, secured by legal rules, rather than linguistic pluralism:

> This benefit of the foren tung, which we use in making their termes to becom ours, with som alteration in form, according to the frame of our speche, tho with the continewing in substance of those words, which ar so used, that it maie appear both whence theie come, and to whom theie come, I call *enfranchisment*, by which verie name the words that are so *enfranchised*, become bond to the rules of our writing, which I have named before, as the stranger denisons be to the lawes of our cuntrie. . . . I think it best for the strange words to yield to our lawes, bycause we ar both their usuaries & fructuaries, both to enjoy their frutes, and to use themselves, and that as near as we can, we make them mere English, as *Justinian* did make the incorporate peple, mere *Romanes* and banished the terms, of both *latins* & *yieldlings*.[20]

For Mulcaster, the legislative frame of English grammar works on foreign words to "bond" them to the "rules of our writing." Such grammatical bondage is positively portrayed as an act of political enfranchisement characterized by alteration and restriction of the 'foren tung.' Analogously, stranger denizens are bound to the "laws of our cuntrie." This enfranchisement results in the foreign word (and the foreigner) being made "mere English," that is to say, *pure* English.[21] Mulcaster's portrait of the linguistic stranger-made-denizen expresses what Jean Howard has characterized as "forced cosmopolitanism, a recognition that one had to undertake certain kinds of negotiations with strangers in order to further one's own interests," including enjoying the fruits borne of linguistic incorporation.[22]

Originally foreign, now enfranchised, Mulcaster's denizen lexicon deconstructs the binary positions that polarized debate in the inkhorn controversy. What emerges, however, is not a celebratory picture of linguistic multiplicity or copious mixedness.[23] Instead, Mulcaster proposes a restrictive and regulated vision of linguistic and cultural assimilation. The successful enfranchisement of foreign words transforms what was foreign out of itself as it is pressed into an English mold. Almost two decades later, William Camden echoes Mulcaster when he writes: "The alteration and innovation in our tongue as in all others, hath beene brought in by entrance of Strangers, as *Danes, Normans,* and others which have swarmed hither, by trafficke, for new words as well as for new wares. . . . It hath beene beautified and enriched out of other good tongues, partly by enfranchising and endenizing strange words, partly by refining and mollifying olde words, partly by implanting new words with artificiall composition, happily containing themselves within the bounds prescribed by *Horace.*"[24] For Camden, the strategy by which foreign words are "enfranchised" includes the process of "endenizing."[25] For both authors, the stranger-made-denizen serves as an exemplar of successful incorporation of foreign vocabulary into English speech precisely because such incorporation attests to the ability of "others which have swarmed hither" to beautify and enrich English.

Unlike the inkhorn, the denizen could be mobilized to support a range of ideological positions within the language debates. Rather than celebrating the "endenizing" of English, Samuel Daniel's *Defense of Ryme* (1603) rejects the positive notion of linguistic enfranchisement by recasting the denizen as a symbol of cultural anarchy:

> Next to this deformitie stands our affectation, wherein we always bewray [*sic*] our selves to be both unkinde, and unnaturall to our owne native language, in disguising or forging strange or un-usuall wordes, as if it were to make our verse seeme an other kind of speach out of the course of our usuall practise, displacing our wordes, or investing new, openly upon a singularitie, when our owne accustomed phrase, set in the due place, would express us more familiarly and to better delight, than all this idle affectation of antiquity, or

novelty can ever do. And I cannot but wonder at the strange presumption of some men, that dare so audaciously adventure to introduce any whatsoever forraine wordes, be they never so strange; and of themselves as it were, without a Parliament, without any consent or allowance, stablish them as Free-denizens in our language.[26]

Such impassioned rhetoric effects a conflation of the subject of the passage (forraine wordes) with its figurative vehicle (the denizen). For Mulcaster the denizen points to the positive stability of the grammatical framework of English (the foreign word made denizen is "bond to the rules of our writing"), as well as the strength of the legislative framework of the English state, which can incorporate and enfranchise the stranger as denizen. For Daniel, the denizen is, conversely, a figure of deceit, an unregulated, "disguised" border crosser who, having arrived, is established, without proper warrant, as a "free-denizen." Whereas the inkhorn's symbolic logic reinforced the binarism of debate, the denizen proved a contested figure—in one instance an exemplar of cultural assimilation, in another an unwanted and deceptive stranger existing outside the laws of English grammar and the English realm.

If branding a term as "inkhorn" expressed a condemnation of English's mixedness with other foreign languages, the denizen was not a wholly celebratory corrective to that critique. Instead, denizen words are once foreign now enfranchised, at once incorporated but not necessarily fully naturalized as native. As a positive figure of linguistic exchange, the denizen demonstrates the flexibility of the English language to accommodate, even adopt, the stranger into its own linguistic economy. Cast in this light, the denizen renders visible the always-transitioning nature of language itself.

Though the inkhorn and the denizen amplify different ideological positions, as expressions of ideals they both emphasized linguistic difference over sameness. In the context of these debates, the non-English-speaking stranger was cast either as an agent of linguistic contamination or as a figure of potential assimilation. The debates, and the figures deployed within them, thus ascribe an essential alterity to both the foreign word and the stranger who carries it into the realm. With the turn of the seventeenth century a different linguistic argument gained sway, one with its own attendant historical narrative that stressed the linguistic and racial relatedness of the English to their "familiar neighbours," emphasizing correspondences, rather than differences, across languages.

The Teutonic Thesis: A Racial Turn in the Language Debates

> Now are we come to the language, in which lieth the maine strength
> of this disputation and the surest proofe of peoples originall. For no
> man, I hope, will deny, that they which joine in communitie of
> language, concurred also in one and the same originall.
> —William Camden, *Britain*, 1610[27]

Whereas sixteenth-century debates depended primarily on an assumption about the differences between languages, early seventeenth-century antiquarians advanced a genealogy of language that made families of neighboring language groups. As historians of the English language have documented, this interest in English's linguistic origins resulted in a pronounced shift, especially among antiquarians in England, who placed "stress upon [English's] Saxon element."[28] Historians of the English language and critics writing on the emergence of early modern national and ethnic identity have long recognized the importance of the Teutonic thesis to constructions of English identity.[29] Richard F. Jones characterizes this interest in narratives of linguistic origins and the broader cosmopolitan conversation about the origins of Europe as a "Teutonic mania" or Nordic craze: "Its chief characteristic was an opinion, which, drawing heavily upon Tacitus, extravagantly praised the Germans and all things German. The history of the Teutons was elaborated upon in connection with the origin and dispersal of human races, and their far-flung migrations were pointed out as evidence of great excellence. . . . Many and long were the treatises on these matters, and intricate and imaginative the theories evolved, but they were always so managed as to redound to Teutonic glory. And more than once the Saxons are singled out as especially blessed with all the virtues attributed to the Germans as a whole."[30]

In 1605 two influential texts asserting the Teutonic origins of the English people were published in English, William Camden's *Remaines of a Greater Worke, Concerning Britain* and Richard Verstegan's *A Restitution of Decayed Intelligence*. Critical work on English nationalism and ethnicity has focused on the fact that both texts propose a revisionist history of the English people, one that emphasizes Saxon influence as predominant in English history and thus reassigns English origins to a Germanic rather than Roman line of descent.[31] Verstegan's *Restitution*, in particular, advances so strong a thesis regarding the Germanic origins of the English people that Mary Floyd-Wilson contends that in it we find "the first stirrings of an English identity that is both 'peculiar' and 'pure'—hence, racialized."[32] *A Restitution* was a seminal work of English Gothicism (also referred to as "Teutonism"), the first devoted explicitly to linking English identity to Germanic origins by drawing on Mosaic foundation myths that were considered key to developing an accurate account of ethnic theology. The German nation, Verstegan argued, had been one of the core groups dispersed at the Tower of Babel. Philological concerns were central to the ethnic theology of English Gothicism. Ethnic theology rooted in the Mosaic paradigm "emphasized affiliation and relationships within the family tree rather than the notions of difference and otherness which we associate with modern nationalism," Colin Kidd underscores.[33] What critics have failed to notice about these writers' reorientation of English toward its Teutonic origins, however, is the way in which the racial argument—coextensive with the linguistic arguments—links the English and the Dutch in a particularly close racial kinship. These links sometimes emerge by direct assertion; other times racial kinship is implied by the historical and geographic discussions within these texts. These embedded theses imply racial kinships that cut across emerging articulations of English nationalism. They thus press to the fore the ways in which cultural proximity can lead to cultural approximations of kind particularly as they advance a linguistic history that identifies English as a part of Dutch linguistic history.

English authors asserting the Teutonic thesis begin doing so at a moment when "British" nationalism depended, in part, on what Paula Blank has characterized as a program of Anglicization: "the process by which English forms began to infiltrate foreign languages abroad . . . [which] proceeded largely without intervention, as a reflex of cultural evolution rather than a consequence of deliberate reform."[34] While, on the one hand, in the political sphere differences between English, Welsh, Scottish, and Irish were often "marginalized or suppressed" in order to unify the realm, on the other hand, "Renaissance English writers incorporate the speech of the Welsh, the Irish, and the Scottish into the province of English letters," and in so doing "dramatize the differences in language."[35] The program of Anglicization and the politics of imagining a linguistically unified Britain are different expressions of nationalism in the making. The Teutonic thesis, which asserts the Saxon heritage of the English as primary, expands claims of linguistic kinship well beyond the domain circumscribed by Britain's monarch and so fails to align with either deliberate or unintentional expressions of British nationhood. Colin Kidd persuasively demonstrates that among English Gothicists, the "national characters and institutions of the Continent [were embraced] as variants of their own culture. Englishness [was] celebrated more as an isomer of a common Gothic heritage than as a unique insular identity."[36] Indeed, Kidd concludes, "the European scope of the influential Gothic concept meant that our received idea of a 'unique' Anglo-Saxon heritage was, in fact, very severely qualified among English literati of the seventeenth [century]. . . . Instead, Gothicism fostered concentric loyalties."[37] Unlike the program of Anglicization, which was inflected by the politics of colonization cast as nation thinking, Teutonism resisted framing English's history within the confines of the realm, drawing connections and forging relations across political, linguistic, and cultural borders and implicating, in particular, the English and Dutch in shared ethnolinguistic heritage—what the period characterized as racial heritage.

Cornelius Tacitus's essay *On the Origin and Geography of Germany*, composed in 98 CE, rediscovered in the fifteenth century, and translated into English in the late sixteenth century, deeply influenced William Camden's narrative of English history, *Remaines . . . Concerning Britaine*.[38] In his earlier chorographical work *Britannia* (1586), Camden had begun to advance a notion of linguistic nationalism. The 1610 English translation, *Britain*, argues that languages were "the surest proofe of peoples originall. For no man, I hope, will deny, that they which joyne in communitie of language, concurred also in one and the same originall."[39] In *Remaines*, Camden underscores the Germanic origins of the English language in an effort to dispel what he characterizes as the culturally dominant but specious Brutus legend that had long served as the founding myth of Britain.[40] Early in his chapter entitled "The Languages," Camden asserts, "the *English-Saxon* tongue came in by the *English-Saxons* out of *Germany*. . . . This English tongue [is] extracted out of the olde *German*."[41] The second edition of the *Remaines* (1614) further stresses the "glorious" German heritage of English, emphasizing the German "nation" as "the most glorious of all now extant in Europe for their morall, and martiall vertues, and preserving the libertie entire, as also for propagating their language by happie victories in *Fraunce* by the *Francs*, and *Burgundians*, in this Isle by the *English-Saxons*, in *Italie* by the *Heruli*, West-*Gothes*, *Vandales*, & *Lombards*, in *Spaine* by the *Suevians* and *Vandales*."[42] In Camden's estimation, the linguistic conquest of the English-Saxons was absolute, "to the honour of our progenitors the *English-Saxons* be it spoken, their conquest was more absolute here over the *Britaines*. . . . The *English-Saxon* conquerors, altred the tongue which they found here wholly."[43] Despite the influence of Latin and the linguistic invasion of the Norman conquest, "ancient *Saxon*, . . . the tongue which the English used at their first arrivall heere, about 440 yeares after Christs birth," was retained due to "our Ancestors stedfastnes in esteeming and retaining their owne tongue."[44] The quality of steadfastness that Camden esteems in his English ancestors is manifest par excellence by "the *Germans* which have most of all Nations opposed themselves against all innovations in habite, and language."[45]

Camden's thesis was echoed in Gerhard Mercator's "General Description of England," published in the 1636 English translation of his *Atlas*: "That English men from Saxons drew descent / Their color white and tongue make evident."[46] At the time of publication, Camden's thesis would have registered as a strong but not original argument. Two years before *Remaines* was first published, John Clain ventured in *Historia Britannica*, "the English tongue is a mixture of many languages, especially German and French, although it is believed that formerly it was altogether German."[47] Clain's qualified assertion of English's indebtedness to the Germanic tongue was politic, for, as Charles Barber points out: "the Tudors had cultivated their Welsh ancestry and the old Celtic legends as part of their mystique, and James I continued this policy: it was no accident that Ancient British and Trojan material played a prominent part in the courtly masques and entertainments of Elizabeth I and James I. An attack on theories of Celtic origins for the English nation was an attack on part of the mythology of the ruling dynasty. . . . There was a period in the first half of the seventeenth century during which the authorities tended to regard antiquarian and Anglo-Saxon studies as something subversive."[48]

Camden's contemporary Verstegan therefore ventured boldly when he dedicated *A Restitution of Decayed Intelligence in Antiquities Concerning the Most Noble and Renowmed [sic] English Nation* to King James, " 'the chiefest Blood-Royal of our ancient English-Saxon Kings,' and thus set aside the Stuart claim to British ancestry and James's vision of himself as a second Arthur."[49] *A Restitution* was the foundational text of English Gothicism and underwent five subsequent editions: 1628, 1634, 1653, 1655, 1673. Verstegan, whose forefathers were of Dutch ancestry, penned his *Restitution* from Antwerp, where he sometimes resided as an English Catholic exile.[50] For Verstegan, the ancestry of "so honorable a race" had been obscured by the prevailing poetic traditions that linked English ancestry to the Britons, descendants of the Welsh, rather than to the Saxons, who, he argues, came out of Germany.[51] The work thus ventures to recover the "true originall and honorable antiquitie"

> [which] lieth involved and obscured, and wee remayning ignorant
> of our own true anceters [sic], understand our descent otherwise
> then it is, deeming it enough for us to heare that *Eneas* and his
> Troyans the supposed anceters [sic] of King *Brute* and his Britans are
> largely discoursed of. . . . And by this meanes cometh it to passe,
> that wee not only fynde Englishmen (and those no idiots neither)
> that cannot directly tel from whence Englishmen are descended, and
> chanceing to speak of the Saxons, do rather seem to understand
> them for a kynd of forreyn people, then as their own true and meer
> anceters . . . for Englishmen cannot but from Saxon originall deryve
> . . . and can lack no honor to be descended of so honorable a race,
> and therefore are the more in honor obliged to know and acknowl-
> edge such their own honorable and true descent.[52]

Questions of English descent, origin, and race are central to Verstegan's project, and language proves the key to recovering this history. Verstegan's revisionist project aims to reorient the English toward their "true," northern,
Saxon origins, an effect of which is the linking of the English not only to the
Germans but, more specifically, to the Dutch.

Verstegan's text is replete with assertions of the Germanic origins of
English, a thesis boldly underscored in the second chapter title: "How the
Ancient Noble Saxons, the True Anceters [sic] of Englishmen, Were Origi-
nally a People of Germanie, and How Honorable It Is for Englishmen to Be
Descended from the Germans." The chapter opens, "That our Saxon ancet-
ers came out of *Germanie,* and made their habitation in *Britaine,* is no ques-
tion; for that therin all agree, but some not content to have them a people of
German race." This moment of arrival is one of the few narrative moments
of the text that Verstegan illustrates for his reader (Figure 1). Original to
Verstegan's text, the image features England's Saxon ancestors landing on
the English shore having journeyed a short distance from their homeland,
"Germanie."

Throughout, Verstegan ascribes value to the German "race" in order that
his readers might not only find persuasive but desirable the genealogy he
insists is their own. Verstegan underscores, "what a highly renowmed [sic]
and moste honorable nation the Germans have always bin, that thereby it

THE ARRIVAL OF THE FIRST ANCETERS
of Englifhmen out of *Germanie* into *Britaine*.

They arryued at *Ippedsfleet* now called *Ebsfleet,*
in the Ile of *Tanet* in *Kent*, in the yeare of our Lord
447. and in the fecond yeare of the raign of king
Vortiger. And albeit venerable *Bede* wryteth that in
the yeare of our Lord 4 2 9. *Marcianus* raigned with
Valentinian, in whofe tyme he faith the Saxons were
P 3
fent

FIGURE 1. "The arryval of the first Anceters [*sic*]" in Richard Verstegan,
A Restitution of Decayed Intelligence (1605).

By permission of the Huntington Library, San Marino, California.

may consequently appeer how honorable it is for Englishmen to bee from them descended."[53] He fortifies this historical narrative by laying out three distinguishing and laudable features of the German people drawn from "testimonies which ancient authors of other nations, do give them":

> The first therefore & moste memorable, & woorthy of moste renowme and glorie, is, that they have bin the only and ever possessors of their countrey, to wit, the first people that ever inhabited it, no antiquitie being able to tel us that ever any people have dwelt in *Germanie* save only the Germans themselves, who yet unto this day do there hold their habitation.
>
> Secondly they were never subdued by any, for albeit that the Romans with exceeding great cost, losse & long trooble, might come to bee the comaunders of some parte thereof; yet of the whole never, as of *Gallia, Spain* & many other countries els, they were.
>
> Thirdly they have ever kept themselves unmixed with forrain people, and their language without mixing it with any forrain toung.
>
> In all which three pointes of greatest, national honor, I doubt whether any people els in the world can chalenge to have equalitie with them.[54]

Imagined as autochthonous, unsubdued by and unmixed with "forrain people," the portrait of the German race that emerges in Verstegan's account draws heavily on Tacitus, whom he cites as having argued, "For mine owne part I hold with them, which thinke that the people of Germanie, not changed and altered by marrying with other nations, have continued the true and pure nation like unto none, but themselves."[55] In being represented as "pure," the Germans escape the very crisis of mixedness that had dogged English efforts to attach value to their vernacular throughout the inkhorn controversy of the previous century. Verstegan's discussion of the Germans emphasizes similitude among the Germanic race of people whose lineage can be testified to by the diverse languages, as Camden asserted, of the "*Francs,* and *Burgundians,* in this Isle by the *English-Saxons,* in *Italie* by the *Heruli,* West-*Gothes, Vandales,* & *Lombards,* in Spaine by the *Suevians* and *Vandales.*" In Verstegan's formulation, these diverse languages share a common linguistic ancestor. Verstegan's Teutonic thesis thus gathers up a multiplicity of cultural, linguistic, and geographic differences under the rubric "the German people." The linguistic map that emerges radically differs from the map of early modern geopolitical domains. In constructing a temporal genealogy, Verstegan deemphasizes the territorial differences between and spatial boundaries of various European states, emphasizing instead their shared historical derivation.

Yet this temporal genealogy had spatial implications too. This "diminish[ed] . . . sense of distance between England and the 'other,'" which, Kidd has demonstrated, shaped ideas of English identity in the period, also affected notions of the interrelatedness of English and Dutch linguistic and racial histories.[56] In tracing the route by which Verstegan ties the English to the Saxons, we discover that the English language, England's history, and its people are directly linked to the territory of the Netherlands. Verstegan posits a linguistic link between Saxonie and the Netherlands by mapping the geography of the Teutonic language family to the western limit of Saxon country: "the river of *Sceld*, (which in passing down along by *Antwerp*, devydeth *Brabant* from *Flanders*)."[57] Furthermore, he asserts, "about 900 yeare past our language and the language of Saxonie and the Netherlands was all one," thus making both a linguistic and a colonial claim.[58] Throughout *A Restitution*, linguistic venerability is measured across geographic territory. The more geography a language once covered on the map, the greater its dominance in the form of historical influence. This emphasis on geographic coverage was prevalent among philologists of the period. The Dutch author Abraham van der Myl (Vander-Mylius) concurred with Verstegan's vision of the linguistic colonization by Teutonic in his *Lingua Belgica* (1612), in which he argued, "Hebrew and its dialects occupied roughly one-half of the world, while Teutonic and its dialects, the other."[59] According to Verstegan, the conquering Saxon armies, those who advanced into Britain, had come out of the Low Countries: "Very probable it is that these two Saxon leaders with their forces, which were of *Westphalia, Friesland* and *Holland*, did (as the chronicles of *Holland* affirme) set foorth from thence & so saile over into *Britaine*, for as I have said in the third chapter, the inhabitants of these provinces were all somtyme generally called by the name of Saxons."[60] Verstegan proposes that the Saxon colonizers of Britain were originally inhabitants of Westphalia, Holland, and Freisland, the latter two being provinces of the Low Countries. The reader who looked up from Verstegan's text to plot Saxon history on a contemporary map would have discovered that the homeland of the ancient Saxons was occupied by the present-day Dutch.

"The Ground of Our Speech": Visualizing
Anglo-Dutch Geo-linguistic Territory

Contemporary with Verstegan's publication was the English translation of
Abraham Ortelius's *Theatrum Orbis Terrarum* (1608), the most important
European atlas of the early seventeenth century. Therein, readers encountered
a detailed description of "the British Isles, now the Empire of Great Britaine"
in which Ortelius makes explicit the Belgic origins of the English people:
"from whence the people and first inhabitants came, whether they were
home-borne (indigenae) or come from other countries, it is not knowen as
Tacitus hath written. The inner partes, higher within the land, are inhabited
of those which they say, were borne and bred there: the sea coasts are possessed of those which came thither from Belgium (the Low Countries)."[61]
This narrative of migration is repeated in the Flemish cartographer's description of the Low Countries. Paraphrasing Caesar, Ortelius writes, "*The sea
coast* [of Britain] *is inhabited of those which by reason of pillage and warre, went
from* Belgium *thither.*" The geographic proximity of England and the Low
Countries and ease of traversing between the two coasts leads Ortelius to
conclude, "they therefore that went from *Belgium,* into *Brittaine,* did only
change coast for coast."[62] Like the bawdy comic puns that I explored in
Chapter 1 for how they represented the fluidity of boundaries between
England and the Low Countries, here the cultural migration that Ortelius
narrates foreshortens geographic distance. In Ortelius's original edition of
Theatrum Orbis Terrarum (1570), a small section of England's southeast coast-
line appears in the margins of the map of "Germania" (Figure 2), making
England and the Netherlands seem so closely situated as to pose a challenge
even to the passage of a ship. In both the maps of "Germania" and "Germania Inferioris" (the Low Countries), a small section of England appears in
the upper left corner, as if to suggest that to recognize the geography of
"Germania," Flanders, and the Brabant is to orient oneself also to the coast
of England (Figure 3).

When the 1608 English edition of Ortelius's *Theatre of the Whole World*
was published, readers encountered a similar representational pattern of situating England, the Netherlands, and France within the mise en page, always
in close relation to one another. Indeed, on the map of "Angliae et Hiberniae" the region is represented as a nearly unified whole, with details of the
geography of Flanders and France appearing along the margins (Figure 4).

FIGURE 2. Detail of "Germania" in Abraham Ortelius,
Theatrum Orbis Terrarum (1570).
By permission of the Huntington Library, San Marino, California.

Four decades after the first publication of Ortelius's *Theatrum Orbis Ter-*
rarum, in John Speed's map of "The Kingdome of Great Britaine and Ireland" in *The Theatre of the Empire of Great Britaine* (1611), the Low Countries
continues to fill the lower right corner of the map of "the Kingdome of
England," serving less as a margin along the edge than as a part of the whole
picture of England. In the 1632 edition, Flanders, Brabant, and Holland are
prominently displayed (Figure 5).

Speed's representation of the Low Countries is especially noteworthy
because his atlas was not a world atlas, like Ortelius's, but an atlas of Great
Britain. Why include the Low Countries at all? Speed provides his readers
with a picture of Great Britain that renders the Low Countries as at once
present *within* the frame of Britain and as a place that stands in for the
wider world beyond it. In European atlases produced in England and the
Netherlands, this kind of "situating shot" onto the neighboring shorelines

FIGURE 3. Detail from "Germaniae Inferioris " in Abraham Ortelius,
Theatrum Orbis Terrarum (1570).

By permission of the Huntington Library, San Marino, California.

was becoming conventional. A case in point is Mercator's *Atlas sive cosmo-graphicae meditationes de fabrica mundi et fabricati figura*, also published in 1623, wherein England (*Anglie*) appears prominently inside the frame of the *Belgii inferioris* map (Figure 6). Early modern world maps represent location not in isolation but by reference to the paratactically situated outside, and in so doing bring into view borders between proximately situated geographies. Sometimes what an atlas reader experiences instead, however, are interconnections. Like Andrew Marvell's paradoxical portrait of the Netherlands, imagined as the "off-scouring of the British Sand," Ortelius's change of "coast for coast" subtly interlaces the two geographies.[63] To cross the narrow passage between England and the Low Countries is to traverse across and, potentially, to *mix* the two sites, a subtle message evident even in the pictorial representation of the coastlines. In Mercator's original Latin edition of *Atlas sive* (1595), for instance, the

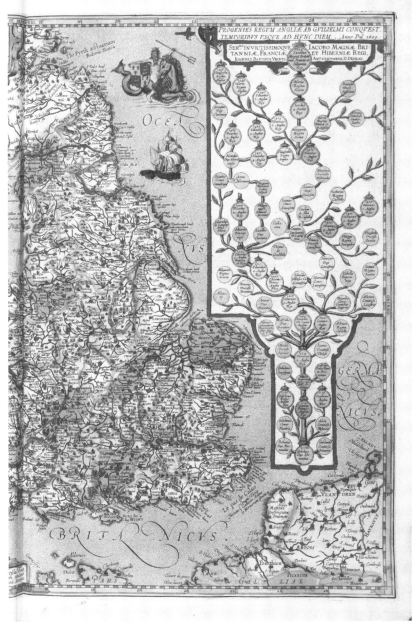

FIGURE 4. Detail from "Angliae et Hiberniae" in Abraham Ortelius,
Theatre of the Whole World (1606, i.e., 1608).

By permission of the Huntington Library, San Marino, California.

FIGURE 5. Detail from "The Kingdome of Great Britain and Ireland" in John Speed,
The Theatre of the Empire of Great Britaine (1632).

By permission of the Huntington Library, San Marino, California.

narrowness of the sea passage between southeast England and the coast of
Flanders forces enjambment of the names of towns on both sides (Figure
7).[64] Here, the coastlines are transformed into intersections that are literally
cluttered with the linguistic detail of town names. Robert Devereux's
inquiry at the end of the sixteenth century—"Is not the Lowe Countries
the Rise, by which shee [Spain] may leape into England?"—seems
answered in the affirmative.[65] Yet a "leape" would be an overstretch, as
Mercator's linguistic land bridge renders England and the Low Countries
so proximate as to seem a mere step apart.

The close tethering of England and the Low Countries in cartographic
representation is most evident in the "Leo Belgicus" (Belgian Lion) maps of
the Low Countries. In one of the earliest versions of this tradition, Anglia
appears to be angling for its conventional position on the periphery of the
map. Nestled into the curl of the Lion's tail, England seems the butt of a

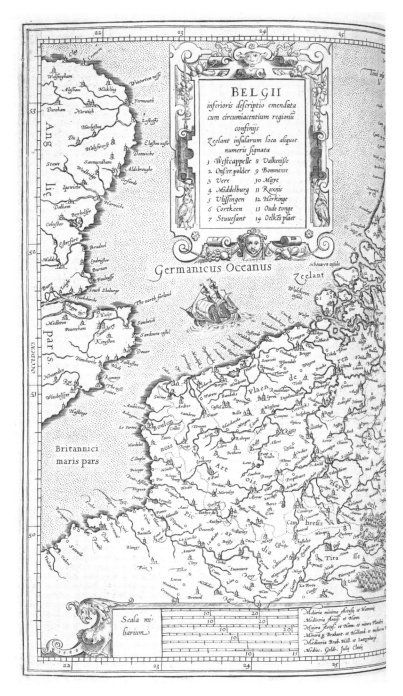

FIGURE 6. Detail from "Belgii" in Gerhard Mercator,
Atlas sive cosmographicae (1623).

By permission of the Huntington Library, San Marino, California.

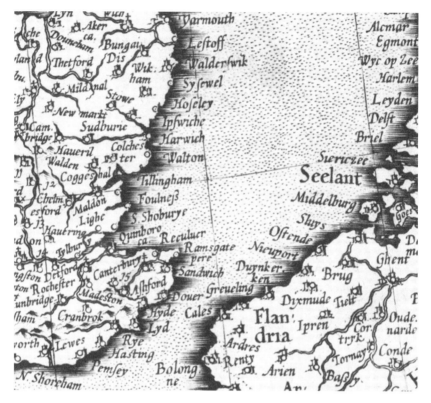

FIGURE 7. Detail from "Britannicae Insulae" in Gerhard Mercator,
Atlas sive cosmographicae (1595).

By permission of the Huntington Library, San Marino, California.

visual joke, one that anticipates the lower-order tropes of geographic proximity and intimacy that would come to animate ideas about Anglo-Dutch relations in English city comedies (Figure 8).[66] The Leo Belgicus cartographic tradition extends into the late seventeenth century and beyond, lending readers of Marvell's description of Holland a vivid, scatologically inflected visual image by which to turn those lines around on England itself. Here Anglia risks appearing as Belgium's lowest organic form of detritus.

The convention of displaying neighboring locations together on maps was primarily an intuitive way of orienting viewers to the larger region of which a place was a part and was not a representational strategy unique to England and the Low Countries. It also characterized representation of other

FIGURE 8. Frans Hogenberg, *Leo Belgicus* (1583).
By permission of Den Haag, Koninklijke Bibliotheek, shelf number KW 1710 B 11.

near neighbors, such as Spain and Barbary. In both the Latin edition of
Ortelius's *Theatrum Orbis Terrarum* and the later English edition, *Theatre of
the World*, for instance, the map of Spain includes the thin stretch of the
"Estrecho de Gibraltar" and the coast of "Barbarie" along the map's southern
margin (Figure 9). In turn, the *Theatre*'s map of Barbarie shows Spain's coast-
line to the north. In this way, European readers were reminded of Spain's
geographic as well as cultural proximity to Africa, a proximity that Barbara
Fuchs has demonstrated richly animated European perceptions of Spain as

FIGURE 9. Detail from the map of Spain in Abraham Ortelius,
Theatre of the Whole World (1606, i.e., 1608).

By permission of the Huntington Library, San Marino, California.

infused with Moorish culture.[67] In cartographic representations of England and the Low Countries as well as Spain and North Africa, each place heralds the other into the margins of its own geographic representation. To know Spain, these maps suggest, is to see North Africa in one's peripheral vision, just as to be situated in England is to experience the Low Countries as a mere step away. The point is not that maps of England and the Low Countries were uniquely displaying the geographic proximity of one another's coastlines in atlases, but instead that the cartographic arts were informing and informed by cultural as well as geographic proximities, displaying waterways between regions as the integrative cultural networks they indeed were. In so doing, atlases of the period lent credence to the casual ease of Ortelius's historical reflection that to move from Belgium into Britain was "only" to "change coast for coast."

"To Draw More Neerer the True Original"

For Verstegan, this local migration from Belgic to British shores could be charted spatially and linguistically. Verstegan advances his case by asserting a linguistic kinship between seventeenth-century "Nether-dutch" (or "Low-duitsh") speech and old Teutonic. It is "East-landish & Low-duitsh, [which] draw more neerer the true original [old Teutonic] then the High-duitsh. And for further proof heerof it is to bee noted, that all such writings as are found in the old Teutonic, do more neerer agree to the speech of these partes, then to the High-duitsh."[68] Here Verstegan presses for a distinction between Nether-Dutch (Low Dutch) and "High-duitsh" (German), categories often rendered interchangeable in the writing of the period. He attributes the differences between Low-and High-Dutch to the internal developments of language as it spreads across territory over time: "the maritime partes of countries were inhabited before the inlands that ly furthest from the sea; the ancient language was their first planted, and is lyke to have bin moste varied by such as went afterward to dwel more higher and dispersed abrode in the countrey, and therefore I hold the East-landish and Low-duitsh, to draw more neerer the true original than the High-duitsh."[69] Writing from Antwerp—the very border of "Saxon country" as he maps it—Verstegan was intimately familiar with the geographic and linguistic territory he charted. Arguing that the Low-Dutch of Holland preserves old Teutonic even more

closely than does "High-duitsh," Verstegan invests the Netherlands with having preserved the origins—both ethnic and linguistic—of *England's* Saxon
ancestry.

"The neernes" of English and Dutch is not merely a theoretical proposi-
tion but is evinced in the spoken language of Verstegan's day:

> And as touching our English toung, which is more swarved from
> the original Teutonic then the other languages thereon also depend-
> ing . . . [a]nd notwithstanding the so much swarving of our toung
> from the original, I durst for a trial of the great dependance which
> yet it holdeth with that which being issued from the same root is
> spoken in the continent, wryte an Epistle of chosen-out woords yet
> used among the people of sundry shyres of *England,* as also of the
> people of *Westphalia, Friesland,* and *Flanders,* and the countries lying
> between them, that should wel bee understood both of Englishmen
> and Duytshmen, so great is the neernes of our unmixed English
> with their yet used Duytsh.[70]

Verstegan's reference to "unmixed English," made on the heels of the inkhorn controversy that had made so much of English's mixedness, may strike
the reader as curious, but here Verstegan refers to an English derived from
old Teutonic *before* its encounter with classical and Continental forms. Such
English, spared from contamination by its isolation in the "shyres of
England," is a relic of the past. Still preserved in much of England's monosyllabic lexicon, this "unmixed English" shares a special nearness to spoken
Dutch. Verstegan elaborates by displaying empirical examples of such propinquity: "It is not long since that an Englishman travailing by wagon in *West-
Flanders,* and hearing the wagoner to call unto his man and say, 𝕯𝖊 𝖘𝖙𝖗𝖎𝖓𝖌
𝖎𝖘 𝖑𝖔𝖘𝖘𝖊/ 𝖇𝖎𝖓𝖉 𝖉𝖊 𝖘𝖙𝖗𝖎𝖓𝖌 𝖆𝖊𝖓 𝖉𝖊 𝖜𝖆𝖌𝖊𝖓 𝖛𝖆𝖘𝖙[,] [p]resently understood him as
yf hee had said, 𝕿𝖍𝖊 𝖘𝖙𝖗𝖎𝖓𝖌 𝖎𝖘 𝖑𝖔𝖔𝖘𝖊/ 𝖇𝖞𝖓𝖉 𝖙𝖍𝖊 𝖘𝖙𝖗𝖎𝖓𝖌 𝖔𝖓 𝖙𝖍𝖊 𝖜𝖆𝖌𝖔𝖓 𝖋𝖆𝖘𝖙/ and
weening the follow [*sic*] to have bin some English clown spake unto him in
English."[71] Verstegan's fieldwork, ostensibly drawn from travelers' reports,
equates Dutch speech with that of clownish English. Verstegan presses further, proffering examples of the phonetic proximity of English and Dutch,
which he articulates in spatial terms as "neernes":

> I have divers tymes in noting the neernes of that and our language,
> observed certaine of our old countrey rymes to accord with theirs,

both in self ryme and self sence, which is a very great argument, of the ancient neernes of our and their language.

As for example.

Wee say,   𝔚𝔦𝔫𝔱𝔢𝔯𝔰 𝔱𝔥𝔲𝔫𝔡𝔢𝔯 𝔦𝔰 𝔰𝔬𝔪𝔢𝔯𝔰 𝔴𝔲𝔫𝔡𝔢𝔯.
They say,   𝔚𝔦𝔫𝔱𝔢𝔯𝔰 𝔡𝔬𝔫𝔡𝔢𝔯 𝔦𝔰 𝔰𝔬𝔪𝔢𝔯𝔰 𝔴𝔬𝔫𝔡𝔢𝔯.
Wee say,   𝔄𝔫 𝔞𝔭𝔭𝔩𝔢 𝔦𝔫 𝔐𝔞𝔶 𝔦𝔰 𝔞𝔰 𝔤𝔬𝔬𝔡 𝔞𝔰 𝔞𝔫 𝔢𝔶.
They say,   𝔈𝔫 𝔞𝔭𝔭𝔩𝔢 𝔦𝔫 𝔐𝔢𝔶 𝔦𝔰 𝔰𝔬 𝔤𝔬𝔢𝔱 𝔞𝔩𝔰 𝔢𝔫 𝔢𝔶.[72]

Ancient kinship is evidenced in contemporary linguistic resemblance, suggesting a special historic and ongoing bond between English and Dutch speech. This passage opens onto yet another layer of complexity inherent to the lexical and regional variations within English itself. On the one hand, a reader might understand Dutch *ey* and English "eye" as (false) cognates: in Dutch, *ey* means egg, not eye, a point that subtly undercuts Verstegan's thesis regarding English and Dutch nearness. From this vantage point, homophones falter in making a case for English and Dutch as kissing cousins. On the other hand, however, Verstegan may have had in mind the word *eyren* in English, which signified "eggs." In that case, English "eye" and Dutch *ey* in fact illustrate his point brilliantly. Verstegan's linguistic example thus enacts the double vision, which here might best be understood in auditory rather than visual terms. English "eye" operates like a pun, pointing to both the difference and similitude across English and Dutch.

Verstegan's observations envisage a language continuum that sets old Teutonic, Dutch, and English in such close relation that even idiomatic expressions are almost identical. Along this continuum, contemporary Dutch speech preserves old Teutonic most closely; the nearness of English to Dutch reveals that English is also derived from Teutonic; the differences between English and Dutch underscore that English has yielded to more linguistic mixing than has Dutch.[73] In its broadest strokes, *A Restitution* contends that the English and Dutch languages reveal their shared derivation from old Teutonic in their evident phonetic approximation to one another.

The notion that a continuum exists between the language of the Saxons, the Dutch, and the English is nowhere more explicitly articulated than in Richard Carew's *The Excellency of English*, 1595/1614: "The ground of our owne appertaineth to the old Saxon little differing from the present low *Dutch*, because they more then any of their neighbours have hitherto preserved that speech from any great forreine mixture; here amongst, the Brittons have left divers of their wordes intersowed, as it were therby making a continuall claime to their auncient possession."[74] What Verstegan refers to as "Nether-dutch" and "old Teutonic" Carew names "low Dutch" and "old Saxon" respectively. Although their terms vary, the authors agree that English, High Dutch, and Low Dutch derived from the same Germanic tongue.[75] According to Carew, the English language "appertaineth" (relates) to the old Saxon, which itself differs little from present Low Dutch. More than neighboring languages (English, German, and French), Low Dutch has preserved itself from foreign mixture. Like English, Dutch also derives from old Saxon, but it has preserved old Saxon more completely than has English, which is fraught with foreign mixture.[76] The implication of the seventeenth-century antiquarian argument was that native English speakers might hear in the speech of their Dutch neighbors an alternative to the history of English. The Dutch language set into relief what the English language might have been, had it not yielded to so much mixing. As a preserver of old Teutonic "from any greate forrayne mixture," Low Dutch stood in elevated contrast to the diluted, mixed, and "doubled-headed" English tongue.

Across the North Sea, the idea that Dutch closely preserved old Teutonic was one vigorously advanced by Flemish authors as well. Johannes Goropius Becanus (1518–72), a Brabant-born physician, made an extreme case, which "even the most ardent Germanophiles for the most part could not follow," that his native Belgian (Flemish) had been the language of Paradise: "it rather than Hebrew was the first language . . . and the one in which the Old Testament was first composed."[77] Other languages, including English and Scottish, were considered by Dutch theologian and linguist Abraham van der Myl to be Teutonic languages, but unlike Belgian "they had lost many indigenous words, and they pronounced, declined and inflected differently," and so, along with Scandinavian languages, "could not claim the purity and unchangeability which characterized Belgian."[78] In so arguing, Van der Myl echoed the anxieties of sixteenth-century English purists who, throughout the inkhorn controversy, worried about the relationship of English to other languages. Van der Myl's argument in effect provincialized English from a northern perspective, rendering it the bastardized kin of its more robust Dutch cousin.

In the context of seventeenth-century English and Dutch antiquarian-ism, Dutch was considered a purer instantiation of Teutonic. Dutch authors occasionally went so far as to disparage English as "broken Dutch." Emanuel van Meteren (1535–1612), who spent most of his life in England, authored *Historie der Nederlandscher ende haerder Na-buren oorlogen* (1614), in which he argued that English was "ghebroken Duyts, vervreement en vermengt met Fransche en Brittaeensche termen ende woorden" ("broken Dutch [i.e. Germanic] estranged and mixed up with French and British phrases and words").[79] The notion of English as Dutch (or broken Dutch) spread well beyond the context of Continental antiquarianism, becoming even proverbial. James Howell's book of collected proverbs, *Paroimiographia* (1659), asserts, for instance, "the *English Language* is *Dutch* embroidered with *French*."[80] A contemporary of Van Meteren's, the Flemish mathematician and engineer Simon Stevin (1548–1620), included in his formidable study on mechanics a treatise entitled "Discourse on the Worth of the Dutch Language." In it Stevin aimed to recover the greatness of the "Dutch race" by revealing the superiority of Dutch to all other languages, especially in "interpreting the profound secrets of Nature."[81] Stevin posits the antiquity of the Dutch language, arguing from extraordinarily creative, often specious, linguistic evidence that "we may safely conclude that the French formerly spoke Dutch, that is that they were Dutch, and consequently that in former days the Dutch were a well-known and powerful nation."[82] Even the Spanish had once been "Dutch or modeled their language on Dutch."[83] The philological perfection of Dutch was evident, according to Stevin, in its economy of monosyllabic words: "denoting single things by single sounds."[84] It is a refrain of Dutch antiquarians that the antiquity (evident in the affinity of Dutch with old Teutonic), economy (predominance of monosyllabic words), and immutability (despite potentially transformative linguistic encounters) of Dutch rendered it the most venerable of Europe's languages.[85] When authors from the Low Countries remarked on the "neernes" of English to Dutch, English was determined to be decidedly more "mixed" and thus less pure in its derivation from Teutonic origins. English had migrated further from its own linguistic roots than had Belgian or Nether-Dutch dialects.

Despite this migration, the nearness, indeed the linguistic kinship, of English and Dutch was propounded by both English and Dutch philological arguments. This linguistic propinquity was evidence of a once-forgotten-now-recalled relatedness, specifically located in a shared Saxon ancestry. The logic of race and affiliation that informed the antiquarian movement insisted on a connection between "kin" or kind when a connection between languages could be demonstrated. Verstegan's argument that that kinship existed between the English and the Dutch, alongside the works of other English and Dutch antiquarians, laid the philological foundation for Thomas Scott's claim that the English and Dutch "come of the same race originally that wee do, as our speech witnesseth." The following chapter explores the how this relational way of thinking about Anglo-Dutch shared linguistic heritage emerges in the drama of the period in the form of meditations on the characterological proximities between the English and Dutch.

CHAPTER 3

Double Dutch Tongues

Language Lessons of the Stage

What is it . . . against law of hospitality, to jest at strangers because
they speak not English so well as we do? What do we learn?
—Sir Philip Sidney, *The Defence of Poesy,* 1595

The broken English of aliens on the English stage has been the focus of significant scholarly attention, much of which contends that broken English enacts
the alien's marginalization.[1] In his study *Languages and Communities in Early
Modern Europe,* Peter Burke argues that the "evidence of plays" as representational records of human speech "especially in comedies . . . was probably styl-
ized and stereotyped" and therefore is not a reliable window onto the spoken
word during the period.[2] "In the cases of Shakespeare, Jonson, and Molière,"
Burke continues, "playwrights exploited sociolects for comic effect, representing marginal communities as funny foreigners who do not know how to
speak."[3] This chapter demonstrates that stage Dutch was particularly funny to
English audiences, but that in this case laughter is not necessarily a response
that marginalizes its object. When audiences laugh they are, as Sir Philip Sidney
suggests, also learning something. While plays do not offer us a "record" of
early modern sociolects—"the distinctive languages of particular social
groups"—they are rich archives for attitudes toward language.[4] More than a
laugh at the other's expense and the consolidation and confirmation of cultural
difference, English comedies offered audiences lessons in philosophies of language that were shaping notions of English's similitude and difference from the

Dutch. In ways that challenge conventional interpretations of foreign speech on the English stage, performances of stage Dutch enacted the consensus of the antiquarian debates: that English and Dutch were related tongues.

Sir Philip Sidney's remarks would have us assume that when a Dutch character spoke "stage Dutch" on the English stage, English audiences both heard and saw a stranger. Undoubtedly, the truth of Sidney's observation about his countrymen's appetite for jesting at strangers finds full expression in early seventeenth-century city comedies, wherein Dutchmen rarely escape the satirization of their native tongue. In the period's first city comedy, William Haughton's *Englishmen for My Money* (1598), Frisco, the play's clown, boasts that he can speak "perfect *Dutch*" but first must stuff his "mouth full of Meate . . . and then you shall heare me grumble it foorth full mouth, as *Haunce Butterkin slowpin frokin*."[5] Later in the play, Laurentia (whose father has promised her to the play's real Dutchman, Vandalle) bemoans, "Shall I stay? till he belch into mine eares / Those rusticke Phrases, and those Dutch French tearmes, / Stammering halfe Sentences dogbolt Elloquence" (929–31). Her sister sympathizes, "Alas poore Wench, I sorrow for thy hap, / To see how that art clog'd with such a Dunce" (943–44). Vandalle's Dutch speech reveals more than his nonnative status as a merchant alien of London. Characterized as "rusticke," incomplete ("half Sentences"), a hybrid ("Dutch French") neither here nor there, and as "dogbolt Elloquence," Vandalle's "belch[ed]" expressions of endearment render him more than merely unintelligible to the English sisters whose ears he "clogs." To speak Dutch in this company of women inevitably assures that one will be dismissed as a "dunce."

Time and again in city comedies Dutch speech is portrayed as clownish, and its speakers rendered unintelligent, even stupid. In *The Weakest Goeth to the Wall* (1600) the Englishman Barnaby Bunch mocks the Flemish innkeeper Yacob van Smelt, who would rent him space in his inn:

> *Bunch:* My head in, and fall to work here, and instead of *parle buon francoys*, learn to brawl out "butterbox, *yaw, yaw*," and yawn for beer like a jackdaw.
> *Yacob: Heare me eance. Ick heb a cleyne skuttell, a little stall, by mine huys dore. Sall dat hebben for a skoppe.*
> *Bunch:* "*Hebben, habben*," quoth'a? What shall I "*hebben*"?[6]

In similar terms, the journeyman Firk of Thomas Dekker's *The Shoemaker's Holiday* (1599) pleads with his master, shoemaker Simon Eyre, to hire the seeming Dutchman Hans on the grounds that laughing at Hans's "gibble-gabble. . . . Twill make us work the faster":

> *Firk:* Ha, ha! Good master, hire him. He'll make me laugh so that I shall work more in mirth, than I can in earnest.
> *Eyre:* Hear ye friend, have ye any skill in the mystery of cordwainers?
> . . .
> *Lacy* (as Hans): *Yaw, yaw, yaw, ik can dat wel doen.*
> *Firk:* "*Yaw, yaw!*" He speaks yawing like a jackdaw that gapes to be fed with cheese curds. O, he'll give a villainous pull at a can of double beer.[7]

As the century progresses, Dutch characters begin to self-censor their native speech, as when in Henry Glapthorne's *The Hollander* (1635) the title character Sconce reasons:

> It shall be so, my English is not compleate enough
> To hold discourse with Ladies of regard, my naturall
> Dutch too is a Clownish speech, and only fit to court
> A leagurer in.[8]

In these productions, Dutch is rendered comic, even—to borrow Richard Verstegan's characterization—"clownish," consisting of repetition ("*yaw yaw*"), rhyme ("*slowpin frokin*"), long open vowels (*aw* and *ow*), and alliteration. Evidently, Dutch characters as well as English characters posing as Dutch "grumble[d]," "stammer[ed]," and "gibble-gabble[d]" their way to the funny bone of English audiences. In many instances, then, when stage Dutch was spoken, audiences were encouraged to see a clown.

When they wish to go undetected in their city business, English characters sometimes temporarily adopt stage Dutch. In Thomas Dekker and John Webster's *Westward Hoe* (1605), for example, Mistress Honeysuckle evades her husband, who has come looking for her at the Stillyard, by suggesting that "sir Gozlin (because he has bin in the low Countries) . . . drive e'm away with broken Dutch" (2.3.50–52).[9] Here Gozlin's linguistic impersonation impedes Master Honeysuckle's inquiry by introducing static into the lines of communication between the men in the play who would restore their wives to their proper homes. This tactic for dissembling identity was not unique to the stage. In *The Gull's Horn-book*, Dekker advises a similar strategy for Londoners interested in evading the law: "If you read a *mittimus* in the Constable's look, counterfeit to be a Frenchman, a Dutchman or any other nation whose country is in peace with your own, and you may pass the pikes; for being not able to understand you, they cannot by the customs of the City take your examination and so by consequence they have nothing to say to you."[10] As in the drama of the period, "counterfeiting" one's Dutch or French identity in London was apparently as easy to do as grumbling forth "slowpin frokin."

As Dekker's advice suggests, the stage provided one of many venues wherein native English speakers listened to and learned about Dutchness. Traveling through the streets of the metropolis, a Londoner might encounter the Dutch language in many of the city's quarters. In Broadstreet Ward, on the Sabbath, Dutch immigrants conversed each week at the Dutch Church of Austin Friars, where services had been conducted in Dutch from its foundation in 1550. Following services, "wealthy, merchant members of Austin Friars" were known to meet for business on the Royal Exchange, a practice that drew the attention of those "pious Englishmen" who generally held a "stricter" notion of sabbatarianism than did the Dutch.[11] Walking along Cornhill Street, passing by the Royal Exchange or nearby taverns such as the "Antwerp," English-speaking Londoners would have overheard conversations between London's Dutch immigrants and Dutch merchants who frequently traveled to London from the Netherlands for business.[12] In St. Katherine's Precinct the majority of strangers were Dutch, lending historical veracity to Ben Jonson's talk of going to "St Katherine's / To drink with the Dutch there and take forth their patterns."[13] Dutch strangers also resided in large numbers in Bridge Ward Without, just across the river Thames.[14] For English-speaking Londoners, passing into St. Katherine's or Bridge Ward Without registered something of a linguistic, as well as juridical, transition. Beyond London, the large presence of Dutch exiles living in Norwich, reaching "almost one-third of the population" by 1581, made encounter with Dutch speakers likely as one traversed the streets and conducted business at shops in the East Anglian town.[15]

In addition to overhearing Dutch in the streets and at the Exchange, English men, boys, women, and girls lived and worked in the homes of Dutch-speaking strangers, drawing English-speaking and Dutch-speaking Londoners into discussion on a daily basis in both the commercial and domestic spheres.[16] The 1593 population return reveals that the majority of the aliens living in and around London were from the Low Countries, and would have spoken one or more languages, including Flemish, Dutch, French, and English.[17] Stranger women and men alike worked in close quarters with English-speaking apprentices, servants, and journeymen, thus creating an environment that, in many instances, necessitated some familiarity with Dutch turns of phrase and terms of trade. The Antwerp-born starcher Dionis Welfes provided work for four English women domestic servants, set four English women to work, presumably as starchers, and additionally employed one Antwerp-born woman servant.[18] The widow Joyce Vanderowe, an immigrant "silk throster," reported residing in England for twenty-six years; she employed two stranger men as servants and one stranger maid servant, kept seven English men and one English maid, and set to work five English men and one English maid, bringing Vanderowe's charges to seventeen people.[19] An exceptional case is that of brewer Mary Jeames, widow and householder, born in Antwerp. Jeames reported employing eight Dutchmen "of the English Church," employing one Englishman and one Englishwoman, and setting to brewing work twenty-three English men and women for wages.[20] Between these three Dutch women, they employed forty-six English people along with twelve strangers, nine of whom are identified as Dutch. It seems likely that these Dutch women, each of whom had resided in England for over two decades, acquired a degree of proficiency in English even as they retained their native Dutch (or Flemish) vocabularies. In such cross-cultural working conditions, English speakers had occasion to learn commonplace sayings, oft-repeated colloquialisms, and terms of the trade, not only from their employers but also from the "stranger" servants with whom they worked. Indeed, Dutch loan words enter English in their greatest number during the sixteenth century; "in contrast to the Latin and French ones, [Low German–Dutch terms] tend to be popular rather than learned or polite."[21] Such loan words include "cambric" (1530), "yacht" (1557), "manikin" (1570), "pawn" (1575),[22] "landscape" (1598), "knapsack" (1603), and "brandywine" (1622), as well as verbs such as "foist" (1545), "ravel" (1582), "snip" (1586), "rant" (1598), "hanker" (1601), and "drill" (1622). Linguistic exchange went hand in hand with the domestic and commercial exchanges of the English and Dutch.

The turn of the seventeenth century also ushered in the possibility of formalized study of Dutch language in the form of Anglo-Dutch dictionaries and grammars. Nine different Anglo-Dutch dictionaries and grammars appeared in seventeenth-century England, six of which underwent multiple editions.[23] Marten Le Mayre's *The Dutch Schoole Master* was entered in the stationer's register on 15 August 1603 and published in 1606. It consists of rules for pronunciation, thirty-eight pages of grammar, and an equal number of pages of dialogue, and it concludes with thirteen pages of religious text. The work's compiler was a "professor of the said tongue" who dwelt in Abchurch Lane.[24] In the "Letter to the Reader," Le Mayre advises: "If you have desire to understand perfectly the hardest and most eloquent Dutch, and to speake it naturally, you must acquaint your selfe with some Dutchman, to the ende that you may practise, with him by dayly conference, and frequent also the Dutch-church, having a Dutch Bible, and marking how the Reader readeth, and hearing the Sermons. The one will confirme and strengthen your pronountiation, & the other to understand when one doth speak."[25] Le Mayre's text envisages a polyglot metropolis in which a native-born Englishman might practice Dutch "daily," even "frequent" the Dutch Church. The city supplements the book by providing daily lessons in Dutch. Le Mayre's preface suggests that Dutch is not a language confined to the study; it is a language of and for the city: "you must not thinke that my Booke will make you a good Dutch-man, except you bee a diligent Student."[26] The mandatory language lessons between Dutch strangers and native English speakers that the preface requires raise important questions about the relationship between language and identity, speech and community affiliation. Le Mayre's ambition, the making of a "good Dutch-man," begs the question: was to speak Dutch to *be* Dutch in early modern London? Did one's linguistic competence in a foreign tongue implicate one in ethnic affiliation? If a dictionary, wordbook, or grammar, together with discussion with one's Dutch neighbors, can make one a "good Dutch-man," what then does one see and hear when the well-practiced Englishman opens his mouth and out flies Dutch?

Thomas Middleton's *No Wit, [No] Help like a Woman's,* performed around 1611 and first published in 1657, takes up questions of the relationship of linguistic to ethnic identity by exploring what George Metcalf characterizes as the "intermingled diversity and similarity of human speech."[27] Middleton's exploration of the polyglot reality of London life challenges the satirical characterization of the Dutch as clownish dunces. So too a close reading of this play requires a revision to the scholarly consensus that foreign speech on the English stage enacts the foreigner's marginalization. In *No Wit,* English and Dutch speech share similar phonologies and approximately the same syntaxes. In dramatizing this similitude, *No Wit* presents English audiences with a complex rehearsal of the antiquarian thesis that English and Dutch speech are related tongues.

Speaking "Double Dutch" in Thomas Middleton's *No Wit, [No] Help like a Woman's*

Stage Dutch is represented in Middleton's *No Wit* in two distinct and opposed forms. This double representation of Dutch happens across two sets of linguistic relations. The first is in the relation between what I will call authentic and inauthentic stage Dutch. Stage Dutch (the authentic form) reproduced the marked characteristics, if not the "real" lexicon and grammar, of the Dutch that Londoners would have heard on the streets. Conversely, counterfeit Dutch (the inauthentic form) was represented as mere gibberish, a collection of sounds that no one—on or off stage—was supposed to understand as "real" speech. In essence, inauthentic Dutch functioned on the early modern stage as an instance of what today we refer to as "double Dutch," a gibble-gabble of unintelligible sounds.

In an extended triangulated exchange between an Englishman, a Dutchman, and an English servant pretending to speak Dutch, Middleton enjoins his audience to identify and distinguish between authentic and inauthentic stage Dutch. As the scene evolves, a second level of linguistic interplay unfolds whereby the resemblances between authentic stage Dutch and English are emphasized over and above their differences. The play thus closely pairs English and authentic stage Dutch and sets their affiliation in opposition to the counterfeit, inauthentic Dutch. This linguistic triangulation structures more than a language lesson per se. A plot that starts as a cross-cultural exchange between an Englishman and a Dutchman ultimately results in a lesson that reorganizes the ethnolinguistic oppositions and affiliations with which the play begins. While an audience familiar with the conventions of city comedy might expect to laugh when the play's Dutchman takes the stage, they find themselves laughing instead at a caricaturization of Dutch speech that is funny precisely because it gets Dutch so very wrong.

Unlike his merchant father, the "little Dutch Boy" of *No Wit* "can speak no English." Having recently arrived in London from Antwerp, the boy's father nevertheless entrusts his Dutch-speaking son to the Englishman Sir Oliver:

> Business commands me hence, but as a pledge
> Of my return I'll leave my little son with you,
> Who yet takes little pleasure in this country,
> 'Cause he can speak no English; all Dutch he.[28]

In the scene that follows, Sir Oliver's man, Savourwit, much abuses the Dutch merchant, putting into question his credibility by conducting a mock interview in which he falsely translates the Dutch boy's speech against the word of his absent father. While the father "wears a double tongue that's Dutch and English" (1.3.141), Savourwit observes, the "little Dutch Boy in great slops" cannot negotiate, control, or contest Savourwit's specious translations. In the case of the boy, spoken Dutch yields no more than a blank script that Savourwit fills with English meaning to advance his deceptive end.

The little Dutch boy is an unusual instance in city comedy of an "all Dutch" character who never attempts to translate his ideas into English. More commonly, the Dutch of English city comedy "wear a double tongue," part English-, part Dutch-sounding speech, coined "stage Dutch" by literary critics. I will refer to stage Dutch when speech is identified as Dutch by the speaker and the listener or by the stage direction ("enter with a dutche songe," for instance). In the anonymous play *An Enterlude of Welth and Helth* (1565), Haunce Berepot, "one of the earliest foreign characters with a specific nationality in nonhistorical drama,"[29] enters the stage singing a "dutche songe":

> Entreth Hance with a Dutche songe.
> Gut nyuen s[ ]ne rutters by the moder got
> It heist ōwne s[ ]hon, for s[ ]aue ye ne[ ]e
> De qus[ ]eker mau iche bie do do
> Uan the groate bnmbarde well ic we[ ]e
> Dartyck dowsant van enhebit mete
> Ic best de ma[ ]ikin van de keining dangli[ ]er
> De grot keyser kind ic bene his busket[ ]r.[30]

Haunce speaks a hodgepodge of Dutch and English: English articles ("the," "a"), prepositions ("with," "for"), and verbs ("got") are interspersed with

Dutch articles ("de"), nouns ("moder"), adjectives ("groate"), and verbs ("bene"). Of course, some words, which might be categorized as English, may have been intended to be understood as Dutch, rendered phonetically into English: "by," for example, is phonetically and linguistically cognate with the Dutch preposition *bij*. The instability of orthography, both in English and Dutch, in addition to the use of cognate words and our inability to know how an actor's speech was delivered in performance, will inevitably undermine attempts at too fine an assessment of the Dutch or English content in stage Dutch. Nonetheless, the mixedness of Haunce's speech clearly anticipates the flexible theatrical formula for representing Dutch speech on the Jacobean stage.

While our earliest Elizabethan evidence suggests that stage Dutch is almost always interspersed with some English or English-sounding vocabulary, a shift in representations of stage Dutch takes place between the mid-Elizabethan and the late Elizabethan to early Stuart periods. In the mid-sixteenth century, stage Dutch was less influenced by English phonology and vocabulary than is the case by the turn of the seventeenth century. An example of this subtle shift can be traced to Lacy's performance of a Dutch song in *The Shoemaker's Holiday*. When Lacy, dressed as the Dutchman Hans, enters scene 4, he, like his predecessor Haunce Berepot, sings in stage Dutch:

Enter Lacy [dressed as Hans], singing	
Der was een boor van Gelderland,	There was a boor [peasant] from Gelderland,
Frolick sie byen.	merry they be.
He was als dronck he could neit stand,	He was so drunk he could not stand,
Upsee al sie byen.	pissed [drunk] they all be.
Tap eens de cannikin	Fill up the cannikin [small drinking vessel],
Drincke, schone mannikin.	Drink my fine manikin [little man].[31]

If Hans's song is more comprehensible than Haunce Berepot's, it is partly due to the use of Anglo-Dutch cognates ("drink," "dronck"; "stand," "staan") and the mobilization of loan words, such as "frolick," a Flemish word that enters English in 1583, and "canniken," a Dutch diminutive of "kan" (from Middle Dutch *kanne*), meaning a small drinking vessel. As Dutch and Flemish words increasingly enter English as the sixteenth century progresses, the likelihood that native English speakers understood stage Dutch as familiar broken English also increased. For instance, in *Englishmen for My Money*, Vandalle, the play's Dutchman, expresses his gratitude: "Seker Mester *Pisaro*, mee do so groterly dancke you, dat you macke mee so sure of de Wench, datt ic can neit dancke you genough" (399–401). While we do not know how the actor playing the part of Vandalle performed his lines, on the page the stage Dutch that Vandalle speaks registers as a variant of English (a point, as I discuss in the following chapter, that even the typography of Vandalle's speech underscores). There are few if any unfamiliar words—not because Vandalle's Dutch has been completely Englished but because his entire lexicon consists of words that have cognates in English.[32] In the case of the examples above, the characters were intended to sound Dutch; Haunce and Vandalle are both Dutchmen and Lacy (as Hans) plays a Dutchman. However, this stage Dutch is doing more than confirming their characterizations as Dutch. These performances also highlight the similarities of Dutch and English speech, the way in which English and Dutch consisted of approximately the same phonologies, and even shared lexicons. Unlike in mid-sixteenth-century drama, in early seventeenth-century city comedies, stage Dutch theatrically represents the resemblances between English and Dutch. In this representation, these comedies perform the thesis of antiquarians like Verstegan who asserted the historical relatedness of English and Dutch. If, as Jonson averred, "no glass renders a man's form or likeness as true as his speech," then on the Jacobean stage, laughter at stage Dutch was potentially a joke at the expense of the English.[33]

Before the arrival of the Dutchman in *No Wit*, Sir Oliver's son, Philip, and man, Savourwit, are confident that their scheme, which has set the plot in motion, has gone off without a hitch. In the opening scene of the play Savourwit reveals that Sir Oliver's wife and daughter were "taken by the Dunkirks, sold both, and separated . . . in nine years' space / No certain tidings of their life or death" had reached Sir Oliver until "five months since, a letter came, / Sent from the mother, which related all / Their taking, selling, separation . . . and withal required / Six hundred crowns for ransom" (1.1.63–73). Sir Oliver promptly secured the ransom, entrusting it to his son and Savourwit who immediately departed for Antwerp. Rather than rescuing sister and mother, however, Philip, "eased" the heavy weight of his gold-filled pockets in "wenches' aprons" at Antwerp (1.1.78–79). Savourwit confesses:

> 'Twas my young master's chance there to dote finely
> Upon a sweet young gentlewoman, but one
> That would not sell her honour for the Indies
> Till a priest struck the bargain, and then half
> A crown dispatched it.
> To be brief, wedded her and bedded her,
> Brought her home hither to his father's house;
> And with a fair tale of mine own bringing up,
> She passes for his sister that was sold. (1.1.84–90)

Philip and Savourwit presumably thought that the distance between London and Antwerp would ensure that their scheme would remain undetected. With the arrival of the Dutch merchant in London, however, the closeness of London to Antwerp and the regularity of commercial and sexual traffic between the two cities threatens their plans.

Having been led to believe by those closest to him that Grace, the Antwerp inn "gentlewoman" now residing in his home, is his recovered daughter and that his wife is dead, Sir Oliver is unprepared for the news the Dutch merchant delivers. Addressing Sir Oliver, the Dutchman speaks in perfect English:

> This is my business, sir: I took into my charge
> A few words to deliver to yourself
> From a dear friend of yours that wonders strangely
> At your unkind neglect. (1.3.48–51)

The merchant brings news that "within this month" he has seen Sir Oliver's wife "talk and eat; and those, in our calendar, / Are signs of life and health." Aghast at the news, Sir Oliver can only concur, "Mass, so they are in ours" (1.3.62–63). Gathering his thoughts and summoning Grace to the scene, Sir Oliver protests that his daughter has been restored to him, returned by means of a ransom paid by his son, Philip. The Dutch merchant examines Grace and contends:

> If my eye sin not, sir,
> Or misty error falsify the glass,
> I saw that face at Antwerp in an inn
> When I set forth first to fetch home this boy. . . .
> I tell you my free thoughts. I fear y'are blinded.

I do not like this story. I doubt much
The sister is as false as the dead mother. (1.3.82–92)

Sir Oliver reasons, "Yea? Say you so, sir? I see nothing lets me / But to doubt so too, then" (1.3.92–93). From Sir Oliver's vantage point, the Dutch doppelgänger playing his "daughter" was, until this moment, unmarked by any difference that might have raised his suspicions of deception. Presumably, Grace arrived speaking fluent English, just as the Dutch merchant of the play does. Sir Oliver's epiphany rests, as he declares, on "nothing"—no sign or mark of difference—but instead on the word of a discerning Dutchman. As in the language debates, wherein "forraine wordes [are disparaged because] . . . of themselves as it were, without a Parliament, without any consent or allowances, [they] [e]stablish them as Free-denizens in our language," here too the foreigner establishes herself within the English household without consent because the Englishman can't tell the difference between neighbor and kin.[34] The audience—momentarily suspended between perspectives—examines Grace with the double vision so often required when the Dutch appear on the English stage. While Grace is scrutinized by both an English and a Dutch onlooker for signs of her true identity the audience is invited to discern difference where instead they find "nothing." This initiates the first of many exchanges in the play where the English and Dutch, Englishness and Dutchness, so closely resemble one another as to seem—to English eyes—interchangeable.

Linguistic, cultural, and moral similarities are established between Sir Oliver and the Dutch merchant during their initial exchange. Both men speak fluent English, thus eliminating the possibility for misunderstanding that so often structures the comic banter between the English and aliens on stage. So too the Dutch merchant and Sir Oliver concur that the greatest deceptions often transpire domestically:

Sir Oliver: Here's strange boggling! I tell you, sir,
   Those that I put in trust were near me too.
   A man would think they should not juggle with me.
   My own son and my servant, no worse people, sir.
Dutch Merchant: And yet, oft-times, sir, what worse knave to a man
   Than he that eats his meat?
Sir Oliver: Troth, you say true, sir. (1.3.73–78)

Their agreement serves not only to elicit a chuckle amid this scene of unraveling domestic deceit but foregrounds a universalism that sets ethnic and cultural difference backstage.[35] Finally, in contradistinction to the moral compass of Philip and Savourwit, who have squandered a hefty ransom for a rendezvous at an Antwerp inn, the Dutch merchant and Sir Oliver appear to share a moral barometer, agreeing that the worst deceptions grow up among familiars. Although the Dutch merchant enters the scene as a stranger, he presents Sir Oliver with news that estranges him from those he considers most near. The rupture introduced by the Dutchman splits not along ethnic or linguistic lines, but winds through the domestic sphere, threatening to divide father from son.[36]

The theme of domestic deception is played out as a game of dissembling translations. Desperate to preserve his employment, Savourwit manages to raise doubt about the credibility of the Dutch merchant and the reliability of his message by conducting a mock interview with the little Dutch boy. The audience is in on the deception as Savourwit confides his intention to play the Dutch boy's word against that of his absent father:

> Savourwit: [aside] All's confounded. . . .
> Sir Oliver: 'Las, he can speak no English.
> Savourwit: [aside] All the better; I'll gabble something to him.
>   (1.3.139–44)

By confessing his plot to speak an early modern version of double Dutch, Savourwit enjoins the audience to hear what Sir Oliver initially does not: the difference between authentic stage Dutch, as represented in the boy's speech, and the "gabble" (inauthentic stage Dutch) of the dissembling Englishman. Savourwit's ruse involves a lengthy comic interlude in which he generates nonsensical, rhyming, and alliterative phrases in an attempt to sound Dutch enough to fool Sir Oliver into believing that the Dutch merchant cannot be trusted:

> Savourwit: Hoyste Kaloiste, Kalooskin ce vou, dar sune, Alla Gas-
>   kin?
> Dutch Boy: Ick wet neat watt hey zacht. Ick un-
>   verston ewe neat.[37]
> Savourwit: Why, la, I thought as much!
> Sir Oliver: What says the boy?

> *Savourwit:* He says his father is troubled with an imperfection at one
> time of the moon, and talks like a madman. (1.3.144–49)

The extent to which the audience was encouraged to translate the boy's
authentic stage Dutch would have been significantly influenced by the actor's
performance: how slowly he spoke each word, whether gesture aided in
meaning making, how the actor paced the line, and his performance of the
phonetics of stage Dutch. Additionally, those audience members who
encountered Dutch in the streets of London, in taverns, on the floor of the
Royal Exchange, or in homes where they apprenticed may have developed a
limited Dutch lexicon useful in glossing the personal pronoun "Ick" and the
negative "neat" (*niet*), for instance.

For that native English speaker who had escaped encounters with Dutch
speech on the streets of London, the scene itself offers practice in glossing the
Dutch boy's speech. Before the Dutch merchant departs, leaving his boy
alone with Sir Oliver and Savourwit, he turns to his son and asks,

> *Dutch Merchant:* Where's your leg and your thanks to the
> gentleman?
>   *War es you neighgen an you thonkes you.*[38]
> *Dutch Boy* [To Sir Oliver]: *Ick donck you, ver ew Edermon vrendly
> Kite.*[39]
> *Sir Oliver:* What says he, Sir?
> *Dutch Merchant:* He thanks you for your kindness. (1.3.103–7)

This exchange is typical of the flexible formula for authentic stage Dutch in
city comedy: real Dutch words, such as "ick," combine with Dutch-sounding
phrases represented in macaronic Dutch-English, such as "donck you"; these
commingle with orthographically English but technically cognate forms,
including ("you" / *je* or *u*), and broken English, as in the father's "thonkes."
In Middleton's script, this initial production of stage Dutch is accompanied
by a gloss that the Dutch merchant provides by translating his son's gratitude
to his host. In the exchange between father and son, the English-speaking
audience is given an opportunity to hear the similarities between Dutch and
English syntax and is familiarized with conventions of stage Dutch. This
gloss establishes a counterscript to Savourwit's "gabble" Dutch: replete with
exaggerated rhyme, alliteration, and repetition, Savourwit's speech includes
recognizably English, scatological words, "*Quisquinikin Sadlamare, alla pisse*

kickin Sows-clows, / Hoff Tofte le cumber shaw, bouns bus boxsceeno" (1.3.157–58). This exaggerated caricature of Dutch speech underscores for the audience what Dutch is *not*. Consisting of nonsense nouns, even romance articles ("le"), Savourwit's clownish speech approximates nothing of Dutch vocabulary or English syntax and is a far cry from the little Dutch boy's speech.

While Middleton has provided the audience a lesson in understanding the Dutch boy, the comic thrust of the exchange between Savourwit and the Dutch boy does not require that the audience literally translate the Dutch boy's line (above), "I do not know what he says; I do not understand you." If laughter erupted at Savourwit's mock interview and false translations, it was because the audience, informed by Savourwit's asides, is already in on the joke and so realizes that the Dutch boy has made no such accusation against his father. As the scene progresses, Sir Oliver grows suspicious of Savourwit's translations and begins to press for clarification:

> *Dutch Boy: Ick an sawth no int hein clappon de heeke, I dinke ute zein*
>   *zennon.*[40]
> *Savourwit:* Oh *zein zennon!* Ah ha! I thought how 'twould prove
>   i'th'end. The boy says they never came near *Antwerp*, a quite
>   contrary way, round about by *Parma.*
> *Sir Oliver:* What's the same *zein zennon*?
> *Savourwit:* That is, he saw no such wench in an inn. (1.3.159–65)

Sir Oliver's question, "what's the same *zein zennon*," reveals the fallibility of Savourwit's performance and Sir Oliver's increasing suspicion that something is awry in Savourwit's translation. Of course, the audience has all along heard the distinction between the Dutch boy's Dutch and Savourwit's speech. The scene gains its comic piquancy because the audience enjoys Savourwit's farfetched mimicry of Dutch speech and awaits Sir Oliver's discovery of the ruse.

Savourwit puts Sir Oliver's gullibility to a final test by expounding a theory of the Dutch language that, fittingly, turns on the word "Gulldergoose," a term suggestive of both the gulling under way and the figurative sense of "goose" during the period: a foolish person or simpleton.[41] Savourwit translates the jibe into evidence of the economy of Dutch speech:

> *Savourwit:* He tells me his father came from making merry with
>   certain of his countrymen, and he's a little steep'd in English Beer;
>   there's no heed to be taken of his tongue now.

Sir Oliver: Hoyda! How com'st thou by all this? I heard him speak
  but three words to thee.
Savourwit: Oh, sir, the Dutch is a very wide language; you shall have
  ten English words even for one. As for example, *Gullder-goose*:
  there's a word for you, master.
Sir Oliver: Why, what's that same *Gullder-goose*?
Savourwit: 'How do you and all your generation?'
Sir Oliver: Why 'tis impossible! How prove you that, sir?
Savourwit: 'Tis thus distinguished; sir: *Gull*, 'how do you'; *Der*,
  'and'; *Goose*, 'your generation'.
Sir Oliver: 'Tis a most saucy language. How cam'st thou by't?
Savourwit: I was brought up to London in an eel-ship; There was
  the place I caught it first by th'tail. (1.3.183–98)

Although Savourwit's Dutch is self-confessed gibberish, the logic of his argument about the economy of Dutch, an economy he characterizes as "wide,"
had precedence in the linguistic debates about the value of Dutch vernacular
in the period. The lesson, despite the teacher, had sound grounding in Dutch
philology of the day.

    In his treatise of 1586 *Uytspraeck vande weerdigheyt der Duytsche tael* (On
the Worth of the Dutch Language), Bruges-born Simon Stevin praised Dutch
for its *rijcheyt* (wealth), evinced in the economy of Dutch speech. Writing in
Dutch on subjects that humanists in the Low Countries conventionally
reserved for Latin (including mechanics, mathematics, and measurement),
Stevin argued that the "structure" of Dutch exhibited "its superiority to all
the other languages": "The object of language is, among other things, to
expound the tenor of our thought, and just as the latter is short, the exposition also calls for shortness; this can best be achieved by denoting single
things by single sounds."[42] Long circumlocutions, particularly polysyllabic
words used for single ideas, obscure the revelation of nature's properties,
Stevin proposed. The Belgian lexicon, richest of all in monosyllabic vocabulary, made it superior to and a model for the world's other languages.[43]
Almost two decades earlier, as noted in Chapter 2, Johannes Goropius Becanus, physician and linguist and enthusiast of the Belgian dialect, had
authored a controversial but major work in the history of lexicographical
thought entitled *Origines Antwerpianae* (1569) in which he too praised the
monosyllabicity of Belgian, going so far as to concoct absurd etymologies
toward the end of "exalting his native Belgian, even presuming it . . . to have

been the language of Paradise."[44] Becanus's contention that Adam spoke a pure Teutonic (extant in the contemporary Belgian dialect) was debated among antiquarians and satirized by playwrights. In *A Restitution,* Verstegan reports discussing Becanus's claim with Abraham Ortelius, who, he alleges, thought Becanus's claims difficult to refute.[45] Ben Jonson, who may have learned of Becanus's ideas from *A Restitution*, recalls the debate in *The Alchemist* (1610) when Sir Epicure Mammon is portrayed as an exponent of Becanus's thesis:

> *Mammon:* Will you believe antiquity? Records?
>   I'll show you a book where Moses and his sister
>   And Solomon have written of the art;
>   Aye, and a treatise penned by Adam.
> *Surley:* How!
> *Mammon:* O' the philosopher's stone, and in High Dutch.
> *Surley:* Did Adam write, sir, in High Dutch?
> *Mammon:* He did,
>   Which proves it was the primitive tongue.[46]

Among his Dutch contemporaries, Becanus's ideas were met with skepticism. In *Lingua Belgica* (1612), Abraham van der Myl refuted Becanus's most controversial claim, "that Belgian rather than Hebrew had been the language of Paradise . . . [but] did agree that the monosyllabicity of Belgian in contrast to the polysyllabicity of Hebrew was a telling argument for Becanus."[47] English humanists encountered these ideas also in Verstegan's *Restitution*, wherein the monosyllabicity of Dutch serves as evidence of its derivation from old Teutonic.[48] Among both English and Dutch authors, the parsimony of Dutch, exhibited in its rich monosyllabic lexicon, set it apart from and elevated it above other languages.[49]

In Savourwit's attempt to pull off a persuasive performance of Dutch he expounds a philosophy of the language that rehearses the assertions of English and Dutch philologists. To support his contention that Dutch is a "wide" language, Savourwit articulates a commonplace comparison between Dutch and English: "you shall have ten English words even for one [Dutch]" (1.3.191–92). Savourwit's case for the wideness of Dutch at once reiterates Verstegan's thesis, which rendered Dutch a less diluted branch of old Teutonic than English, and implies an inadequacy of English to express ideas with economy. In this moment, the play's double portrayal of (authentic and inauthentic) Dutch overlaps as the purveyor of inauthentic Dutch expounds an authentic linguistic lesson. And yet Savourwit's linguistic argument is ironically undercut by his summoning of a polysyllabic nonsense word, "Gulldergoose," to illustrate his point. Even his linguistic performance—rife with polysyllabic constructions ("Quisquinikin sadlamare")—undermines the intended illustrativeness of his argument. The audience is meant to understand that Savourwit's counterfeit Dutch is not only not Dutch, but that it also does not conform to the conventions of authentic stage Dutch established during the exchange between the Dutch merchant and his boy and developed more broadly in other stage plays. It will take a real double tongued Dutchman to expose the truth about the relation of English to Dutch.

Having left Sir Oliver "tossed between two tales," knowing "not which to take, not which to trust" (1.3.208–9), Savourwit exits confessing to the audience, "We are undone in Dutch; all our three-months' roguery / Is now come over in a butter-firkin" (206–7).[50] Sir Oliver, still suspicious of Savourwit's self-professed bilingualism, ponders whom he should trust:

> The boy here is the likeliest to tell the truth,
> Because the world's corruption is not yet
> At full years in him. Sure he cannot know
> What deceit means; 'tis English yet to him. (1.3.210–14)

Sir Oliver's double entendre imbricates English speech and deceit. On the one hand, because it is an English word, the little Dutch boy is quite literally unable to understand "deceit." On the other hand, Sir Oliver's rumination also implies that deceitfulness is an English *trait*, a characterological description nowhere more manifestly displayed than in Savourwit's false translation of the boy's speech. Upon the Dutch merchant's return, Sir Oliver's curiosity is piqued, compelling him to interrogate the merchant:

> *Sir Oliver:* Pray resolve me one thing, sir:
>   Did you within this month with your own eyes
>   See my wife living?
> *Dutch Merchant:* I nev'r borrowed any.
>   Why should you move that question, sir? Dissembling
>   Is no part of my living. (1.3.222–26)

The merchant quickly demonstrates that "dissembling" and deceit are not Dutch but English practices. Sir Oliver maintains that his man "questioned your boy in Dutch" who said "that you / Had imperfection at one time o'th'moon, / Which made you talk so strangely" (1.3.230, 1.3.232–34). With this, the Dutch merchant turns to his son, thus replaying the interview that Savourwit, moments earlier, had conducted in counterfeit Dutch:

> *Dutch Merchant:* How, how's this!—
>   *Zeicke yongon, ick ben ick quelt medien dullek heght, ee untoit*
>   *van the mon, an koot uram'd.*
> *Dutch Boy: Wee ek heigh lieght in ze Bokkas, dee't site.*[51]
> *Dutch Merchant:* Why, la you, sir! Here's no such thing.
>   He says he lies in's throat that says it. (1.3.233–38)

Sir Oliver presses the merchant for further confirmation of the news of his wife's survival, inquiring if indeed he "came near Antwerp" and spotted his wife there (1.3.243). Ultimately, the revelation of the nature and source of the deception pivots on the very word Savourwit introduced as evidence of his skill in Dutch:

> *Sir Oliver:* Pray tell me one thing:
>   What's *Gulldergoose* in Dutch?
> *Dutch Merchant:* How, *Gulldergoose?* There's no such
>   thing in Dutch; it may be 'an ass' in English.
> *Sir Oliver:* Hoyda! Then am I that ass in plain English; I
>   am grossly cozened, most inconsiderately. (1.3.249–54)

With the help of the honest Dutchman, whose true bilingualism sets him apart from everyone else onstage, Sir Oliver discovers that he has indeed been made an "ass in plain English." The "all Dutch" boy, the "gabbling" Savourwit, and the gullible, monolingual Sir Oliver are all at the mercy of the "double tongue[d]" Dutch merchant to shed light on the facts. That the bilingual Dutch merchant is characterized as wearing a "double tongue that's Dutch and English" proves accurate, as he speaks both unbroken English and authentic Dutch.

Ironically, in a play that performs an early modern instance of double Dutch as gibble-gabble, the "double-tongue[d]" Dutchman never speaks a line of it. Instead, he emerges as the only character with the combined moral

constitution and linguistic ability to set matters straight. He can do so precisely because his work renders him doubly situated (both a man of London
and a man of Antwerp) and bilingual (fluent in English and in Dutch).
While English dramatists of the sixteenth century had regularly exploited
the monolingualism of strangers on stage, characterizing them as essentially
untranslatable and inassimilable others, Middleton's Dutchman turns this
older dramatic convention on its head, exposing instead the monolingualism
of Sir Oliver as the impediment to his desire to reunite his family.[52] By the
scene's conclusion, it is evident that even a rudimentary knowledge of Dutch
would have spared Sir Oliver from Savourwit's cozening.

If the audience laughs at Savourwit's ridiculous performance of Dutch
speech, the laughter simultaneously ridicules Sir Oliver, whose ignorance of
the differences between authentic and counterfeit Dutch makes all the difference in the realization of his desire. To garner the audience's laugh, Middleton tutored his English-speaking audience, teaching Londoners to tune their
ears to the shared characteristics between authentic stage Dutch and English
and to identify as absurd Savourwit's exaggerated linguistic performance. The
audience's knowledge of the variety of kinds of Dutch staged within the play
provides an epistemic advantage. The play not only tunes its audience's ears
to the conventions of authentic stage Dutch and its caricature; it also offers
lessons regarding the proximate syntax and phonology of English and authentic stage Dutch. More, the audience is exposed to a philosophy of language
that classifies Dutch as "economical" and straightforward, an idea extended
to the characterization of the Dutch merchant's moral stature as the one who
speaks the truth and does so precisely. The Dutchman stands in for moral
virtue, against which the morally wayward Savourwit is set into negative
relief. Not simply "funny foreigners who do not know how to speak," the
Dutch on Middleton's stage resist xenophobic caricatures as they emerge
"honest" bulwarks against "the world's corruption."[53]

City comedy was multiplying the meaningful categories of speech on
stage and complicating ideas about the relation of linguistic and ethnic identity. By expanding the range of categories that pertain to the representation
of Anglo-Dutch relations to include stage Dutch, counterfeit Dutch, English,
and broken English, comedy complicates the binary of English versus foreign.
In this theater of linguistic multiplicity, affiliations emerge across languages
as audiences begin to hear correspondences between English and authentic
stage Dutch. The image of London that Middleton sketches situates the
city as part of a larger northern European network wherein the scope of its

citizens' "linguistic competence" is expanded to include a bit of basic Dutch.[54] Without it, one risks being gulled even out of reunion with one's family. In the end, Middleton's play reveals that it is not the Dutch stranger but the monolingual Londoner whose linguistic limitations threaten to marginalize him in London's ever-expanding linguistic emporium.

The language lessons of the early seventeenth century, which uncovered, emphasized, and dramatized the propinquity of English and Dutch, enjoy a legacy throughout the seventeenth century in the emerging market of Anglo-Dutch vocabularies, grammars, and dictionaries that lent English readers more formal access to the study of the Dutch tongue. When, for instance, Edward Richardson publishes his grammar and vocabulary *Anglo-Belgica: The English and Nether Dutch Academy* (1677), he markets his work in terms that underscore the proximities that also characterize Anglo-Dutch relations in English stage plays: "My present work is to make an Essay towards the conjoining of two Languages of those Nations whom Nature by the propinquity of their situation, and Providence by mutuall traffick, and an intermixture of the Inhabitants, have brought to a necessity of endeavoring the understanding of one anothers speech" (*To the Reader*). London playwrights were dramatizing just the kind of Anglo-Dutch cultural "intermixture" and propinquity touted in Richardson's seventeenth-century dictionary. The next chapter turns to the history of print to reveal how Anglo-Dutch linguistic relations as featured on playbook and dictionary pages invited supple interpretive engagements and sparked new questions for how England represented itself in the context of its northern European identifications.

CHAPTER 4

Dutch Impressions

The Narcissism of Minor Difference in Print

Language most shows a man: Speak, that I may see thee. . . .
No glass renders a man's form or likeness so true as his speech.
—Ben Jonson, *Timber or Discoveries*

Ben Jonson imagines the revelation of identity in speech as a visual rather than solely auditory process. "Speak, that I may see thee" is a catachrestic construction that reveals why language was so central to debates regarding cultural identity in early modern England. Language, Jonson believes, lays the epistemological foundation upon which man's identity comes into view. Literary critics have largely echoed Jonson, arguing that the imprint of accent on the early modern stage was an indelible sign of one's foreign origins and the mark of difference against which notions of a linguistically rooted English nationalism emerged. As I have argued, these characterizations capture only partially the rich linguistic landscape of the early modern stage and in so doing obscure the sophisticated language tutorials present therein. The theater's representation of polyglot London raised the important question of how to mark the difference between self and other when the other is a proximate neighbor whose mother tongue was prized for preserving the Teutonic origins of English's past. If on the stage when a Dutch merchant speaks he *sounds* like a native Englishmen, Jonson invites us wonder, might he therefore *look* like one too?

In previous chapters, I have explored a multiplicity of responses to this question as it pertains to the drama, stressing the ways in which English characters find themselves so "jumbled" with Dutchness that they fail to display an inherent or "natural" Englishness. This chapter takes up the question of the relation of language to ethnic identity from the vantage point of print, reorienting our site of inquiry to the mise en page of both playbooks and what I will refer to as "wordbooks": dictionaries, word lists, vocabularies, and grammars that recorded and represented the English and Dutch languages in dialogue. Building on the period's debates about language and the dramatic productions that thematized their contours, this chapter explores the semiotics of language in print. A close study of the typographic representations of English and Dutch in playbooks and wordbooks puts Jonson's calculus to the question of whether and how the printed word affirmed, denied, or qualified the logic that grafts language to ethnic identity. What literal or conceptual impression did being Dutch, speaking Dutch, or recording the Dutch language leave on English texts? I contend that the domain of print was as richly animated by the tensions that structure representation of Anglo-Dutch relations as was the early modern theater. Far more than critics generally have imagined, the printed page proves a dynamic and experimental site for exploring ideas of language's role in signifying ethnic identity, and nowhere is this more evident than in the typographic experiments exhibited in early modern playbooks themselves.

Characters with a Difference: Dutch Impressions on the Playbook Page

The loquacious Hans van Belch of *Northward Hoe* (1607) enters act 2, scene 1, expressing himself in terms that unambiguously emphasize his Dutch identity: "Dar is vor you, and vor you: een, twea, drie, vier, and vive skilling."[1] In naming the play's "Flemish Hoy" Hans van Belch, Thomas Dekker and John Webster draw on a long stage history of naming Dutch and Flemish characters "Hans."[2] Indeed the character's performance conforms to many of the stereotypes that the stage circulated about the Dutch, not the least of which was a love of drink, here manifest in a patronymic that renders Hans *of the belch.* As the scene between Van Belch, Doll, the play's common woman, and her crew unfolds, Hans's stage Dutch sparks laughter when phonetic similarities between Dutch and English result in semantic confusion:

Horn: Is your father living Maister *Hans.*

Hans: Yau, yau, min vader heb schonen husen in *Ausburgh:*[3]
   groet mine heare is mine vaders broder, mine vader heb land, and
   bin full of fee, dat is beasts, cattell.

   . . . .

   Min vader bin de groetest fooker in all *Ausbourgh.*

Doll: The greatest what?

Lever: Fooker he saies.

Doll: Out upon him. (2.1.92–101)

What Hans means, indeed what he attempts to clarify ("dat is beasts, cattell" / that is, beasts and cattle), is that his father is a "fokker," a "cattle breeder" in Dutch. What Doll presumably hears is altogether another claim that links the Dutch to sexual appetite, a commonplace in English drama at the turn of the seventeenth century. Freighted with derogatory and sexual connotation, the word "fucker" comes into English, according to the *Oxford English Dictionary*, in 1598 when it appears in John Florio's wordbook *A Worlde of Wordes.*[4] Less than a decade later, when Hans gives the word its comic debut on the English stage, Dutch meaning is already lost in translation as English and Dutch phonetic similarities occlude significant semantic differences.[5] Hans's linguistic performance is characteristic of the way in which stage Dutch induced laughter among English audiences not for its differences from English but because it so closely approximated the phonology of English as to create comic homophony. When the Dutch speak on the English stage—particularly in city comedies—the laughter their speech sparks almost always points to the failure of minor differences to secure a distinction between English and Dutch.

In performance, Hans's speech is meant to sound at once familiar and foreign and is thus illustrative of the tension of approximation characteristic of English playwrights' representations of Dutchness. On the early modern playbook page, however, Hans's speech looks like a typographic experiment in setting stark difference into play. In the 1607 quarto edition of *Northward Hoe*, the only extant early modern print edition of the playbook, the play's Dutchman looks quite unlike any other character in print (Figure 10). In the early modern quarto, all of the Dutchman's speech is printed in black letter and his is the *only* speech in the playbook that consistently appears in black letter type.[6] Hans's stage Dutch is thus given a look all its own. If, for the theater-going audience, laughter erupted in recognizing semantic ambiguity where the Dutchman himself does not, when the joke plays out across the printed page, does the typographic contrast between Hans's stage Dutch and Doll's common English resolve this comic ambiguity? I will return to this question below. Here I want to highlight that the mise en page of *Northward Hoe* provides a striking instance of the way typography could make a difference between languages that were comically approximated at the level of the aural pun. In this instance, the punning exchange emphasizes resemblances between English and Dutch while print signals their difference.

That critics have largely overlooked the typographic peculiarity of Hans's speech is partly unsurprising given the modern editorial convention of printing critical editions of plays exclusively in roman and italic type, a practice that effaces Hans's early modern typographic embodiment. What is more, as Jennifer Richards and Fred Schurink argue, such a significant body of scholarly work on the "material dimensions of books and reading" has been produced in recent years that a call for "renewed focus on the 'textuality' of reading alongside the materiality of the book" is much needed.[7] This chapter responds to this call by attending to the dynamic interaction between text and content through exploring how dramatic content comes to bear on the mise en page partly constituted by typography, and how, in turn, typography informs the reader's engagement with the narrative content of the play.

Black letter stage Dutch is an important case of what D. F. McKenzie classifies as a "dialect of written language—graphic, algebraic, hieroglyphic and, most significantly for our purposes, typographic—[which] have suffered an exclusion from critical debate about interpretation of texts because they are not speech-related."[8] The interplay between the mise en page and the content it relays has been largely neglected in critical discussions of typography, particularly discussions of black letter, which have until recently focused primarily on whether and how type font indicates the social rank of a text's intended readership.[9] For the early modern reader, however, the mise en page of *Northward Hoe* created a complex matrix of relations between the stage and the page, language as speech and language as print; it thus redirects critical attention to the way in which typography functions as an expressive form that pluralizes the practice of reading. As Julie Stone Peters has argued in relation to the style of speech prefixes and the placement of stage directions in later sixteenth- and early seventeenth-century dramatic texts, the "accidentals" of typography offer us evidence of "exploratory attempts to use typography meaningfully" at a moment when typography was "not yet bound to diue skilling, drinke Skellum vpse fræse: nempt, dats b drinck gelt.

Leut. Till our crownes crack agen Maister *Hans van Belch.*

Hans. How ist met you, how ist bro? brolick?

Doll. Ick vare well God dancke you: Nay Ime an apt schol-ler and can take.

Hans. Datt is good, dott is good: Ick can nét stay long: for Ick heb en skip come now vpon de vater: O mine scho-men bro, wee sall dauce lanteera, teera, and sing Ick brincks to you min here, van: —wat man is dat bro.

Hor. Nay pray sir on.

Hans. Wlat honds foot is dat Dorothy.

Doll. Tis my father.

Hans. Gotts Sacrament! pour vader! why seyghen you niet so to me! mine heart tis mine all great desire, to call you mine vader ta for Ick loue dis schonen bro your dochterkin.

Hor. Sir you are welcome in the way of honesty.

Hans. Ick bedanck you: Ick heb so ghe founden vader.

Harn. Whats your name I pray.

Hans. Bun nom bin Hans van Belch.

Horn. Hans Van Belch!

Hans. Pau, yau, tis so, tis so, de dronken man is alteet re-menber me.

Horn. Doe you play the marchant, sonne *Belch.*

Hans. Pau vader: Ick heb de skip swim now vpon de vater if you endouty, goe vp in de little Skip dat goe so, and bæ puld vp to Wapping, Ick sal beare you on my backe, and hang you about min neck into min groet Skip.

Horn. He Sayes *Doll,* he would haue thee to Wapping and hang thee.

Doll. No Father I vnderstand him, but maister *Hans,* I would not be seene hanging about any mans neck, to be counted his Iewell, for any gold.

Horn. Is your father liuing Maister *Hans.*

Hans. Pau, yau, min vader heb schonen husen in Aus-burgh groet mine heare is mine vaders broder, mine vader heb land, and bin full of fæ, dat is beasts, cattell

Char. He's lowzy be-like.

Han

Hans. Min vader bin de grotest fooker in all Ausbrough.

Dol. The greatest what?

Leuer. Fooker he saies.

Dol. Out vpon him.

Han. Paw paw,fooker is en groet min here hees en elberman vane Citty,gots sacrament,wat is de clock:Ick met stay. *A watch.*

Hor. Call his watch before you,if you can.

Doll. Her's a pretty thing:do these wheeles spin vp the houres! whats a clock.

Han. Acht: paw tis acht.

Dol. We can heare neither clock,nor Iack going,wee dwell in such a place that I feare I shall neuer finde the way to Church, because the bells hang so farre ; Such a watch as this , would make me go downe with the Lamb , and be vp with the Larke.

Hans. Seghen you so,doz it to.

Doll. O fie : I doe but iest, for in trueth I could neuer abide a watch.

Han. Gotts sacrament,Ick niet heb it any moze.

Exeunt Leuer-poole *and* Chartly.

Dol. An other peale ! good father lanch out this hollander.

Horn. Come Maister *Belch*, I will bring you to the water-side, perhaps to Wapping,and there ile leaue you. *Exit.*

Han. Ick bedanck you vader.

Doll. They say Whores and bawdes go by clocks , but what a Manasses is this to buy twelue houres so deerely , and then bee begd out of 'em so easily? heele be out at heeles shortly sure for he's out about the clockes already : O foolish young man how doest thou spend thy time?

Enter Leuer-poole *first,then* Allom *and* Chartly.

Leur. Your grocer.

Dol.eNay Sfoot , then ile change my tune : I may cause such leaden-heeld rascalls ; out of my sight : a knife, a knife I say : O Maister *Allom* , if you loue a woman , draw out your knife and vndo me,vndo me.

Allo.Sweete mistris *Dorothy*,what should you do with a knife, its ill medling with edge tooles , what's the matter Maisters ! knife God blesse vs.

Leuer.

printerly protocols."[10] Typographic variations—what Sir Walter Greg classified as "accidentals"—errors, inconsistencies, and exceptionalisms of the kind that I consider throughout this chapter—are not merely the scars of print's rough apprenticeship through the first century and a half of its evolution but instead provide evidence of the experimental liveliness of the semiotics of the early modern printed page.[11] Attending to the semantic mobility of typographic experiments in playbooks and wordbooks opens onto the conjunctions and disjunctions in the period's developing ideas regarding the relation of English and Dutch. I aim to attune our critical sensitivity to typography as a "dialect of written language" by exploring the experimental aspects of its use and by charting the interplay between the materiality of the printed page and the dramatic, linguistic, and ideological content it conveys. In what follows, the dramatic nature of the printed page, what Stone Peters aptly characterizes as "the theatre of the book," comes sharply into focus, together with a fresh understanding of the history of print and its role in shaping representations of Anglo-Dutch relations.[12]

Scholars agree that conventions for printing dramatic texts were by no means settled, even as late as the turn of the seventeenth century when conventions had started to firm.[13] The use of black letter for playbook printing was not unusual in itself.[14] Black letter had been widely used by printers in the mid-sixteenth century, as it was, during that period, the dominant typeface in England.[15] By 1595, however, black letter began to be replaced by the use of roman type in printed plays. Zachary Lesser calculates: "From 1576, when the first play from the professional theater was printed, through 1594, when the market for playbooks experienced its first rapid expansion, black letter was used in almost half of all editions of professional plays. From 1595 to 1608, however, the typeface began to disappear, used in only 12.4 percent of editions, and in no first editions after 1605."[16] Printed primarily using roman typeface, the 1607 quarto of *Northward Hoe* stands as evidence of this typographic transition in playbook printing. However, insofar as black letter stage Dutch appears within the otherwise all-roman playbook as a feature of a single character's speech, *Northward Hoe* proves unusual in early modern playbook printing.

How exceptional or conventional is the mise en page of *Northward Hoe*? In my study of the typographic arrangement of dramatic texts printed in England from 1564 through 1657 in which Dutch characters, Dutch-speaking characters, or English characters pretending to be Dutch are featured (seventeen dramatic works in all), I have located three instances of black letter stage Dutch, all of which appear in the first two decades of the seventeenth century. These include: Thomas Dekker and John Webster's *Northward Hoe*, Thomas Middleton and Thomas Dekker's *The Roaring Girl* (1611), and Ben Jonson's *Masque of Augures* (1621). More often, stage Dutch appears similar to the surrounding speech in early modern playbooks. In plays such as the anonymous *The Weakest Goeth to the Wall* (1600) and *The London Prodigal* (1605), Thomas Dekker and John Webster's *Westward Hoe* (1607), John Marston's *The Dutch Courtesan* (1605), and later printed playbooks, including John Ford's *The Ladies Triall* (1639), Henry Glapthorne's *The Hollander* (1640), and Thomas Middleton's *No Wit, [No] Help Like a Woman's* (1657), all of which include the appearance of a Dutch-speaking character, roman type was used for all speech in the playbook (Table 1).[17] Among the texts in which black letter stage Dutch appears, none share printers,[18] nor were any performed originally by the same theater company,[19] nor have editors reached consensus on which dramatist (if any) provided the printer's copy.[20] In short, no clear and compelling pattern emerges from the variables of production that would determine with certainty *who* selected the use of black letter typeface for stage Dutch in these three dramatic playbooks.[21]

Why, then, might black letter have been selected for stage Dutch when, in most English playbooks of the first decade of the seventeenth century, italic was used to indicate foreign speech on the printed page? Asking the question in the period's own terms opens onto the complexities of this inquiry. In England's earliest manual of printing, *Mechanick Exercises on the Whole Art of Printing* (1683–84), Joseph Moxon unveils the "printer's dialect" of the English printing house and in so doing further complicates the terms by which we understand the typographic experiment under way in early modern playbooks: "That I may be the less unintelligent to the Reader, I will inform him that in the *Printers* Dialect . . . *Language* is understood *Letter*; For the *Compositor* does not say, I shall use a Word or two of *Greek Letter*, or *Hebrew Letter*, or *Saxon Letter*, &c. but I shall use a word or two of *Greek*, a Word or two of *Hebrew, Saxon*, &c. so that the Word *Letter*, is in *Compositers* [sic] Dialect, understood by naming the Language."[22] When a compositor reached for the letterforms with which to set Hans's stage Dutch for *Northward Hoe*, he would have imagined the mechanical process in terms of "using a word or two of *English*." In the parlance of the printing house, "letter" and "language" are interchangeable categories, generating a paradox in signification. In the "printers dialect," Hans's lines are "English," even as this "English" impression imprints Hans's difference from the English-speaking characters on the page. That black letter typeface was referred to as

Table 1. Typographic Arrangement of Plays with a Dutch Character, Dutch-Speaking Character, or English Character Pretending to Be Dutch

Title	Author	Date	Typographic arrangement
1. *Enterlude of Welth and Helth*	Anon.	ca. 1565	Black letter
2a. *Like will to Like*	U. Fulwell	ca. 1568	Black letter; Roman stage directions & some characters' names
b. *Like will to Like*		1587	Black letter; Roman stage directions & some characters' names
3. *Tyde Taryeth No Man*	G. Wapull	1576	Black letter
4a. *Life and Death of Jack Straw*	Anon.	1594	Roman; King's Pardon in black letter
b. *Life and Death of Jack Straw*	Anon.	1604	Entire play in black letter
5a. *Shoemakers Holiday*	T. Dekker	1600	Black letter; Roman for characters' names & italic for stage directions (Black letter stage-Dutch, but by default, as the entire play is printed in black letter).
b. *Shoemakers Holiday*		1610	This typographic arrangement is consistent throughout all seventeenth-century editions of this play.
c. *Shoemakers Holiday*		1618	
d. *Shoemakers Holiday*		1624	
e. *Shoemakers Holiday*		1631	
f. *Shoemakers Holiday*		1657	
6a. *Weakest Goeth to the Wall*	Anon.	1600	Roman and italic
b. *Weakest Goeth to the Wall*		1618	Roman and italic
7. *A Larum for London*	Anon.	1602	Roman and italic

8. *London Prodigall*	Anon.	1605	Roman and italic
9a. *Dutch Courtesan*	J. Marston	1605	Roman and italic
b. *The Works of John Marston* (including *Dutch Courtesan*)		1633	Roman and italic
10. *Westward Hoe*	T. Dekker & J. Webster	1607	Roman and italic
11. *Northward Hoe*	T. Dekker & J. Webster	1607	Roman with some italic & **black letter stage-Dutch**
12. *The Roaring Girle*	T. Dekker & T. Middleton	1611	Roman with some italic & **black letter stage-Dutch**
13a. *Masque of Augures*	B. Jonson	1621	Roman with some italic & **black letter stage-Dutch**
b. *Masque of Augures* in *Works* vol. 2		1631	Roman with some italic & **black letter stage-Dutch**
14a. *English-men for My Money*	W. Haughton	1616	Roman and italic
b. *English-men for My Money*		1626	Roman and italic
c. *[English-men for my Money] A pleasant comedie called, A woman will have her will*		1631	Roman and italic
15. *The Ladies Triall*	J. Ford	1639	Roman and italic
16. *The Hollander*	H. Glapthorne	1640	Roman and italic
17. *No Wit / [No] Help Like a Woman's*	T. Middleton	1657	Roman and italic

"English letter" complicates the matter further. Reframing our inquiry in terms of the "printers dialect" of the period reorients our inquiry, directing attention not only to the difference that the "written dialect" of black letter sets into play across the page but also to the overlap between English and Dutch in the "printers dialect" of the printing house. Rather than ask why black letter was used for stage Dutch, I want to consider what typographic logic informed the choice to print the Dutchman's speech in "English letter" and how English readers might have interpreted the typographic distinction that adheres to Hans's speech.

First we must consider whether a conventional connection existed between the spoken word on the English stage and the printed word of the playbook page. Does Hans's speech look different on the playbook page because in performance it sounded foreign? Did black letter function as "visualized speech," as Yvonne Schwemer-Scheddin has proposed regarding black letter in post–World War II Germany?[23] Scholars working on the material history of the playbook have drawn various conclusions regarding the question of the relation of theatrical performance to the printed play. In his influential essay "What Is an Editor?," Stephen Orgel asserts: "if the play is a book, it's not a play."[24] David Scott Kastan expands: "Although they have often been imagined as two halves of a single reality, as the inner and outer aspects of the play, the printed text and the performed play are not related as origin and effect (in whatever order one might conceive it). Indeed, in any precise sense, they do not constitute the same entity. Performance no more animates the text than does the text record the performance. They are dissimilar and discontinuous modes of production. . . . The printed play is neither a pre-theatrical text nor a post-theatrical one; it is a *non*-theatrical text, even when it claims to offer a version of the play 'as it was played.'"[25] *Pace* Kastan and Orgel, Marta Straznicky argues that "the early modern play could be play and book at one and the same time. This is not to say, however, that reading plays was meant to be a straight-forward replication of playgoing."[26] Straznicky critiques the framing of the debate—as page verses stage—and reorients critical inquiry toward a consideration of the "matrix within which such a history [of play reading] might emerge: that is, the relationship between the material forms of playtexts, their production and modes of circulation, and their interpretations, uses, and appropriations by various reading publics."[27] Shifting inquiry from a binary dividing stage from page toward the relation of the page to its readers opens a different and more productive question for our purposes: in what ways might the allocation of black letter or "English letter" to stage Dutch have informed how readers interpreted a text? This question returns us to a long history of critical work on English texts printed in black letter.

Numerous theories aim to explain the conventional use of black letter type in early modern texts, but none has been quite so influential in the last half century as that proposed by Charles Mish, who argues that black letter served as a "social discriminant" in the seventeenth century, a "determining criterion" for indicating that a text was produced for a middle-class audience.[28] That "cheap print" (chapbooks, romances, broadside ballads) was often printed in black letter pointed subsequent critics to evidence of an indexical relationship between the typography of a text and its intended readership. Black letter survived well into the seventeenth century as the "dominant font" of "prayer books, primers, ABCs, hornbooks, early chapbooks, law books, published laws, and statutes—texts issued in the voice of authority, whether divine or civil; texts which instilled obedience, singularity of opinion, and uniformity of action," observes Sabrina Alcorn Baron.[29] The books "essential in early modern childhood education . . . were printed in black letter"; even books, such as Edmund Coote's *The English School-master*, "designed for teaching tradesmen's apprentices or small children, followed [a] pattern [of printing] roman for the teacher, black letter for the student."[30] Throughout the sixteenth century and early seventeenth century, Bibles were regularly printed in black letter. Coverdale's New Testament, the Great Bible ("the English translation authorized by Henry VIII to supplant Coverdale in 1539"), the Bishops' Bible (1568–1610), and King James I's Bible (1611) were all printed in black letter.[31] In addition to an almost fifty-year history of state-sanctioned black letter English Bibles, black letter "had become identified with 'common' vernacular texts designed for 'circles untouched by humanistic studies.'"[32] On the basis of such evidence, Baron, Keith Thomas, and John King come to related conclusions that in England black letter "transmitted the voice of authority";[33] it was "the type for the common people";[34] and "typography differentiates learned readers capable of reading text set in roman and Greek typefaces from the *hoi poloi*, who do not go beyond vernacular wording set almost wholly in black letter."[35] In such analyses, black letter functions indexically, pointing beyond itself to a target readership, "hoi poloi," the everyman and child of early modern England or those in need of instruction from above. In other words, black letter indexes a "low" or common readership.

In his critique of these prevailing interpretations of black letter, Zachary Lesser admonishes that "we must resist the reductionism that would see only a single meaning to the typeface, which was used in a wide variety of contexts, or that would see no meaning at all in it, only an index to 'popular culture.'"[36] We come closer to understanding the polyvalence of black letter when we approach type not as an index but as a *signifier*: "While black letter appears to be the material index to a class of readers, the specifics of these class formations are never stable. What this instability reveals is that black letter is in fact not an *index* but a *signifier*, a sliding signifier of the 'low' that depends on how the critic defines the total spectrum of readers" (102–3). In approaching black letter as a sliding signifier, Lesser rightly emphasizes the inherent instability of typography in serving as a transmitter for the voice of authority or as a stable material index to a class of readers.[37] Instead, he suggests, the study of "low" or popular culture reveals the critical "desire *for* popular culture" (my emphasis, 100).[38] One of the "dominant meanings of black letter in this period," Lesser contends, "was the powerful combination of Englishness ('the English letter') and past-ness (the 'antiquated' appearance of black letter by the seventeenth century)," what he calls "typographic nostalgia" (107).[39]

Black letter conveyed and created nostalgia not only for the English past but also for the Teutonic past of English's history. As I traced in Chapter 2, while language purists and archaizers argued that English's Teutonic past had long been marred by the adoption of foreign word stock, antiquarians of the early seventeenth century were arguing that English's Teutonic history had indeed been preserved beyond the shores of England in the Dutch vernacular of the Netherlands. In listening to the speech of their Dutch neighbors the English could hear evidence of their own linguistic past. So too, Richard Verstegan argued in *A Restitution of Decayed Intelligence* (1605), relics of English's "unmixed" past live on in remote "shyres of England," where English sounds much like "West-Flanders" Dutch.[40] Verstegan goes further yet, mobilizing black letter to underscore the historical relatedness of English and Dutch. The majority of the text is printed in roman, but at the moment when Verstegan makes his most explicit argument for the proximity of "unmixed English" and Dutch, black letter is introduced into the mise en page, simultaneously differentiating recorded speech from narration and visually underscoring the "ancient neernes" of English and Dutch by means of typographic similitude (199). In the exchange recounted in Chapter 2, Verstegan represents an imagined dialogue between a traveling Englishman and a West Flanders Dutchman: "It is not long since that an Englishman travailing by wagon in *West-Flanders*, and hearing the wagoner to call unto his man and say, 𝕯𝖊 𝖘𝖙𝖗𝖎𝖓𝖌 𝖎𝖘 𝖑𝖔𝖘𝖘𝖊/ 𝖇𝖎𝖓𝖉 𝖉𝖊 𝖘𝖙𝖗𝖎𝖓𝖌 𝖆𝖊𝖓 𝖉𝖊 𝖜𝖆𝖌𝖊𝖓 𝖛𝖆𝖘𝖙[,] presently understood him as yf hee had said, 𝕿𝖍𝖊 𝖘𝖙𝖗𝖎𝖓𝖌 𝖎𝖘 𝖑𝖔𝖔𝖘𝖊/ 𝖇𝖞𝖓𝖉 𝖙𝖍𝖊 𝖘𝖙𝖗𝖎𝖓𝖌 𝖔𝖓 𝖙𝖍𝖊 𝖜𝖆𝖌𝖔𝖓 𝖋𝖆𝖘𝖙/ and weening the follow [fellow] to have bin some English clown, spake unto him in English" (198–99). Verstegan comments on the "neernes" of England's old country rhymes and the Dutch language, stressing the similitude in phonology ("ryme") and semantics ("sence") (Figure 11). Here, typography dramatizes the linguistic argument that English and Dutch are "issued from the same root" (198). For Verstegan, who oversaw the print production of his work in Antwerp, even creating its illustrations, the choice to set this linguistic exchange in black letter serves two related arguments. First, it visually emphasizes English's ("ancient") Teutonic roots by casting it in the typeface that conjures both the look of English's past and the print history of the Germanic north. Second, the typographic arrangement formally enacts the cross-cultural linguistic argument of the passage: English and Dutch are so nearly alike that they sound less like distinct languages than like dialects of one another. An argument regarding Anglo-Dutch shared linguistic history emerges, formally speaking, in the shape of shared typographic embodiment. The difference that emerges in graphic form is not the difference between England and Dutch, but the difference between dialogue and exposition.

In *A Restitution* black letter recalls English's past and is mobilized to demonstrate the relatedness of that past to contemporary Dutch. If we use this insight to reconsider the playbook page of *Northward Hoe,* black letter stage Dutch can be understood to signify not only cross-cultural Anglo-Dutch linguistic differences but also the internal historical differences within English itself. The point, in this instance, is hardly a subtle one—since black letter was better known during this period as "English Letter." Stage Dutch printed in black letter awakens English readers to an alternative history of the English language, one that played out across the North Sea in the now Dutch- and Flemish-speaking Low Countries. As I argued in Chapter 2, Verstegan heralded the close relation between "unmixed English" and Dutch in positive terms, as he understood linguistic "neernes" to demonstrate a forgotten, but desirable, racial kinship. On the stage, however, speakers of stage Dutch often elicited pejorative responses, whenever their speech was used to render them as "English clown[s]." Even so, by not representing stage Dutch as an incomprehensible barbarous tongue but, instead, as broken English, the theater implicitly suggests Verstegan's thesis: that English and Dutch are related tongues that exist on a continuum. Read within this frame that an Englishman trauailing by wagon in *VVest-Flanders*, and hearing the wagoner to call vnto his man and say, **De ſtring is loſſe/ bind de ſtring aen de wagen vaſt.** preſently vnderſtood him as yf hee had ſaid, **The ſtring is looſe/ bynd the ſtring on the wagon faſt/** and weening the follow to haue bin ſome Engliſh clown, ſpake vnto him in Engliſh. I haue diuers tymes in noting the neernes of that and our language, obſerued certaine of our old countrey rymes to accord with theirs, both in ſelf ryme and ſelf ſence, which is a very great argument, of the ancient neernes of our and their language.

As for example.

Wee ſay, ⎰ **Winters thunder is ſomers wunder.**
They ſay, ⎱ **Winters donder is ſomers wonder.**

Wee ſay, ⎰ **An apple in May is as good as an ey.**
They ſay, ⎱ **En apple in Mey is ſo goet als en ey.**

Our particular language albeit it could not by the Normannes be changed, but that both the noble name of Engliſhmen, and their Engliſh ſpeech did ſtil remaine, yet became it by their coming among them to bee much mixed with French: & heer concerning this language which now beareth the name of Frech, I hold it not amiſſe to take occaſiõ, to giue the reader ſome knowlege more then is vulgar. The countrey of *Gallia*, now called *France*, was anciently inhabited of the Gaules, but what language the Gaules did ſpeak is now in ſome queſtion, *Ceaſar* ſaith in the begining of his comentaries, that they had amõg them three languages, but I ſhould rather think that they only differed as the High-duitſh, Low-duitſh,

Bb 4   and

of reference, Hans of *Northward Hoe* offers English readers a glimpse of the Other *they might have been*, as he is cast in the typographical likeness of the Other *they once were*. As the Dutchman's speech looks like that of English's not-so-distant past, so too it sounds so much like English that Hans unwittingly finds himself playing the "English clown." Whether audiences understood Hans to be speaking stage Dutch or broken English is a question that even the differential type of the playbook page will not definitively resolve. While the minor differences between Hans's stage Dutch and Doll's common English ensured a hearty laugh, so too the language lesson that takes the form of a joke directs attention to the failure of minor differences to secure an abiding distinction between English and Dutch.

Before readers of *Northward Hoe* opened their playbooks to discover stage Dutch printed in black letter, they would have regularly encountered variation in typographic arrangement on playbook pages in the form of italic. As playbook printing increasingly shifted away from black letter toward roman typeface, italic was deployed to make broad classificatory distinctions, indicating unnarrated dramatic action such as character entrances and exits, character prefixes, all proper names, often place names, and sometimes songs.[41] Italic was also sometimes mobilized to create a visual distinction between foreign and English speech. Indeed, in seventeenth-century English playbooks, stage Dutch was more often printed in italic than in black letter. In such cases, italic indicated foreign language, not a character's foreignness per se. Even so, given the indeterminacy of the linguistic categories the plays themselves explore (as well as the many variables and opportunities for interpretation in print production), slippages between speech and speaker, foreign language and foreignness, were introduced by the very typographic arrangements that were apparently intended to stabilize distinctions between them. A close study of the typographic arrangements across three print editions of William Haughton's comedy, *Englishmen for My Money* (1598), London's earliest city comedy, reveals the various ways type proved a sliding signifier of the linguistic difference it was also impressing on the page.

Throughout *Englishmen for My Money*—a play rich in instances of foreign speech—three foreign suitors vie in marriage for three English women, who much prefer their English suitors. What the women negotiate in the context of courtship, the exclusion of the foreigner from the marriage market, the playbook page conveys as a typographic mediation. In the first three surviving editions of Haughton's play (1616, 1626, 1631),[42] the use of italic is carefully managed to differentiate between foreign speech (set in italic) and broken English (set in roman), differences that may not have always been self-evident in the spoken performances of the play. In all three print editions, Italian, Dutch, and French speech is printed in italic type.[43] The distinction between broken English and foreign speech is evident, for instance, when the play's Italian, Alvaro, addresses the other foreigners and Englishmen using both broken English and stage Italian (Figure 12). Typographically speaking, Alvaro's speech, printed in roman on the top half of the page, looks exactly like that of the Englishmen with whom he converses. Nine lines up from the bottom of the page, however, Alvaro launches into his native Italian. With this shift from broken English to foreign speech, Alvaro's lines alter typographically from roman to italic type.

The look of Alvaro's foreign speech is characteristic of the way type underscores the distinction between English and foreign speech when all three of the play's foreigners speak. The Frenchman, Delio, remarks, "*Oh de brave de galliarde devise:* me sal come by de nite and contier faire de Anglois Gentlehomes dicte nous ainsi monsieur *Pisaro*" (E3r). Just why the first half of this sentence signifies as French enough to require italics while the second half of the sentence, so rife with French vocabulary, is typographically represented as broken English is unclear—clearly the semiotics of typography in the period were fluid. The point is not that the arbitrariness of such distinctions should disqualify these textual and typographic "anomalies" from our close analysis, but that these moments demonstrate just how powerful an instrument typography could be for creating both differences and resemblances between English and foreign speech on the playbook page.[44] While on stage Delio apparently sounds French, on the page he often looks English.

The typographic arrangement of the speech of the play's Englishmen makes plain that italic indicates foreign language, not foreign characters. In the following parley, for instance, two English characters exchange lines in French, Italian and Dutch and their foreign speech appears in italic type:

> *Frisco:* Can you speake French? *Content pore vous monsier Madomo.*
> *Anthony:* If I could not sir, I should ill understand you: you speake the best French that ever trode upon Shoe of Leather.
> *Frisco:* Nay, I can speak more Languages then that: This is *Italian,* is it not? *Nella slurde Curtezana.*
> *Anthony:* Yes sir, and you speake it like a very Naturall.

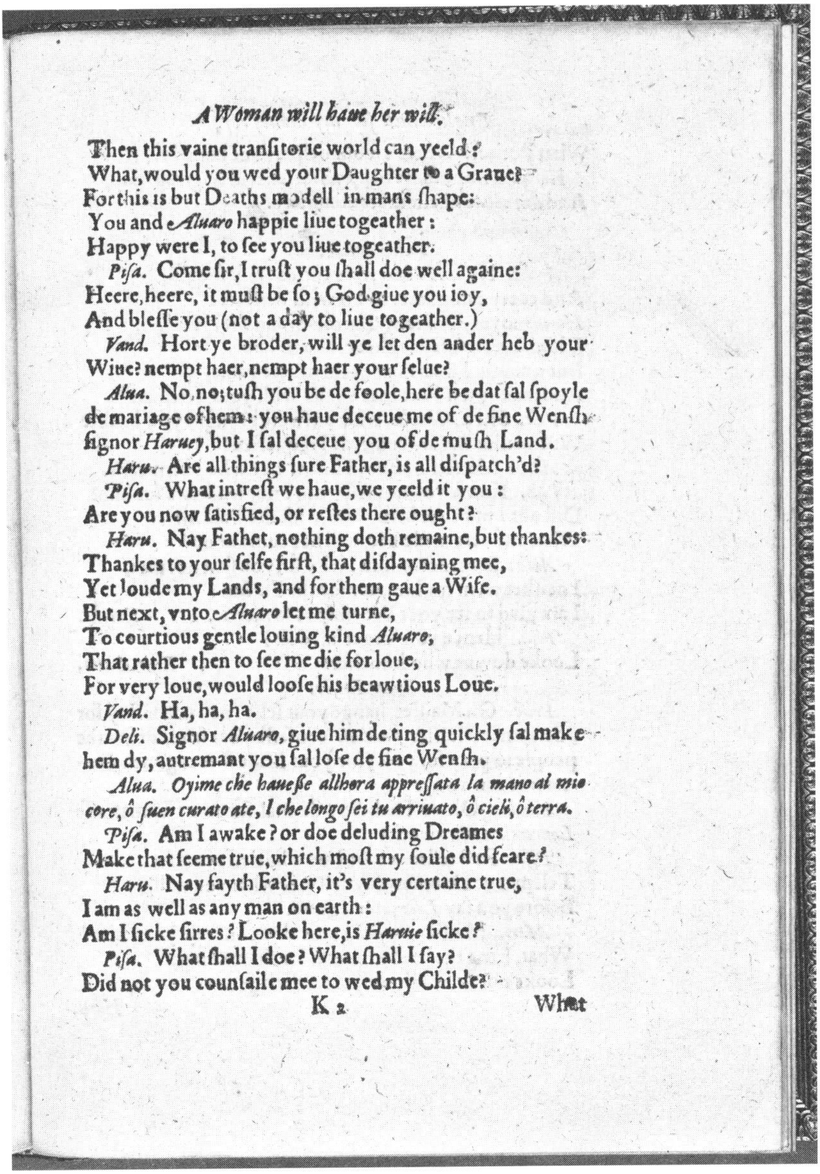

Then this vaine tranfitorie world can yeeld:
What, would you wed your Daughter to a Graue?
For this is but Deaths modell in mans fhape:
You and *Aluaro* happie liue togeather:
Happy were I, to fee you liue togeather.

   Pifa. Come fir, I truft you fhall doe well againe:
Heere, heere, it muft be fo; God giue you ioy,
And bleffe you (not a day to liue togeather.)

   Vand. Hort ye broder, will ye let den aader heb your
Wiue? nempt haer, nempt haer your felue?

   Alua. No, no; tufh you be de foole, here be dat fal fpoyle
de mariage of hem: you haue deceue me of de fine Wenfh,
fignor *Haruey*, but I fal deceue you of de mufh Land.

   Haru. Are all things fure Father, is all difpatch'd?

   Pifa. What intreft we haue, we yeeld it you:
Are you now fatisfied, or reftes there ought?

   Haru. Nay Fathet, nothing doth remaine, but thankes:
Thankes to your felfe firft, that difdayning mee,
Yet loude my Lands, and for them gaue a Wife.
But next, vnto *Aluaro* let me turne,
To courtious gentle louing kind *Aluaro*,
That rather then to fee me die for loue,
For very loue, would loofe his beawtious Loue.

   Vand. Ha, ha, ha.

   Deli. Signor *Aluaro*, giue him de ting quickly fal make
hem dy, autremant you fal lofe de fine Wenfh.

   Alua. Oyime che haueffe allhora appreffata la mano al mio
core, ô fuen curato ate, I che longo fei tu arriuato, ô cielt, ô terra.

   Pifa. Am I awake? or doe deluding Dreames
Make that feeme true, which moft my foule did feare?

   Haru. Nay fayth Father, it's very certaine true,
I am as well as any man on earth:
Am I ficke firres? Looke here, is *Haruie* ficke?

   Pifa. What fhall I doe? What fhall I fay?
Did not you counfaile mee to wed my Childe?

K 2

Whet

FIGURE 12. William Haughton, *English-men for My Money* (1616).

Frisco: I believe you well: now for *Dutch:*
  Ducky de doe watt heb yee ge brought. (D3r)

On the page, foreign speech—even inauthentic stage Dutch ("ducky de doe")—is printed in italic type. Conversely, when the play's three foreigners speak broken English it appears as English, in roman type.

The distinction that the typographic arrangement of all three editions of *Englishmen for My Money* underwrites is broadly conceived, separating foreign and English speech. Distinctions that are central to the comedy of cross-cultural encounter in theatrical performance—between English and broken English, for instance—are effaced by a typographic arrangement that renders English and broken English identical on the page. This is nowhere more in evidence than when the play's Dutchman, Vandalle, bemoans his linguistic inadequacy in the following terms: "Mester *Pisaro*, de Dochter maistris *Laurentia* calle me de Dyel, den Asse, for that ic can neit englesh spreken" (E3v). Here broken English and English, both rendered in roman type, look alike, suggesting that broken English counts *as* English, according to the typographic logic of the playbook page. So where does the difference between Vandalle's English and Dutch reside? The point, the printed playbook suggests, is less about distinction than its lack. What counts as English or Dutch is less important to the comic thrust of representations of Anglo-Dutch relations in English city comedies than is the overlap between them. As the play's Dutchman toggles back and forth across the typographic landscape of the playbook, in one instance his speech is Englished, in another it is Dutched. "Ic can neit englesh spreken" proves as much a joke at English's expense as it is at that of the beleaguered Dutchman, whose lexicon and typographic embodiment enacts the breaking of English. In the typographic drama playing out across the printed page, the characters' written and spoken dialects collide. Any secure sense of a difference between broken English and stage Dutch—potentially salient in comic performance—collapses when Vandalle's confession, "ic can neit englesh spreken," is set in roman type. Within the typographic conventions of the playbook, Vandalle appears to be attempting *English* in this moment, even as he strains it to the breaking point with a lexicon so plainly Dutch.

The predominant order of the play's typographic arrangement conveys the implicit message that Englishmen speak English because they *look* to do so. So too the play's foreigners speak their native tongues when they look to do so. In addition to revealing that language rather than character functions as the organizing principle of the play's typographic arrangement, *Englishmen for My Money* demonstrates that typographic arrangements could function as the toggle whereby dialogue passes back and forth from foreign-identified (italic) to English-identified (roman) speech. In this way, typographic arrangements enact the dramatic movements across ethnic categories that the play itself thematizes as threatening to the stability of the English language: "Ah Gentlemen," Frisco the play's clown admonishes the English suitors, "doe not suffer a litter of Languages to spring up amongst us" (338–39). English, however, is already "littered" with the language of the play's aliens. While type appears to have been mobilized to draw categorical differences between foreign and English speech, the difference it encodes does not exist a priori. Only once early modern readers attune themselves to the conventions of type established within the playbook itself does type emerge as a powerful signifier of the differences it inscribes. In other words, roman and italic typefaces do not record linguistic differences so much as they *create* them. They do so by demarcating English from even the most ambiguous instances of speech: broken English, foreign-accented English, and sometimes stage Dutch. Even in those instances wherein type is mobilized to draw broad distinctions between English and *not English*, it proves far from an exacting instrument. For the playbook reader, typographic variation encourages close attention to the imprinting of Englishness and Otherness, in no small part because it exposes the fragility of the distinctions it imprints.[45] The typographic logic of Haughton's city comedy reverses the assumption of Jonson's epigram, suggesting that characters must first be "seen," they must become typographically manifested, in order that a reader might *hear* and so categorize their speech as either foreign or English. "Speak, that I may see thee" becomes "appear that I may hear thee." On the playbook page, where typographic similitude powerfully suggests proximity of kind, the difference between the foreigner and the Englishman may be utterly effaced.

Returning to the case of black letter stage Dutch in *Northward Hoe*, a striking typographic experiment appears to have been under way. Upon the Dutchman's arrival in act 2, the English character, Doll, offers her impression of stage Dutch, and in so doing alters the typographic look of the page (Figure 13). The double typeface of Doll's half-Dutch, half-English sentence is a remarkable instance of how the technology of print could transform an aural into a visual pun. To be "apt," in early modern English, was not only to be quick witted or intelligent but also "susceptible to impression." The typographic arrangement of Doll's sentence literalizes her susceptibility to

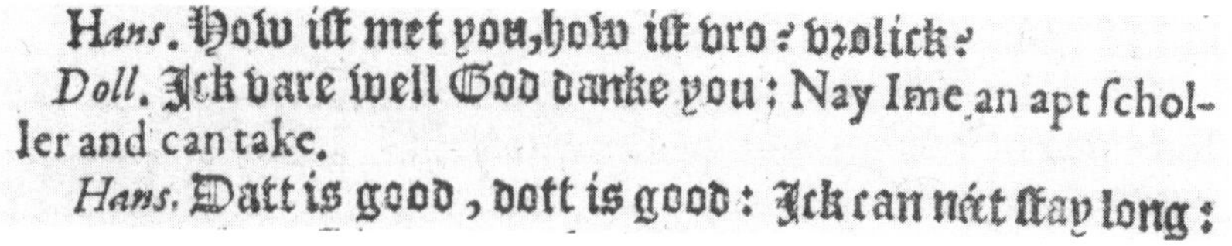

Hans. Ｈｏｗ iſt met you, how iſt bro ꞉ bꞛolick꞉
Doll. Ick bare well God danke you ; Nay Ime an apt ſchol-
ler and can take.
Hans. Ｄatt is good , doſt is good : Ick can net ſtay long ꞉

FIGURE 13. Thomas Dekker and John Webster, *Northward Hoe* (1607).
By permission of the Huntington Library, San Marino, California.

impression as her linguistic aptness with stage Dutch leaves its typographic
impression on the page. Whoever made the choice to set forth Doll's line in
two typefaces was clearly counting on a sophisticated readerly engagement
with the semiotics of type. Doll's double typographic embodiment and the
visual pun it engenders bears witness to the ways in which typography invited
readers to engage the material cues of the playbook page together with the
dramatic and linguistic content of the play.

If the appearance of Hans's black letter speech in a playbook otherwise
printed in roman is conspicuous, the double typeface of Doll's line is also
striking as this is the only instance in the playbook of black letter and roman
typefaces being used *within the same line* to convey the speech of a single
character. This arrangement involved additional effort on the part of the
compositor, requiring him to determine that he has type of equal body size,
to draw that type from the separate cases where roman and black letter were
stored, and then to set the type in his compositor's stick to form a single line
on the playbook page. This was not an uncommon practice in printing
houses, but it was one that might slow the process of setting type, particularly
if another compositor was using the black letter of that body size at the same
time. In terms of the mise en page, the allocation of black letter for Doll's
stage Dutch emerges prominently because of how it is juxtaposed against
roman type, focusing the reader's attention by means of spatial proximity on
the visual difference of roman and black letter. As she takes up Hans's native
Dutch, her lines are set down in a type that effaces her English difference.
On the page, Doll momentarily sounds *and looks* Dutch. If in performance
stage Dutch was made to sound similar to English, as we have discovered in
Hans's unwitting malapropism (𝖋𝖔𝖔𝖐𝖊𝖗), here Dutch and English are made
to look as different as the technology of print would allow. And yet no
sooner has Doll's typographic metamorphosis occurred than she snaps back,
demonstrating that while she can "take" to Dutch as "an apt scholler," so

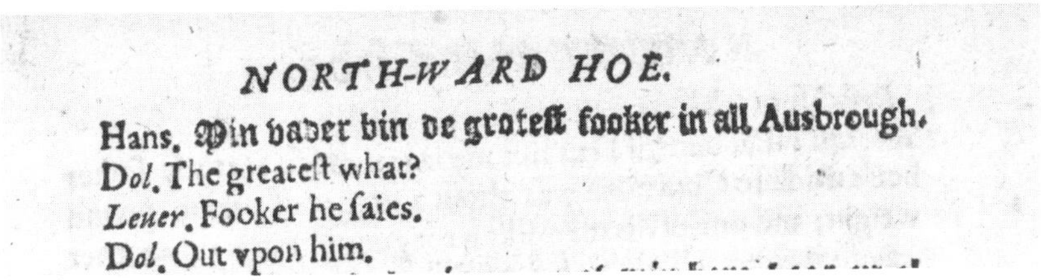

NORTH-WARD HOE.

Hans. Min vader bin de groteft fooker in all Ausbrough.
Dol. The greateft what?
Leuer. Fooker he faies.
Dol. Out vpon him.

FIGURE 14. Thomas Dekker and John Webster, *Northward Hoe* (1607).
By permission of the Huntington Library, San Marino, California.

too can she translate herself back into English, both linguistically and typographically. The material manifestation of Doll's line reveals one way in
which typography introduces difference onto a page, even as it creates the
effect of its own impermanence. The theater of the page raises the stakes of
what it means to impersonate another through linguistic impression since, in
so doing, one reveals the mutability of the signifiers of one's ethnolinguistic
identity.

Like Doll's typographic metamorphosis as an "apt" scholar, Lever's
English response puts the notion of linguistic identification itself to the question by introducing confusion about the etymological origins of the word
"fooker." The mise en page of cross-cultural linguistic exchange suggests that
when Hans speaks, the word is Dutch, but just two lines later when Lever
repeats what he has heard, the word has been (typographically) Englished
(Figure 14).[46] Is Lever's use of the word "fooker" meant to be interpreted as
if it were Dutch, or English, or both? The answer hinges on whether the
reader understands Lever to be parroting or translating Hans's Dutch. If, on
the one hand, Lever is merely repeating Hans, then the compositor has
missed the chance to manifest that repetition in the typographic arrangement
of the line. The double typographic appearance of Doll's lines on the facing
playbook page suggests that the printer or compositor(s) could have opted for
such an arrangement, but instead chose roman type. Given the typographic
arrangement of *Northward Hoe*, Lever appears to be translating Hans's Dutch
into bawdy English. What registers in performance as an English-Dutch
homophone typography exposes as a cognate relation. The relation between
homophones and etymology was a close one in this period, as Margreta de
Grazia emphasizes: "etymologies in this period served to blur the distinction
among words of similar sounds rather than differentiate them with an origin

and history of their own."[47] In the case of this exchange, similar sounding words also blur semantic distinction. As the English-speaking characters fail to recognize the contextual specificity of Hans's semantic meaning, they expose just why this witty confusion unfolds. Hans's "**fooker**" and Lever's "fooker" are cognates, thought to derive from the Middle Dutch *fokken*. While it is unknown whether the verb "to fuck" comes directly into English from the Middle Dutch verb *fokken*, Hans—the first character on the English stage to speak the word—memorably dramatizes its importation. And yet even with its comic debut, the very fact that the word can serve as the punch line of a dramatic joke is evidence of its circulation in English *as* English. The double typographic appearance of "fooker" suggests that Hans, whose speech is printed in "English letter," unwittingly speaks with a lexicon that recalls the Dutch origins of the English language. What makes Hans's speech so entertaining—both on the page and on the stage—is not its difference or its sameness from English, but the way in which his lexicon displays the slippages of the in-between.

If Hans both *is* and *isn't* speaking Dutch, so too Lever both *is* and *isn't* speaking English. The specter of Dutch on the early modern stage sparks category confusion not only about national difference—as Dutch characters appear as the Englishmen's double—but also about the very linguistic difference that, however forged, fictionalized, and created it was, was nonetheless essential to underpinning claims of English identity. That this instance of category confusion is engendered by Hans's stage Dutch cast in or as "English letter" makes this brief exchange one of the finest examples of typographic wit (and linguistic insight regarding English and Dutch) in early modern drama.

While *Northward Hoe* offers a rare instance of the typographic finesse of Anglo-Dutch linguistic exchange in dramatic playbooks, a similar case occurs in another of Thomas Dekker's coauthored plays, *The Roaring Girl* (1611).[48] In act 5, scene 1, the English-speaking Tearcat temporarily takes on Dutch speech and the look of the page transforms in the process (Figure 15). One of the play's many "base rogue[s]," Tearcat adopts stage Dutch as part of a ruse to extract sympathy and swindle money from the street-smart Moll and her companions, Sir Beauteous and Jack Dapper. Having claimed injury in both "nether limbs," Tearcat pretends to be a wounded soldier whose service has taken him from Hungary to Venice to "Dutchlant." Having primed his audience with commonplace geographic puns on the Netherlands, Tearcat is imagined in derogatory terms that further entrench him in associations with

T. Cat. In both our neather limbs.

Mol. Come, come, *Dapper*, lets giue 'em something, las poore men, what mony haue you? by my troth I loue a souldier with my soule.

Sir Bewt. Stay, stay, where haue you seru'd?

T. Long. In any part of the Low countries?

Trap. Not in the Low countries, if it pleafe your manhood, but in *Hungarie* againft the *Turke* at the fiedge of *Belgrad*.

L. Nol. Who feru'd there with you firra?

Trap. Many *Hungarians*, *Moldauians*, *Valachians*, and *Tranfiluanians*, with fome *Sclauonians*, and retyring home fir, the *Venetian* Gallies tooke vs prifoners, yet free'd vs, and fuffered vs to beg vp and downe the country.

Iack. Dap. You haue ambled all ouer *Italy* then.

Trap. Oh fir, from *Venice* to *Roma*, *Vecchio*, *Bononia*, *Romania*, *Bolonia*, *Modena*, *Piacenza*, and *Tufcana*, with all her Cities, as *Piftoia*, *Valteria*, *Mountepulchena*, *Arrezzo*, with the *Siennois*, and diuerfe others.

Mol. Meere rogues, put fpurres to 'em once more.

Iack. Dap. Thou look'ft like a ftrange creature, a fat butter-box, yet fpeak'ft Englifh,
What art thou?

T. Cat. Ick mine Here. Ick bin den ruffling Teare-Cat,
Den braue Soldade, Ick bin dorick all Dutchlant.
Gueresen: Der Shellum das meere Ine Beafa
Ine woert gaeb.
Ick flaag bin ftroakes ou tom Cop:
Daftick Den hundred touzun Diuell balle,
Frollick miue Here.

Sir Bewt. Here, here, let's be rid of their iobbering,

Moll. Not a croffe *Sir Bewtious*, you bafe rogues, I haue taken meafure of you, better then a taylor can, and I'le fit you, as you (monfter with one eie) haue fitted mee,

Trap. Your Worfhip will not abufe a fouldier.

K 3   *Mol.*

FIGURE 15. Thomas Middleton and Thomas Dekker, *The Roaring Girle* (1611).
By permission of the Huntington Library, San Marino, California.

things Dutch. Prompted by Jack Dapper's observation that he looks like "a fat butter-box," a negative characterization of the Dutch used frequently both on and off the English stage, Tearcat launches into a performance of language aimed at authenticating his counterfeited professional and national identities. In attempting to pass as Dutch, Tearcat hopes to transform into the "fat butter-box" Dapper derides. On the page, he appears to succeed. However, within the dramatic exchange of the play, Tearcat's brief adoption of stage Dutch fails to resolve the question "what art thou?" Sir Beauteous's response, "let's be rid of their jobbering" (i.e., jabbering), reveals that Tearcat has succeeded only in perturbing his audience. Moll concludes that he is not a soldier but a "skeldering varlet," a swindler and thief (5.1.113).[49] Unlike Sir Beauteous and Moll, the playbook reader experiences Tearcat's typographic transition as a linguistic costume change, a visually compelling display of his linguistic doubleness. Tearcat's performance of stage Dutch tests the limits of Jonson's calculus, "speak that I may see thee," as his speech is exposed as an instrument of disguise rather than the sine qua non of his origins. Tearcat's performance in effect denies response to Dapper's query "what art thou," as he demonstrates how authentic stage Dutch and the identity it bespeaks, according to Jonson's logic, can be taken up and discarded at will. Although the page momentarily suggests that speaking Dutch makes one appear Dutch, Tearcat's various typographical embodiments—from roman to black letter and back to roman—impress on the reader a countervailing hypothesis: that speech, even speech set down in print, is a far less stable signifier of identity than Jonson would wish.

Type proves a nimble instrument of meaning making on the pages of these early modern playbooks. In fostering a tension between difference and sameness, the Hans of the early printed page enlists readers in an interpretive process that requires sustaining focus on the multivalent fields of evidence (form and content) that pull meaning in more than one direction. Hans's stage Dutch, as well as Doll's and Tearcat's temporary impression of stage Dutch, catalyzes a double vision for the playbook reader. Just as type could import alterity into the mise en page of the playbook, impressing the speech of the other with the look of difference, it also exposes the constructedness of the alterity it works to establish. In mastering Dutch linguistic difference, the characters I have explored play double "types"—both English and Dutch—and in so doing imprint the page with compelling but impermanent impressions of ethnolinguistic identity in the making.

Typography and Typology in Jonson's *Masque of Augures*

Nowhere was Jonson's idea challenged more than in his own *Masque of Augures* wherein stage Dutch, printed in black letter, signifies an infection of the tongue due to travel. Presented to King James's court on Twelfth Night, 1622, the opening antimasque is set in the court buttery hatch where a brewer's clerk, a "Lighterman," an alewife, "her two women," a "rare Artist," a bearward, and his "three dancing Beares" have arrived in hopes of performing their masque for the king. The artistic principal among this band of "St. Katherine's" thespians (who "stincke like so many bloat-herrings newly taken out of the chimney!") is named *Van Goose*, the "rare Artist" of the crew. Eager to persuade "Groome of the Revels," who works in the court buttery, that the king and his company might enjoy their performance, Van Goose begins:

> *Van:* Dat is all true, exceeding true, de Inventors be barren, lost,
>   two, dre, vour mile, I know that from my selva: dey have no
>   ting, no ting. . . . Now me vould bring in some dainty new ting,
>   dat never vas, nor never sall be in de rebus natura! dat has never
>   van de mater, nor de vorme, nor de head nor de hoof, but is a
>   mera devisa of de braine—
> *Groom:* Hey-da! what HANS FLUTTERKIN is
>   this? what do's this *Dutchman* build, or talk of?
>   Castles in the ayre?
> *Not:* He is no *Dutchman* Sir, he is a *Brittaine* borne,
>   but hath learned to misuse his owne tongue in travell,
>   and now speakes all languages in ill English; a rare Artist
>   he is sir, & a Projector of Masques.[50]

On the page, Van Goose looks like Hans of *Northward Hoe* and the counterfeit "butter-box" of *The Roaring Girl*. Except for his Latin lexicon, all of Van Goose's words appear in black letter. His speech prompts Groom to rename him Hans Flutterkin, a name no less satirical than Van Goose, which, like Middleton's rendition of Savourwit's pontifications on the nonsense word "gulldergoose," has the effect of linking Dutchness with intellectual simplicity. Van Goose's name, the look of his speech on the page, and his Dutch-accented English coalesce, urging the reader to concur with Groom's identification of him as Dutch. More, the opening of the masque makes reference to both geography and foodstuffs commonly linked to the Dutch. The members of Van Goose's troupe confess they are from "St. Katherines," a precinct beyond London's wall where, according to population surveys of the latter half of the sixteenth century, a significant population of Dutch immigrants settled, inter-married, and buried their dead in what was known as the "Flemish cemetery."[51] More, Van Goose's motley crew stinks of herring, a fish the Dutch were said to savor. Upon first spotting the unexpected players, Groom exclaims, "Hey-da! what's this! A hogshead of beere broake out of the Kings Buttry, or some *Dutch* hulke!" This proliferation of references to things Dutch sets the scene before the presumed "Dutch hulke" ever speaks a line and spills his typographic difference onto the page.

Notch's insistence that Van Goose "is no Dutchman . . . , he is a *Brit-taine* borne," together with the black letter appearance of Van Goose's speech, raises the question of whether this translated Englishman is now English or Dutch, neither or both? Notch claims that Van Goose's lexicon is a symptom of perambulation, not birth. His "misuse[d]" English is a "learned," rather than an inborn, affectation. His travels, even to the proxi-mate outskirts of St. Katherine's, have infected his English speech in word and inflection, thus bringing to life Thomas Wilson's foreboding depiction of England as the land of Babel, "Some seeke so farre for outlandish Englishe, that thei forget altogether their mothers language. And I dare swere this, if some of their mothers were alive, thei were not able to tell, what thei say."[52] Though Notch claims that he "now speakes all languages in ill English," the typography of the page portrays Van Goose as having a particularly Dutch case of "mingle-mangle." Indeed, though a "*Brittaine* borne," he looks, talks, even smells like a Dutchman. When Van Goose speaks the reader does not *see* an Englishman. Quite the contrary, the clues of the page suggest that Van Goose is neither performing in nor passing as Dutch. On the page and by the page, Van Goose has become Dutch.

Is the medium the message? In Jonson's masque, black letter impresses difference onto Van Goose's speech, apparently foreclosing the interpretive wiggle room the theater almost always left open, indeed exploited for comic effect, when a Dutchman spoke on the stage. Unlike Tearcat and Doll, the British-born Van Goose does not transition in and out of his black letter appearance. Cross-cultural engagements, even those that transpire *within* and around London—as is the case with Van Goose and his "St. Katherine's" troupe of players—can translate one out of one's native "type," impressing such border crossers through and through with apparent Dutch difference. Here identifications *with* the Dutch render Van Goose identified *as* Dutch, as ethnic identity proves particularly amendable to witting or unwitting adoption. In this case, typography seems aimed at settling the question of Van Goose's identity. At least this is the story *on the page.* The verbal exchanges within the masque—especially Notch's insistence that Van Goose is a "Brittaine borne," together with Van Goose's predominately *English* lexicon, which, as Notch rightly characterizes, is much "misuse[d]"—resists interpretive foreclosure on questions of Van Goose's ethnic identity, even as typography, in this instance, consistently underscores his difference from other English characters. Audiences are left toggling between possibilities, engaging in the double vision engendered by the paradoxes of Van Goose's linguistic and typographic performance.

In all three instances of black letter stage Dutch that I have explored here, black letter does not foreclose questions of a character's ethnic identity so much as it underscores the elective, temporary, and sometimes-unwitting identifications that perplex claims of identity, particularly those staked to the English language. Speak that I may see thee? On the English stage and on the playbook page, Dutch characters, English "apt schollers," street-savvy rogues, and British-born wayfarers who speak stage Dutch prove themselves slippery characters. Their typographic embodiments bespeak the fungibility of linguistic and ethnic identity, as well as the fragility of the bond between them.

"The Narcissism of Minor Difference" in Print

At the turn of the seventeenth century, black letter stage Dutch introduces a seeming difference into a relation increasingly characterized by resemblance both in the language debates and on the public stage. This experimental use of typographic variation is a symptom of a larger cultural concern about the ways the English and Dutch languages are rendered approximate in cultural performance. In Chapter 2, I explored these debates for how the antiquarian movement, taking place on both sides of the North Sea, stressed the linguistic relatedness of English and Dutch and, on this ground, erected a history of the racial relatedness of the English and Dutch as Germanic peoples. Black letter stage Dutch appears in playbooks at precisely this historical moment, introducing difference into a relation increasingly characterized—within the

language debates and on the public stage—by propinquity and resemblance.
Across the landscape of the dramatic page, the experimental use of black
letter stage Dutch is illustrative of what Sigmund Freud characterized as the
"narcissism of minor difference." In his 1921 essay "Group Psychology and
the Analysis of the Ego," Freud's ruminations on the idea of the narcissism
of minor difference are triggered by a reflection on Arthur Schopenhauer's
parable of the freezing porcupines: "'A company of porcupines crowded
themselves very close together one cold winter's day so as to profit by one
another's warmth and so save themselves from being frozen to death. But
soon they felt one another's quills, which induced them to separate again.
And now, when the need for warmth brought them nearer together again,
the second evil arose once more. So that they were driven backwards and
forwards from one trouble to another, until they had discovered a mean
distance at which they could most tolerably exist.'"[53] Huddling together for
warmth only to discover themselves soon agitated by their proximity, the
porcupines come together as a group and pull apart as individuals, eventually
learning to strike a "mean distance," that balance between separation and
proximity necessary to "tolerably exist" as a group. I want to linger for a
moment on Schopenhauer's parable for what it reveals about how Freud was
thinking about proximate relations and for how it casts light on the case of
black letter stage Dutch as one especially compelling instance of English
culture seeking that "mean distance" between Englishness and Dutchness.

Like Schopenhauer's story, which begins by presuming sameness across
"a company of porcupines," Freud's ruminations on the narcissism of minor
difference are predicated on his vision of "closely related races" or "peoples
whose territories are adjacent": "Of two neighbouring towns each is the other's most jealous rival; every little canton looks down upon the others with
contempt. Closely related races keep one another at arm's length; the South
German cannot endure the North German, the Englishman casts every kind
of aspersion upon the Scot, the Spaniard despises the Portuguese."[54] In *Civilization and Its Discontents* (1930), Freud returns again to this concept and to
his reflections on the ethnic relations of "closely related" peoples: "I once
interested myself in the peculiar fact that peoples whose territories are adjacent, and are otherwise closely related, are always at feud with and ridiculing
each other, as, for instance, the Spaniards and the Portuguese, the North and
South Germans, the English and the Scotch, and so on. I gave it the name
of 'narcissism in respect of minor differences', which does not do much to

explain it. One can now see that it is a convenient and relatively harmless form of satisfaction for aggressive tendencies, through which cohesion amongst the members of a group is made easier."[55] Freud's insight is not that narcissism exhibits as rivalry when proximity between neighboring but different and distinct groups sparks the need for further distinction. Rather, identifications fostered by conditions of proximity (whether between or within closely related groups) are characterized by the narcissism of minor difference, an inherently relational and dynamic impulse that endlessly defers the settling and solidification of group identity even as it is an essential aspect of it. In cultural contexts, the narcissism of minor difference exhibits when the process of ethnicity in the making is at work. Feuding, ridiculing, and other aggressive tendencies of rivalry are not merely negative expressions of individuation against a group but the necessary expression of engagement with it. The golden mean of group psychology, Freud suggests, entails the ongoing negotiation toward the "mean distance" whereby identification with the Other does not threaten self-identity. Here relations defined by proximity (adjacent territories) and similitude (peoples who are otherwise closely related) carry within a dis-ease that conjures the desire for distance, distinction, and differentiation. Freud's narcissism of minor difference lends a name to the way in which the forging of identity and self-definition is always in tension with the identifications that help to define that self, be they familial, ethnic, or national.

For cultural anthropologist Anton Blok, who considers the explanatory power of the narcissism of minor difference for "clarify[ing] contemporary cases of extremely violent confrontations," the anxiety produced when sameness threatens can trigger the forging of fine-grained distinctions between groups who otherwise "share many social and cultural features."[56] When identification and self-identity risk collapsing, minor differences, either invented or discovered, hold this collapse at bay. For Blok, Freud's narcissism of minor difference anticipates René Girard's contention that "it is not the differences but the loss of them that gives rise to violence and chaos."[57] If proximate relations are characterized by the narcissism of minor difference, then Girard's insight entails what Freud characterized elsewhere as *doppelgängerscheau*, the fear of the double. The double upsets the premise of identification as an outreach beyond the self to a "second self," insofar as the double appears identical with the self. The double—the doppelgänger—is the sign of a potential collapse in the tension between identity and identification. The narcissism of minor difference characterizes just that self-preserving tension in conditions of proximity—what in the context of representations of Anglo-Dutch relations we have been exploring as a cultural double vision.

As Schopenhauer's parable foretells, and as Freud's and Girard's reflections on ethnic proximity suggest, proximity requires constant adjustments, which take place across a wide range of cultural performances, including the appearance of language on the early modern playbook page. While for Freud and Girard violence threatens when the mean distance is not maintained, the theater of the early modern playbook stages the narcissism of minor difference as experimental play. Typographic arrangements point to an experimental process of approximation that reveals both the wish for distinction and the fact of interconnection. By characterizing this dynamic tension as "play," I mean to hold open the possibility that rivalries among proximate groups, or within the same group, do not necessarily work themselves out through "violence and chaos." Attending only to those tensions wherein violence threatens risks obscuring the significant labor performed by "play" and experimentation in the process of forging cultural constructions of identity. In the case of English representation of the relation of English and Dutch tongues, when "sameness threatens" in the form of philological arguments that assert the nearness of English and Dutch, typographic arrangements introduce a minor difference across this fluid linguistic landscape. As my close readings reveal, in playbooks black letter stage Dutch fails to secure the distinction it appears to assert. Instead, the mise en page of early modern playbooks directs attention to the pervasive evidence that the English understood themselves to be huddled closely together with the Dutch. In like company, they experimented endlessly with striking a mean distance. On the page, that distance was aptly struck by means of letterforms that imprinted stage Dutch with a difference known as "English letter."

Typographic Relativism and the Anglo-Dutch Wordbook

In the year 1607, a Londoner sitting down to read Thomas Dekker and John Webster's *Northward Hoe* might have had near at hand a copy of Professor Marten Le Mayre's *The Dutch Schoole Master, Wherein Is Shewed the True and Perfect Way to Learne the Dutch Tongue,* published the previous year. Both texts opened onto the relation of the English and Dutch languages, in speech and in print, and offered London's reading public a gateway into

engagement with questions of ethnic heritage. Over the course of the seventeenth century, Le Mayre's *The Dutch Schoole Master*, together with a series
of other Anglo-Dutch grammars, vocabularies, phrasebooks, and dictionaries
printed in both London and the Low Countries, provided English readers
with a resource for the formal study of Dutch when they were not learning
about it through the theater's language lessons, on playbook pages, in philological debates, and in their daily exchanges with the Dutch population on
the streets of London. In *Dictionaries in Early Modern Europe: Lexicography
and the Making of Heritage*, John Considine traces the ways in which lexicography became a powerful instrument in the forging of ideas of cultural history
in early modern Europe:

> The study of the development of vernacular languages was seen as a
> particularly important key to the past. "Every people and nation has
> a particular chronicle in its language and traditional wisdom," wrote
> the German historian Aventinus. Jean Bodin agreed that one of the
> three best means of determining the origins of peoples was "in the
> traces of language." William Camden put the case more strongly,
> seeing language as "the surest proofe of peoples originall," and was
> still being quoted with approval a century later. . . . Lexicography
> then became a means by which to understand heritage, and a more
> powerful one than, for instance, even the study of genealogy.[58]

While lexicography was a project increasingly essential to forging cultural
heritage, the heretofore-unexplored typographic arrangements of dictionaries,
grammars, vocabularies, and grammars also generated powerful ideas about
the intertwining of linguistic and cultural relations. In this final section on
representation of Anglo-Dutch relations in print, I explore the lessons
English readers were learning about the relatedness of English and Dutch as
they consulted the Anglo-Dutch lexicons of the seventeenth century. In what
ways did these texts challenge or shore up the double vision onto Anglo-
Dutch linguistic relations that the theater of the playbook page so nimbly
explored?

In Le Mayre's *The Dutch Schoole Master* (1606), the first bilingual Anglo-
Dutch grammar published in England for English readers, Dutch words are
printed in black letter beneath corresponding English translations, which
appear in roman (Figure 16). Despite the English reader's tendency to read a
single line from left to right, the reader of Le Mayre's text is encouraged

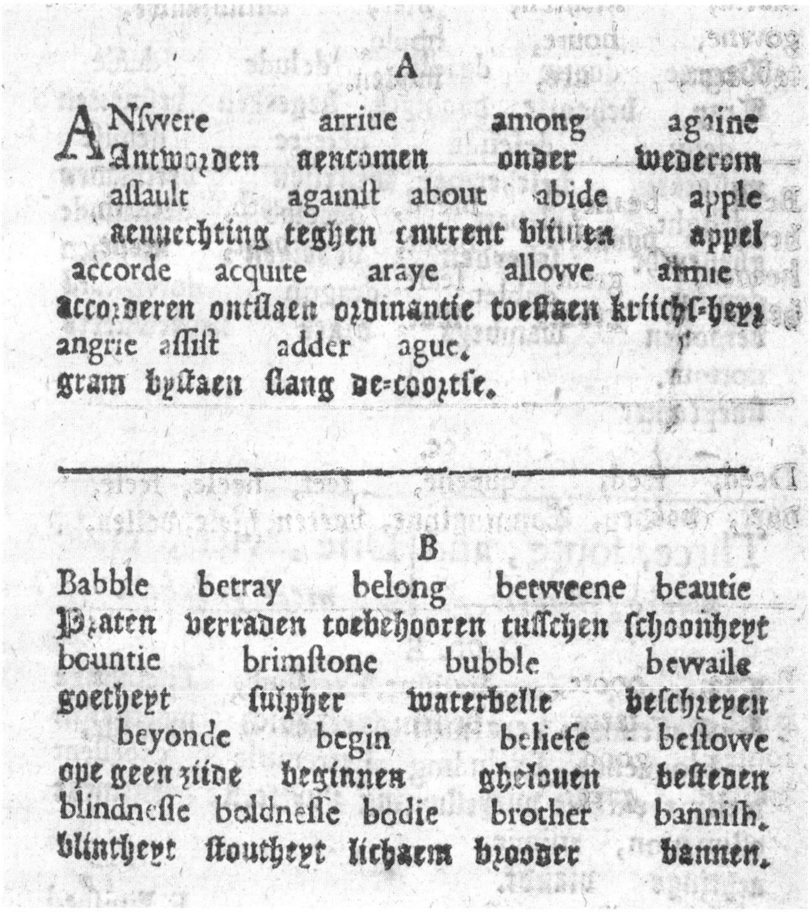

A

ANſwere arriue among againe
Antwoorden aencomen onder wederom
aſſault againſt about abide apple
aenuechting teghen omtrent blijuen appel
accorde acquite araye allowe armie
accorderen ontſlaen ordinantie toeſlaen krijchſ-heyr
angrie aſſiſt adder ague.
gram bijſtaen ſlang de-coortſe.

B

Babble betray belong betweene beautie
Praten verraden toebehooren tuſſchen ſchoonheyt
bountie brimſtone bubble bewaile
goetheyt ſulpher waterbelle beſchreyen
beyonde begin beliefe beſtowe
ope geen zijde beginnen ghelouen beſteden
blindneſſe boldneſſe bodie brother banniſh.
blintheyt ſtoutheyt lichaem brooder bannen.

FIGURE 16. Marten Le Mayre, *The Dutch Schoole Master* (1606).
By permission of the Bodleian Library, University of Oxford.

by the consistency of the typographic arrangement to register typographical difference as signifying linguistic difference and so navigate both left to right and up and down. The dialogues also distinguish English (roman) from Dutch (black letter), but organize the lexical data left to right across the columns (Figure 17). Was the typographic arrangement of Le Mayre's *The Dutch Schoole Master* characteristic of seventeenth-century Anglo-Dutch wordbooks? Or was the mise en page of this Anglo-Dutch wordbook an arbitrary arrangement aimed simply at differentiating the two languages? Just how pervasive was the association of black letter with the Dutch language in the lexical resources of the period? My survey of all extant bilingual Anglo-Dutch dictionaries, grammars, phrasebooks, and vocabularies printed in England and the Netherlands throughout the seventeenth century reveals a remarkable consistency in the distinctive use of black letter and roman type. When black letter appears in seventeenth-century Anglo-Dutch grammars and vocabularies it *always* attaches to Dutch rather than English words, as is evident in eight different wordbooks in twenty editions (see Table 2 and examples in Figures 18 and 19).

The consistency of this arrangement across seventeenth-century word-books printed in both England and the Low Countries suggests that English and Dutch printers shared a typographic dialect, one that enabled and encouraged readers to distinguish English from Dutch before ever *reading* a word. Like playbooks from the same period, here too linguistic categories are figured by means of typographic organization, fostering a strong association of black letter with Dutch and roman with English. This is not, however, a case of typographic "inevitability."[59] As I will show, this typographic pattern is highly determined by context and by the linguistic relations in play. Indeed, to characterize this pattern as inevitable would be to miss the contextual conditions that inform typographic arrangements. A study of the typographic mise en page of early modern wordbooks directs attention to a high degree of what I characterize as "typographic relativism"—a dynamic system of linguistically driven typographic organization that is relative both in the sense of being context specific, and so subject to change within limits, and in the sense that it forges and underscores relations between languages across the mise en page. On first glance, wordbooks of this period invited readers to enter a *visual* rather than exclusively lexical matrix. Typography played an important role in expanding and contracting the categorical associations across languages that early modern wordbooks both represented and produced. In early modern wordbooks, the medium is the message, at least upon a reader's initial engagement, as typography proves a powerful conveyor and generator of information about the relatedness of various tongues.[60]

Before I turn to a case study of the typographic arrangement of polyglot wordlists to demonstrate the context-specific relativism of early modern word-lists, it is important to stress that typography alone does not constitute a wordbook's mise en page. Situating English and Dutch side by side in columns (see Figure 17), or in parallel rows, one word atop another (see Figure 16), bilingual Anglo-Dutch wordbooks *structurally* suggest a parallelism

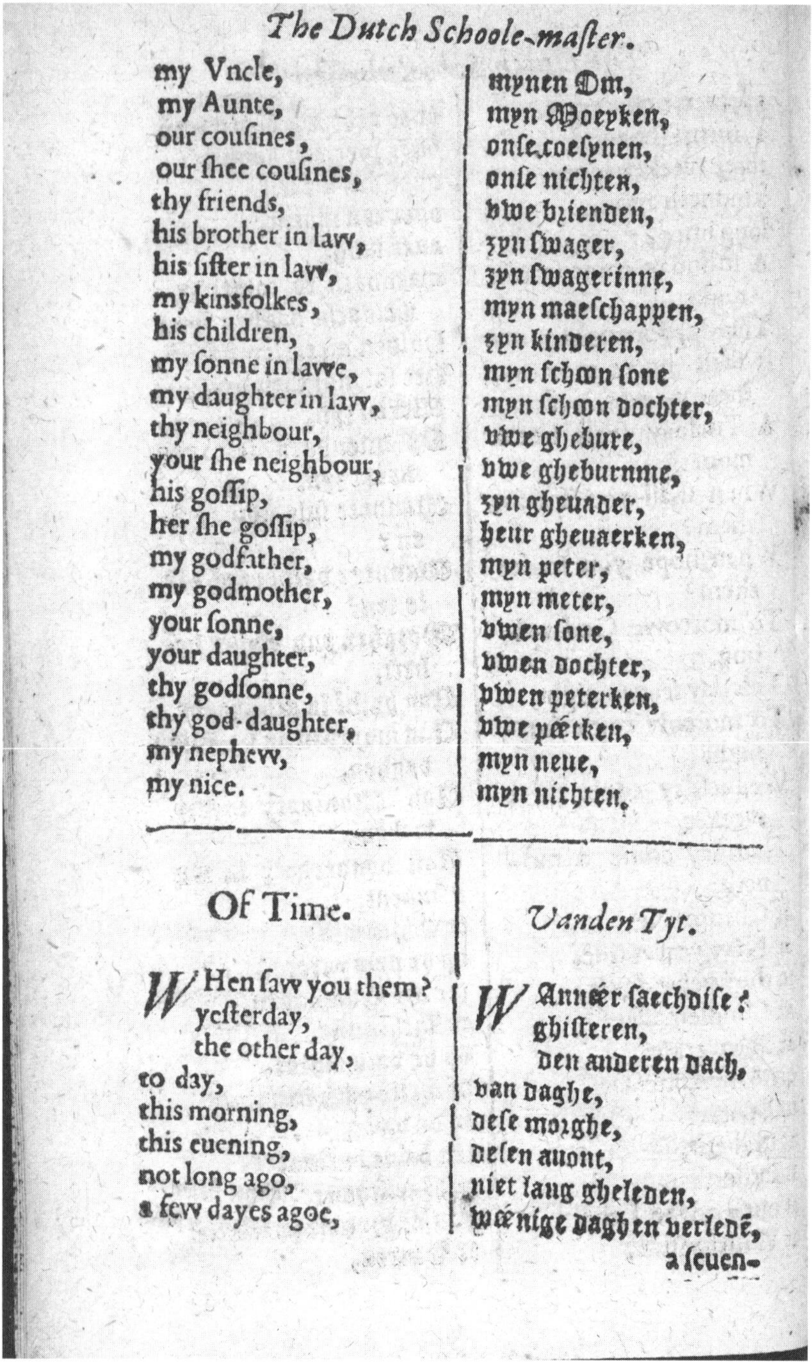

The Dutch Schoole-maſter.

my Vncle,	mynen Om,
my Aunte,	myn Moeyken,
our couſines,	onſe coeſynen,
our ſhee couſines,	onſe nichten,
thy friends,	vwe vrienden,
his brother in lavv,	zyn ſwager,
his ſiſter in lavv,	zyn ſwagerinne,
my kinsfolkes,	myn maeſchappen,
his children,	zyn kinderen,
my ſonne in lavve,	myn ſchoon ſone
my daughter in lavv,	myn ſchoon dochter,
thy neighbour,	vwe ghebure,
your ſhe neighbour,	vwe gheburnne,
his goſſip,	zyn gheuader,
her ſhe goſſip,	heur gheuaerken,
my godfather,	myn peter,
my godmother,	myn meter,
your ſonne,	vwen ſone,
your daughter,	vwen dochter,
thy godſonne,	vwen peterken,
thy god-daughter,	vwe peetken,
my nephevv,	myn neue,
my nice.	myn nichten.

Of Time.	*Vanden Tyt.*
WHen ſavv you them?	WAnneer ſaechdiſe?
yeſterday,	ghiſteren,
the other day,	den anderen dach,
to day,	van daghe,
this morning,	deſe morghe,
this euening,	deſen auont,
not long ago,	niet lang gheleden,
a fevv dayes agoe,	weenige daghen verledẽ,

a ſeuen-

FIGURE 17. Marten Le Mayre, *The Dutch Schoole Master* (1606).
By permission of the Bodleian Library, University of Oxford.

a feauen night agoe,	ouer acht daghē verledē,
a fortnight agoe,	ouer viertien daghen
three weekes agoe,	ouer dʒy weken,
a moneth agoe,	ouer ēn maent,
long fince,	ouer lang,
A Monday come feauen night,	maendach to comende fhalt acht dagheu zyn,
This day fortnight,	huiden vieertien daghē,
It fhall be to morrow, three weekes,	het fal moʒghen dʒy, weken zyn,
A Tuefday fhall bee a moneth	Op difendach falt een maext zyn.
When fhall you fee them?	Wanneer fult ghy fe fi-en?
When hope you to fee them?	Wanneer verhopt ghy fe te fen?
To morrowe God wil-ling,	Moʒghen eud Godt be-lieft,
This day feauen night,	Aan huidē in acht daghe.
To morrow come fort-night.	Aan moʒghen in verthiē daghen,
Wednefday come three weekes,	Aan Wonfdach in dʒy weken,
Thurfday come a mo-neth,	Aan donderdach in ēn maent,
at Chriftmaffe,	te Chʒiftmiffe,
at New yeares tide,	op de new yare,
in the twelue dayes,	ter dʒy Coninghen,
at Candlemaffe,	te Lichtmiffe,
at Shrouetide,	op de vaftelaueut,
on Afhwednefday	dē ērftē dach vāde vaftē,
in Lent,	in de vafte,
at midlent,	ten halue vaften,
at Eafter,	te Paeffchen,
at our Lady in Lent,	t'onfer vʒouwe in mærte
at Whitfontide,	te Sinxeū,

Table 2.   Typographic Arrangement of Anglo-Dutch Dictionaries and Grammars

Date	Title/Place of publication	Black letter	Roman	Italic
1606	*The Dutch Schoole Master* London	Dutch	English	
1639 (reprinted: 1658, 1663)	*Den grooten vocabulaer Engels ende Duyts . . . The great vocabuler, in English and Dutch* Rotterdam	Dutch	English	
1646, 1658, 1663	*The English Schole-master . . . Den Engelschen School-Meester* Amsterdam	Dutch	English	
1647–1648	*Het Groot Woorden-boeck / A copious English and Netherduytch Dictionarie* Rotterdam		English	Dutch
1660, 1669	*Dutch-tutor; or, A new-book of Dutch and English* London			
	"Rules" & Dialogues	Dutch	English	
	Vocabulary		Dutch	English
1664, 1671, 1677, 1678, 1686	*Den Engelschen ende Ne'erduitschen onderrichter. . . The English, and Low-dutch Instructer* Rotterdam	Dutch	English	
1675	*An English and Nether-dutch Dictionary* Amsterdam			
	Dictionary		Dutch	English
	Letter to reader		English	Dutch
1677, 1689, 1698	*Anglo-Bel[g]ica. . . The English and Netherdutch Academy* Amsterdam			
	Dialogue	Dutch	English	

Den grooten Uo-
cabulaer/ Engels ende Duyts :
**Dat zijn ghemeyne Spraken op alderhan-
de manieren/ oock Brieven ende Obligatien
te schrijven. Met eenen Dictionarium/
ende de Conjugatie.**

THE GREAT VOCABVLER,
in Englifh and Dutch :
That is to fay common fpeaches of all forts, alfo
Lettres and Obligations to write. With a Dictionarie
and the Conjugation.

**Defen leften Druck/ op nieus overfien ende ghebetert/
van vele honderde grove fouten.**

TOT ROTTERDAM,

**Bp Pieter van Waes-berge/op't Stepgher/
inde Swarte Klock. Anno 1639.**

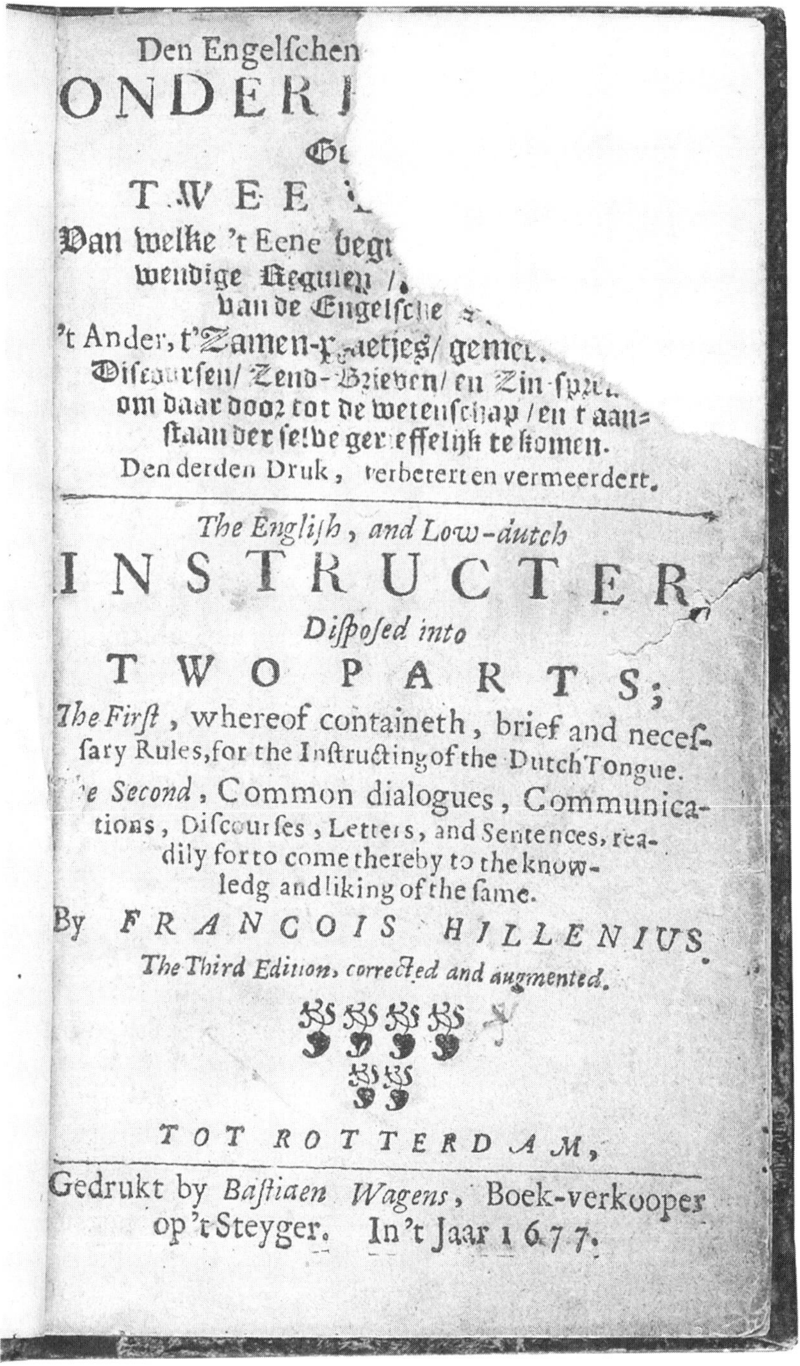

Den Engelfchen

ONDER[

Gr

T.WEE [

Van welke 't Eene begi
wendige Regulen /
van de Engelfche s
't Ander, t'Zamen-p.aetjes/ gemee.
Difcourfen/ Zend-Brieven/ en Zin-fpre.
om daar doo2 tot de wetenfchap /en t aan=
ftaan der felve ger effelyk te komen.
Den derden Druk, verbetert en vermeerdert.

The Englifh, and Low-dutch

INSTRUCTER,

Difpofed into

TWO PARTS;

The Firft, whereof containeth, brief and necef-
fary Rules, for the Inftructingof the DutchTongue.
e Second, Common dialogues, Communica-
tions, Difcourfes, Letters, and Sentences, readily forto come thereby to the know-
ledg and liking of the fame.

By *FRANCOIS HILLENIUS.*

The Third Edition, corrected and augmented.

TOT ROTTERDAM,

Gedrukt by *Bastiaen Wagens*, Boek-verkooper
op't Steyger. In't Jaar 1 6,7 7.

FIGURE 19. *Den Engelschen ende Ne'erduitschen onderrichter* (1677), title page.
Courtesy of the Beinecke Rare Book and Manuscript Library, Yale University.

between the languages represented on the page. Indeed, many of these word-books are not dictionaries, in a now-conventional sense of offering a defini-tion of words, but synonym lists. Considine contends that such synonym lists, particularly polyglot wordlists, conveyed the message that "the languages of Europe could all express the same range of concepts, and hence that, whatever the linguistic difference of Europe might be, Europeans shared a heritage of concepts, and all, in that profound sense, spoke the same lan-guage."[61] The structural organization of the mise en page also reinforces the notion that for every English word a likeness (in the form of a synonym) can be identified in Dutch, French, Latin, and so on. While the structural organization of the mise en page bespeaks linguistic parallelism, then, the typographic arrangements on these same pages underscore linguistic distinc-tion. If we imagine the wordlist in Figure 16 without typographic variation, for instance, the challenge of distinguishing English from Dutch on the page becomes immediately apparent, particularly in instances of the appearance of cognates, like "apple" and 𝖆𝖕𝖕𝖊𝖑, at a historical moment when English orthography was not fixed. Consistently allocating black letter type to the Dutch language and roman to English in Anglo-Dutch wordbooks encour-aged readers to decipher Dutch from English not by means of the lexical and semantic content of the page, but by means of its graphic codes. Wordbooks, like playbooks, encourage readers to *look* first and then *read* the languages set on the page before them. Wordbooks of the period subtly induce readers' double vision, requiring them to register similarity and difference simultane-ously in decoding the lessons on the page.

Throughout the seventeenth century, English readers who consulted bilingual Anglo-Dutch wordbooks likely anticipated finding the typographic arrangements that so consistently appeared within. They thus would have had to adjust such expectations when leafing through polyglot vocabularies that displayed a different principle of typographic organization. Polyglot wordlists and phrasebooks had been circulating in Europe for over a century before the appearance of the first Anglo-Dutch bilingual wordbooks and pro-vided the source text for some of England's early Anglo-Dutch vocabularies. *Den Grooten Vocabulaer,* or *The Great Vocabuler, in English and Dutch* (1639), for instance, was based on one of the most popular and widely reproduced of these phrasebooks, Noël de Berlaimont's *Colloquia et Dictionariolum,* the earliest extent version of which is the Antwerp 1536 edition.[62] Noel Osselton calculates that over the course of the one and three-quarter centuries of its print history, this polyglot phrasebook enjoyed beyond one hundred editions and "more than twenty editions had appeared before the first one to include English was published at Antwerp in 1576."[63] The print history of twenty-five editions of the text, ranging in date from 1585 to 1639, published in the Low Countries, Germany, Italy, and England, provides an intriguing case study of the semiotics of type.[64] Its typographic arrangements suggest that, even before the "Teutonic thesis" of the antiquarians began to hold sway in the language debates of the early seventeenth century, printers, compositors, and publishers understood English and Dutch as closely related languages. This relatedness plays out across the mise en page of polyglot wordlists in the form of typographic similitude.

Within the scope of my study of the *Colloquia*, black letter type appears for the first time in the 1593 Leiden edition, in which it is used to print Dutch ("Flamen").[65] The other six languages (including English, German, Latin, French, Spanish, and Italian) alternate between roman and italic type across columns that facing pages. Five years later, an edition printed in Delft expands the list to eight languages by including Portuguese. In this edition, both English and Dutch are printed in black letter while all other languages, including High Dutch or German ("Alleman"), appear in columns that alternate roman with italic typefaces (Figure 20). Typographically and structurally the mise en page of the Delft edition forges a visual parallel between English and Dutch. Both languages appear in black letter in the third column of facing pages.[66] As the *Colloquia* expands, and English and Dutch are entered into a broader matrix of linguistic relations with Classical, Romance, and Germanic languages, English and Dutch appear regularly in black letter font. We might imagine that the printer or compositor was merely reproducing the black letter print history of the European north in selecting this typographic arrangement—but the use of italic for German troubles such a hypothesis.[67] As the reader's eye moves from column to column across rows of foreign words, typography provides a visual key to the various languages on the page. For instance, an English speaker who wishes to locate a word in Dutch need not look to the top of every column to find "Flamen" and then "Anglois" and then scan down the page to the row in which the English word appears and finally scan across the columns to find the same word in Dutch, as that reader would have in the all-roman typeface editions of the *Colloquia* printed in Venice in 1606 and 1627. To read these typographically varied texts is, in the first instance, to decipher the key of type. To read requires that the word-book user *look* first, decipher the typographic organization of the page, and then engage with its semantic content. In turn, the semiotics of type implies

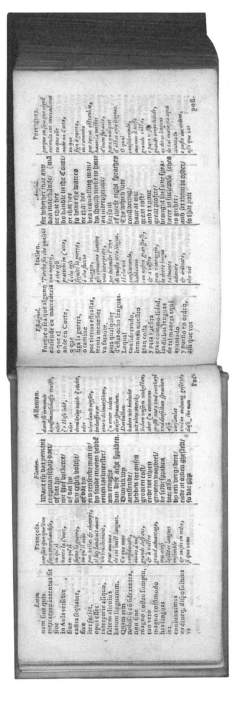

Figure 20. *Colloquia et dictionariolum octo linguarum* (1598).

Courtesy of the Rare Book & Manuscript Library, University of Illinois at Urbana-Champaign.

relations and distinctions across languages that a reader who habitually con-
sults such word lists may come to naturalize.

Following the 1598 edition, the subsequent four editions of the *Colloquia*
printed in the Low Countries before the 1620s use black letter type exclusively
for English and Dutch.[68] Not until the Antwerp edition of 1630 are all three
of the text's Germanic languages (German, English, and Dutch) printed in
black letter (Figure 21). For readers familiar with earlier editions of the text,
the introduction of black letter for German has the effect of altering the
organizational pattern of rotating fonts—column by column—across the
page.[69] What is more, this edition reorganizes the languages that it implicitly
relates by means of type. Here, English, German, and Dutch all look alike.
This typographic arrangement is not repeated in any of the three editions that
appear the following year, printed in Delft, Amsterdam, and Middleburg. As
in the earlier Dutch editions, English and Dutch appear in black letter while
the other six languages on the page, including German, alternate between
roman and italic type.

Lexicography was forging ideas about cultural heritage in this period and
the typographic arrangement of parallel wordlists was refining the message
by suggesting which languages shared a close affinity. As the Antwerp edition
of the *Colloquia* suggests, in polyglot wordbooks English, Dutch, and German were the languages most commonly printed in black letter, while
Romance and Classical languages tended to be printed in roman or italic.
Across a survey of over one dozen English and Romance- and Classical-
language vocabularies of the latter half of the sixteenth century and the seventeenth century, I have found none that set Romance or Classical languages
in black letter.[70] Moreover, when black letter appears in these vocabularies
and dictionaries, it is used exclusively for *English*.[71] While English was sometimes printed in black letter when it appeared in polyglot sources that
included only Romance and Classical languages, when English appears in
polyglot sources together with other Germanic languages, very often English,
Dutch, and German were jointly printed in black letter; it is more common,
though, to see English and Dutch printed in black letter. For instance, in
Sex linguarum Latinae, Gallicae, Hispanicae, Italicae, Anglicae & Teutonic[a]e
(1579), in which languages are organized in columns across the page, both
English and Dutch appear typographically alike, distinct from their romance
counterparts. In this way, typography forges visual correlations across the
page, affiliating some languages as if they were, philologically speaking, more
closely related to one another than to the other languages represented.

FIGURE 21. *Colloquia et dictionariolum octo linguarum* (1630).

By permission of the Folger Shakespeare Library.

As the Dutch and English print history of the *Colloquia* suggests, an intriguing contradiction emerges. When Dutch and English appear exclusively as the languages of bilingual wordbooks (whether printed in England or in the Low Countries) Dutch *always* appears in black letter font. This pattern of printing Dutch in black letter sometimes extends even to trilingual wordbooks, such as André Madoet's *Thesaurus theutonicae linguae* (1573), published by the Antwerp printer Christophe Plantin, in which Flemish words appear in black letter, French in roman, and Latin in italic.[72] The same typographic arrangement occurs nearly a century later in Guillaume Beyer's *La vraye instruction des trois langues la Francoise, l'Angloise, & la Flamende . . . Right instruction of three languages French, English and Dutch* (Dordrecht, 1661), wherein black letter is used predominately for Dutch, roman for French, and italic for English (Figure 22). And yet when English and Dutch appear together on the same page and in the context of a wider range of Classical and Romance languages, Dutch and English very often share a black letter appearance. Taken together with more expansively inclusive polyglot wordlists, the choice to differentiate English from Dutch depends on the extent to which English and Dutch appeared alongside or in the context of other European languages. When printed face-to-face as the only linguistic relation represented in a text, black letter most often came to stand in for Dutch difference, roman for English difference. Set among the larger field of Europe's *lingua matrix*, English and Dutch more consistently appear alike on the page. There is, in other words, an accordion effect to the typographic relativism, a flexible calibration of typography that points to variations within limits.

There were exceptions, of course. Editions of the *Colloquia* printed in London, in particular, diverge from the typographic pattern established in Continental editions. In 1637 an edition of the *Colloquia* is printed in London for the first time under the title *The English, Latine, French, Dutch, Schole-master; or, An Introduction to Teach Young Gentlemen and Merchants to Travel or Trade.* In it, English is the only language to appear in black letter. Dutch and Latin appear in roman type, while French is printed in italic (Figure 23). This exception demonstrates that while patterns of typographic arrangements can be identified, assertions of firm axioms will be belied by the typographic relativism that obtains in these texts, particularly in the case of black letter. Two years later when the same London printer released an expanded edition of the *Colloquia*—including Latin, French, Low Dutch, High Dutch, Spanish, Italian, English, and Portuguese—English and Low Dutch appear in

GRAMMAIRE
FRANCOISE.

Inſtruction de la langue Françoiſe, en François, Anglois, & Flamend.

Inſtruction of the French tongue, written in French, Engliſh and Dutch.

Onderwijſinge ban de Franſche tale/ in Franſch/Engels en Nederdupts.

Regles neceſſaires à la naïfve prononciation de quelques lettres & ſyllabes, qui ſonnent autrement en Françoys que dans les autres langues.

Neceſſary rules for the due pronunciation of certain letters and ſyllables, which ſound otherwiſe in the French, than in other languages.

Noodige regelen tot de rechte uptſpꝛaeck van eenige letteren en ſpllaben / die anders in 't Franſch als in andere talen lupden.

L'Lphabet ſe diviſe en voyelles & conſones : les voyelles ſont des lettres qui ſonnent par elles-mémes, ſans l'ayde d'aucune autre, & ſont ſix en nombre ; *a, e, i, o, u,* & *y* ou *u* Grec. Les conſones ſont des lettres qui ne ſonnent point par elles-mémes, mais par l'aſſiſtance des autres, & en compagnie avec les autres, & ſont toutes les autres horsmis les voyelles, *b, c, d, f, g, h, l, m, n, p, q, r, ſ, t, x, ʒ.*

THe Alphabet is divided into vowels and conſonants : the vowels are letters that ſound by themſelves ; without the help of any other, and are ſix in number ; a, e, i, o, u, and y or the Greek u. The conſonants are letters which doe not ſound by themſelves, but by the aſſiſtance of others, and in company with others, and are all the other except the vowels, b, c, d, f, g, h, l, m, n, p, q, r, ſ, t, x, z.

Het A/B/C woꝛt gedeelt in klinckers en mede-klinckers : de klinckers zijn letters die klincken dooꝛ haer ſelben/ſonder de hulp van eenige andere / en zijn ſes in 't getal / a, e, i, o, u, en y ofte Gꝛieckſche u. De mede-klinckers zijn letters / die niet en klincken dooꝛ haer ſelven / maer dooꝛ bpſtant en in geſelſchap van andere/ en zijn 't alle uptgenomen de klinckers / b, c, d, f, g, h, l, m, n, p, q, r, ſ, t, x, z.

AI & ay ſe prononcent comme l'*e* long ou dur,
(Orth. Pron.)
faire, fére.

Ai and ay are pronounced as a long or hard e :
faire, to doe.

Ai en ay woꝛt uptgeſpꝛoken als een lange of te harde e.
faire, doen.

Aou ſe prononce comme ou,
ſaouler, ſouler.

Aou is pronounced as ou :
ſaouler, to ſatiſfie.

Aou als ou,
ſaouler, verſadigen.

Au comme un *o* long,
Fraude, haut, Frode, hoot.

Au like a long o :
fraude, deceit ; haut, high.

Au als een lange o,
fraude, bedꝛog, haut, hoog.

C Avec une queuë comme une double ſſ,
garçon, garſſon.

C with a taile, as a double ſſ.
garçon, boy.

C met een ſteert ç als een dubble ſſ,
garçon, jongen.

A
E' avec

FIGURE 23. *The English, Latine, French, Dutch Schole-master* (1637).
By permission of Cambridge University Library.

black letter, repeating the typographic arrangement of earlier editions printed
in the Low Countries. Here, again, German is printed in italic. Both English
and Dutch were languages regularly printed in black letter, and England and
the Low Countries had a long history of printing with black letter type.[73] In
the case of the 1637 *English, Latine, French, Dutch Schole-master*, it is not
difficult to imagine that in the mind of the printer or compositor, English
was fittingly printed in "English letter." Within the *lingua matrix* of early
modern word lists, where a flexible pattern of linguistic relations comes to
the fore, the *Schole-master* provides a case in point. It limits the number
of languages represented to four, cutting by half the languages available in
Continental editions of the *Colloquia* on which it is based. This restriction
may have resulted in the choice to distinguish English from Dutch. Grouped
together on the verso of each leaf, English and Dutch appear much as they
do in Anglo-Dutch bilingual wordbooks. So too English and Dutch are two
Germanic vernaculars in a text that otherwise includes Classical and

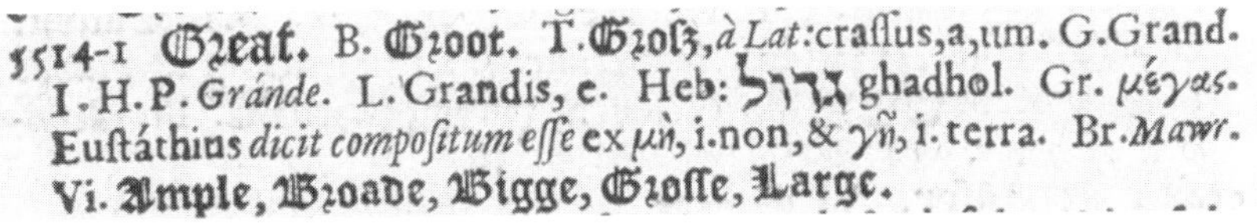

5514-1 **Great.** B. **Groot.** T.**Grots,** *à Lat:* craſſus,a,um. G.Grand.
I.H.P. *Gránde.* L. Grandis, e. Heb: גָּדוֹל ghadhol. Gr. μέγας.
Euſtáchius *dicit compoſitum eſſe* ex μὴ, i.non,& γῆ, i. terra. Br.*Mawr.*
Vi. **Ample,** **Broade,** **Bigge,** **Groſſe,** **Large.**

FIGURE 24. John Minsheu, *Hēgemōn eis tas glōssas id est, Ductor in linguas,*
The guide into tongues (1617).

By permission of the Huntington Library, San Marino, California.

Romance languages. The typographic arrangement of this text reverses the particular allocation of type to language that prevails in bilingual Anglo-Dutch wordbooks from the same period. What it *repeats* is the structural principle of difference introduced by typography when English and Dutch are represented on the bilingual mise en page of wordbooks. Like any expression of reversal, this one preserves the logic of difference within which it works.

The print history of the *Colloquia* suggests something that scholarship on the black letter print history of the European north has not underscored: English and Dutch shared a particularly close linguistic correspondence that was both reflected in and manufactured by the Dutch and English printers and compositors responsible for producing the polyglot vocabularies. The typographic arrangements of the *Colloquia* impressed on readers an implicit message that English and Dutch philologists, antiquarians, and playwrights of the period were theorizing and thematizing more explicitly: English and Dutch are so closely related that they sometimes appear alike.

As the production of wordbooks expanded throughout the seventeenth century, the increasing sophistication of the mise en page suggests that readerly engagement was finely attuned to the semiotics of type. Ambrogio Calepino's *Dictionarium Undecim Linguarum,* which underwent 211 editions between 1502 and 1779 and was the "best selling Latin dictionary of the sixteenth century," aids the reader's engagement with the page by organizing word entries with the help of typographic differentiation and by means of abbreviated language headers, such as GERM for German and BELG for Low Dutch.[74] So too a particularly sophisticated typographic arrangement guides the eye through John Minsheu's *Hēgemōn eis tas glōssas* or *The Guide into Tongues* (Figure 24), which, unlike Calepino's *Dictionarium,* employs typography to help the reader quickly spot and distinguish between the various languages on the page.[75] Unlike many polyglot wordbooks, such as *Sex linguarum* and the *Colloquia,* which organize languages in columns across facing pages of the open book, here typography alone does the initial work of linguistic classification. Readers of the *Guide* must first engage the page as a visual rather than lexical field, decipher its typographic logic (wherein Teutonic, English, and Belgic look the same), and increasingly refine their engagement by sifting through keyed categories that distinguish languages and dialects (B for Belgic, L for Latin, and so on). Only then do readers focus on the text's semantic content. English readers searching for the Belgic equivalent of the English word "great" need not read each word in the entry. Instead, they can scan only those words in black letter, bypassing all others. Then they would search for "B.," which stands as the key for Belgick, to find 𝕲root. Typography thus provides a key into the wordbook's various lexical categories. By encouraging an early modern version of smart textual "surfing," typography enabled readers to move past an otherwise daunting amount of lexical data by learning to engage the text, initially, as a visual rather than semantic medium.

My survey of early modern wordbooks and playbooks yields a number of findings that highlight the flexibility of the typographic relativism structuring the appearance of multilingual texts during this period. First, in bilingual Anglo-Dutch wordbooks in which black letter appears, both English and Dutch printers appear to have shared a typographic dialect in which the Dutch language *always* takes on the black letter typeface. To my knowledge, an example of the opposite typographic arrangement does not exist. Second, in bilingual and polyglot dictionary printing, when English is positioned next to Romance and Classical lexicons, Dutch is absent, and black letter is used, then English takes on the black letter typeface. In the course of my study, I have not come across a single example of the opposite typographic arrangement, wherein Romance languages appear in black letter and English in roman. Third, in polyglot vocabularies that include English and Dutch and that use black letter type, Dutch and English are the languages most commonly and consistently printed in black letter. Fourth, in polyglot vocabularies that include English and Dutch, the more languages represented on the page, the more likely it is that *both* English and Dutch appear in black letter type. Sometimes this is true of German too, but less commonly than with English and Dutch. Fifth, in the sixteen plays and single masque from the mid-sixteenth century to the mid-seventeenth century in which English and Dutch characters appear or stage Dutch is spoken, we find no instance of English being set in black letter, except in one instance (Dekker's *Shoemaker's Holiday*) when the entire playbook is printed in black letter.[76] Finally, when black letter appears in the context of Anglo-Dutch linguistic exchange in early modern English playbooks and masques otherwise printed in roman font, black letter *always* signifies stage Dutch. To frame these findings in Schopenhauer's terms, what we witness across this broad survey of representations of Anglo-Dutch linguistic relations in print is the process whereby print seeks that "mean difference" between the closely-related English and Dutch.

Over the course of the seventeenth century, and with the arrival of the first truly monumental Anglo-Dutch dictionaries, roman and italic type replace black letter (a trend that also characterizes the print history of monolingual English wordlists).[77] *The Dutch-Tutor*, an Anglo-Dutch grammar, phrasebook, and vocabulary printed in London 1660 and again in 1669, evidences this typographic transition. The first section follows the pattern of similar books printed in the Netherlands: its grammar and dialogues print Dutch in black letter and English in roman. However, in the vocabulary that appears toward the end of the book, English headwords appear in italic and Dutch words in roman type.[78] Though a number of Anglo-Dutch wordlists and vocabularies were published in the first half of the seventeenth century, the first to aim at comprehensiveness was Henry Hexham's Anglo-Dutch dictionary, *Het groot Woorden-boeck . . . A Copious English and Netherduytch Dictionarie* (Rotterdam, 1647).[79] Compared with any English dictionary available on the market at the time, Hexham's dictionary was a magnificently comprehensive text, arriving at nearly thirty-one thousand word entries, a feat unsurpassed by any English dictionary throughout the seventeenth century.[80] Throughout all of its seventeenth-century editions, *Het groot Woorden-boeck* never uses black letter.[81] So too in J. G. van Heldoren's *An English and Nether-dutch Dictionary* (Amsterdam, 1675), a grammar, phrasebook, and vocabulary, and his *A New and Easy English Grammar . . .* [and] *a Nomenclature, English and Dutch* (Amsterdam, 1675; London, 1690), English is printed in roman and Dutch in italic throughout the text.[82] When Willem Sewel publishes his *New Dictionary English and Dutch* (Amsterdam, 1691) and *Nieuw Woordenboek der Nederduytsche en Engelsche Taale* (Amsterdam, 1691), his late seventeenth-century dictionary borrows more than word lists from Hexham. The frontispiece to his *New Dictionary* depicts Sewel as copying directly from other texts in his library (Figure 25). No doubt one of the reference works within arm's reach was Hexham's dictionary, which, like Sewel's, set English and Dutch in roman and italic type. By the end of the century, Anglo-Dutch wordbooks displayed a very different typographic face than that with which the century opened.[83]

FIGURE 25. Willem Sewel, *A New Dictionary English and Dutch* (1691), frontispiece.
By permission of the Huntington Library, San Marino, California.

The turn of the seventeenth century was a moment when knowledge of Anglo-Dutch linguistic proximity was actively produced in philological debates, in the performance and printed publication of London drama, and in bilingual and polyglot wordbooks. While Richard Verstegan and others were busily advancing claims for the racial kinship between the English and Dutch people, the theater and its playbooks capitalized on the humorous ways Dutch could be made to sound a lot like English. In these instances, the effect was one of similitude. On the printed pages of playbooks and in Anglo-Dutch wordbooks, however, typographic arrangements point to an experimental play characteristic of the narcissism of minor differences. As we have seen, even as black letter could introduce difference into an all-roman play text, so too it subtly reveals that its difference is a fiction of the page. Although typographic arrangements could make a difference between English and Dutch on the page, even there—where we might expect to discover only stark opposition—the fine line between English and Dutch identity is exposed. These various cases of philologists, antiquarians, playwrights, printers (compositors), and lexicographers exploring—even playing—with signs of difference and sameness provide us a window onto the process of ethnicity in the making. Just as English characters demonstrate how "apt" they are in "taking up" Dutch, so too one imagines the reader of a wordbook learning the language as a process of identifying resemblance alongside (sometimes minor) linguistic difference. In moving back and forth between Dutch and English, and in demonstrating just how fine a line is crossed in that movement, the theater's characters—on the stage and on the page—together with the dictionary printers of the period did more to knit together the English and the Dutch, the English and Dutch languages, than they did to tease them apart.

CHAPTER 5

London as Palimpsest

The Anglo-Dutch Royal Exchange

Architecture is neither here nor there . . . neither purely specific nor
purely abstract, neither purely social nor purely formal, neither
purely local nor purely global. Architecture, all architecture, is here
and there, specific *and* abstract, social *and* formal, local *and* global.
It is only a question of how and to what degree it attempts to enact
this here and there-ness.
—Mark Rakatansky, "Why Architecture Is Neither Here nor There"

The skyline of London was transformed in March 2000 as the world's largest
observation wheel was set in motion on the south bank of the river Thames.
From atop, viewers survey London twenty-five miles in each direction. The
objective of the architects of the London Eye was to offer "an exciting new
way to see and understand one of the greatest cities on earth." The official
website of the London Eye boasts, "London Eye has become, quite literally,
the way the world sees London."[1] While the architects, designers, and corporate financiers extolled the innovation of the project, they could not rightly
claim it as the first Eye of London. In the mid-sixteenth century the world's
merchants would observe the city from inside another London Eye, London's
Royal Exchange. Completed in 1568, the Royal Exchange was the first building devoted exclusively to mercantile exchange within London (Figure 26).[2]
It was a quadrilateral structure with a central court open to the sky, located
within the city walls at the intersection of Threadneedle Street and Cornhill.

FIGURE 26. Frans Hogenberg, The Royal Exchange, exterior view (1569).

The ground level of the interior consisted of an open-air square and an arcade with marble pillars, above which stood a story of one hundred small merchant shops called "pawns." In his 1598 *Survey of London*, John Stow reveals that the Royal Exchange had earned the appellation "The Eye of London."[3]

In walking to the site, sixteenth- and seventeenth-century Londoners indeed could eye much of their world. A structure designed to organize and shelter London's merchants, who until 1568 had met in open-air markets along nearby Lombard Street, it showcased far more than worldly goods. Inside the open square, merchants traded commodities twice daily, loaned and borrowed capital from European traders, arranged transportation for goods, and caught up on city gossip and world news.[4] A German visitor in 1598 declared, "it has a great effect, whether you consider the stateliness of the building, the assemblage of different nations, or the quantity of merchandise."[5] Initially intended as a space in which mercantile exchange might be organized, the daily use of the Royal Exchange quickly expanded beyond its intended purpose (Figure 27). During nonbusiness hours Londoners played football within the building.[6] Outside the Exchange gates "boyes and children, and younge rougues" were often heard "shoutinge and hollowinge"; women were reported "selling oranges, apples, and other things at the Exchange-gate . . . amusing themselves in cursinge and swearinge, to the great annoyance and greif [*sic*] of . . . passers by."[7] The artist Wenceslaus Hollar captured the hustle and bustle of commercial and social interactions at London's Royal Exchange by showcasing the European cast of merchants who regularly gathered within (Figure 28). Hollar's image stages the vibrancy of the Royal Exchange as a place of commerce and entertainment where licit and illicit activities transpired and domestic and foreign merchants met to transact business. It was even the site of business exchange on Sunday, as London's Dutch merchants were known to ignore conventional business hours, transacting business there following their church service at Austin Friars to the chagrin of their more piously self-fashioned English hosts.[8] Prior to its destruction in the Great Fire of 1666, the Royal Exchange served as a stage for the spectacles of early modern commercial and social life.

Before Londoners began migrating to the Royal Exchange for business, the building itself had made its own migration. Arriving figuratively on the scene from across the North Sea, London's Exchange was an architectural copy of Antwerp's Nieuwe Beurs; as such, it was a material outgrowth of the shuttling of people, products, and capital between these two northern European cities. The Royal Exchange quite literally materializes the metaphorical

Byrsa Londinensis *vulgo* the Royal Exchange

FIGURE 27. Wenceslaus Hollar, Royal Exchange (date unknown).
Courtesy of the Thomas Fisher Rare Book Library, University of Toronto.

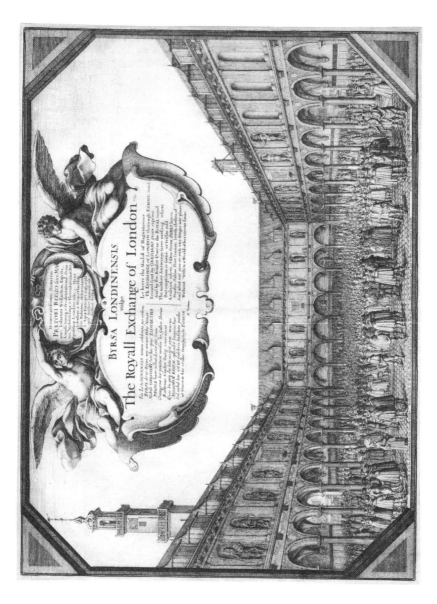

FIGURE 28. Wenceslaus Hollar, Interior of the Royal Exchange (1644).
By permission of Guardian Royal Exchange Collection, the Mercers' Company, London.

overlaying of the Low Countries onto London that I have been exploring as transpiring within puns, double entendres, and tropes of Anglo-Dutch nearness, proximity, and kinship. In previous chapters, I have attended to the semiotics of Dutchness as circulated in stage plays, in language debates, in polemical discourse, and on the printed page. This chapter directs attention to how Dutchness comes to inhere within London's built environment and to the ways in which representation of ceremonial engagements with the Royal Exchange open onto how the Dutch of London engaged the semiology of their host city by strategically adopting the double vision that was so central to English constructions of Dutchness.

Architecture/Migrancy: Reading for the Drift of Culture

Prior to its fiery demise in 1666, London's Royal Exchange was materialized on the pages of dramatic texts, pamphlet literature, political speeches and in records of civic pageantry. This chapter considers three performances *at* or *of* the Exchange: Queen Elizabeth's visit to and renaming of the site in 1571, King James's royal progress by the Exchange in 1604 as recorded in Thomas Dekker's *The Magnificent Entertainment of King James*, and the mayoral pageant of 1605, which begins with the fictional arrival of a ship named the *Royall Exchange* into London. I explore these performances for how they reveal the affiliations and tensions between the space of the Royal Exchange and the dynamics of early modern Dutch immigration. By setting Dutch immigration into London side by side with the importation of this Dutch-inspired architectural site, I bring to the fore the relations of Dutch migrancy to commercial architecture, urban pageantry, and cultural identity in early modern London. Throughout, I approach the Royal Exchange as a site of interaction, one animated by and in turn generative of domestic and foreign, particularly English and Dutch, interplay. In so doing, I aim to recover cultural interactions as they are housed in textual representations of London's cityscape. The Royal Exchange is both a real and symbolic site, a space where Anglo-Dutch relations transpire and a place whose symbolic resonances make it productive of knowledge about Dutchness in London city life. More than snapshots of the once real Royal Exchange, the representations I explore are productive of a "poetic geography" that reveals London as palimpsested with Dutchness, both past and present.[9]

The immigration of the Dutch community to London and the migration of Dutch-inspired architecture are intertwined, but not as our contemporary understandings of migrancy might predict. In such cultural narratives, architectural theorist Stephen Cairns has pointed out, the link between architecture and migrancy is often figured as causal; architecture is imagined as built *by* migrants or *for* migrants.[10] For example, ethnic enclaves—what sociologists refer to as the "ethnopolis" (such as Little Italy or Little Saigon)—are thought to spring up as a result of the concentration of "permanent immigrants from relatively coherent ethnic backgrounds . . . within particular sectors of the city."[11] The little city within points beyond the parameters of the host city, which acts as "an 'urban portal' that opens onto larger diasporic networks of association."[12] Architecture *for* migrants, in our current sociopolitical moment, conjures more traumatic associations of the refugee camp or temporary structures of disaster relief. In both cases, architecture is imagined as a by-product of trends in migrancy—a material reality derived from social conditions. As such, the intersection of architecture and migration yields the perception that architecture announces the presence of the foreign within.

The Royal Exchange and the cultural contests it catalyzed—including contests about representation—do not fit comfortably into these narratives. The relation between people and London's built environment that this chapter explores challenges a central line of thought in conventional scripts of migrancy's relation to architecture. Notably, the Royal Exchange was not a by-product of Dutch immigration, at least not initially so. As I explain below, the concept for and politics behind the building of the Exchange preceded the first significant wave of Dutch refugees into London in the mid-sixteenth century. Nevertheless, the Exchange's indebtedness to its Antwerp predecessor sparked anxieties about the site that erupted in contests over its signification. These contests affirm Michel de Certeau's insight that "stories . . . carry out a labor that constantly transforms places into spaces."[13] For de Certeau, place "implies an indication of stability"; it is ruled by the law of the "proper[:] the elements taken into consideration are *beside* one another, each situated in its own 'proper' and distinct location, a location it defines."[14] Space, on the other hand, is "*a practiced place*" and "actuated by the ensemble of movements deployed within it. Space occurs as the effect produced by the operations that orient it."[15] In early modern London, discursive, representational, and ceremonial networks intersect with architecture, transforming the place, the Royal Exchange, into space. Throughout this chapter, I trace the various ways in which the Exchange's embeddedness in and production of such networks rendered it a vital space through which Anglo-Dutch relations within London were represented, contested, and revised. In so doing, I reanimate the ways in which the Exchange came to signify the complexities of Anglo-Dutch cultural approximation, and explore the interpretive questions that arose as a result of the site being doubly situated in the imaginations of those who engaged with it, particularly in the ceremonial context of London pageantry. I argue that representational efforts to "English" the Royal Exchange induced a palimpsestic perception of London's commercial center and gave rise to new possibilities for how the Dutch stranger community in London represented their civic belonging.

From "Gresham's Bursse" to "The Royal Exchange"

Beyond a shared appellation and prominence on the London skyline, both the sixteenth- and the twenty-first-century London "Eyes" are architectural monuments whose material history bespeaks Anglo-Dutch commercial relations. In building the twenty-first-century London Eye, the Dutch steel company Hollandia was contracted to engineer the world's largest wheel rim, which would serve as the infrastructure of the Eye. The finished rim was shipped in sections along the same waterways used in the sixteenth century when three ships, also laden with iron as well as stone, glass, and wainscot (oak panels), sailed from the Low Countries into the river Thames to deliver the materials with which London's Exchange would be built.[16] In addition to its materials, the building owed its architectural design to the Dutch. "Gresham's Bursse," as the Exchange was initially named, was an architectural copy of Antwerp's Nieuwe Beurs ("new marketplace"), erected in 1531. Thomas Gresham, the English merchant who proposed the building of and orchestrated the financing for the Burse in London, spent much of his young adult life successfully trading and negotiating debts on behalf of the English Crown in Antwerp.[17] In the mid-sixteenth century, merchants from around the globe met at Antwerp's Nieuwe Beurs to negotiate matters relating to foreign trade and local commercial exchange. Both products and people flowed regularly in and out of Antwerp, and at the center of this commercial exchange stood the Nieuwe Beurs.[18] Gresham was intimately familiar with the structure as he transacted business there regularly for over twenty years and, when residing in Antwerp, lived within three hundred yards of it.[19] His own agent in Antwerp, Richard Clough, urged on Gresham's plans for a

London copy in a letter written from Antwerp (31 December 1561) in which he pinpointed London's lack of a Burse as a symptom of its arrested development: "consyderyng whatt a sittey London ys, and that in so many yeres they have nott founde the menes to make a Bourse! but must wallke in the raine when ytt raineth, more liker pedlers then marchants; and in thys countrie, and all other, there is no kynde of pepell that have occasyon to meete, butt they have a plase meete for that pourpose."[20] Given his own ambitions and the provocations of friends and colleagues in Antwerp, it is hardly surprising that Gresham, whose reputation and fortunes were largely reaped from the success he enjoyed as merchant-adventurer in Antwerp (1543–51) and later as the English Crown's royal agent in the Netherlands (1551–64), would select a Flemish architect, Hendryck van Paesschen, to realize his vision of erecting a Burse in London.[21]

The often-heated mercantile tensions that would partly characterize Anglo-Dutch relations during the sixteenth and seventeenth centuries were prefigured in the labor conflicts that arose around the building of Gresham's Burse.[22] The Flemish architect who oversaw its construction brought with him "masons, bricklayers, and other foreign workmen" along with materials imported from Flanders.[23] English artisans and bricklayers were incensed at the loss of potential income to Dutch aliens; they angrily protested the use of foreign labor and the loss of potential English jobs. The Lord Mayor of the city of London was forced to respond to reports of abuse and vandalism of Gresham's Burse by issuing a proclamation in which we learn that the crest of Thomas Gresham on the building's south side had been "cut mangled and defaced" and that the bricklayers committed "misdemeanors . . . both in words and also in deeds" against "Sr Thomas Gresham."[24] In order to prevent subsequent vandalism, Gresham agreed to give the English bricklayers a "parcel of his work at the said Bursse."[25] Given the impassioned nature of the bricklayers' protests, one might suspect that city officials would have registered concerns regarding the building project. There are, however, no extant records of city officials querying the logic of building a copy of Antwerp's marketplace in London by means of a significant presence of foreign workmen.[26] The silence in official records suggests that for Gresham, the city authorities, and Queen Elizabeth, the building was not a cultural anachronism. On the contrary, London's appropriation of the architecture that symbolized Antwerp's economic prowess seems to have been an act of intentional political posturing, which called for nothing short of a royal visit by the queen. Foregrounding a nascent cultural fantasy, the building signaled to London's merchants and their prosperous northern European neighbors that London was prepared to surpass Antwerp's more powerful position in an increasingly global world market.[27]

Despite hopes that London's merchants would prefer to avoid the elements of weather, which they regularly suffered in the open-air markets, merchants did not take quickly to the new building that opened for business on 22 December 1568. The "pawnshops" within the Burse remained mostly empty and unrented for almost two full years.[28] This changed when, in 1571, Queen Elizabeth's visit to the building transformed it into a site of spectacle. In preparation for the queen's visit, Gresham devised a way to foreground the success of his Burse at a moment when the building had, in reality, received only a lukewarm reception from London's merchants. John Stow's *Chronicle* (1604) records that since only a few shops about the pawn had been rented, Gresham negotiated with his tenants an agreement that on the evening of the queen's visit, they would "furnish and adorn with wares and wax-lights as many shops as they either could or would, and they should have all those shops so furnished rent-free that year, which otherwise at that time was forty shillings a shop by the year."[29]

According to Stow's *Survey of London* (1598), Gresham's backstage negotiations with tenants resulted in a successful production of the Burse's commercial promise: "After dinner, her Majestie returning through Cornehill, entered the Bursse on the southside, and after that she had viewed every part thereof above the ground, especially the Pawne, which was richly furnished with all sorts of the finest wares in the Citie: shee caused the same Bursse by an Herauld and a Trumpet, to be proclaimed the *Royal Exchange*, and so to be called from thenceforth, and not otherwise."[30] The queen's visit became urban legend, retold in Thomas Heywood's play *If You Know Not Me, You Know Nobody, Part II* (1606), and later recalled after the building was lost to the Great Fire in *Great Britains Glory; or, A Brief Description of the Present State, Splendor, and Magnificence of the Royal Exchange* (1672).[31] The visit was visually commemorated on coins, in engravings, and on murals.[32]

The renaming of Gresham's Burse was a creative act of royal English appropriation. As Gresham's Burse, the building evidenced both the profitable drift of Dutch material culture and Dutch craftsmanship into London and the necessary shuttling of England's merchant class from London to Antwerp and back. As Gresham's Burse, the building further underscored

London's commercial interdependence with Antwerp. In calling the building a "Royal Exchange," Elizabeth attempted a two-fold revision of the building's signifying potential. First, she suppressed the emphasis on the economic prowess of the individual merchant, Gresham, whose wealth, ambition, and penchant for business was instantiated by the "richly furnished" monument that bore his name. She also countered the potential for London's marketplace merely to set into relief Dutch commercial enterprise. As the "Royal Exchange" London's new marketplace shed the Dutch-derived title (*Beurs /* "Bursse"), which linguistically recalled the building's foreign architectural influence and inspiration.[33] With this act, Elizabeth attempted to cast off the Burse's derivative, foreign origins, urging on its status as a fully English site.

Elizabeth's speech served simultaneously as an act of erasure and inscription, thereafter charging the site with a double signification, a doubling that both affiliated and set into opposition England and the Low Countries, English and Dutch commercial life. On the one hand, as the Royal Exchange, the building signified London's pretension to ascend as the new European center of global trade, a fate that Antwerp's increasing troubles with Spain would soon thereafter help bring about. Despite the foreign craftsmanship and materials that made possible the construction of the building, the Royal Exchange would become an English monument whose ultimate success depended not on Anglo-Dutch collaboration (or the wealth Englishmen raised in Antwerp's Nieuwe Beurs), but on the English whose most prominent political signifier was the monarch herself. On the other hand, as a "copy," the building necessarily retained its affiliation with Antwerp. Indeed, despite the queen's insistence that the structure be called the Royal Exchange "from thenceforth, and not otherwise," the original name stuck and the building was called both the Royal Exchange and Gresham's Burse until its fiery demise. Volume 1 of the Gresham *Repertories*, housed in London's Mercers' Company, records the minutes of the committee responsible for administrating the business relating to the Exchange during the years 1596–1625; the committee's reports refer to the building both as the "Gresham Bourse" and the Exchange throughout this period.[34] Likewise, in drama and public pamphlet literature, both nomenclatures were used interchangeably.[35]

The ideological imperative implied by Elizabeth's renaming was never fully actualized. Well after its pawns were all rented and merchants were meeting on the main floor twice daily to loan and borrow money as well as sell merchandise, the building's assimilation into London's commercial geography continued to be challenged by its association with the Netherlands. Indeed, the cities' two almost identical exchange structures made potential doppelgängers of London and Antwerp, underscoring in material form the long-standing "complementary [trade] relationship" between them.[36] This doppelgänger effect seems not to have been Gresham's intention. Rather, London's Burse was to outshine its Continental inspiration. In political discourse, the project's merit is framed in terms that underscore a competition between London and Antwerp. In his address to the Merchant Taylors on 12 January 1565, Sir William Chester averred that "Sir Thomas Gresham knight . . . had . . . promised . . . to build and plant within this City a burse to be more fair and costly builded in all points than is the burse of Antwerp."[37] Antwerp's Nieuwe Beurs is regularly compared with London's Exchange in travel writing and drama as well. Thomas Platter, a foreign visitor to London, was prompted to compare London and Antwerp precisely because of their similar exchanges: "the Exchange is a great square place like the one in Antwerp."[38] In 1606, Thomas Heywood's *If You Know Not Me, You Know Nobody, Part II* features two characters who admire London's Exchange as if it were Europe's latest cultural accomplishment:

> *2 Lord:* The nearest that which most resembles this,
>   Is the great Burse in Anwerpe, yet not comparable
>   Either in height or widness: the faire Sellerage,
>   Or goodly shoppes above: O my Lord Major,
>   This Gresham hath much grac't your Cittie London,
>   His fame will long out-live him. (1371–76)

The play's characterization of Gresham, like the Lord's analogy of Burses, works to shake London's commercial and urban history free from links with Antwerp. For instance, Gresham's historical role as Royal Agent in Antwerp is geographically revised so that his business dealings connect him instead with investments in North Africa and the Levant.[39] On the one hand, the comparison of Antwerp's Beurs as the "nearest . . . which most resembles" London's reinforces the Anglo-Dutch affiliation, even as it hints at a cultural anxiety that London might signify not its own place in European trade relations, but prove instead a satellite city, an Antwerp affiliate.[40] On the other hand, by affiliating Gresham with Morocco and the Levant instead of Antwerp, this play simultaneously attempts to efface the effect of Antwerp's influence on and material presence within London.

Elizabeth's renaming of Gresham's Burse sparked a representational quandary for those authors who would lionize Thomas Gresham and his architectural legacy in their praise of London as a commercial trade center. Representation of the Royal Exchange was built on an erasure at its center— that of Antwerp's material and cultural migrations into London. This erasure proved difficult to maintain, especially as the sixteenth century drew on and Antwerp suffered the Spanish Fury of 1576 and then the devastating "siege of Antwerp" in 1585, which catalyzed the exile of half of Antwerp's population (nearly thirty-eight thousand people), many of whom found safe harbor in London.[41] As Dutch immigrants increasingly settled in London and were trading at the Royal Exchange, the cultural memory of the site's Antwerp predecessor was lent a new vocabulary and a renewed cultural force.

The civic category of denizenship that attempted to govern the relationship of strangers living within London to the material culture they participated in producing provided a powerful trope for representing the relationship of the Royal Exchange to the Antwerp Beurs. Donald Lupton's 1632 characterization of the city, for instance, mobilizes this category to subtend his depiction of the city's marketplaces. When Lupton was writing his *London and the Country Carbonadoed and Quartered into Several Characters*, there were two exchanges in London, the "Old," or Royal Exchange, and a "New Exchange," which opened in 1609 along the Strand and showcased more fashionable and costly products than were sold at the Royal Exchange.[42] Lupton's comparison of the "Old" and "New" Exchanges recalls the foreign origins of the Old Exchange: "The one of these came from *Antwerpe*, the other from a Stable; the one was *Dutch*, yet made *Denison*; the other was not so at the beginning, but did Exchange his name and nature."[43] By evoking the legal terminology of denizenship, more conventionally employed to categorize the status of enfranchised immigrants in London, Lupton anthropomorphizes the Old Exchange; the building, like a Dutch stranger once from Antwerp, shares with that stranger the ability to be "made Denison." As in the context of the language debates, here too the figure of the denizen serves as a nimble emissary for and exemplar of ethnic assimilation. What is most interesting in this context is what Lupton's analogy does *not* do. Lupton does not mobilize an insider-outsider or citizen-alien dichotomy to locate the Old Exchange in opposition to the New. The Old Exchange, Gresham's Burse, is characterized as once "Dutch now Denison," which is not to claim it as a fully Englished site. The status of the Old Exchange as "denizen" reveals less about where on the continuum of cultural affiliation it stands than that a continuum, rather than a dichotomy, is necessary to represent the place of the Royal Exchange in London. The logic underpinning Lupton's comparison of the Old Exchange with Dutch immigrants suggests that the success of London's Old Exchange is measured by the degree to which it effaces evidence of its original Dutchness. It is here that the story of architecture's migrancy implies something in turn about the migrant. As the building's incorporation into London underwent a process of assimilation, in Lupton's view, so too the successful Dutch immigrant is one who, having once been Dutch, is now denizen. Dutch immigrants, linked by means of a vocabulary of citizenship to the story of the Old Exchange, are rendered figures of partial immigration—their migrancy is characterized as *always heading toward* but *never fully arriving at* Englishness. Put differently, what Queen Elizabeth's performance attempted to efface (the sign of "Antwerp" thriving within London), Lupton imaginatively accommodates.

The paradox of the Royal Exchange's double signification—born in Elizabeth's ceremonial renaming and reaccommodated in Lupton's representation—came forcefully to bear on its textual representations. The difficulty of using the site to symbolize London's commercial success resided in how to domesticate that success when its most prominent signifier was anxiously and repetitively associated with Antwerp, and with a Dutchness both within and elsewhere. Despite its Englished royal title, the building continued to spark comparison to its foreign antecedent. As the Royal Exchange, it was imagined as Europe's superior place of commerce, but as Gresham's Burse, it continued to belie its foreign origins—indelibly marked, through a lexicon of citizenship, as denizen.

The Denizen Reimagined: Staging Dutch Belonging

As England mourned the death of Queen Elizabeth, London citizens undertook extensive preparations for the royal progress of her successor.[44] London at this time was a "ceremonial city" whose established processional routes were inflected by what Lawrence Manley has identified as a "ceremonial syntax" upon which the ritual meaning of London's civic pageants depended.[45] Pageantry's ceremonial efficacy and cultural legibility depended on its proceeding along particular streets and stopping at conventional sites along the way. For the stranger communities, civic pageantry occasioned a rare opportunity for direct address both to the London citizenry and to

English royalty. By focusing on the participation of a community of people who had long lived *in* but were not *of* England, I aim to reconstitute a perspective of King James's progress of 1604 that, while partial, reanimates a denizen perspective of the pageant.

Scholarship on civic pageantry has conventionally attended to the thematic trends of an entire pageant;[46] in so doing, we implicitly read civic pageantry from the perspective of the guest of honor who, along with the entourage, would have experienced not only a privileged perspective but one unavailable to most of the city's inhabitants, who clustered around particular pageant arches. Such reading practices have tended to obfuscate the contribution of those participatory and interpretive communities for whom pageantry's emphasis on social unity and budding English nationalism may have proved illusory. Additionally, in reading the entirety of the progress as the thing, critics have missed the opportunity to excavate the local and spatial context of each performance in order to consider how the history and everyday use of a site along the "central civic axis" might have served as a meaningful part of that spectacle.[47] In James I's royal progress the Dutch creatively deployed the "ceremonial syntax" of their host city to showcase the social contributions and commercial success of London's Dutch inhabitants. Even more, their performance as depicted in Thomas Dekker's "Magnificent Entertainment Given to King James"—our most complete account of James's royal progress—amplifies the Scottish king's implicit status as a stranger and in so doing extends the politics of the Dutch strategy for self-representation by implicitly connecting the king's immigration to London with their own.[48] In Dekker's account of the Dutch pageant, London's Dutch denizens greet England's recently crowned denizen with a savvy series of performances that stress their communion as strangers made denizens.

As James wound his way from Grace Church Street to Cornhill on the morning of 15 March 1604 he traced the path of England's queens and kings before him.[49] But on this day James's ceremonial landmark at Cornhill would differ from that of his predecessors. When Queen Elizabeth progressed through London in 1559, plans for the Royal Exchange had not yet taken hold; additionally, the Dutch community that would spring up in London, in part due to the Low Countries' battles with Spain, had not yet begun immigrating to London in significant numbers.[50] James was the first king for whom the Royal Exchange was incorporated into a royal progress and he was the first whose royal progress included an arch sponsored by the Dutch stranger community.[51] On this day, the Royal Exchange and the Dutch community emerged as fledgling participants within London's ritual zone. Though new to the context of royal progresses, the building was already a loaded signifier in London life, and the Dutch community that erected its arch "by the Royall Exchange" creatively mobilized the interplay of domestic and foreign significations activated by it.

David Bergeron emphasizes that "no English pageant previously studied so depends on triumphal arches as this one, and they embody highly embellished architectural achievements,"[52] an assessment that extends to the Dutch arch (Figure 29). The strangers collected funds enough through the Dutch Church in London to afford the building of an arch eighty-seven feet high and thirty-seven feet wide that rivaled in scale and design those other "wonders of Wood [that] clymed . . . into the clowdes" designed and funded by the London guilds (lines 175–76). While English architect Stephen Harrison designed most of the pageant arches, the craftsmen, designers, and architects of the Dutch arch were drawn from the Dutch and Walloon communities.[53] The architect, Conraet Jansen (Coenraet Janszoon), was a Protestant refugee who arrived to England in 1567 from 's-Hertogenbosch and was made denizen in 1571. A joiner by trade, Jansen "prospered, employing four English employees in 1593" and baptizing five children in the London Dutch Church in the 1570s.[54] Jansen married twice in London; his first wife and mother of his five children was "a widow of another Netherlandic refugee" and his second, "Elizabeth Garland, [he] married [outside the Dutch Church] at the church of St. George the Martyr, Southwark."[55] As much a part of the London world of Anglo-Dutch culture as any man of his time, Jansen built an arch whose design reveals his sophisticated understanding of Anglo-Dutch political relations, especially pertaining to the context of London.

Dekker's account highlights the divide between the domestic and foreign communities participating in the pageant. "The Magnificent Entertainment" refers to the arches funded by London guilds according to *where* they appeared along the pageant route: the Fenchurch arch, the "Device at Soperlane end," the arch of triumph "above the Conduit in Fleetstreete," or Pageant in the "Strond." These arches are immediately decipherable as creations by English subjects for their king. In contrast, the strangers' contributions are distinguished from the London guilds by largely printed title headings that emphasize the community that sponsored the arch: "The Italians Pageant" and "The Pageant of the Dutch-men, by the Royal Exchange." What

FIGURE 29. Stephen Harrison, "The Dutch Arch at the Royal Exchange," from
The Arch's of Triumph Erected in Honor of the High and Mighty Prince James (1613).

By permission of the Folger Shakespeare Library.

Dekker's title headings set apart—domestic from foreign participation in London's ceremonial and economic life—the Dutch arch itself creatively and strategically confounds.

On the day of James's progress, London was transformed in anticipation. "The Sunne over-slept himselfe," Dekker reports,

> and rose not in many houres after, yet bringing with it into the very bosome of the Cittie, a world of people. The Streets seemde to bee paved with men: Stalles in stead of rich wares were set out with children, open Casements fild up with women.
>
> All Glasse windowes taken downe, but in their places, sparkeled so many eyes, that had it not bene the day, the light which reflected from them, was sufficient to have made one: hee that should have compared the emptie and untroden walkes of *London*, which were to be seen in that late mortally-destroying Deluge, with the thronged streets now, might have believed, that upon this day, began a new *Creation*, and that the Citie was the onely Workhouse wherein sundry Nations were made. (177–89)

Dekker portrays London's rebirth from the recently devastating plague as also a birthing of nations: the city is envisaged as the generative agent of and spatial context out of which "sundry Nations" are made. From our historical perspective—so entrenched in nationalism—it is difficult not to gloss this line as a simple poetic inversion that gains its piquancy by flying in the face of the obvious: cities exist within the domain of national territory and therefore Dekker's observation gathers poetic charge by inverting that order. But as Dekker's account of the pageant itself unfolds, it seems that in more ways than one, on the day of a royal progress, the city *was* the workhouse wherein sundry nations were made—not the least of which was England.

Having passed through two of the pageant's arches (Fenchurch arch and then beneath and past the Italians' pageant at Grace Church Street), James wound his way toward Cornhill: "Having hoysted up our Sailes, and taken leave of this *Italian* shore, let our next place of casting anker, be upon the Land of the 17. Provinces; where the *Belgians*, (attired in the costly habits of their own native Countrey, without the fantasticke mixtures of other Nations) but more richly furnished with love, stand ready to receyve his Maiestie: who (according to their expectation) does most gratiously make himselfe and his Royall traine their Princely ghests" (437–43). The king's movement through the city is figured as travel among nations as he sails from Italian to Belgic shores. Even before readers arrive at Dekker's description of "The Pageant of the Dutch-men, by the Royall Exchange," the Seventeen Provinces are imagined as a shoreline. The nautical metaphor suggests the geographical reality that underscored much of Anglo-Dutch exchange, an exchange mediated and facilitated by the North Sea waters they shared. Like those cartographic representations that reinforce the sense of spatial proximity between England and the Low Countries in atlases from the period, which I discussed in Chapter 2, here the king's arrival to the "Belgic shore" merely requires his traversing of the *London* landscape. Within Dekker's "Entertainment," the king's approach to the Royal Exchange renders him both at home and abroad (in London and "upon the Land of the 17. Provinces"), a geographical paradox that interlocks London and the Seventeen Provinces as the king passes through "the house . . . these *Strangers* have builded." In this reconfigured space, the king plays the part of foreigner and honored "ghest." Dekker's imagery subtly reverses the more evident guest-host relationship at work; although the Dutch are guests in London, the British king is rendered a guest within his own nation and a stranger among his nation's strangers.[56]

For Londoners, James's Scotland was in practice farther away than the Low Countries. The "Entertainment" was designed to open with a device that attempts to resolve James's status as a "stranger" by entering him into a pact of brotherhood with England: "Saint *George*, Saint *Andrew*, (the Patrons of both Kingdomes) having a long time lookt upon each other, with countenances rather of meere strangers, then of such neare Neighbours, upon the present aspect of his Maiesties approach toward *London*, were (in his sight) to issue from two severall places on horsebacke, and in compleate Armour, their Brestes and Caparisons suited with the Armes of *England* and *Scotland*, (as they are now quartered) to testifie their leagued Combination, and newe sworne Brother-hood" (31–38). What the device enacts—a resolution between "neare Neighbours"—prefigures that which James's kingship must achieve. James, once stranger to England, must make a "sworne Brotherhood" of "neare Neighbours," that is, England and Scotland, whose people were more often than not "meere strangers." That the "*Genius* of the Cittie" is "call[ed] up" to aid these strangers in their pact of brotherhood is a fitting role, given the city's history of making neighbors of strangers—a fact on full display in the Dutch strangers' participation in the royal celebration.

In their address to the king, the Dutch make the implicit request that their status as strangers in the realm be accommodated and protected. The request was not merely rhetorical. Following James's coronation a bill was introduced in the House of Commons that aimed to restrict strangers from selling retail and to limit the economic rights of the children of strangers. Though the bill did not pass through Parliament, London's Dutch strangers no doubt were keen to secure their favor under the new king.[57] Through their "speaking instrument," a "Boy, attired all in white Silke," the Dutch remind King James that his authority derives from God and thus admonish against ambitions of political overreaching. Furthermore, the Dutch address cautiously extends the king-as-stranger leitmotif. Like the new king, the Dutch "likewise come" into London; they too have been brought to new kingdoms:

> Great KING, those so many Scepters, which even fill thy right hand, are all thine owne, onely by the providence of Heaven . . . for to sway onely but one Empire (happily) as it is a labour, hard; so none can undergoe the waight [*sic*]; But . . . to controule many Nations, (and those of different dispositions too) O! the Arme of man can never doe that, but the finger of GOD. . . . It is hee, whose beames, lend a light to thine: It is hee, that teaches thee the Art of *Ruling*; because none but hee, made thee a *King*. . . . Wee (the *Belgians*) likewise come . . . a Nation banisht from our owne Cradles; yet nourcde [*sic*] and brought up in the tender boo-some of Princely Mother, *ELIZA*. The *Love*, which wee once dedi-cated to her (as a Mother) doubly doe wee vow it to you, our Soveraigne, and Father; intreating wee may be sheltred under your winges now, as then under hers: our Prayers being that hee who through the loynes of so many Grand-fathers, hath brought thee to so many Kingdomes, may likewise multiply thy years. (664–701)

The Dutch community asserts its part in recognizing the British king's authority, even as it seeks his political protection. The community's formal address serves as a communal oath of allegiance to the new king and simulta-neously calls on his protection in reciprocation. The implication of the address is twofold: on the one hand, as strangers the Dutch recognize King James's authority as their sovereign (and so seemingly relinquish loyalty to their homeland); on the other hand, the sovereign himself is a stranger (and so, ironically, requires recognition from the city's strangers). These are not mutually exclusive perspectives, of course. Rather, in so fashioning the king as "ghest" and as "meere stranger," the *Entertainment* accommodates both the Dutch and King James as strangers who belong. In granting the Dutch the role of hosts of the king, Dekker's text enfranchises the members of the Dutch community by making them denizen subjects of Britain, subjects who can publicly declare their allegiance to the British king.

The Dutch arch functioned as a stage concealed by curtains until the royal entourage approached the Royal Exchange at Cornhill. Dekker details the dramatic aspect of the Dutch pageant: "(being [at] the heart of the *Trophee*) was a spacious square roome, left open, Silke Curtaines drawne before it, which (upon the approach of his Maiestie) being put by, 17. yng *Damsels* (all of them sumptuously adorned, after their countrey fashion,) sate as it were in so many Chaires of State, and figuring in their persons, the 17. *Provinces of Belgia"* (479–84). A stage so densely packed showcases the density of the Dutch stranger population in London.[58] Dutch merchants, artisans, religious leaders, and apprentices lined up along Cornhill, flanking the arch their community had sponsored. As the king approached and passed beneath it, he would have seen, carved in high relief, images everywhere of Dutch artistic and agrarian industry: "Over the other Portall, . . . men, women and children (in Dutch habits) are busie at other workes: the men Weaving, the women Spinning, the children at their Hand-loomes, &c. Above whose heads, you may with little labour, walke into the *Mart,* where as well the *Froe,* as the *Burger,* are buying and selling, the praise of whose industrie (being worthy of it) stands publisht in gold" (584–90). Even the artifice of the arch itself reveals the truth of Dutch creative industry: "In the square Field, next and lowest, over one of the Portals, were the Dutch Countrey people, toyling at their Husbandrie; women carding of their Hemp, . . . such excellent Art being exprest in their faces, their stoopings, bendings, sweatings, &c. that nothing is wanting in them but life (which no colours can give) to make them bee thought more than the workes of Paynters" (569–74). Images of commercial productivity and mercantilism are featured prominently on the arch (images that regularly ornament Dutch maps as well). But one image on the backside of the arch stands out among the others. With London's Royal Exchange looming in the immediate background, the backside of the arch features the *Dutch* Exchange, the Antwerp Beurs: "Lift up your eyes a little," Dekker implores, "and beholde their *Exchange*; the countenaunces of the Marchants there being so lively, that bargaines seeme to come from their lippes" (575–77).

Four different contemporary reports concur that the Dutch arch stood near or "by" the Royal Exchange.[59] Dekker's description of the arch's breadth raises the question of whether these two exchanges—one, the stone building, the other, a temporary edifice—did not in fact abut, in effect creatively condensing the spatial distance between the two historically and textually interlocked Bourses.[60] The picture that Dekker's text paints of the adjacent Bourses invites the reader to imagine the city as an open book. For those standing along Cornhill facing the backside of the arch, the verso page of the city street was filled by the Royal Exchange, while an image of Antwerp's Beurs was featured on the recto. Of course, the Royal Exchange at Cornhill was already richly palimpsested with Dutchness. There too onlookers glimpsed the phantom presence of Antwerp's Beurs, a history of Dutch labor in London, and evidence of Anglo-Dutch commercial and cultural exchange.[61]

The Dutch arch renders spatially what Dekker's nautical metaphor had accomplished poetically: a foreshortening of the distance between Antwerp and London and their commercial centers. It draws together Antwerp and London not only by setting a representation of Antwerp's Beurs into relief against the backdrop of London's Exchange but also because the Dutch community that occupied the street alongside the Royal Exchange suggested both the cause and outcome of such interlocking of northern European trading spaces. There, at the center of London's burgeoning metropolis and almost midway through the king's ceremonial procession, stood a creative amalgam of the Dutch presence: London's Dutch stranger community, its impressive triumphal arch, and the legacy of Dutch cultural influence as evinced in London's own Royal Exchange.

As if tearing a page from the book of English perspectives onto Dutchness, the Dutch stranger community of London (as Thomas Dekker represents it) appears to have willfully embraced and strategically mobilized the double vision that rendered Dutchness an uncanny likeness with Englishness. The performance at Cornhill optimized the representational doubleness of the Royal Exchange, challenging the new king both to identify with the Dutch denizens of London as the precursors to his own successful migration to England and to experience London as a "world city" infused with a Dutchness as inextricable as the stones and pillars of the London Burse.[62] The strategy at the center of this performance might best be characterized as strategic proximity: this is a performance that maximizes the opportunity to create meaning out of temporary realignments of bodies in the urban sphere.[63] The proximity of Dutch bodies to London's built environment—particularly *this* charged space—makes possible the fantasy of Antwerp's presence *within* London, and Dutch presence as integral to Englishness. The Dutch who were present and performing that day were not the Dutch of Antwerp, but the Dutch of contemporary London: a people built in to (and partly responsible for building) the economic, social, and material fabric of London life.

If Queen Elizabeth's visit to and renaming of Gresham's Burse attempted to settle the site as English—to cut off the shuttling of signification between England and the Low Countries catalyzed by the building's doppelgänger effect—the Dutch performance builds on the royal erasure at the center of the Exchange's representational history. The Dutch immigrants mobilize architecture to stage a broader representational contest already animating that building's meaning, and their performance sets into question the way that meaning underpins the logic of Dutch enfranchisement in London. The community's arch and performance of strategic proximity frustrates distinctions that depend on discursive and geographic references framed by a logic of here or there, home or abroad, us or them. Fundamentally, it is not Anglo-Dutch *difference* that has agitated and threatened to unravel the production of an Englished Royal Exchange; it has been a lingering sense of sameness, an unshakeable doppelgänger effect, which undercuts the fantasy of national difference and frustrates any easy national consolidation of "Britain" that Dekker's text (and civic pageantry) aim to create. If, as Dekker declared, on this day London was the workhouse in which sundry nations were made, then those nations—including once "strangers," now "neere neighbors"—were made to look as if they were in the city to stay.

A Floating Signifier: The *Royall Exchange* at Sea

We construct, we make every city a little in the image of the ship *Argo*, whose every piece was no longer the original piece but which still remained the ship *Argo*, that is, a set of significations easily readable and recognizable. In this attempt at a semantic approach to the city we should try to understand the play of signs, to understand that any city is a structure. . . . [T]he city is a poem . . . but it is not a classical poem, a poem tidily centered on a subject. It is a poem

which unfolds the signifier and it is this unfolding that ultimately the semiology of the city should try to grasp and make sing.
—Roland Barthes, "Semiology and the Urban"[64]

The year following James's royal progress, Anthony Munday, pageant director and author, staged a spectacular entry of "The Shippe called the *Royall Exchange* . . . laden with *Spices, Silkes* and *Indico*" returning from its voyage to the East as the opening act of *The Triumphes of a Re-united Britannia* (1605).[65] The first extant mayoral pageant of King James's reign, *Triumphes* untethers the Royal Exchange and its significations from the material site and releases Dutchness from inhering in London's Dutch community per se. By tracing this lexical signifier, we witness how the meaning of the Royal Exchange began to float free from its material sign (the building), even as it continued to register English and Dutch commercial competition.

The pageant opens with a narration of the Brutus-Troy myth of English history. Over the course of the pageant, this myth transforms James into "our second Brute . . . by whose happye comming to the Crowne, England, Wales, and Scotland, by the first Brute severed and divided, is in our second Brute re-united, and made one happy Britania again."[66] If the story of Brutus focused spectators' minds on King James, whose royal progress must have been fresh in memory, the spectacular entrance of "the Shippe called the Royall Exchange" returned attention to the city's new mayor and to the economic life of the city that his office helped to oversee. The arrival into port of the *Royall Exchange* occasions the pageant's initial address to the Lord Mayor and serves as an important stage for figuring the parameters of his juridical and economic domain. The shipmaster's address to the city of London provides the narrative context for the ship's arrival in London:

All hayle fair London, to behold thy Towers.
After our voyage long and dangerous:
Is Seamens comfort, thankes unto those powers,
That in all perils have preserved us.
Our *Royall Exchange* hath made a rich returne,
Laden with *Spices, Silkes,* and *Indico,*
Our wives that for our absence long did mourne,
Now find release from all their former woe. (108–15)

On the ship's return from the East Indies, its cargo hold brims with valued goods. Mayor Leonard Halliday is cast as the ship's owner, a role revealed when the ship's mate calls out, "Maister good newes, our Owner, as I heare, / Is this day sworne in Londons Maioralty" (116–17). At this moment in the performance fact and fiction are tightly intertwined, since Halliday was indeed a founder of the East India Company and would later become a Treasurer. In so linking the wealth of the East Indies with London, London's trade success with the ship the *Royall Exchange*, and the *Royall Exchange* with Leonard Halliday, Merchant Taylor, whose inauguration the pageant was designed to celebrate, the pageant expands the Lord Mayor's interests and influence well beyond London's horizon.

The spectacle of an English ship's return from the East Indies alludes to the successful return of the first English East India Company fleet two years previous, in September 1603.[67] The four ships in that fleet collected pepper from south Sumatra and Bantam in western Java. Upon their return, the ships "were almost entirely laden with pepper . . . the consignment [of which] was estimated to amount to 1,030,000 [pounds]," a staggering quantity, which had the result of throwing the market "completely out of balance."[68] The market surplus of pepper had implications for Anglo-Dutch economic relations because English success in reaching Sumatra and Java transformed England from an indirect to a direct importer of pepper. This transformation posed a challenge to the Dutch market in pepper, which, like the English, was profitable largely due to its re-exportation of pepper to other European markets, including England.[69] Following the East India Company success, all pepper that had not been imported directly by the company was sequestered, hence limiting Dutch re-exportation of pepper into England. Thus, at the time of Halliday's mayoral inauguration, London's markets were clamoring to adjust to the unprecedented influx of pepper. When the master of Munday's *Royall Exchange* orders his boy and mate to "Take of our Pepper, of our Cloves and Mace, / And liberally bestow them round about," the London audience, whose market had been literally peppered by the 1603 fleet, was invited to participate as consumers in the recent success of the English East India Company's venture.

The opening dramatic sequence enacts a London so rich with spices that the ship's entire crew showers the London crowd with the ship's "luggage." Such a strewing of spices was the convention of mayoral shows and played an important part of the "gift exchange" enacted between the company and the city.[70] Given the surplus of pepper in London in the year 1605, we can have little doubt that actors tossed pepper into the London crowd. The master of the ship also boasts "Cloves and Mace" among his cargo. This claim functions as a proleptic appropriation of Dutch export commodities. While "between 1599 and 1634 . . . mace [was] regularly imported from the Nether-lands," it is not until 1607 that "the first mention of a clove sale in the [English East India] Company's records occurs."[71] The exchange vignette of the mayoral pageant nonetheless celebrates England's emergence as a direct importer of East Indies spices. Mundy thus creatively scripts into the mayoral inauguration a triumph over a much-disliked dependence on European, par-ticularly Dutch, middlemen.[72] Munday's ship of pepper, cloves, and mace depends on the audience's association of it with London's central market-place—where merchants ventured capital on just such risky ventures—to harness its fullest signification. Within this fictional framework, the *Royall Exchange* sails beyond the geographical territory of northern Europe, drawing with it the Anglo-Dutch commercial competition that has adhered to its London counterpart.

By carrying the Royal Exchange out to sea, Munday's pageant liberates Anglo-Dutch commercial exchange from the parochialism of Europe, extend-ing it into the global economy of imperial ventures. Just as the king (and his court) are king and court regardless of their location, so too, this performance suggests, wherever the Royal Exchange is—in London, or at sea—so too are London's mercantile powers and, implicitly, commercial competition with the Dutch. In so translating the Royal Exchange, Munday resituates Anglo-Dutch competition, locating it in the corporate bodies of the English East India Company and its Dutch competitor, De Vereenigde Oost-Indische Compagnie. The mayor's power is also refigured as exceeding the city's walls insofar as this mobile, global marketplace registers the success of the city he governs. In drawing that ship back home, Munday figures an English tri-umph over England's Dutch competitors, a triumph that the English would, in fact, not enjoy in their subsequent trade ventures to the Spice Islands, as we will see in the following chapter. As James brings with him Scotland into the fold of Britain, *The Triumphes of a Re-United Britannia* presents the *Royall Exchange* as a floating, imperial marketplace whose centrifugal commercial force draws the spices of the East into London, even as its centripetal political force figuratively extends the Lord Mayor's domain even to the East Indies.

Neither Munday nor his London audience could have anticipated that fifteen years after Mayor Halliday's inauguration, an eight-hundred-ton ship, named the *Royal Exchange*, would indeed venture to the very edges of Brit-ain's trading outposts.[73] According to East India Company shipping lists, the *Royal Exchange* was among England's largest trade vessels and sailed three expeditions to Batavia (Jakarta) between the years 1620 and 1640. During the early years of competition between De Vereenigde Oost-Indische Compagnie and the East India Company, England's *Royal Exchange* carried highly profitable spices from the Indonesian archipelago back to England. The arrival of the *Royal Exchange* into England's ports was, as Munday's pageant had boldly presaged, a triumph of the English company in its battle to curb Dutch domination of the Indonesian spice trade. With the turn of the seventeenth century, the symbolic commercial charge of the Royal Exchange was unmoored from London, to become a floating signifier of Anglo-Dutch commercial competition on the world's seas.

CHAPTER 6

Doppelgänger Dilemmas

The Crisis of Anglo-Dutch Interchangeability in the East Indies and the Imperfect Redress of Performance

Ysabinda: Fly this detested Isle,
  where horrid Ills so black and fatal dwell,
  as *Indians* cou'd not guess, till *Europe* taught.
. . . .
Towerson: But dry your tears, these sufferings all are mine.
  Your breast is white, and cold as falling Snow.
  You still as fragrant as your Eastern Groves.
          —John Dryden, *Amboyna*, 4.5.15–17, 32–34

Before the "horrid Ills" of Anglo-Dutch rivalry are played out on the body of Ysabinda in John Dryden's *Amboyna* (1673), the play's native Amboyner makes a promise that the changing conditions of her world will refuse to let her keep. The intended wife of the English East India Company captain, Gabriel Towerson, Ysabinda has waited three years for his return to Amboyna, a clove-producing "Spice Island."[1] Their anticipated nuptials are tragically marred when Harmon Junior, son of the island's Dutch East India Company governor, sets his sights on Ysabinda and declares his competition for her in marriage. In terms that presage the central crisis of the play, Ysabinda dismisses Harmon's suit:

Ysabinda: If this be earnest, you've done a most unmanly and
ungrateful part, to court the intended Wife of him, to whom you
are most oblig'd.

Harmon: Leave me to answer that: assure your self I love you
violently, and if you are wise, you'l make some difference 'twixt
Towerson and me.

Ysabinda: Yes, I shall make a difference, but not to your advantage.[2]

Harmon's "violent" love will be horrifically realized when, in act 4 of the
play, he pursues Ysabinda into the island's clove forests, binds her to the tree
that has drawn Europeans to her island, stops her screams with a rag, and
rapes her. Before Ysabinda's tragedy unfolds, Harmon urges Ysabinda to
make a different choice in marriage. Pressing his case by appealing to mercantile and colonial logics that test the limits of overseas cosmopolitanism, Harmon asserts Dutch primacy in trade on the island as a reason for Ysabinda's
affectionate realliance. He scoffs at Ysabinda's choice of "an *Englishman*, part
Captain, and part Merchant" because "his Nation [is] of declining interest
here: consider this, and weigh against that fellow, not me, but any, the least
and meanest *Dutchman* on this *Isle*" (2.1.21–24). As a Dutchman, he boasts,
he is worth more than any Englishman from a "nation of declining interest."
Indeed, as the play reminds its audience, the English and the Dutch had
reached a controversial agreement regarding their trade relations in the East
Indies' Spice Islands, ratified in the treaty of 1619, which guaranteed the
Dutch Vereenigde Oost-Indische Compagnie (VOC) two-thirds of the trade
in the region, the English East India Company (EIC) one-third.[3] The play
takes place after the treaty and in the days running up to one of the most
notorious Anglo-Dutch East Indies conflicts of the seventeenth century, the
Amboyna massacre of 1623. From the position of the EIC merchants, the
treaty of 1619, which had been negotiated in the complex political atmosphere
of Anglo-Dutch relations back home, secured Dutch domination of the spice
trade and foreclosed English opportunity to compete in "fair and free commerce" in the Spice Islands.[4] In local matters of trade, being Dutch makes
all the difference of economic advantage on Amboyna. Therefore, Harmon
Junior reasons, he should enjoy an advantage in his suit for Ysabinda's hand.

Ysabinda's response to Harmon's suit, "I do not weigh by bulk," though
"I know your Countreymen have the advantage there," suggests that she is
knowledgeable of but indifferent to the Anglo-Dutch negotiations that structure European commercial contests on Amboyna (2.1.25–26). Though

profitable cloves, weighed and distributed in bulk, draw the play's Europeans to the island, Ysabinda maintains that the logic and politics of trade, worked out between the English and the Dutch, do not govern her relations with the strangers on her island. In effect, Ysabinda positions herself outside the conditions of trading enterprise that she has played no role in brokering. From her standpoint, what meaningful difference can be drawn between the Dutchman and her betrothed English captain, both European traders on her island? Recent literary scholarship has done much to shed light on how Dryden's most underexplored play responds to this question. Critical consensus converges around Ysabinda's role in the play, asserting the centrality of the native Amboyner in forging English *national* self-definition in opposition to the play's portrait of the dissembling Dutch rival. Ysabinda's role has been understood as symbolic; as an object of an Englishman's and a Dutchman's desire, she functions primarily to distinguish the national character of the English from that of the Dutch, especially as these national identities are expressed in very different modes of colonial engagement. The contest over and ultimately the violence against Ysabinda is "a metaphor for colonial aggression";[5] she "is herself a symptom of Dryden's recasting of international economic conflict into a binary political morality";[6] more, "this feminization of Asian culture in the figure of Ysabinda thus writes out of existence both Asian men and those Europeans who do not conform to a manichean politics of English virtue and Dutch vice."[7] While critics agree that conflicted projections of national ideology circulate in the play, Ysabinda's place in that conflict has largely been understood as helping to stabilize the difference the play aims to constitute. Ysabinda serves not as the sign of "Indian" difference or as the exoticized Other that raises the specter of miscegenation, familiar tropes of Anglo-Indian encounter in Restoration drama.[8] Instead, she has been understood as the fulcrum around which Anglo-Dutch national difference turns. In the play's terms, she is understood as keeping her promise to "make a difference"—a national difference between European men.

In this chapter I look at Ysabinda afresh to consider how positioning her not only within a matrix of masculine European desire but also alongside Julia, another female character in the play, complicates, on the one hand, the play's project of fashioning intra-European national difference and, on the other, critical understanding of the intersection of gender and national self-definition in the play. In so doing, I offer a reading that makes visible the structural contradictions in Ysabinda's subject position as the native object of Anglo-Dutch common interest in the form of sexual desire. Ysabinda's

story, one that unfolds both before and after the rape, taken together with
that of Julia's, the other, less-often noted female character on the island,
reveals a more complex, less successful vision of distinct national definition
than has heretofore been argued. If Ysabinda is a "symptom" of a kind, as
critics have argued, she proves a symptom of a broader cultural problem that
plagued Anglo-Dutch mercantile relations, politics, and identity in the Spice
Islands: the crisis of Anglo-Dutch interchangeability.

    En route to this rereading of Dryden's *Amboyna*, I argue that the enmity
that generated some of the early seventeenth century's most explosive rivalries
between the English and Dutch in the Spice Islands was catalyzed not by the
differences between the Dutch and English but by their apparent likeness.
Though often critically explored for England's encounter with the exotic
Other, English travel writing, journals, and letters abound also with stories
in which the English discover themselves rendered interchangeable with the
Dutch, both from the perspective of the indigenous population and from
that of other Europeans. Such stories of confused or mistaken identity have
garnered little critical attention in part because Anglo-Dutch relations in the
East Indies are often cast as a "rivalry" from the start.[9] As if forged in commercial competition, the English and the Dutch have too often been understood as essentially commercial identities, and the Anglo-Dutch relation
solely as mercantile or political in nature. Consequently, a powerful anxiety
that shaped this rivalry has been obscured: a sense—drawn with the English
and the Dutch into the East Indies, which experiences there magnified—that
cultural affinities, linguistic correspondences, and reciprocal political obligations between the English and the Dutch blurred distinctions between them.
As Anglo-Dutch relations are transplanted to the Spice Islands, so too is the
anxiety that the doppelgänger might be mistaken for the self.

    In early English accounts of voyages to the East Indies, the ubiquitous
figure of the Dutch proves a dangerously unstable signifier. In so being, the
Dutch function somewhat like the figure of the Spaniard in English New
World discovery narratives. As Louis Montrose has argued, in discourses of
New World discovery the Spaniard is the proximate Other who problematically shares an "ambient" "cultural, moral and intellectual" tradition with
the English. The Spaniard is the Other who is always already there:

    he is, at once, an authority to be followed, a villain to be punished,
    and a rival to be bested. For the Englishmen in the New World, the
    Spaniards are proximate figures of Otherness: in being Catholic,

Latin, and Mediterranean they are spiritually, linguistically, ethnically, and ecologically alien. At the same time, however, England and Spain are intertwined with each other in an encompassing European system of economic, social, and political structures and forces; and they share an ambient Christian and classical cultural, moral, and intellectual tradition. The sign of the Spaniard in English discovery texts simultaneously mediates and complicates any simple antinomy of European Self and American Other.[10]

Eric Griffin has recently nuanced this story, demonstrating the deep-seated English ambivalence about the figure of the Spaniard, which enabled England to emulate Spanish imperialism even as its Hispanophobic perspectives paradoxically emphasized the ethnic differences between the English and Spanish.[11] In English-authored East Indies travel narratives the Dutch are similarly ubiquitous and unsettling figures. However, the Dutch were imagined as being spiritually, linguistically, and ethnically similar to the English and, thus, emphatically unlike the Spaniard of New World discovery narratives, who was represented as alien to the English by these measures. As Protestant, northern, Teutonic neighbors, the Dutch share with the English affiliations, qualities, characteristics, even racialized histories,[12] which would have more definitively distinguished an Englishman from a Spaniard in a European context. Alison Games has recently argued for the importance of exploring the effects of an intertwining of enmity and amity in Anglo-Dutch oversees enterprises: "Relations forged in Europe and memories of solidarity against a common enemy followed the English and Dutch to their trading posts and commercial ventures on the other side of the globe. There a shared faith and history of alliance shaped hopes for support and shadowed the animosities of the age. Dutch and English relations vacillated constantly between different extremes, as commercial rivalry was always shaped, mediated, and muted by a common faith and an ongoing history of military alliance in Europe."[13] While commercial rivalry with the Dutch was certainly in play, early English accounts of Anglo-Dutch relations in the East Indies provide a more multivalent picture of how the English experienced their relations with the Dutch. On the one hand, the theater of Anglo-Dutch relations in the East was much like that back home, where the double process of identification with and differentiation from the Dutch characterized England's relations with its nearest neighbors. On the other hand, in the Spice Islands the perception of Anglo-Dutch interchangeability—a phenomenon explored as comic on

London stages and as a social and political advantage in London civic pageantry—proved an explosive problem as the minor differences that signify so
powerfully in the northern European context fail to secure ethnic, national,
or corporate difference abroad. Uprooted from the geographies of England
and the Netherlands, where minor differences, however fragile and fluidly
constituted, nonetheless signify, the English and the Dutch discover themselves compelled to identify—and create anew—signs of their difference.

Yet "Neere Neighbours," So Far from Home

At ten o'clock at night, on 5 August 1603, Dutch captains of the VOC
knocked on the door of the English house in Bantam, Java. The first ship
flying under a Dutch flag had arrived at the port city of Bantam in 1596,
prior to the formation of the VOC in 1602 and predating the EIC arrival by
six years. When the first of England's East India Company ships arrived in
the region, the English found themselves part of a volatile political arena. As
Michael Neill explains, English efforts to establish a factory at Bantam were
"complicated [by] already violent rivalries between the Dutch and Portuguese
trading empires, and at the local level between Chinese, Indian, and Javan
merchants, while it also added to the tensions created by local power struggles, including ethnic, factional, and dynastic rivalries that the newcomers
did not well understand."[14] Situated east of the city walls, Bantam's market
was an emporium for Asian worldly goods: "fine spices from the islands of
eastern Indonesia, Chinese silks and porcelain, Japanese lacquer, precious
stones, carpets, strange drugs and gourmet foods, dyestuffs, rare gums and
essences, scented woods, ingredients for incense and . . . a bewildering variety
of textiles from India."[15] The English, hoping to trade their heavy woolen
broadcloth for pepper, cloves, and other rare spices, rented space for their
factory west of the city walls, in the Chinese part of town and close to the
Dutch factory there. Half a world away from their northern European homelands, the Dutch and English discovered themselves intertwined by a historical sense of affiliation engendered by their proximate cultural relations back
home, and anew by their spatial propinquity on the island and their shared
status as strangers there.

   Edmund Scott's *An Exact Discourse of the Subtilties, Fashishions* [*sic*]*, Policies, Religion, and Ceremonies of the Indians as Well Chyneses as Javans, There
Abiding and Dweling . . . Since the 2 of February 1602 Until the 6 of October*

1605, published in London in 1606, provides one of our three earliest printed accounts of the English East India Company experience in the Indonesian archipelago.[16] Scott was among the less than two dozen factors left behind in Bantam by the first fleet of East India Company ships.[17] Following the death of two senior merchants, Scott became chief of the English factory, where he attempted to trade and preserve goods for the next English fleet. His account of his almost three years' residence on the island reveals just how perilous, complex, and explosively violent England's early Asian trading ventures were. On the evening of 5 August, however, the Dutch captains at the English house door came bearing goodwill toward the English. Under the cover of darkness the Dutch share intelligence with Scott about the ever-changing politics of commerce on the island: "There came to our House Capt. *Spylbeck*, Capt. *John Powlson*, and some other *Dutch* Captaines, who told us they had that day bin with the *Protector* about some busines, who asked them if they would take our parts, if he should do any violence to us? To the which they answered (as they sayd) that we and they were neere neighbours, wherefore they might not see us wronged."[18] The "Protector" was one of the island's principal governors with whom the Dutch, Portuguese, and English, as well as Chinese, Indian, and Javan merchants on the island, negotiated for trade privileges.[19] The suspicion that the protector might be plotting against English interests would have been grave news. Scott and his fellow Englishmen nonetheless take seriously the Dutch-delivered rumor, suggesting that in these early years of EIC and VOC interactions at Bantam, the English also believed themselves to be "neere neighbours" with the Dutch, both in a geographic and affective sense. As the Dutch captains make clear, Anglo-Dutch interests at Bantam are not simply aligned but intertwined.

Scott's *Discourse* is replete with evidence of Anglo-Dutch strategic and affective alliances. In addition to the "shared history of military alliance and Reformed Protestantism in Europe," which Games has argued "helped to produce the historical character [of] . . . the 'Dutch friend'" in many of England's overseas experiments, so too the realities on the ground at Bantam encouraged the English to foster this friendship.[20] The need for a strategic alliance is evident in the arrangement of the storage of goods and spices on the island. The English stocked their overflow of goods and pepper in the Dutch house, suggesting that there was no distinct separation between the Dutch and English commercial infrastructure on Bantam.[21] An attack against the English house might snowball into an attack against the Dutch. Therefore, the English and Dutch volunteered to defend one another's property when they found themselves assaulted by other players in the region. Scott reports that on an evening when the Chinese were suspected of setting fire to the English house, "the *Dutch* merchaunts . . . came verie kindely with their weapons, and sware they would live and die in our quarrell" (Fɪv). The Dutch are not only tactical allies, but trusted messengers who bring important news from England. It was, in fact, the Dutch who "tolde us of the death of the late *Queene Elizabeth,* and of the great plague and sicknesse that had beene over all Christendome. . . . [T]hey tolde us the king of *Scots* was crowned, and that our land was in peace, which was exceeding great comfort unto us" (Kɪv). Acting as strategic allies, the Dutch offer military and infrastructural support; as neighbors, they bring news of "great comfort" to the English. Such episodes suggest that the Dutch at Bantam were not merely rivals in trade; they also provided an essential lifeline to the English as they adopted the role of the helpful neighbor, and sometimes friend.

Affective bonds were displayed and nurtured in Anglo-Dutch social exchange on the island too. Scott recounts how the Dutch offered succor when his factors were weakened by disease: "We are very much beholding to this Generall [Wyborne van Warwycke] for Wine, Bread, and many other necessaries and curtisies received of him." More than victuals, the Dutch general also shared conversation and friendship with Scott's men: "He would often tell us how *Sir Richard Luson* relieved him when he was likely to perish in the Sea: for the which (he would say) he was bound to be kind to *English* men where soever he met them: and to speake the thruth [*sic*], there was nothing in his Shippes for the comfort of sicke men, but wee might commaund it, as if it had been our owne. Also, he in his owne person did verie much reverence the *Queenes* Majestie of *England,* when he talked of her" (A4r–Bɪv). So closely bonded were Van Warwycke and the English merchants that when an Englishman at Bantam knew himself to be dying, "hee thought it good . . . to spend the rest of his time with *Generall Warwicke*" (Bɪr). Upon the Englishman's death, General van Warwycke "caused [him] to be honored with a voley of Shot and Pikes, the which with the Cullours were trayled upon the ground, according to the order of Souldiers buriall" (Bɪr). So imbricated are the English and Dutch at Bantam that they participate in one another's ceremonies of honor and mourning. Not all Anglo-Dutch relations were catalyzed by crises, however. The groups regularly dined together, fostering a sense of friendship between them: "after dynner the Hollanders and wee parted exceeding great friends" (Eɪv); "the 8. of September, the Dutch Merchants invited our Generall and all his Merchants & Masters to a feast, where there was great cheere, and also great friendshippe was made betweene us" (M1r); "the third day of October our Generall made a feast for his farewell, whereunto hee invited the *Dutch-Admirall*, with also all the rest of his *Captaines, Maisters*, and *Marchants*, where we were all exceeding merry, and great frendshippe was made betweene us" (M2r).

These snapshots of strategic alliance, festive merriment, and displays of "great friendshippe" bring into focus a picture of neighbors bonded in affectionate alliance. As we have seen, the notion that the English and the Dutch were near neighbors was a long, continuous thread in their centuries-long history. When the Dutch report telling the protector of Bantam that they and the English are "neere neighbors," the Dutch are not speaking in the idiom of local politics or with the lexicon of commercial rivalry; instead, they are deliberately calling up the idiom of Anglo-Dutch Protestant alliance back home. In this way, the Dutch and the English attempt to transplant to the East Indies a conceptual framework that had long structured their relations. In the Anglo-Dutch context of northern Europe, "neere neighbours" are those whose proximity implies shared political, religious, even cultural investments, as well as reciprocal obligations. And yet, just as they are near, neighbors are also—ideally—just beyond the home. When the English and Dutch use the phrase to characterize their relations abroad, they imply that theirs remains a relation defined at once by the geographic proximity of their homelands, by affection and bonds of reciprocal obligation, and by the important recognition that there remains some distinction between them. "Neere neighbors" are not the same as kin.

Even as the English and Dutch share a degree of communion in their struggles for survival at Bantam, they are troubled by events that imply a lack of distinction between them. In the context of Reformation politics of the European north, English and Dutch identities had long been closely approximated. The proximate identities of the English and Dutch, especially "the Dutch" who resided on English soil, were regularly represented on the English stage as fallible, fluid, potentially counterfeited, or unintentionally jumbled. Both English and Dutch accounts of the first two decades of VOC and EIC engagement in Asia report episodes in which the English and Dutch experience not merely a blurring of identities but a complete loss of distinction between them. Strategic alliances between the English and Dutch, their social interconnectedness, and their similar position as trading strangers in the region reinforced perceptions of similitude. These near neighbors, in other words, discover themselves rendered as disquieting doubles.

"They Thought Wee Had Beene *Hollenders*"

In February 1605, the Englishman Sir Henry Middleton, general of the second East India Company voyage, sailed his ships, the *Dragon* and *Ascension*, into view of the island of Amboyna. Situated farther east than Java, Amboyna, an island rich in clove production, sat just south of the Moluccas, also called the Malukan Islands: Ternate, Tidore, Moti, Makian, and Bacan, each ruled by local kings or chieftans. Together these islands, and the Banda group (Lontor, Neira, Api, Ai and Run), constituted the "Spice Islands" of eastern Indonesia.[22] The events that transpired off the coast of Amboyna are narrated in *The Last East-Indian Voyage* (1606), an anonymous account of Middleton's ventures to the East Indies published for his brother-in-law, Walter Burre, for whom Edmund Scott's *Exact Discourse* was also published the same year.[23] *The Last East-Indian Voyage* recounts the day of the crew's arrival at Amboyna when, before Middleton's men even set anchor off the island, an "Indian" approaches the fleet to deliver a letter from the Portuguese captain, controller of the island's fort and the clove trade. The story, a tale of a missive delivered into the wrong hands, foretells much about the potential challenges the English would face in the East Indies: "The tenth day wee weyed anker, and stood to the Easter[n] ende of *Amboyna*, and came to an anker in an hundered fadomes water, fayre by the shoare, fayre by a towne called *Mamalla*. Before we came to an anker, there came an *Indian* aboard of us which spake good Portugese, also there came a letter to our Generall from the Captaine of *Amboyna*, but it was directed to the Generall of the *Hollenders*, or any other Captaine of his fleete, supposing us to be *Hollenders*. The effect of his Letter was, to desire them to certifie them of some newes of *Portingale*" (D2r). That the Portuguese misidentified the English as Dutch "was not uncommon in the early days" of East Asian intra-European encounter, according to Rui Manuel Loureiro, historian of Portuguese commercial involvement in Asia.[24] This story compounds the source of mistaken identification: both the Portuguese, who sent the letter from the shores of Amboyna, and the messenger, who boards the English ship, apparently are unable to tell an Englishman from a Hollander. If distance befogged the Portuguese view, proximity did little to clear things up from the Indian's perspective. Once aboard the English ship, the Portuguese-speaking Indian apparently did not see or hear anything to cause him to hesitate before delivering the letter to the men he assumed were Hollanders. If the English were sailing with their flags flying, if they first spoke English to the Indian stranger, then these signs failed to give the messenger pause. In accepting the letter, perhaps hoping to gain some beneficial intelligence thereby, the English general happily plays the part of the Hollander that the Portuguese captain and the Indian messenger suppose him to be. In so doing, the English turn a case of mistaken identity to their advantage.

Instances of mistaken identification at sea were not limited to the point of view of the Portuguese or to that of the indigenous peoples of the Spice Islands. *The Last East-Indian Voyage* reveals that in battles along the coasts of the Moluccan Islands the Dutch themselves could mistake an English vessel for their own. Before the English arrived in the region, the Dutch built an alliance with the sultan, or "king," of Ternate against the sultan of Tidore, who was allied with the Portuguese. The Dutch and the Portuguese were engaged in a battle for trade dominance in the region, one in which the English—with fewer ships, fewer men, and less financing—could not realistically compete. As Middleton and his men sailed toward the clove island of Tidore in hope of negotiating trade relations there, the author reports that the English spotted seven Tidore galleys "rowing betwixt us and the shoare, to chase the *Turnatanes* Galleys . . . they in the *Tarnate* Galleys did all they might to overtake our Ship weaving [*sic*] with two or three flags at once to tarie for them, which our Generall seeing, caused the top-sayles to be strucke, and lay by the lee to know what was the matter" (E2r). Hastening to the side of the English ship, "the King of *Tarnata*, and divers of his Noble-men, and three Dutch Marchants . . . shewed themselves to us looking pale, and desired our Generall for Gods sake, to rescue the caracole that came after us, wherein were divers *Dutch-men*, which were like to fall into the enemies handes, where there was no hope of mercie, but present death: whereupon our Generall caused our Gunner to shoote at the *Tydore* Galleys" (E2r). At the time of this fray, the English were aligned neither with the sultan of Tidore nor the sultan of Ternate. But in this moment, as the pale-with-fear Dutchmen approach the English ship and plead for aid, the English position themselves as allies of the Dutch and, by extension, allies of the Ternatans. Believing many more Dutchmen to be aboard other Ternate galleys under attack, and that if the Dutch were captured they would have "no hope of mercie, but present death," the English turn their guns on the Tidore galleys that pursue them. As it turns out, however, "there were no *Dutch-men*" on the Ternate galleys, "as they [the Dutch had] reported, but all *Tarnatanes*" (E3v). Intending to defend the Dutch, the English instead turned their weapons on the Tidorans in defense of the Ternatans. Not only were there no Dutchmen facing "present death," as the Dutchmen reported, but their desperate approach to the English ship was, the Dutch later claim, itself a case of mistaken identification: "The Dutch-marchants comming aboard, told our Generall they thought wee had beene *Hollenders*, and bound for *Tarnata*, and that was the cause they had put themselves in such danger" (E3v).

Whether the Dutch tricked the English into coming to their defense against the Tidore galleys or whether they indeed believed the English ship to have been their own vessel in danger of attack, the text does not ponder. That the explanation—"they thought wee had beene *Hollenders*"—raises no suspicion in the English text suggests that the author found the Dutch story plausible. Such stories from *The Last East-Indian Voyage* reveal that in the context of the East Indies, mistaking an English for a Dutch ship, an Englishman for a Hollander, was a reasonable mistake, for Europeans as well as islanders.

Letters written by Dutch factors in the East to VOC members in the Netherlands describe similar episodes of mistaken identity.[25] Dutch letters spanning the years 1602–1626 report numerous problems relating to the perception that the English and the Dutch might unwittingly or strategically stand in as one another. In a letter written by Jeronimus Woudaraer on 5 June 1602, we learn that the Dutch were concerned that the Portuguese were deliberately conflating English and Dutch identities to gain a trade advantage with China and Japan. Woudaraer relays a story told to him by the king of Linoa Basso, with whom the Dutch were allied against the Portuguese. He reports that the king admonished the Dutch "that we should be careful, whenever we came, either in China or in Jappan," because a Portuguese priest had "tried to make [the Japanese] believe . . . that we were English and . . . aliens of God's commandments and of faith, [and] had assisted the King, who was heathen" (2.VIII). In an atmosphere of constantly rotating players, the Portuguese strategize to secure trade relations with Japan by deliberately conflating the English and Dutch into one group of English "heathens." More than a case of mistaken identity, in this instance the Portuguese jumble the Dutch and English with the intent of stirring up trouble for the "English[ed]" Dutchmen. If, as the letter goes on to suggest, the Japanese had poor relations with the English and if the Portuguese priest could persuade the Japanese that the Dutch "were English," then, the letter forewarns, the Portuguese might maintain a position of strength in Japan and the Dutch could find themselves at a particular disadvantage: "The same Japonese also advised us not to come in Japan, for the King would make thieves [of] all of us, as he had once with some English three years ago, who had visited that country" (2.VIII). The problem, which Woudaraer's letter anticipates but does not explore, is how the Dutch might compel the Japanese to recognize the difference between a Dutch and an English crew. Once cast as the English, how might the Dutch, in effect, reclaim their status and signification as Dutch?

Strategic counterfeiting of identity became part of the game in the East Indies as the English learned that they could "play Dutch" both at sea and on land. In his letter written from Bantam to the director at Amsterdam (15 December 1616), the Dutchman P. Van der Broeck writes, "The English act very often in our name here in the Indies, as appears herefrom and as I also heard they had hoisted our flag when at Mocha" (4.LXXVIII). Almost two decades into trade relations in the Indonesian archipelago, the Dutch continue to express concern that the "English act very often in our name." At sea too the English apparently counterfeited their national and corporate identity by flying the Dutch flag. That one European company might fly the flag of another was, as the tone of Van der Broeck's letter suggests, an affront to the intra-European politics of Asian trade. However, it was doubtless a savvy strategy for securing safe passage through a region so divided—island by island—in their European alliances. If by taking on another's moniker or flag, or somewhat more opportunistically accepting a misdirected letter, one could disorder the signifiers of ethnic and corporate identity, then there was little hope that either company might gain a definitive stronghold in the region.

What then could be done about such representational confusion? How might the problem of the representational legitimacy of national and corporate identity be redressed? Scott's *Discovery* offers a rare and colorful snapshot of the English response to the problem. Scott and his men stage a pageant—what I characterize as a "ceremony of distinction"—that showcases both the props of English nationhood and ethnic signifiers of Englishness. Scripted with the indigenous audience in mind, staged and performed on a specific ceremonial date, and consciously constructed down to every detail in an attempt to reveal an essential English difference, the ceremony is a highly theatrical production.

A Ceremony of Distinction at Bantam

Ten months into their stay at Bantam, late in October 1603, Edmund Scott foresees that he and his men face imminent danger due to the changing political landscape of the island and to a misunderstanding about who's who among its European strangers:

> About this time also, there was much falling out betweene the *Hollanders* and the Countrey people, by meanes of the rude behaviour of some of their Marriners, and manie of them were stabbed in the eveninges: and at that time, the common people knew not us from the *Hollanders,* for both they and wee were called by the name of *English*-men, by reason of their usurping our name at their first coming thither to trade: and as wee passed along the Stree[t]s wee might heare the people in the Market rayling and exclaiming on the *English*-men, although they meant the *Hollanders:* wherefore fearing some of our men might be slaine in stead of them, wee beganne to thinke how wee might make our selves knowne from the *Hollanders.* (C3v)

Scott paints a scene of social and political disorder sparked by the usurpation of the "name of *English*-men."[26] Cast as usurpers, the Dutch attain illegitimate power by operating as Englishmen. In so doing, they subvert the ability of the island's real Englishmen to authenticate their political, commercial, even social identities. Importantly, this usurpation is not strictly a displacement per se. The English at Bantam have not been ousted. Rather, the more troubling problem in need of redress is that the English find themselves implicated in and defined by the actions of the Dutch masquerading as Englishmen.

While usurpation conventionally implies the replacement of one body by another within a strict framework of power—that of kingship, for instance—here the act of usurpation pressures the framework itself. Names, not bodies, have been usurped, kicking up a crisis regarding the very definition of Englishness. The manner of usurpation matters to what is at stake in Scott's account of this crisis. An example from the London theater clarifies the important and nuanced difference in the kind of usurpation that Scott's performance attempts to redress. On the early modern London stage, interchangeability is often dramatized as the replacement of one body for another. To take one well-known instance, in Shakespeare's *The Comedy of Errors* the play's twin Dromios share a name and visage, facilitating its plot of mistaken identities. So long as the two Dromios do not appear to the same character *at the same time*—as long as both bodies are not present together on the stage—episodes of mistaken identity compound. However, when "these two Dromios, one in semblance" appear together in act 5, scene 1, their double-bodied presence catalyzes the comic conclusion (5.1.349).[27] Even as Dromio of Ephesus recognizes himself in the face of Dromio of Syracuse ("methinks you are my glass and not my brother"), the Dromios are set straight, realigned with their original, unmistaken selves (5.1.419). As a comic device, it is not that the play effaces the fact of there being two Dromios that makes the comedy work; instead, it is the clever rotating of one body into the position of the other that lends the plot its comic charm. In contrast to the logic of replacement that structures Shakespeare's comedy, the performance that Scott and his men enact attempts to avert a tragedy induced by an operation of supplementation. In usurping the name "English-men," the Dutch have added too broad a range of meaning to the category. In short, to be an Englishman at Bantam has lost the definitional and representational legitimacy that makes the category "English" mean anything at all, from the English point of view.[28] From Scott's perspective, if the actions of the Dutch can define the "English-men" at Bantam, then the English have lost more than their commercial footing there. This kind of usurpation threatens not individual identities but national categories, and it is this category confusion that Scott and his men design their performance to redress.

Scott's men select the anniversary of Queen Elizabeth I's coronation to stage a pageant designed to impress on Bantam's "countrey people" the English difference. Significantly, the English do not first attempt to explain their difference from the Dutch—they do not, for instance, send an ambassador to the king of Bantam with letters from the queen—instead they take up props, put on new apparel, and, like players at a theater, *perform* their difference:

> Wee all suted our selves in new Apparrell of Silke, and made us all Scarffes of white and redd Taffata, beeing our Countries Cullours. Also, we made a Flagge with the redde Crosse thorow the middle: and because wee that were the Marchants would be knowne from our men, wee edged our Scarffes with a deepe Fringe of Golde, and that was our difference.
>
> Our day beeing come, wee set up our Banner of *Sainct Gorge* upon the top of our House, and with our Drumme and Shott wee marched up and downe within our owne grounde, beeing but fourteene in number, wherefore wee could march but single one after another. (C3v)

The sign of Saint George hoisted atop the English house, a sartorial display of England's "Countries Collours," the sound of drums and shot, together with the marching bodies of fourteen Englishmen on "our owne grounde" at Bantam, become the signifiers of Englishness. As if restaging a pageant for the queen's royal progress through London, the English use familiar, iconic signifiers of Englishness; nothing here is invented specifically for the Javan audience in Bantam. Even as the express agenda of this ceremony of distinction is to make a difference between the English and Dutch on the island, internal differences of rank are also in play. Marked by "a deepe Fringe of Golde," the merchants among the fourteen parading Englishmen are determined that rank be visibly manifest. Content that their gilded scarves represent the hierarchy among the English, Scott concludes, "that was our difference." Despite the seemingly more pressing issue that prompted the performance—that the English are not known from the Hollanders—the English ceremony at once stages both international and intranational codes of difference.

The English ceremony is a success insofar as it draws the audience it was designed to entice. Scott continues: "The *Sabyndar,* and divers of the chiefest of the Land, hearing our Peeces, came to see us, and to enquire the cause of our triumph. Wee told them, that that day six and fourtie yeare our *Queene* was Crowned, wherefore all *English*-men, in what Countrey soever they were, did triumph on that day. Hee greatly commended us for having our *Prince* in reverence in so farre a Countrey" (C3r). Having drawn a considerable audience, the English performance transforms into a kind of animated *Wunderkammer* in which the English on display are prompted to respond to the curiosities their performance has engendered in the Bantam audience: "Many others did aske us, Why the *English*-men at the other House did not so? Wee told them they were no *English*-men but *Hollanders,* and that they had no King, but their Land was ruled by *Governours.* Some would reply againe and say, They named them selves to be *English*-men at the first, and therefor they tooke them to be *English*-men: but we would tell them againe, they were of another Countrey neere *England,* and spake an other Language; and that if they did talke with them now, they should heare they were of an other Nation" (C3r). When an emphasis on sartorial style fails to make clear the English difference from the Dutch, government and language emerge as seemingly self-evident and stable signifiers of English and Dutch difference. The English pageant is itself an expression of pride in English monarchal government; the Hollanders' lack of pageantry on this particular day, by contrast, not only marks them as a people from "another Nation," but from a nation of another kind, one that "had no King" but is "ruled by Governours." The English ceremony becomes an expression of English commitment to their "Prince" and, as a ritual of remembrance, participation in the ceremony is meant to differentiate members of the nation of England from those who merely counterfeit that membership in name. In the absence of such rulers, however, the notion that a people might be ruled differently by a monarch than by a governor was rather an abstraction. Despite the ceremoniously articulated distinction between the political landscapes of England and Holland, the Bantam audience's questions continue, revealing, unsurprisingly, that the attempt to attach English identity to an absent monarch fails to clarify the difference between authentic and inauthentic Englishmen at Bantam.

Scott's men shift emphasis from the sartorial, emblematic, and political to the ethnolinguistic. Surely, Scott seems to believe, language will make clear their essential difference from the Dutch. For the reader of Scott's narrative, this registers as a jarring reminder that such a difference has all along been in play. When the English first arrived to Bantam, they negotiated the polyglot commercial atmosphere in Portuguese; since the Portuguese had captured Malacca in 1511, the language was familiar to many in the region. But then the English began learning Malay, the lingua franca used by the Chinese prior to Europe's arrival in Southeast Asia.[29] In a city that drew "Arab, Turkish, Persian, Gujarati, Tamil, Bengali, Malay, Javanese and Chinese merchants," as well as the English and Dutch, the linguistic exchange must have been as rich as the commercial.[30] And yet nowhere in Scott's recordings of the many exchanges he and his men have with the Dutch at Bantam is a linguistic divide between the English and the Dutch apparent. To the contrary, in all the cultural and commercial exchanges that transpire between the English and the Dutch, nowhere does Scott report a communication breakdown due to a failure of translation. What the text puts into evidence instead is the fluency of Anglo-Dutch linguistic exchange. On the page, the English and Dutch appear to sound the same. Of course, the English and Dutch did speak different languages. However, the question of whether the difference between English and Dutch registered as a salient difference in an environment where Chinese, Japanese, Portuguese, Malay, English, and Dutch were spoken—to name only a few of the world's languages spoken at Bantam—does not worry Scott. Unlike his contemporaries writing for the London stage, Scott was confident that the linguistic difference between English and Dutch was robust; it thus should be perceptible.

The pageant travels from the English grounds at Bantam to the town and marketplace: "In the after noone I caused our men to walke abrode the Towne and the Market, whereby the people might take notice of them. / Their redd and white Scarffes and Hatbandes, made such a shew, that the Inhabitants of those partes had never seene the like: so that ever after that day, wee were knowne from the *Hollanders*; and manie times the Children in the Streetes would runne after us crying, *Oran Enggrees bayck, oran Hollanda iahad:* which is, The *English*-men are good, the *Hollanders* are naught" (C3r). While in Bantam the performance was a success, from Scott's point of view, he expresses concern that the display of English difference on which that success depended risked rendering his crew "fantasticall" in England: "I stood in doubt many times," he acknowledges, "whether I should put this in practise or no, for feare of being counted fantasticall, when it should be knowne in *England*" (C3r). This anxiety is itself characteristically English. The English had long worried about their susceptibility to what John Deacon in *Tobacco Tortured* (1616) characterized as a "fantastic foolerie," a particularly English penchant for all things foreign:

> Our carelesse entercourse of trafficking with the contagious corrup-
> tions, and customes of forreine nations . . . from whence cometh it
> now to passe that so many of our English-mens minds are thus
> terriblie *Turkished* with *Mahometan* trumperies; thus rufully *Roman-
> ized* with superstitious relickes; thus treacherously *Italianized* with
> sundry antichristian toyes; thus spitefully *Spanished* with superfluous
> pride; thus fearefully *Frenchized* with filthy prostitutions; thus fan-
> tastically *Flanderized* with flaring net-works to catch English fooles;
> thus huffingly *Hollandized* with ruffian-like loome-works, and other
> like Ladified fooleries; thus greedily *Germandized* with a most glut-
> tenous manner of gormandizing; thus desperately *Danished* with a
> swine-like swilling and quaffing; thus sculkingly *Scotized* with Mach-
> iavillian projects; thus inconstantly *Englished* with every new fantas-
> ticall foolerie.[31]

As Scott reflected on the show that he and his spiffed-up crew staged for the Bantam audience, he expresses a characteristically English anxiety: that accusations of "fantasticall foolerie" might be cast against them. In his case, however, it is not the Englishmen's taste for the foreign but the anxiety that

that which is foreign might masquerade as English which prompts the pageant. The display of English fashion, an emphasis on color and icons, a display of hierarchy within the group, and the phonetics lesson that the English offer to the people of Bantam attempt to clarify essential English identity. He and his men risk "being counted fantastical"—in other words they risk self-parody—in order that they might stabilize the national categories too much in flux. Unlike Deacon's critique of English character, then, Scott and his men aim to delimit the category "English-men" to its rightful bearers. From Scott's point of view, the "present danger" of Anglo-Dutch interchangeability at Bantam is not the result of English taste for things foreign; it is a result of the Dutch "usurping our name."

An Exact Discourse offers a window onto one way in which the English attempted to disentangle English from Dutch identity in the Moluccas. Though Scott declares his crew's performance a success, the text belies this conclusion when, at the beginning of the New Year, 1604, Scott writes: "Because at that time there was much quarrelling and brabling betweene the *Javans,* and the *Hollanders:* I charged our men that if they were sent out in the evening about any businesse they should take their weapons with them, for feare some *Javans* that knewe them not, might doe them a mischiefe in the darke" (D2r). Composed just four months after the ceremony of distinction, this entry reveals that the Hollanders and the Englishmen apparently remain more alike than different from the perspective of the Javans. Neither a sartorial nor linguistic display of Englishness will spare Scott's English crew from Javan "mischiefe." Despite their "fantasticall" attempts to make their English difference known, the English find themselves compelled to live and die in the Hollanders' quarrel because, as they discover time and again, they are not always clearly "knowne from the *Hollanders.*"

Both *An Exact Discourse* and *The Last East-Indian Voyage* reveal that, when abroad, the English and Dutch are vexed by the problem of a seeming sameness. For the English, a long-standing characterization of the Dutch as, on the one hand, friends, nearest neighbors, and allies and, on the other hand, enemies, dissemblers, and usurpers featured prominently in reports regarding the competitive trading context of the East Indies. These contradictions are symptomatic of the cultural double vision engendered by and entailed in representations of Anglo-Dutch relations in the period. Such reports might have more immediately cast the Dutch, far more simply, as mere rivals. However, even after the Dutch usurpation of the name "Englishmen," Scott continues to imagine Anglo-Dutch relations not as a binary rivalry between two stable kinds but as a relation animated by distinctions and approximations, disputes and affections. In his own words, Scott makes sense of the push and pull of Anglo-Dutch relations at Bantam: "for it is to bee noted, that though wee were mortall enemies in our trade, yet in all other matters wee were friends, and would have lived and dyed one for the other" (H3r). Rivals in trade, friends in all other matters: this construction suggests that, for Scott, English engagement at Bantam was not entirely structured by trade and commercial enterprise. In the interstitial spaces between a trading life—at dinners, during funerals, and in the exchange of news from home— the Dutch remained vital friends. Despite the many instances of mistaken and usurped identity, Scott's cultural double vision helped him to make sense of the new world the Dutch and English were navigating. The representation of the doubly figured Dutch in Scott's text is precisely what complicates English expressions of national self-definition. Since English alliance with, proximity to, and social intercourse with the Dutch rendered them an affili-ated crew of trading strangers, so long as the English considered the Dutch friends "in all . . . matters" other than trade, the English and Dutch were, from the English perspective, primarily closely knit allies and, from the per-spective of the native Javans and "Indians," an interchangeable cast of Euro-pean trading strangers. If the English were to distinguish themselves more decisively from the Dutch in the Moluccas, expressions of rivalry would have to outweigh acts of neighborly alliance. A definitive expression of English difference would have to emerge in repeated and sustained opposition to the Dutch.

From "Tender Amity" to "Unjust, Cruell, and Barbarous Proceedings": The Amboyna Massacre of 1623

Situated southeast of Java, among the central Moluccas, the island of Amboyna was one of the few places on earth suitable for clove cultivation. The Dutch VOC had reached Amboyna in the year 1599, catalyzing a violent intra-European contest for domination of the island's rich clove harvests. In the European marketplace cloves yielded twice the profit of pepper and the Dutch were eager to secure an advantage as importers of this rare spice.[32] Upon their arrival, the Dutch established alliances with the Ambonese against Portuguese traders who had built a fort on the island's southern peninsula. By 1605, the Dutch captured the fort and moved in as the island's primary

European traders.[33] Nestled midway along the island's southern leg, the Dutch fort would become the stage for the most notorious massacre of English merchants to occur in the East Indies in the seventeenth century. The "Amboyna massacre" transpired in February 1623 and quickly sparked a massive publication campaign that began with a three-part pamphlet: the English "relation" of events at Amboyna (*A True Relation of the Unjust, Cruell, and Barbarous Proceedings Against the English at Amboyna*), the VOC justification of its actions (*A True Declaration of the News That Came out of the East Indies with the Pinnace Called the Hare*), and the English East India Company's rebuttal of the VOC account (*an Answer to the same Pamphlet*).[34] Upward of two thousand copies of the 1624 three-part pamphlet circulated in England; another one thousand were translated into Dutch and sent into the Netherlands.[35] From its inception as a newsworthy event, the Amboyna massacre was structured as a discursive debate among nations and their corporate bodies.[36] For both the English and the Dutch, "Amboyna" fast became a tragic keyword in the lexicon of Anglo-Dutch relations.

Throughout the seventeenth century the massacre was serialized in pamphlets, recounted in ballads, censured in plays, and depicted in the visual arts.[37] Even sermons were preached about it.[38] In English versions, the Dutch are almost always represented as figures of ingratitude, dissembling friends driven by self-interest. Even so, the earliest publications express ambivalence about whether to consider the massacre a Dutch plot or that of a few misguided "boors." The letter to the reader that opens the *True Relation,* authored "by the English East-India Company," begins on a reticent note: "The truth is, the English East-India Company have ever been very tender of the ancient amity and good correspondence held between this Realm and the Neatherlands [*sic*], and have been very loth, by divulging of the private injuries done them by the Neatherlands East-India Company to give the least occasion of any distaste or disaffection, which might haply growe between these two Nations, for the sake of and on behalf of the two Companies respectively" (A1r–A2v). Until the recent discovery of a Dutch publication of events on Amboyna, the author continues, the EIC had "contented themselves with informing his Majestie and his Honourable Privy Councell" of their grievances against the Dutch "privately in writing" in order not to "stir up or breed ill blood between these Nations, which are otherwise tied in so many reciprocall obligations." The ambivalence expressed in the letter is symptomatic of the difficulty the English faced when attempting to revise their double perspective on the Dutch. In *A True Relation* (1624), the author separates the public politics of the English and Dutch nations from the "private" politics of their fledgling corporations, thus drawing a distinction between national and corporate identities. This division holds open a gap between the politics and policies of the Dutch nation and the "private" injuries executed by the servants of the VOC: "Thus, Reader, thou seest . . . what now enforceth the Dutch East-India Company, or their servants in the Indies, against the common *Genius* of their Nation, and the wonted firm affection between these two Nations mutually, thus to degenerate, and break out into such strange and incredible outrages against their neerest allies and best-deserving friends" (B1v). Though bound by "firm affection" and "otherwise tied in so many reciprocall obligations" in the context of northern Europe, the English characterize themselves as "grosely overtopped, outraged & vilified" by the Dutch in the East Indies. As national neighbors the Dutch and the English are "best-deserving friends," but as corporate bodies the Dutch are degenerate and strange, while the English characterize themselves as lawful and innocent of corruption.

The text also underscores a difference between English and Dutch models of colonial engagement, a point made expressly in the letter to the reader (which appears in both the 1624 *True Relation* and in the 1672 *Emblem of Ingratitude*, two texts Dryden may have had at arm's reach as he composed his *Amboyna* for the English stage). The letter urges the reader to "consider the different end and design of the English and Dutch Companies trading in the Indies":

> The English being Subjects of a peaceable Prince, that hath enough
> of his own, and is therewith content, without affecting of new
> acquests; have aimed at nothing in their East-*India* Trade, but a
> Lawful and competent gain by Commerce and Traffick with the
> people of those parts. And although they have in some places
> builded Forts, and setled some strength, yet that hath not been done
> by force or violence, against the good will of the Magistrates or
> people of the Country; but with their desire, consent, and good
> liking, for the security only of the Trade, and upon the said Magis-
> trate and peoples voluntary yielding themselves under the obedience
> and Sovereignty of the Crown of England; their own antient [*sic*]
> Laws, Customes and Priviledges, nevertheless reserved. . . . On the
> other side, the Netherlanders, from the beginning of their Trade in
> the *Indies*, not contented with the ordinary course of a fair and free

Commerce, invaded divers Islands, took some Forts, built others;
and laboured nothing more, than the Conquests of Countries, and
the acquiring of new Dominion.[39]

A True Relation seeks to construct a reader who identifies the Dutch not
ethnically (by what they eat or wear, how they talk, or where and how they
worship—those minor differences that prove such a rich resource for early
seventeenth-century comic playwrights). Instead, the text encourages the
reader to identify the Dutch by what they do abroad. John Dryden's theatrical rendition of the massacre at Amboyna will amplify similar binaries of
English and Dutch colonial engagement. While for the "peaceable" English,
whose prince "hath enough of his own," moderation and collaboration are
the ideals of colonial engagement, for the Netherlanders, "conquest" and
full "dominion" are the colonial imperatives. Insofar as the relation between
corporate bodies comes to stand in for Anglo-Dutch relations as a whole, *A
True Relation* works to shift attention away from approximations, similitudes,
and correspondences to draw stark oppositions instead between the English
and Dutch.

The English version of events begins on the evening of 11 February 1623,
when a "*Japoner* soldier," "walking in the night upon the wall" of the Dutch
castle of Amboyna, "came to the Sentinell (being a *Hollander*,) and there,
amongst other talk, asked him some questions touching the strength of the
Castle, and the people that were therein" (*A True Relation* B4v). The Japanese
soldier's questions spark suspicion among the Dutch that the Japanese of the
island are conspiring with the English to take over the castle.[40] The Japanese
soldier is tortured and, in an effort to save his own life, confirms Dutch
suspicions. Days pass and Abel Price, a prisoner in the Dutch castle, is also
tortured into "confess[ing] what ever they asked him." With two torture-
coerced confessions on record, the Dutch lay a trap for the English captain
Towerson. They invite Towerson to bring his men "to speak with the Governour in the Castle" (B4v), and, when the English captain and his company
arrive, they are forcibly imprisoned and their merchandise, including the
"Books, Writings, and other things in the *English* house," is confiscated. One
by one Towerson's men are tortured into giving testimony that confirms
Dutch suspicions that Towerson was masterminding a joint English and Japanese plot to overthrow the Dutch on Amboyna.[41] What follows paints a vivid
and horrifying image of the suffering the English and Japanese endured at
the hands of their Dutch examiners:

First they hoised him up by the hands with a cord on a large dore, where they made him fast upon two Staples of Iron; fixt on both sides, at the top of the dore posts, haling his hands one from the other as wide as they could stretch. Being thus made fast, his feete hung some two foote from the ground; which also they stretcht asunder as far as they would retch, and so made them fast beneath unto the dore-trees on each side. Then they bound a cloth about his necke and face so close, that little or no water could go by. That done, they poured the water softly upon his head untill the cloth was full, up to the mouth and nostrills, and somewhat higher; so that he could not draw breath, but he must withall suck-in the water: which being still continued to be poured in softly, forced all his inward parts, came out of his nose, eares, and eyes, and often as it were stifling and choaking him, at length took away his breath, & brought him to a swoune or fainting. They then tooke him quickly downe, and made him vomit up the water. . . . Afterwards they hoised him up againe as before, and then burnt him with lighted candles in the bottome of his feete, untill the fat dropt out the candles; yet then applied they fresh lights unto him. They burnt him also under the elbowes, and in the palmes of the hands; likewise under the arme-pitts, until his inwards might evidently be seene. (10–11)

This scene of immolation and drowning was graphically illustrated in *A True Relation* (Figure 30). Here, the English double vision that so often held Anglo-Dutch similitudes and differences in tension is expunged, replaced by an image of "barbarous" Dutch cruelty. With nearly three thousand copies of the 1624 pamphlet in circulation across England and the Netherlands, the woodcut frontispiece fast became an unforgettable emblem of Anglo-Dutch colonial rivalry. In the foreground (bottom third) of the illustration, an Englishman appears to plead for his life while in the background another Englishman is tortured simultaneously by water and fire. The 1624 frontispiece depicts two Dutchmen torturing one Englishman. Another illustration multiplies the Dutch agents of torture, filling the page with a more theatrical scene (Figure 31). No fewer than eight Dutch agents immolate a single Englishman while the faces of the other prisoners, presumably English and Japanese, peer from behind bars beneath the floor. These differences in visual representation (the depiction of two "barbarous" Dutchmen versus that of a

FIGURE 30. Frontispiece, *A True Relation of the Unjust, Cruell, and Barbarous Proceedings against the English at Amboyna* (1624).

By permission of the Folger Shakespeare Library.

Figure 31. Frontispiece, *A True Relation of the Unjust, Cruell, and Barbarous Proceedings against the English at Amboyna* (1632).

Courtesy of the Master and Fellows of Trinity College, Cambridge, UK.

whole gang of Dutchmen torturing a single Englishman) point to the ambiva-lence I have explored in the texts themselves: whether to attribute the Amboyna massacre to a few badly behaved boors or understand it as a collective Dutch plot to usurp England's "fair and free trade" in the East Indies. As publications regarding the event multiplied over the course of the century, and as three Anglo-Dutch wars erupted in the years 1652–54, 1665–67, and 1672–74,[42] the double vision still operative in the 1624 letter to the reader gave way to ever-increasing anti-Dutch sentiment, until the tyrannous Dutch emerge in John Beaumont's 1672 account as a very "emblem of ingratitude."[43]

The "Endless Jars of Trading Nations": Staging *Amboyna*

> The doteage of some Englishmen is such
> To fawn on those who ruine them; the Dutch.
> . . . How they love England, you shall see this day:
> No Map shews Holland truer then our Play.
>
> Prologue to *Amboyna* (1673)[44]

The audience attending Dryden's *Amboyna; or, The Cruelties of the Dutch to the English Merchants*, staged three months into the Third Anglo-Dutch War, no doubt anticipated the broad strokes of the play's narrative contours, as the title evoked one of the most widely publicized events in Anglo-Dutch seventeenth-century history. Despite Dryden's own apologies for his play's "imperfections," an assessment echoed by most of the play's subsequent crit-ics, the show was an apparent success.[45] *Amboyna* did not disappoint those who expected to witness the horrific massacre of their English forefathers, half a century past and half a world away.[46] In depicting the "cruel sport" of the Dutch at Amboyna, Dryden drew much from the 1624 *True Relation* and from John Darrell's 1665 pamphlet, *A True and Compendious Narration; Or Second Part of Amboyna*.[47] Dryden's source pamphlets, as well as *The Emblem of Ingratitude: A True Relation of the Unjust, Cruel and Barbarous Proceedings against the English at Amboyna*, envision Amboyna as an exclusively male, almost exclusively European theater of Anglo-Dutch conflict. Dryden intro-duces two prominent female characters: Ysabinda, a native Amboyner, who is betrothed to the English captain Towerson and is the unlucky object of desire of the Dutchman Harmon Junior; and Julia, a Spanish woman, wife of Captain Perez and mistress of both Fiscal (the evil Dutch sidekick of

Harmon Junior) and Beamont (an English merchant).[48] Together the women
of Dryden's *Amboyna* breathe life into the gaps of the historical narrative,
expanding the imaginative framework of social relations on the island while
complicating the binary structure and adversarial national stance of the pamphlet literature.

   While Julia has garnered little critical attention, critics have focused on
Ysabinda as the character whose engagements with the English and Dutch
forge important distinctions between them.[49] In characterizing the play's construction of national self-definition, Robert Markley argues that English and
Dutch national differences are cast in terms of moral economy: English "strategic weakness" in Amboyna becomes a form of moral superiority witnessed
in the desire for "fair and free commerce" between civil gentleman; the
Dutch, by contrast, represent the tyrannical, illegal drive toward monopoly
in the Spice Islands and the exploitation of its natural and human resources.
Markley contends that Harmon Junior's "violence directed against Ysabinda
stands synecdochically for the illegal, tyrannical appropriation of the East
Indies by the Dutch, just as her love for Towerson justifies English trade and
colonization as a mutual desire for harmonious, and hierarchical, relations
between British merchants and dutiful East Indians."[50] In *Framing "India,"*
Shankar Raman argues that a similar binary is developed in the play: "Dryden
strategically coalesces English national identity with ideals of court patronage,"[51] as the English and England are (through the figure of Towerson)
agents "characterized by an idealized disinterestedness, whose marks are generosity, gratitude, honor, heroism, and true religious faith. The Dutch, on
the other hand, incarnate a pure commercial interest that excludes all forms
of faith, justice, and reciprocity."[52] Ysabinda thus makes a difference between
the English and the Dutch by standing in, Raman contends, for the colonized
land, enacting "in refracted form the colonial myth of the native freely yield-
ing him/herself up to the colonizer's protection and sovereignty."[53] Towerson's marriage to Ysabinda, portrayed as "mutually desired," is thus symbolic
of the reciprocity of patronage, while Harmon Junior's violence against her
becomes an expression and confirmation of the "uncivilized" nature of the
Dutch.[54] Recent criticism has thus coalesced around the notion that the
moral economies that distinguish the English from the Dutch result in por-
traying the English as heroic, gentleman merchants and the Dutch as upstart
"boors."[55] In these readings, Ysabinda makes good on her promise to "make
a difference" between European men.

While I find especially persuasive Markley's argument that *Amboyna* reveals "the inconsistencies, gaps, and anxieties that constitute the fiction of an essential transhistorical national identity," his reading of Ysabinda as a "symptom of Dryden's recasting of international economic conflict into a binary political morality" occludes the ways in which Ysabinda actively deconstructs the binary she seems poised to inscribe.[56] I propose, instead, that Ysabinda amplifies precisely those anxieties about Anglo-Dutch interchangeability that plagued Anglo-Dutch relations in the East Indies, particularly in the early decades of engagement there. The women of *Amboyna* reveal national and characterological differences between English and Dutch men, to be sure, but they do so even as they threaten to render interchangeable English and Dutch colonial identities.

As the play opens, the Dutchman Fiscal announces his plot to eliminate the English from the island in terms that express his monopolistic impulse: "This now gives encouragement to a certain Plot, which I have long been brewing, against these *Skellum English* . . . to cut all their Throats, and seize all their Effects within this Island. I warrant you we may compound again . . . we must our selves be ruin'd at long run, if they have any Trade here; I know our charge at length will eat us out; I wou'd not let these *English* from this Isle, have Cloves enough to stick an Orange with, not one to throw into their bottle-Ale" (1.1.40–45, 72–76). The division between English and Dutch models of colonial engagement emerges early in the play as an expression of competing logics regarding the availability and distribution of the island's resources. For the Dutch, a logic of scarcity informs their monopolistic pursuits; in Fiscal's imagination, it is as if every ounce of clove on an English vessel depletes Dutch reserves. In an economy of scarcity, the elimination of English competition ensures that Dutch profits will "compound."[57] According to Donald Lach and Edwin Van Kley, historically speaking, "it was this emphasis upon *control* and *monopoly* which characterized the VOC's policies at all levels. The Seventeen were determined to buy the fine spices at fixed prices, exclude all others from the commerce, and manage the supplies put on the market in Europe in the hope of selling them at constant prices."[58] The notion of market saturation never enters Fiscal's considerations; simply put, the more cloves he packs onto Dutch vessels, the wealthier the Dutch become, both abroad and at home.

The plot to drive the English from Amboyna would have posed a serious threat to England's investments in the Moluccas in the early seventeenth century. Broadly speaking, in the first two decades of VOC and EIC ventures, pepper, not cloves, was the commodity reaping the greatest profits in Europe. This was true for the EIC through the year 1617, when pepper prices peaked and then began to decline.[59] As pepper prices fell because of a glutted European market, profits from cloves increased. Among the rare spices of cinnamon, nutmeg, mace, and cloves, only cloves were directly imported by the EIC from the Indies into England: "this in effect meant that cloves were the only item of importance on the Company's list of spice imports," K. N. Chaudhuri underscores.[60] While the English regularly imported mace and nutmeg from the Netherlands, they managed to maintain their direct importation of cloves. The year of the Amboyna crisis was a peak year for Dutch and English clove importation to Europe. The supplies were on such unprecedented scales that the VOC "felt itself able to supply the whole of Europe for 7–8 years," a claim that was "echoed in London where it was stated that the Dutch had 'cloves at Amsterdam sufficient to serve all Christendom for four or five years.'"[61] With such substantial clove cargos, there was concern that the European market would again become glutted, thus driving down the profits of EIC investors. It is at the height of clove importation into Europe that the Amboyna massacre takes place and accounts of it begin circulating in England and the Low Countries. Fiscal's threat—that he would not "let these *English* from this Isle, have Cloves enough to stick an Orange with"—reveals a plot with far-reaching implications for England's global commercial enterprise. If Fiscal's plot to eliminate the English from the trade in cloves at Amboyna is successful, then England's status as a direct importer of any rare East Indies spice is gravely threatened.

Fiscal's scheme to oust the English is a direct challenge to the treaty of 1619. As he discusses his plot with Harmon, the Dutch captain at Amboyna, they review the terms of the treaty, and in so doing inform Dryden's audience of its details:

> *Fiscal:* After many long and tedious quarrels, they were to have a third part of the Traffick, we to build Forts, and they to contribute to the charge.
>
> *Harmon:* Which we have so increas'd each year upon 'em, we being in power, and therefore Judges of the Cost, that we exact what e're we please, still more then half the charge, and on pretence of their Non-payment, or the least delay, do often stop their Ships, detain their Goods, and drag 'em into Prisons, while our

Commodities go on before, and still forestall their Markets.
(1.1.63–71)

Neither Fiscal nor the Dutch captain expresses interest in complying with the terms of the treaty. Instead, if they can fool the English by using the very terms laid out in the treaty, then they can "forestall" English ships arriving to market, monopolize the European market in cloves, and secure their status as the supplier to the English market in spices. The Dutch policy of noncompliance is here depicted as of a piece with the VOC drive toward monopoly. What the English audience watching Dryden's play would have known (and what the English represented in Dryden's play do not) is that the English will in fact be driven from the clove market following the Amboyna massacre, here represented as Fiscal's plot.[62] Ironically, efforts to bring about this plot depend on sustaining the fiction among the English that the Dutch are England's friends.

From the very start of the play, the Dutch strategy for securing a monopoly of the clove trade depends on a form of doubling that allows them to dissemble their friendship with the English. Fiscal advises that in order to bring about his murderous plot, "we must put on a seeming kindness, call 'em our Benefactors, and dear Brethren, pipe 'em within the danger of our Net, and then we'l draw it o're 'em: when they are in, no mercy, that's my maxime" (1.1.79–82). Unlike the Dutch of early English travel writing, the Dutch in Dryden's play are neither impersonators (who through an operation of replacement cast a seeming similitude across English and Dutch difference) nor usurpers (who through an operation of supplementation threaten to efface categories of difference that matter in ordering social relations). Instead, Fiscal's instructions for Dutch dissembling—"to put on a seeming kindness"—restricts the operation of doubling to the Dutch themselves. Dryden represents the Dutch ability to play a double self as that which distinguishes them from the English in terms of national character. The English emerge as a coherent collective—a people who *are what they seem*, while the Dutch, conversely, put on what they seem by being two things at once: the seeming friend and the menacing dissembler. Importantly, this "double Dutch" character no longer emerges as the result of an English double vision. Instead, as a representation of national character, it is the Dutchman's ability to play two parts at once—to double himself—that distinguishes him from the English in Dryden's play.

While a logic of scarcity informs the Dutch model of colonial engagement at Amboyna, a logic of abundance informs the English model of moderate gain. Having arrived at Amboyna after a three-year absence, the English
captain Towerson expresses this model of moderate gain in the following
exchange:

> *Harmon:* [embracing Towerson] Oh my sworn Brother, my dear
>   Captain *Towerson*; the man whom I love better then a stiff gale,
>   when I am becalm'd at Sea; to whom, I have receiv'd the
>   Sacrament, never to be false-hearted.
> *Towerson:* You ne'er shall have occasion on my part: the like I
>   promise for our Factories, while I continue here: This Ile yields
>   Spice enough for both; and *Europe*, Ports, and Chapmen, where
>   to vend them.
> *Harmon:* It does, it does, we have enough, if we can be contented.
> *Towerson:* And Sir, why shou'd we not, what mean these endless jars
>   of Trading Nations? 'tis true, the World was never large enough
>   for Avarice or Ambition; but those who can be pleas'd with
>   moderate gain, may have the ends of Nature, not to want: nay,
>   even its Luxuries may be supply'd from her o'erflowing bounties
>   in these parts: from whence she yearly sends Spices, and Gums,
>   and Food of Heaven in Sacrifice. (1.1.210–26)

For Towerson, Amboyna's "o'erflowing bounties" yield "spice enough for
both" trading nations, echoing the sentiments expressed in the letter to the
reader in *True Relation*, wherein the English prince is said to "hath enough
of his own" that he need not vie for domination in the East. Harmon's
qualified agreement, "if we can be contented," hints at Dutch ambition for
more than moderate gain. In this initial exchange between Towerson and
Harmon, Towerson invites his Dutch "friend" to reconfirm their commitment to "fair Commerce and Friendliness of Conversation here" (1.1.235–36).
Harmon, who earlier endorsed Fiscal's murderous plot, dissembles in his
reply: "you ask too little friend, we must have more then bare Commerce
betwixt us: receive me to your bosom, by this Beard I will never deceive you"
(1.1.239–41). Beamont, the eavesdropping Englishman, remarks, "I do not
like his Oath, there's treachery in that *Judas* colour'd Beard" (1.1.242–43);
and, indeed, the audience, knowledgeable of the events to come, knows there
is. Beamont is unique among his English cohort because he sees early in the

play a stark division between the character of the English and that of the Dutch at Amboyna. Of Towerson, he worries, "if he has any fault, 'tis only that, to which great minds can only subject be, he thinks all honest, 'cause himself is so, and therefore none suspects" (1.1.132–34). In contrast to his concerns about the English captain's honesty and naiveté, Beamont worries about the Dutch for other reasons: "I do not like these fleering *Dutchmen*, they over act their kindness" (1.1.144–45). From Beamont's perspective, the obsequious grins of the Dutch mask their vicious plots, a perception confirmed by Fiscal, who boasts, "'tis fit we guild our Faces; the troth is, that we may smile in earnest, when we look upon the *Englishman*, and think how we will use him" (3.2.159–61).

As the play begins, then, the Dutch and English adopt different models of colonial engagement, revealing the characterological distinctions between them. The Dutch are double-faced while the English are what they seem. The Dutch emerge as monopolists, driven by their perception that they operate in an economy of scarcity; the English, conversely, are confident in the abundance of the East, and limit their mercantile goals to moderate gain. Structurally speaking, in the economy of scarcity, an either-or framework prevails; in the economy of abundance, a both-and framework prevails. Women's engagements with European men are similarly cast as either exclusive or inclusive—by analogy, monopolistic/monogamous or open market/ polyamorous. Dryden's female characters do not stand apart from the opposed logics of colonial engagement but are trafficked through them in ways that complicate English self-congratulatory innocence regarding their engagements in the East by undermining the difference between Englishness and Dutchness on which that picture of innocence depends.

The two primary female characters of the play make their first appearance together. Ysabinda and Julia enter to find Harmon, Harmon Junior, Fiscal, and Towerson conversing. Ysabinda catches the eye of Harmon Junior who, overcome with desire, confesses, "She's a most charming Creature, I wish I had not seen her . . . oh happy, happy *Englishman*, but I unfortunate" (1.1.75–76, 87). In love as in trade, Harmon Junior's calculations are based on his logic of scarcity. Towerson's riches in love stand not apart from but in relation to Harmon Junior's emotional reserves. If Towerson is the "happy, happy Englishman," then Harmon Junior is "unfortunate," a word that resonates along both affective and economic chords.

When Ysabinda and Harmon Junior meet privately at the beginning of act 2, Ysabinda believes that his declarations of affection are a test: "a plot betwixt you: my *Englishman* is jealous, and has sent you to try my faith"; she believes, "he might have spar'd the experiment after a three years absence; that was a proof sufficient of my constancy" (2.1.4–7). Ysabinda's instinct is wrong, a fact that becomes apparent as Harmon Junior presses her to leave Towerson and choose him instead:

> *Harmon Junior:* If you are wise, you'l make some difference 'twixt *Towerson* and me.
> *Ysabinda:* Yes, I shall make a difference, but not to your advantage.
> *Harmon Junior:* You must, or falsify your knowledge: an *Englishman*, part Captain, and part Merchant; his Nation of declining interest here: consider this, and weigh against that fellow, not me, but any, the least and meanest *Dutchman* in this Isle.
> *Ysabinda:* I do not weigh by bulk: I know your Countreymen have the advantage there. (2.1.18–26)

As she foretells, the difference Ysabinda will make is *not* to Dutch advantage, insofar as she is indifferent to the economic and political realities that give rise to Dutch preeminence in the region. From the start, Ysabinda's affections for Towerson translate Harmon Junior out of his position of advantage and her choice reverberates on local and global levels. In choosing the English captain, Ysabinda inverts the national hierarchy that organizes Anglo-Dutch trade relations on the island. If Ysabinda is the prize to be won, the English win all by her choice—a clear challenge to the politically negotiated distribution of commodities arranged in the 1619 treaty. In contracting herself to Towerson, Ysabinda chooses English protection and English sovereignty, despite the fact that the English have negotiated themselves out of a position whereby they might offer her either. Paradoxically, Ysabinda rejects Harmon Junior by ventriloquizing the logic of scarcity that is primarily associated with his (Dutch) model of colonial engagement. Her response to Harmon Junior—"of all Mankind, you shou'd not be my choice"—echoes closely the all-or-nothing ambition that characterizes Dutch engagement on Amboyna. She is all Towerson's wife, or no one's at all.

When Towerson arrives on the scene, the spurned Dutchman bemoans, "You have no reason *Towerson* to be sad, you are the happy man" (2.1.48–49). Towerson replies in terms informed by his logic of abundance, "If I have any, you must needs some," revealing that, in love as well as in trade, Towerson operates according to a model of moderate gain. For Towerson, his love of

Ysabinda does not preclude Harmon Junior's happiness; instead—though he cannot yet know the implications of his statement—Towerson urges Harmon Junior to "have some" of that which makes the English captain the "happy man." Harmon Junior responds, "No, you are lov'd, and I am bid despair" (2.1.51), echoing Fiscal's earlier assertion regarding Dutch colonial interest in the region: "we must our selves be ruin'd at long run, if they have any Trade here" (1.1.73–74). Though the case he makes to Ysabinda—to consider union with a Dutchman as a strategy of socioeconomic advancement—falls on deaf ears, Harmon Junior is undeterred. For him, the real obstacle to his plot is Towerson, not Ysabinda. So he tries his logic again with Towerson, propositioning him in similarly mercantilist terms:

> *Harmon Junior:* Now I consider on't, it shall be yet in your free
>   choice, to call me, one or other [friend or rival]; for, *Towerson*, I
>   do not decline your Friendship, but then yield *Ysabinda* to me.
> *Towerson:* Yield *Ysabinda* to you?
> *Harmon Junior:* Yes, and preserve the Blessing of my Friendship; I'le
>   make my Father yours, your Factories shall be no more opprest,
>   but thrive in all advantages with ours; your gain shall be beyond
>   what you cou'd hope for from the Treaty: in all the Traffick of
>   these Eastern parts, ye shall—
> *Towerson:* Hold, you mistake me *Harman*, I never gave you just
>   occasion to think I wou'd make Merchandise of Love; *Ysabinda*
>   you know is mine, contracted to me e're I went for *England* and
>   must be so till death. (2.1.72–84)

In this exchange Ysabinda functions symbolically as a commodity subject to the operations of colonial trade. Despite Towerson's refusal to "make Merchandise of Love," his evocation of the "contract" of their love weaves Ysabinda ever more tightly into both the political context and discourses of mercantilism from which he means to exclude her. Moreover, Towerson's defensive stance forces him to adopt Dutch ideas of colonial possession, whereby no part of Europe's engagement in the East can be amicably shared, no amount of merchandise can be equitably distributed between English and Dutch hands. Of course, Ysabinda's fate (not those divisible natural resources of the island) is what is at stake, making Towerson's model of moderate gain tragically inapplicable. Yet as the plot progresses, Ysabinda is increasingly associated with and represented as the spice for which the Dutch and English vie at Amboyna. The native Amboyner thus blurs distinctions between person and place, woman and commodity, in ways that had long been conventional in discourses of "discovery."[63] Like the abundance of cloves on Amboyna, Ysabinda too is "exceeding rich" (2.1.141). More, in a scene to which we will return, Harmon Junior tries on the English logic when, in act 4, he pursues Ysabinda into the woods: "You are a Woman; have enough of Love for him and me; I know the plenteous Harvest all is his: he has so much of joy, that he must labor under it. In charity you may allow some gleanings to a Friend" (4.3.30–33). Ysabinda and the clove forests are rendered as plenteous "harvests" for Dutch sexual and colonial appetite. As Towerson defends his "contract" with Ysabinda, he shifts toward the Dutch logic of colonial engagement (Ysabinda is either mine or yours), and in so doing foreshadows the inevitable violence of the ensuing conflict. Harmon Junior warns, "the sum of all is this, you either must Resign me *Ysabinda*, or instantly resolve, to clear your Title to her by your Sword" (2.1.100–102).

The contest over Ysabinda introduces chiastic interplay between the Dutchman and his self-articulated logic of scarcity and the Englishman and his self-articulated logic of abundance. In defending his right to Ysabinda's exclusive affections—by asserting his power to remove Ysabinda from the sexual marketplace—Towerson expresses a Dutch-identified model of colonial engagement, here figured as marital monogamy. Harmon Junior's attempt to "make merchandise of" Towerson's love by entering Ysabinda into the broader terms of commerce and trade between the two nations renders Ysabinda as another of the island's commodities to be divided among European men. Harmon Junior extends his commodification of Ysabinda by applying the English-identified logic of abundance when he presses her to "allow some gleanings to a Friend." This structural crossing emerges as an ideological entanglement, as the exchange of Dutch and English models of colonial engagement directs attention to the instability of the "difference" that critics have argued Dryden's play constitutes.

Like Ysabinda, Julia is also made "merchandise." Unlike Ysabinda, however, Julia and her lovers embrace this characterization. In her first speech of the play, Julia reflects on the dynamics of her relations with the men on the island:

> *Julia:* Yonder's my Master, and my *Dutch* Servant, how lovingly they
>   talk in private; if I did not know my Don's temper to be
>   monstrously jealous, I shou'd think, they were driving a secret

> Bargain for my Body. . . . If my *English* Lover, Beamont, my
> *Dutch* Love the *Fiscall*, and my *Spanish* Husband, were Painted
> in a piece with me amongst 'em, they wou'd make a Pretty
> Emblem of the two Nations, that Cuckold his Catholick Majesty
> in his *Indi's*. (2.1.220–30)

By the play's conclusion, a secret bargain will be driven for Julia's body, a fact she cannot foresee in this moment as she relishes the emblematic sketch of international relations that her dalliances with men on the island images forth. Julia's emblem refers at once to the sexual as well commercial and political cuckolding of Spain.[64] The Dutch ousting of the Portuguese at Amboyna was the first major Dutch success over the Portuguese in the East Indies. That both the Dutchman Fiscal and Englishman Beamont share Julia's affections and enjoy her sexual favors renders Julia an embodied palimpsest of European trade rivalry. Her sexual relations with men on the island record the layered history of European colonial conquest at Amboyna.

In yet another appropriation of the nationally specific discourses of colonial engagement with which the play began, Julia's lovers vie for her affections in terms that express the English-identified logic of abundance:

> *Beamont:* Mr. Fiscall, you are the happy Man with the Ladies, and
>   have got the precedence of Traffick here too; you've the *Indie's* in
>   your Arms, yet I hope a poor *English* Man may come in for a
>   third a part of the Merchandise.
> *Fiscal:* Oh Sir, in these Commodities here's enough for both, here's
>   Mace for you, and Nutmegg for me in the same Fruit; and yet
>   the owner has to spare for other friends too.
> *Julia:* My Husband's Plantations like to thrive well betwixt you.
>   (2.1.281–84)

The English logic of abundance and philosophy of moderate gain informs Beamont's tongue-in-cheek reference to the 1619 treaty that secured for England one-third of the merchandise of rare spice in the region. In the above exchange, the treaty's division of natural resources is recast as an enabling contract for the Englishman, inasmuch as it allows Beamont to come in for a "part" of the gain. Fiscal does not counter with claims of his rights to Julia. Instead, the Dutchman, who had earlier declared that the Dutch lose all in giving over even some of the island's clove crop to the

English, here adopts the English logic. Echoing Towerson, Fiscal claims "in these Commodities here's enough for both." Julia, the self-fashioned plantation of Amboyna, concurs. Like the island's fruitful abundance, there is "enough" of Julia to "thrive" in use. In a familiar trope of colonial engagement, the land is feminized and divided up by masculine desire. In this exchange, Julia's abundance seemingly mitigates Dutch and English commercial rivalry and feelings of sexual competition. Through Julia, the "Indi's" are fashioned as Europe's mistress. The Englishman and the Dutchman's sexual relations with Julia further disorder, through chiastic interplay, the drama's tidy alignment of Dutchmen with the Dutch logic of colonial engagement and Englishmen with the English logic. Julia's sexual availability apparently converts even the most ardent of the play's Dutch monopolists into something of an Englishman.

Although she is compared to the Indies, Julia is *not* the play's indigenous woman. Rather, she is a European transplanted to the East Indies as a result of Spain's engagements there. That she is nonetheless imagined to be the "Indi's" makes her something more than a palimpsest recording first Spain's and Portugal's, then the Netherlands', then England's commercial pursuits in Amboyna. Her traffic with men disorders the hierarchy of national relations that this layered history of intra-European conquest establishes. Her sexual relations with *all* the various kinds of Europeans on Amboyna raise the specter of interchangeability that had so long plagued especially English and Dutch relations in the Moluccas. Like the prostitutes and sexually available tavern wives of London city comedies, Julia thrives by her indifference to the national affiliation of the men whose sexual desires she satisfies. In their sexual relations with her, the Dutchman, the Englishman, and the Spaniard are rendered interchangeable. Their equal (shared) access to her body is a unique instance of an exchange that is not dictated by the intra-European colonial politics that determine so much of what transpires on the island.

In their mutual cuckolding of the Spanish husband, however, the English and the Dutch (though opposed in national self-definition) share a structural position as Julia's interchangeable lovers. Structurally speaking, their particular interchangeability is expressed as rotation, wherein each replaces the other in subsequent encounters with Julia. Thematically speaking, Anglo-Dutch interchangeability is thematized as northerly similitude when, for instance, Beamont and Fiscal share a rare moment of ideological alignment in their caricature of the Spaniard. Beamont avers, "the whole

Nation of 'em is generally so Pocky, that 'tis no longer a Disease, but a second nature in 'em"; Fiscal rejoins, "I have heard indeed, that 'tis incorporated among 'em, as deeply as the *Moors* and *Jews* are; there's scarce a Family, but 'tis crept into their blood like the new Christians." Extending their shared racializing epistemology from blood to skin, Beamont recalls "what pleasant lives . . . Spaniards . . . live in England" (2.1.293–97): "We observ'd 'em to have much of the nature of our Flies, they bus'd abroad a month or two I'th'Summer, wou'd venture about Dog dayes to take the Air in the Park, but all the Winter slept like Dormice, and if ever they appear'd in publick after Michaelmas, their Faces shew'd the difference betwixt their Countrey and ours, for they look in Spain as if they were Roasted, and in England as if they were Sodden" (2.1.304–10). Out of place and far from home, the Spaniard in the north is a laughing matter for the Dutchman and the Englishman alike. The Spaniard's travels north render him lethargic and his once "roasted" skin pale and "sodden." For Beamont, the difference between the Englishman and the Spaniard can be read across the Spaniard's face—a notion that at once draws on a long history of geohumoral discourse distinguishing the southerner from the northerner and also touches on an emerging racial epistemology that will, eventually, insist that "faces shew . . . the difference betwixt" kinds. The Dutchman and the Englishmen share a geohumoral position as northerners and draw on that northerly status to naturalize their opposition to the Spaniard.[65] So too they share the Spaniard's wife, and in so doing share the same object of (sexualized) colonial desire. For Fiscal and Beamont, colonial desire emerges not as desire for the native (as it has for Towerson and Harmon Junior), but as a desire for the (re)conquest of the European woman who—before their arrival—was already there.

A matrix of colonial desire is figured forth in the affairs that govern the play's plot and subplot. Towerson and Harmon Junior's desire for the native woman is also an expression of Anglo-Dutch commercial rivalry articulated in terms of the *Dutch* logic of scarcity: either one or the other will have all. Fiscal and Beamont's desire for the Spanish woman is also an expression of Anglo-Dutch ideological proximity and structural interchangeability, articulated in terms of the English logic of abundance: both will share Julia. As these affairs develop, a tension builds that threatens to wrench the English from the ideology of colonial engagement that underwrites their very Englishness on Amboyna, and challenges the viability of the English model of colonial engagement itself. Towerson and Harmon Junior's competition for Ysabinda not only represents the perniciousness of the Dutch drive toward monopoly; it raises the question of whether the English model of moderate gain is at all viable. Also, Beamont and Fiscal's dalliances with Julia present a fissure in the play's representation of Dutch colonial desire. If Fiscal can share Julia with Beamont, then the Dutch—even the most malevolent and scheming dissembler among them—might be absolved of what the play represents as the very nature of the Dutchman abroad: his insatiable monopolistic drive to conquer all.

As events unfold in the tragic second half of the play, the fate of the women of *Amboyna* is directly linked to how they negotiate the matrix of Anglo-Dutch colonial desire. Both Ysabinda and Julia differently attempt to negotiate their relations with the European men, and both women suffer tragic consequences. Following the offstage marriage of Towerson and Ysabinda, Julia and Ysabinda stroll into the clove forest at dusk. Having been lured by another of Fiscal's schemes, Towerson has left the wedding party before he and Ysabinda consummate their nuptials, and Ysabinda and Julia follow in search of him. Before Ysabinda locates Towerson, Harmon Junior appears and offers to lead her to her bridegroom. Convinced that Harmon Junior and her husband have reached a peace brokered by the island's Dutch governor, Ysabinda accepts the offer of assistance and slips away from Julia. No sooner is Ysabinda alone with Harmon Junior than he unmasks his true intentions, pleading with her that she might offer him some part of the love she so freely gives Towerson: "You are a Woman; have enough of Love for him and me; I know the plenteous Harvest all is his: he has so much of joy, that he must labor under it. In charity you may allow some gleanings to a Friend" (4.3.30–33). Ysabinda recognizes the Dutchman's deceit and her resistance grows increasingly ardent, "Now you grow rude: I'le hear no more" (4.3.35). As she turns to leave, Harmon Junior warns, "Pray resolve to make me happy by your free consent; I do not love these half Enjoyments, t'enervate my delights with using force, and neither give my self nor you that full content, which two can never have, but where both joyn with equal eagerness to bless each other. . . . You know you were now going to your Bridal Bed. Call your own thoughts but to a strict account, they'l tell you all this day, your fancy ran on nothing else; 'tis but the same Scene still you were to act; only the person chang'd, it may be for the better" (4.3.40–51). The "strict account" that Harmon Junior proposes untethers desire from its object, redirecting even a bride's consummation of marriage away from her bridegroom. Of course, this difference in person makes all the difference to Ysabinda, whose desire for Towerson expresses both her "free consent" and the "contract" of marital monogamy that underwrites their union. This rupture of desire from its object depends on the Dutchman's willingness to portray himself as the architect of yet another instance of Anglo-Dutch interchangeability. He will act the "same Scene . . . only the person chang'd." Like the Dutch of Edmund Scott's *Exact Discourse*, Harmon Junior will act in the Englishman's name, thus usurping from the Englishman his own contracted wife. The notion that Ysabinda's object of desire might be exchanged, or divided in half—that in love she might engage in the *English* model of colonial engagement—is exposed as an impossible and tragic fiction. So too Anglo-Dutch interchange-ability is revealed as a plot of *Dutch* design, a tactic in the game of colonial domination, rather than a phenomenological or epistemological mistake.

Indeed, only in forcibly seizing Ysabinda can Harmon Junior achieve his "half Enjoyment." Ysabinda's attempts to resist him fail. The audience overhears her pleas for mercy as well as Harmon Junior's insidious continuing "negotiations" from offstage:

> *Harmon Junior:* [within] Now you are mine; yield, or by force I'le
> take it.
> *Ysabinda:* [within] Oh kill me first.
> *Harmon Junior:* [within] I'le bear you where your crys shall not be
> heard.
> *Ysabinda:* [as farther off] Succor sweet Heaven, oh succor me.
> (4.3.71–74)

For the play's only Amboyner, no relief will be found. Ysabinda will not escape the gendered violence of colonial aggression. "Ty'd to a Tree and Gagg'd," she is "ravish'd" and in ravishing her Harmon Junior is left "noth-ing . . . of Manhood. . . . I am turn'd Beast of Devil" (4.4.39–40). Following the rape, Harmon Junior returns again to his self-fashioned position as the Englishman's proxy. Cruelly insisting that Ysabinda's honor is still safe so long as she recognizes his possession of her, the Dutchman reminds her that in his ravishment of her "the Husband only alter'd" (4.5.107–8).

If Ysabinda's rape strikes in Harmon Junior a momentary inability to reconcile his "Manhood" with his devilish "actions," in Towerson, the first glimpse of his ravished bride induces visions of "some illusion of the Night . . . some Spectre, such as in these *Asian* parts more Frequently appear" (4.5.6–7). Ysabinda appears both tragically embodied and hauntingly disem-bodied in Towerson's mind's eye; she seems to him to flutter between worlds, at once an illusion and his ravished lover. The crime, writ across her body, leaves Towerson speechless. Having unbound and ungagged her, he remains mute as the powers of language return first to Ysabinda. Her first words to Towerson powerfully recast the differences that matter on her island. Though all along she has played her part in the Anglo-Dutch contest that consumes her land, in this moment—the most tragic and dramatic yet in the play—as the play's ravished subaltern speaks she casts a general condemnation across the whole of Europe's colonial enterprise:

> *Ysabinda:* No longer Bridegroom thou, nor I a Bride: those names
> are vanish'd; Love is now no more. Look on me as thou wou'dst
> on some foul Leper; and do not touch me: I am as polluted, all
> shame, all o're dishonour; fly my sight, and, for my sake, fly this
> detested Isle, where horrid Ills so black and fatal dwell, as *Indians*
> cou'd not guess, till *Europe* taught. (4.5.13–17)

Ysabinda's speech collapses the distinction that matters most to English colonial self-definition by framing the fundamental violence, the real difference at stake, as that between Indians and Europeans. If, for the English, national and colonial self-definition depends on the distinction between the English and the Dutch, then nothing threatens more than Ysabinda's epistemological standpoint as the victim of *Europe's* colonial aggression. In this moment, Ysabinda fails to keep the promise she first made to Harmon Junior, "to make a difference" between Towerson and him, that is, to make Europe's national differences matter in the context of colonial enterprise.[66]

Significantly, Towerson cannot hear Ysabinda's condemnation of Europe's colonial aggression. He slips into a momentary state of aporia (way-less-ness) induced first by the sight of her ravished form and then by a condemnation that, should he register it, would leave him bereft of any hope of reconciling with Ysabinda. His response, "Speak plainer, I am recollected now," reveals that he has not heard his bride. He has not seen from the perspective of her native eyes the full horror of Europe's "horrid Ills." Though Towerson has not heard her, the lingering effect of Ysabinda's perspective—the sense that in their colonial pursuits the English and Dutch may be far more alike than they are different—sends a deep rupture through the play's portrait of English colonial identity. In this moment, the structural inconsistencies of English colonial desire, as the play has fashioned it, are exposed. As Dryden writes Ysabinda into the gaps in the historical narrative, his self-fashioned native—the only figure in the play who has overtly been asked to make a difference between the Dutch and English colonizers on her land—fills those gaps by speaking with another voice. In so doing, she fails to sustain the ideological imperative of her structural position in the play and threatens to rewrite the history that she had been introduced merely to animate. Ysabinda's story does not make a difference between the English and the Dutch, and so cannot, indeed must not, be heard.

If Ysabinda's tragedy cannot be heard, Julia's story of polyamorous and cross-national desire cannot be sustained if the Dutch are to emerge as fully fledged figures of colonial domination, driven by their insatiable and uncompromising monopolistic impulses. By the play's end, Julia is forced to withdraw herself from the circuit of desire that renders interchangeable her English and Dutch lovers. In other words, Julia is ultimately forced to make a difference between those lovers who had once seemed so eager to share her. In coming to the aid of the English against the Dutch at Amboyna, the Spanish captain Perez ties himself to their fate. Upon discovering that her husband has been taken captive by the Dutch, an enraged Julia condemns Fiscal: "Oh you have ruin'd me, you have undone me, in the Person of my Husband!" (5.1.223–24). Fiscal expresses no concern for his lover's pending position as a Spanish widow, victim of yet another round of intra-European colonial competition. Instead, echoing his countryman Harmon Junior, Fiscal avers, "If he will needs forfeit his Life to the Laws, by joying the English in a Plot, 'tis not in me to save him; but dearest *Julia* be satisfy'd, you shall not want a Husband" (5.1.225–27). Once again, in sexual as well as colonial conquest, the Dutch strategize to take the place of other European men. In this instance, the Dutchman renders himself the proxy even for the Spaniard who had previously evoked Fiscal's deepest antipathy. Like Harmon Junior's cruel logic expressed after his rape of Ysabinda—"the Husband only alter'd"—here too Fiscal's promise that Julia shall "not want a Husband" emerges as a particularly pernicious Dutch tactic for "overtopping" their European competition. If in her earlier engagements with the island's European men Julia raised the specter of interchangeability that had long vexed Anglo-Dutch relations in the East, then as the play concludes she is compelled to "driv[e] a secret Bargain for [her] Body" that brokers her body and her allegiances on *Dutch* terms.

Quick to understand Fiscal's implication that he will take her as his wife, Julia retorts, "Do you think, I'le ever come into a Bed with him, who rob'd me of my dear sweet Man?" Fiscal responds, "Dry up your Tears, I'me in earnest, I will Marry you, yfaith I will; it is your destiny" (5.1.228–31). Julia accepts this "destiny" on condition; she brokers a deal with Fiscal that secures her English lover's release:

> *Julia:* Nay if it be my Destiny: but I vow I'le ne're be yours but
>   upon one condition.
> *Fiscal:* Name your desire and take it.
> *Julia:* Then save poor Beamonts Life.
> *Fiscal:* This is the most unkind Request you cou'd have made, it
>   shews you Love him better: therefore in prudence I shou'd hast
>   his Death.
> *Julia:* Come, I'le not be deny'd you shall give me his Life, or I'le not
>   love you. (5.1.232–37)

Fiscal agrees to this exchange of the Spanish wife for the English lover. He spares Beamont's life, but in order to ensure that he himself does not become the cuckold that the Spaniard so easily proved, he exiles Beamont from the island, never to return. This resolution resolves more than Beamont's fate. It reinscribes the Dutch ideology of monopolistic engagement in the East, here expressed as a threatening imposition of forced monogamy with the Dutchman. The play thus suppresses the expression of Anglo-Dutch interchangeability (as that which is beyond the control of the Dutch) by foreclosing the sexual agency of the woman who had most exposed such interchangeability. In making Julia the instrument of the cuckolding of the Spaniard and the ousting of the English, the play refashions her symbolic role. No longer an emblem of the shared Anglo-Dutch cuckolding of Spain, her contract with Fiscal draws her into the Dutch economy of monopoly and renders her an emblem of Dutch colonial desire realized. With her assistance, the Dutch lover indeed overtops the other European men at Amboyna.

The massacre of the English at Amboyna, staged in the final act of Dryden's play, moves the English and England into the structural position of the play's native woman and thus attempts to efface the division that Ysabinda's rape has driven between Europe and her "Eastern Groves." The English are made to suffer "like Ladies" as they have "an Oyl'd Cloath put underneath [their] Chins, then Water pour'd above; which either [they] must drink or must not breath" (5.1.140–42). Even the region's natural resources are brought to bear to remind the English of their defeat: "we have two Elements at your Service," Harmon preens, "Fire, as well as Water; certain things call'd

Matches to be ty'd to your Fingers ends, which are as soveraign as Nutmegs, to quicken your short Memories" (5.1.144–47). In the final moments of the play, Fiscal echoes Harmon, "They shou'd have Fires of Cloves and Cinamon, we wou'd cut down whole Groves to Honour 'em, and be at cost to burn 'em nobly" (5.1.360–62). Despite their torture, the English do "not confess one word to shame [their] Countrey" (5.1.218–19).[67] Even in this final act wherein the English find themselves utterly victimized by the Dutch, the history of Anglo-Dutch proximity enters to figure England and the Netherlands as two spaces always potentially entangled by the intimate relations of their people. An English page, put to the torture of fire, boasts, "Sure you think my Father got me of some *Dutch* Woman, and that I am but of a half straine courage; but you shall find that I am all o're *English*, as well in Fire as Water" (5.1.189–91). In this moment, the paradox of Anglo-Dutch proximate relations is writ large. The rub of the page's claim to being all over English is that beneath this assertion lurks the long history of Anglo-Dutch friendship, alliance, intimacy, and kinship that makes real the possibility that in murdering the English crew at Amboyna, the Dutch inadvertently slay their kin. The page implicitly reminds Dryden's audience that England had once provided refuge and succor to the Dutch and, in so doing, had yoked together the fate of England and the Netherlands, if but for a while. The massacre of the English at Amboyna, unfolding before their eyes, reminds the English now only of Dutch "ingratitude" for England's offer of safe harbor. So too it raises the question, yet again, of what it might mean to be "all o're English."

Finally, as "the scene opens, and discovers the English Tortur'd, and the Dutch tormenting them," Towerson's men literally share the same space on the stage that Ysabinda last occupied when, in act 4, the scene was drawn to discover Ysabinda bound and ravished. Despite Towerson's protests that, "we are not here your Subjects, but your Partners; and that Supremacy of power you claim, extends but to the Natives, not to us," the Dutch prove otherwise (5.1.266–68). In their subjection to the Dutch, the English are made to share the humiliation of "the natives." This subjection rehearses a familiar trope in English imperial discourses, particularly travel writing and literature, that of the vilified *other* European. As Bridget Orr has demonstrated in *Empire on the English Stage, 1660–1714,* there is a "strong tendency to figure English colonial activity indirectly and in the context of a comparison by which another European empire suffers."[68] Similarly, Louis Montrose has shown that in the "discourse of discovery" within New World travel writing, the *other* European is the Spaniard whose "atrocities against the Indians" allowed the Englishman, Sir Walter Raleigh, to "represent his own imperialist venture as a holy and humanitarian war of liberation against Spanish oppression."[69] For Dryden, it is of course the Dutch whose atrocities against the East Indian Ysabinda and then against the English themselves enable the English audience watching the play to disavow, *albeit* imperfectly, the negative aspects of England's colonial endeavors. The Dutch are ultimately characterized, in Towerson's terms, "as if not made of the same Mould . . . not Christians, nor Allies, nor Partners . . . but as if Beasts, transfix'd on Theatres" (5.1.320–24). Towerson thus renounces the approximations and correspondences that have so long been a constitutive part of representations of Anglo-Dutch relations in early modern English culture. In the play's final moments, aporia is again sparked in Towerson as he confronts what has been and what has come to characterize Anglo-Dutch relations. Forced to imagine a new vocabulary for England's relations with the Dutch, Towerson grasps at the tragic negative to articulate the apocalypse of this "friendship": "Not Christians, nor Allies, nor Partners," the Dutch emerge instead as if "not made of the same Mould." Riddled with negations, Towerson's speech suggests that he cannot yet articulate a new vision, a new lexicon or analytic for representing and understanding Anglo-Dutch relations. He can only speak the death of the double vision he once knew. As the play concludes, the Dutch are represented not merely as a different *national* kind; they have so debased themselves in their aggression toward the English that they have shown themselves to be "Creatures of another kind" (5.1.322). Dryden's play thus works to expunge the discourses of Protestant alliance and cultural "friendship" from the lexicon of Anglo-Dutch relations by demonstrating that such notions of affiliation are but outdated chimeras of the English imagination, nullified by the Dutch at Amboyna.

Coda

A View from Antwerp

Two decades before the first English East India Company ship set sail for Asia, the crisis of Anglo-Dutch interchangeability that plagued the English in the Indonesian archipelago was writ large across a landscape much closer to home. From atop the tower of the English House at Antwerp, the Elizabethan courtier and dramatist George Gascoigne watched in horror as smoke engulfed the city's gable-roofed skyline. On a crisp November evening, the Spanish army was sacking the city below in what Geoffrey Parker, historian of the Dutch Revolt, characterizes as "one of the worst [intra-European] atrocities of the sixteenth century," the Spanish Fury of 1576.[1] With a panoramic view of the city before him, Gascoigne cast a surveying eye over the cityscape to discover that the trenches built to prevent the Spanish attack had failed. Fires blazed throughout the city, illuminating the grim reality of Antwerp's darkest hour. Gascoigne swiftly became embroiled in events that he feared would prove a harbinger of London's fate. His pamphlet *The Spolye of Antwerpe* (1576) initially presents its English readers with a bird's-eye view, the vantage point of an observer whose safe harbor is temporarily secured by his position aloft a tower, then suddenly shifts to the perspective of an Englishman caught in the fray.[2]

Racing down the tower and onto the streets, where the "shot was so thick, as neyther ground, houses, nor people could be discerned for the smoke thereof," Gascoigne winds his way through the city, passing by townsmen who stand in their doorframes "with such weapons as they had" to meet the Spanish troops, and their almost certain deaths. Others rush past Gascoigne in a frenzied dash for safety. But Gascoigne presses on determined to make his way "toward the marketplace," the Antwerp city Burse. Exactly why Gascoigne feels compelled to hazard his life to arrive at the Burse remains a mystery: perhaps he wants to see, hear, or learn something particular that he believed he could not from atop his tower. At street level, Gascoigne certainly catches a clearer glimpse of the particular players in this bloody, intra-European drama. From this new vantage point, he is no longer only an eyewitness but also a participant-observer. Yet such an objective might have drawn him to any corner of the city. Why head for the city's Burse?

The answer, I believe, lies not in what Gascoigne saw upon his arrival, but rather in what his readers were encouraged to imagine for having been taken there. As Gascoigne rounds a corner and the Antwerp Burse comes into view, London readers would have recognized something of themselves in Gascoigne's encounter with that façade. In both real and symbolic ways, Antwerp's Burse was London's Burse. To stand inside one was to glimpse the other, since this piece of Antwerp's built environment had been assimilated, less than a decade earlier, into London's own. Of course, some English merchants would have recognized Antwerp as well, for they may have traded within the city's stately edifice, a symbol of the southern Low Countries' economic prosperity and mercantile prowess. But Gascoigne's readers need not have traveled from London to Antwerp to feel a chill of foreboding run down their spines. From the moment Thomas Gresham's Burse opened for business in London, the mercantile landscapes of Antwerp and London were rendered doppelgängers. The buildings presented one face doubly figured in two cities, an urban *Unheimliche*. By narrating *The Spoyle of Antwerpe* from within Antwerp's Burse, Gascoigne encourages his London readers to imagine—as if the events were transpiring simultaneously—the spoiling of London too. His account transforms his reader into what Frances Dolan characterizes as "the reader as relator," one who "participate[s] imaginatively, thus . . . closing the opposition between reading and doing" in an engagement with "true reports."[3] In this instance, such an "imaginative reenactment" fosters a bifocal perspective on the event, what I have called the English double vision on Anglo-Dutch proximate relations. Situated at the Antwerp Burse, the reader encounters the proximate as that which is also at home.

Like so many representations of Anglo-Dutch relations explored throughout this study, Gascoigne's pamphlet construes England and the Netherlands as neighbors who do not enjoy a distanced view of one another's landscapes. Their geographic propinquity, mutual struggles against Spanish domination, and complexly intertwined mercantile, religious, colonial, sexual, linguistic, and ethnic histories engendered on-going cross-cultural identifications. Often, English efforts to put distance between Englishness and

Dutchness—attempts at dis-identification and differentiation—failed to produce distinct boundaries. Like fires that engulf neighboring rooftops, the Spanish Fury sparked in Antwerp risked igniting London too. The "burning houses of so neare neighbors," Gascoigne warns, ought to rouse fear in the hearts of Englishmen, lest England fall into a like calamity (A3r).[4] If this disquieting sentiment calls to mind Edmund Scott's conviction, explored in my final chapter, that the survival of the English and Dutch at Bantam required that they live and die in one another's foreign quarrels, it is because Gascoigne returns us to the scene of northern European proximate relations that gave rise to Scott's belief that the English and Dutch remained "neere neighbors," even when living halfway around the globe.[5]

The sense that England and the Netherlands, Englishness and Dutchness, were rarely more than a mere step apart was a commonplace whose broad range of representational manifestations and cultural implications I have traced throughout this book. For the English, taking that step entailed taking measure of the sometimes small distance—and minor differences—between self and Other, calibrating degrees of sameness and difference with a double vision that put matters of ethnicity at the forefront of representations of Anglo-Dutch relations. So too, as Gascoigne's account illuminates, the process of forging Englishness through both real and imagined relations with Dutchness involved grappling with the positive and negative effects of such cross-cultural approximation.

In the days following the Spanish Fury, Gascoigne reveals just how attuned the English were to the problems that arise when the play of difference and similitude no longer animates proximate relations, when identities are rendered so closely approximated as to seem alike. Trapped within the city for days in the aftermath of the siege, Gascoigne reports the dangers he faced: "At least all the world wyll beare mee witness, that ten (yea twenty dayes) after, whosoever were but pointed at, and named to bee a Walloon, was immediatlye [sic] massacred without furder [sic] audience or tryall. For mine owne part, it is wel known that I did often escape very narrowly, because I was taken for a Walloon" (C3v). As the fires burned out in Antwerp, Gascoigne finds himself mistaken for the city's Walloons: French-speaking Dutch Protestants whose "heresies" the Spanish were intent on suppressing. While we might imagine that this Englishman should easily have been distinguished from a Walloon—since his English tongue and post at the English House set him apart, linguistically, politically, diplomatically, and spatially—Gascoigne insists otherwise. He fears for his life not because he is a foreigner, an Englishman, or a suspected Protestant sympathizer, but because he is (mis)taken for a native. Gascoigne's plea that "all the world" might bear witness to his narrow escape touches the quick of a characteristically English anxiety that one might be "taken for" one's nearest neighbor, rendered as a double. As I have argued, if to be English was to understand Englishness in relation to a complexly layered and often shifting set of correspondences between Englishness and Dutchness, it also entailed resisting unwelcome conflations. While Gascoigne abhors the atrocities of the Spanish troops and urges his English readers to identify with the fate of their Protestant neighbors, he pulls up short of identifying as a "Walloon." This "taken" likeness is threatening—indeed potentially deadly—precisely because it proves so difficult to deny.

This episode opens onto the darker side of the comic puns about Anglo-Dutch proximity with which my book began. Wordplay, I have argued, is an archive of culture in action, animating questions of ethnic identification in the period's drama by showcasing the role of linguistic play in the construction of ethnicity. Ethnicity is a process that lives in relation, whether on the streets of London, Antwerp, and Bantam; on the London stage; on the printed pages of playbooks, dictionaries, and vocabularies; or in impromptu performances enacted by upstart players in the Indonesian archipelago. In the early modern texts I have considered and in contemporary critical practices as well, the collapsing of salient minor differences into sameness and, conversely, the overlooking of similitudes in order to emphasize difference both ossify the elastic nature of ethnicity by denying the movement between identification and dis-identification. In the context of northern European proximate relations, there is more at risk than an Englishman's mistaken identity. To refuse the play of approximation between Englishness and Dutchness is to deny the double vision on which the possibility of Gascoigne's identification *as English* depends. To (mis)take Gascoigne as a Walloon or to read him critically as merely an Englishman untethered to the Dutch is not simply to get the *what* of his identity wrong, it is to efface the *how*—that is, the relational dynamics by which identity categories emerge as culturally salient.

As the broader scope of this study demonstrates, categorical confusions and conflations of kind were not limited to the fog of war in the sixteenth and seventeenth centuries or to the colonial contexts that engendered intra-European rivalries and alliances. The English double vision on Dutchness and its attendant modes of expression—puns, double entendres, cognates, homophones, copies, palimpsests, doppelgängers, and other doublings of character and kind—made representing Dutchness vital to imagining Englishness in virtually every aspect of social life. For the English, this double vision sparked laughter as often as fear, gave rise to great pleasure as well as anxiety, and produced identification in one moment and dis-identification in the next. It is out of such doppelgänger dilemmas that we encounter English ethnicity in the making.

NOTES

INTRODUCTION

Epigraph: William Shakespeare, *The Norton Shakespeare,* ed. Stephen Greenblatt, Walter Cohen, Jean E. Howard, and Katharine Eisaman Maus (New York: W. W. Norton, 1997). Unless otherwise noted, all quotations from Shakespeare are drawn from this source.

1. Thomas Middleton and Thomas Dekker, *The Roaring Girl,* ed. Paul A. Mulholland (Manchester: Manchester University Press, 1987), 2.1.226–28, 302–5.

2. Irene Scouloudi, ed., *Returns of Strangers in the Metropolis 1593, 1627, 1635, 1639: A Study of an Active Minority* (London: Huguenot Society, 1985). Later in the Introduction, I address the complexities of categorizing strangers in London during this period.

3. This survey records aliens living in London, the Liberties, and Westminster. See Scouloudi, *Returns of Strangers.*

4. Ibid.

5. Max Eastman, *Enjoyment of Laughter* (London: Hamish Hamilton, 1937), 133.

6. For Roland Barthes, the figure of Folly personifies the effect of double entendre: "the *double understanding*, the basis for a play on words, cannot be analyzed in simple terms of signification (two signifieds for one signifier); for that there must be the distinction of two recipients; and if, contrary to what occurs here, both recipients are not given in the story, if the play on words seems to be addressed to one person only (for example, the reader), this person must be imagined as being divided into two subjects, two cultures, two languages, two zones of listening (whence the traditional affinity between puns and 'folly' or madness: the Fool, dressed in motley, a divided costume, was once the purveyor of the *double understanding*" (*S/Z: An Essay* [Paris: Editions du Seuil, 1970], 145).

7. An important collection of essays edited by Ton Hoenselaars and Holger Klein draws attention to the topic of the Low Countries, but does not focus primarily on questions of identity: *Shakespeare and the Low Countries,* Shakespeare Yearbook 15 (Lewiston, N.Y.: Edwin Mellen Press, 2005). Anglo-Dutch relations have drawn significant attention from historians of the period. Simon Schama's *The Embarrassment of Riches: An Interpretation of Dutch Culture in the Golden Age* (New York: Knopf, 1987) remains for many literary critics the most influential monograph on Anglo-Dutch cultural relations in the period. When drawing on English sources to make his case for the zeitgeist of the Dutch "Golden

Age," Schama often stresses the rivalry and antipathy in Anglo-Dutch relations, a point that my argument about England's double vision on the Low Countries challenges and complicates. Recently, in *Going Dutch: How England Plundered Holland's Glory* (London: Harper Press, 2008), Lisa Jardine explores how the English and Dutch benefited from and wrestled with their "shared mentality" over the course of the seventeenth century. My book offers a period-specific prequel, drawing attention to different texts and contexts than Jardine's predominately mid- to late seventeenth-century materials, and also places greater emphasis on the range of cultural texts and contexts through which the English explored identification and lack of identification with the Dutch.

8. For example, Queen Elizabeth discusses the "mutuall love" of the peoples of England and the Low Countries, whose bonds tie them "in perpetuall union," in *Declaration of the Causes Mooving the Queene of England to give aide to the Defence of the People afflicted and oppressed in the Lowe Countries* (London, 1585): "By which mutual Bondes, there hath continued perpetuall unions of the peoples heartes together, and so by way of continuall entercourses, from age to age the same mutuall love hath bene inviolablie kept and exercised, as it had bene by the woorke of nature, and never utterly dissolved, nor yet for any long time discontinued, howsoever the kinges and the Lordes of the countries sometimes (though very rarely) have bene at difference by sinister meanes of some other Princes their Neighbours, envying the felicitie of these two Countries" (rpt. in *A Collection of Scarce and Valuable Tracts,* ed. John Somers and Walter Scott, vol. 1 [London: Cadell and Davies, 1809–15], 411; hereafter Somers's *Tracts*).

9. On negative characterizations of the Dutch in political polemic, see Schama, *Embarrassment of Riches,* 221–88.

10. Laura Hunt Yungblut, *Strangers Settled Here Amongst Us: Policies, Perceptions, and the Presence of Aliens in Elizabethan England* (London: Routledge, 1996). On England's "Hollandophobia" in particular, see Schama, *Embarrassment of Riches,* 257–64. Alan Stewart argues that hostility to the denizens of London animates the central tension of London's first city comedy (" 'Every Soyle to Mee Is Naturall': Figuring Denization in William Haughton's *English-men for My Money,*" *Renaissance Drama* 35 [2006]: 75). Joseph Ward questions the limits of popular xenophobia in London in "Fictitious Shoemakers, Agitated Weavers and the Limits of Popular Xenophobia in Elizabethan London," in *From Strangers to Citizens: The Integration of Immigrant Communities in Britain, Ireland and Colonial America, 1550–1750,* ed. Randolph Vigne and Charles Littleton (Brighton: Sussex Academic Press, 2001), 80–87.

11. See especially Yungblut, *Strangers Settled Here*; see also Lien Bich Luu, " 'Taking the Bread out of Our Mouths': Xenophobia in Early Modern London," *Immigrants and Minorities* 19 (2000): 1–22.

12. Nigel Goose, " 'Xenophobia' in Elizabethan and Early Stuart England: An Epithet Too Far?," in *Immigrants in Tudor and Early Stuart England,* ed. Nigel Goose and Lien Luu (Brighton: Sussex Academic Press, 2005), 110–35.

13. Kenneth Harold Dobson Haley, *The British and the Dutch: Political and Cultural Relations Through the Ages* (London: George Phillip, 1988), 8.

14. I employ the words "stranger" and "alien" to refer to the Dutch residing in London. "Foreigner" was a word more often used to refer to native-born English men and women who migrated from areas outside London.

15. Jonathan Israel, *The Dutch Republic, Its Rise, Greatness, and Fall, 1477–1806* (Oxford: Clarendon Press, 1995), 129–54. On the social, economic, and religious backgrounds of the Dutch revolt, see also Geoffrey Parker, *The Dutch Revolt* (Ithaca, N.Y.: Cornell University Press, 1977). On the years leading to the Dutch Revolt, see Maarten Prak, *The Dutch Republic in the Seventeenth Century: The Golden Age* (Cambridge: Cambridge University Press, 2005), 7–24.

16. See Israel, *Dutch Republic*, 155, 160.

17. Nigel Goose, "Immigrants in Tudor and Early Stuart England," in Goose and Luu, *Immigrants in Tudor and Early Stuart England*, 1. Goose notes that in the seventeenth century, "the Moriscos expelled from Spain in 1609 and the Huguenots who fled Louis XIV's France during the 1680s" exceeded in number the Protestants who fled the Spanish Netherlands. At the time of their exodus from the southern Netherlands, however, the Protestant migration was indeed the "largest emigration movement" that early modern Europe had yet experienced.

18. It lies beyond the scope of this book to do justice to the complexities of the confessional debates (and religious identifications) that shaped Anglo-Dutch relations in this period, a topic that has received significant attention in the historiography. However, I address certain aspects of this complex history when the literature thematizes or dramatizes religious issues (as with the representation of the Family of Love in Chapter 1). I refer the reader to two dense and nuanced historiographies: Israel, *Dutch Republic*; and Benjamin Kaplan, *Divided by Faith: Religious Conflict and the Practice of Toleration in Early Modern Europe* (Cambridge, Mass.: Belknap Press of Harvard University Press, 2007). On the cross-pollinations and conflicts among the Dutch stranger communities of London and English and Continental Protestantism(s), see especially Charles Littleton, "The Strangers, Their Churches and the Continent: Continuing and Changing Connexions," in Goose and Luu, *Immigrants in Tudor and Early Stuart England*, 177–91; Andrew Pettegree, *Foreign Protestant Communities in Sixteenth-Century London* (Oxford: Clarendon Press, 1986); and Ole Peter Grell, *Dutch Calvinists in Early Stuart London: The Dutch Church in Austin Friars, 1603–1642* (Leiden: E. J. Brill, 1989). Further references, cited below, relate to specific aspects of religious exchange between the English and Dutch.

19. On this period, see Haley, *British and the Dutch*.

20. See Michael Duffy, *Englishman and the Foreigner: The English Satirical Print, 1600–1832* (Cambridge: Chadwyck-Healey, 1986). For a persuasive exploration of the interrelated expressions of Hispanophobia and Hispanophilia in England, see Eric J. Griffin, *English Renaissance Drama and the Specter of Spain: Ethnopoetics and Empire* (Philadelphia: University of Pennsylvania Press, 2009); on the links between "Maurophilia" and ideas of Spain in the broader European context, see Barbara Fuchs, *Exotic Nation: Maurophilia and the Construction of Early Modern Spain* (Philadelphia: University of Pennsylvania Press, 2009).

21. On England's uneven Protestant Reformations, see Christopher Haigh, *English Reformations: Religion, Politics, and Society Under the Tudors* (Oxford: Clarendon Press, 1993); on the Dutch Reformations, see Kaplan, *Divided by Faith*.

22. For the long view of Anglo-Dutch relations, see J. F. Bense, *Anglo-Dutch Relations from the Earliest Times to the Death of William the Third* (The Hague: Martinus Nijhoff, 1925); and William Cunningham, *Alien Immigrants to England* (1897; New York: Augustus M. Kelly, 1965).

23. Bense, *Anglo-Dutch Relations*, 97.

24. This statistic reflects only the portion of people who applied for denization; the number of immigrants who did not seek denization but who were living in England is unknown. Raymond Fagel, "The Netherlandish Presence in England Before the Coming of the Stranger Churches, 1480–1560," in Vigne and Littleton, *From Strangers to Citizens*, 9.

25. Ibid., 10.

26. Immigrants from Antwerp served as elders and deacons of the three stranger churches in statistically significant numbers. Twenty of the Dutch Church's elders and deacons (1567–85) were from Antwerp, almost twice the representation of any other Netherlandish city or town in the Dutch Church's governing body. Thirteen immigrants from Antwerp served as elders and deacons of the French Church (1567–85), second in representation only to all those immigrants who claimed "France" as a place of origin. Among those who served as elders and deacons of the Italian Church (1568–91), immigrants from Antwerp equaled those from Italy. Raymond Fagel, "Immigrant Roots: The Geographical Origins of Newcomers from the Low Countries in Tudor England," in Goose and Luu, *Immigrants in Tudor and Early Stuart England*, 48.

27. Fagel, "Netherlandish Presence," 12.

28. Ibid.

29. Fagel finds that marriage between Dutch men and English women "was the case in more than 60 percent of the new denizens in 1541, that is, 112 persons" (ibid., 14). Regarding marriage between strangers and English during the second half of the sixteenth century, see Charles Littleton, "Social Interactions of Aliens in Late Elizabethan London: Evidence from the 1593 Return and the French Church Consistory Actes," *Proceedings of the Huguenot Society* 26.2 (1995): 153–55; and Lien Bich Luu, "Assimilation or Segregation: Colonies of Alien Craftsmen in Elizabethan London," *Proceedings of the Huguenot Society* 26.2 (1995): 168–70.

30. John J. Murray, "The Cultural Impact of the Flemish Low Countries on Sixteenth- and Seventeenth-Century England," *American Historical Review* 62.4 (1957): 837–85; and Bense, *Anglo-Dutch Relations*, 94.

31. On the Anglo-Dutch exchange of ideas in print in the seventeenth century, see Cornelis W. Schoenveld, *Intertraffic of the Mind: Studies in Seventeenth-Century Anglo-Dutch Translation* (Leiden: E. J. Brill, 1983). For a broader exploration of the exchanges that characterized Anglo-Dutch intellectual history in the seventeenth century, see the following collections: Simon Groenveld and Michael Wintle, eds., *The Exchange of Ideas: Religion, Scholarship and Art in Anglo-Dutch Relations in the Seventeenth Century* (Zutphen: Walburg Instituut, 1994); J. A. van Dorsten, J. van den Berg, and Alastair Hamilton, eds.,

The Anglo-Dutch Renaissance: Seven Essays (Leiden: E. J. Brill, 1988); and Susan Roach, ed., *Across the Narrow Seas: Studies in the History and Bibliography of Britain and the Low Countries: Presented to Anna E. C. Simoni* (London: British Library, 1991).

32. M. Evers, "Religionis et Libertatis Ergo: Dutch Refugees in England and English Exiles in the Netherlands," in *Refugees and Emigrants in the Dutch Republic and England: Papers of the Annual Symposium, Held on 22 November 1985* (Leiden: Sir Thomas Brown Institute, 1986), 8.

33. On the political complexities of these proposals, from the perspective of Queen Elizabeth I and her councilors, see Haley, *The British and the Dutch*, 27–49, here 38.

34. Somers's *Tracts* 1.417.

35. Ibid., 1.416.

36. Robert Devereux, Earl of Essex, *An Apologie of the Earle of Essex . . . 1598* (London, 1603), D3r. It was commonplace among those who supported Elizabeth I's military intervention in the Netherlands that the Spanish invasion there was "not undertaken against the Netherlands, but with a further intent and meaning to make a greater conquest [of England]" (Jean François Le Petit, *A Generall Historie of the Netherlands . . . by Ed. Grimeston* [London, 1608], 889).

37. Regarding the debates at court for and against military intervention in the Low Countries, and Elizabeth's preference for diplomatic engagement, see Roy Strong and J. A. van Dorsten, *Leicester's Triumph* (Leiden: Sir Thomas Brown Institute and University Press, 1964). On Leicester's reception in the Netherlands, see Israel, *Dutch Republic*, 219–32.

38. On the legal position of strangers in England, see Daniel Statt, "The Birthright of an Englishman: The Practice of Naturalization and Denization of Immigrants Under the Later Stuarts and Early Hanoverians," *Proceedings of the Huguenot Society* 25.1 (1989): 61–74; and Scouloudi, *Returns of Strangers*, 3–18. An important collection of essays that spans two centuries of English history on this subject is Vigne and Littleton, *From Strangers to Citizens*.

39. Lien Bich Luu, "Natural-Born Versus Stranger-Born Subjects: Aliens and Their Status in Elizabethan London," in Goose and Luu, *Immigrants in Tudor and Early Stuart England*, 57–75.

40. On the "freedom" conferred by the City, see John Michael Archer, *Citizen Shakespeare: Freemen and Aliens in the Language of the Plays* (New York: Palgrave Macmillan, 2005), 1–22.

41. Israel in *Dutch Republic* summarizes the three-pronged movement of Protestant emigrants in the years 1567–68: "Those fleeing the Netherlands moved in three main directions. From Amsterdam, the West Frisian towns, Friesland, and Groningen, the flow was towards the north-western corner of Germany, especially Emden. From Flanders and Zeeland, emigration was chiefly by sea to England. From Brabant, southern Holland, and Utrecht, the exiles gravitated mainly to Cleves and the Rhineland" (160). Fagel further details the specific geographical origins (town and city roots) of London's Protestant immigrant population over the course of the sixteenth century in "Immigrant Roots."

42. For book-length studies on the stranger communities and their churches, see Pettegree, *Foreign Protestant Communities*; Grell, *Dutch Calvinists*; and William John Charles Moens, ed., *The Marriage, Baptismal, and Burial Registers, 1571–1874 and Monumental Inscriptions, of the Dutch Reformed Church, Austin Friars, London* (Lymington: n.p., 1884), i–xliii. Essential articles include Littleton, "Strangers"; Goose, "Immigrants"; and Ole Peter Grell, "The French and Dutch Congregations in London in the Early Seventeenth Century," *Proceedings of the Huguenot Society* 24.5 (1987): 362–77.

Not all immigrants who arrived in England during this time were religious refugees. Some came for economic reasons and many did not join the strangers' churches; see Andrew Spicer, " 'A Place of Refuge and Sanctuary of a Holy Temple': Exile Communities and the Stranger Churches," in Goose and Luu, *Immigrants in Tudor and Early Stuart England*, 91–109. While I focus on the Dutch immigrants in London, there were other significant communities of Dutch strangers in southern England. Nigel Goose estimates, "it is very likely that collectively the provincial immigrant communities outnumbered those in London in the late sixteenth century, and in total there may have been as many as 23,000–24,000 aliens in England by the 1590s" ("Immigrants," 18). In Norwich the alien population reached over 40 percent of its population in the early 1590s: "by 1571 it numbered as many as 3,999 (Dutch and Walloon), and 4,679 by 1583 despite the death of 2,482 strangers in the plague of 1579–80" ("Immigrants," 18). On Norwich's stranger population, see also Douglas Rickwood, "The Norwich Strangers, 1565–1643: A Problem of Control," *Proceedings of the Huguenot Society* 24.2 (1984): 119–28. Towns with significant immigrant settlements included "Norwich, Canterbury, Colchester, Sandwich, Maidstone, Southampton, Great Yarmouth, Dover, Thetford, Kings Lynn, Stamford, Halstead, Rye, Winchelsea, and later also on Canvey Island in Essex and in the fens of Lincolnshire and Cambridgeshire, at Sandtoft and Thorney respectively" (Goose, "Immigrants," 17).

43. Though referred to as the "Dutch" and "French" Churches, the congregations of both churches consisted predominately of Dutch-and French-speaking people who originated from the Netherlands, not France. The distinction was primarily linguistic, as French (or local dialects Picard, Rouchy, and Walloon) was the speech native in much of the southern Low Countries. The French Church congregation consisted "mostly of Walloons from the southern Netherlands until the St. Bartholomew massacre in 1572 brought the first significant number of French refugees to London" (Grell, "French and Dutch Congregations," 363). Charles Littleton, historian of the French Church in London, estimates that in 1593, "of the 417 individual members of the French Church whose place of birth is listed in the Dugdale [manuscript], 54 percent came from what was the Spanish Netherlands and 39 percent from the Kingdom of France," suggesting that the French Church continued to count Netherlanders among the majority of its congregation even after the St. Bartholomew massacre ("Social Interactions," 149). Patrick Collinson further notes: "not all adherents, or even members, of the various stranger churches [of London] were of the appropriate and designated nation or language. In the 1560s an actual minority of the members of the Italian congregation, an extreme case, were Italian by birth. The majority were Dutch, in 1568 numbering at least 63" ("Europe in Britain: Protestant

Strangers and the English Reformation," in Vigne and Littleton, *From Strangers to Citizens*, 62).

44. The Dutch and French Churches also served "as a kind of ecclesiastical Trojan horse," Collinson has argued: "In effect, the strangers were exempt from the terms and requirements of the Act of Uniformity" (Ibid., 57). For French and Dutch alien settlement within England, see Yungblut, *Strangers Settled Here*; and Bernard Cottret, *The Huguenots in England: Immigration and Settlement c. 1550–1700* (Cambridge: Cambridge University Press, 1991). A number of related essays appear in Goose and Luu, *Immigrants in Tudor and Early Stuart England*. For foreign Protestant settlement within London, see especially Pettegree, *Foreign Protestant Communities*; and Ian Archer, *The Pursuit of Stability: Social Relations in Elizabethan London* (Cambridge: Cambridge University Press, 1991), 131–40.

45. Grell, *Dutch Calvinists*, 3.

46. Jean Howard, *Theater of a City: The Places of London Comedy, 1598–1642* (Philadelphia: University of Pennsylvania Press, 2007), 10. Jacob Selwood underscores the divergent responses of the City and Crown to foreign immigration into London, emphasizing the ways in which the central government encouraged immigration to an extent the City government sometimes resisted. Selwood emphasizes that the powers that "forced" cosmopolitanism on London's English subjects also came from within England, as well as beyond it (*Diversity and Difference in Early Modern London* [Burlington: Ashgate, 2010]).

47. On the mobility of the Dutch scientific community, for instance, see Deborah Harkness, *The Jewel House: Elizabethan London and the Scientific Revolution* (New Haven: Yale University Press, 2007).

48. R. E. G. Kirk and Ernest F. Kirk, eds., *Returns of Aliens Dwelling in the City and Suburbs in London from the Reign of Henry VIII to That of James I*, vol. 1 (Aberdeen: University Press, 1900–1908), 293.

49. Yungblut, *Strangers Settled Here*, 16.

50. Goose, "Immigrants," 16; cf. Yungblut, *Strangers Settled Here*, for a more conservative estimate. On the location of aliens in and around London, see Luu, "Natural-Born."

51. Pettegree, *Foreign Protestant Communities*, 182. Pettegree estimates that "the members of the French and Dutch churches would have made up less than half the total foreign population of the capital" (78).

52. Marten Le Mayre, *The Dutch Schoole Master.* . . . (London, 1606).

53. Scouloudi, *Returns of Strangers*, 209.

54. Ibid., 199.

55. Of course we cannot know for certain what Strete said, or even if she did in fact answer the door on the day the censor knocked. That the *Returns* record this answer *as if* it were derived from an encounter with Strete is what most interests me.

56. I have derived this figure from Scouloudi, *Returns of Strangers*, 145–221.

57. On local, regional, and religious identity in the early modern Netherlands, see Judith Pollmann and Andrew Spicer, eds., *Public Opinion and Changing Identities in the Early Modern Netherlands: Essays in Honour of Alastair Duke* (London: Brill, 2007).

58. *Oxford English Dictionary Online* [hereafter, *OED*], s.v. "Dutch."

59. Ibid. See also C. A. J. Armstrong, "The Language Question in the Low Countries: The Use of French and Dutch by the Dukes of Burgundy and Their Administration," in *Europe in the Late Middle Ages*, ed. J. R. Hale, J. R. L. Highfield, and Beryl Smalley (Evanston: Northwestern University Press, 1965), 386–409.

60. William Z. Shetter and Inge van der Cruysse-van Antwerpen, *Dutch: An Essential Grammar* (New York: Routledge, 2002), 1.

61. Armstrong, "Language Question," 386.

62. Alastair Duke, "The Elusive Netherlands: The Question of National Identity in the Early Modern Low Countries on the Eve of the Revolt," in *Dissident Identities in the Early Modern Low Countries*, ed. Judith Pollmann and Andrew Spicer (Burlington: Ashgate, 2009), 24.

63. Ibid., 11.

64. Ibid., 24.

65. Abraham Ortelius, *Theatrum Orbis Terrarum . . . The Theatre of the Whole World* (London, 1606 [i.e., 1608]), 34. When date or place of publication is false on the imprint, I have entered the corrected information in brackets as it appears in the English Short Title Catalogue (hereafter, STC).

66. Of course the Netherlands was not a monolingual place. Flemish; Frisian, a low German dialect; Dutch; and French were all spoken in various regions and, at the University of Leiden, Latin was the lingua franca.

67. "Nether-dutch" (translation of *Nederduits*) appears on the title page of J. G. van Heldoren's *An English and Nether-dutch dictionary* (Amsterdam, 1675). For "netherland language," see the prefatory letter in Richard Verstegan's *Newes from the low-countreyes. . . .* (Saint-Omer, 1622).

68. Armstrong, "Language Question," 397.

69. Le Mayre *Dutch Schoole Master*.

70. *Den grooten vocabulaer Engels ende Duyts . . . The great vocabuler, in English and Dutch* (Rotterdam, 1639).

71. *The English Schole-master or certaine rules and helpes whereby the natives of the Netherlandes, may bee, in a short time, taught to read, understand, and speake, the English tongue . . . Den Engelschen School-Meester* (Amsterdam, 1646).

72. François Hillenius, *Den Engelschen ende Ne'erduitschen onderrichter . . . The English, and Low-dutch instructer,* 3rd ed. (Rotterdam, 1677).

73. J. G. van Heldoren, *An English and Nether-dutch Dictionary. . . .* (Amsterdam, 1675).

74. Duke, "Elusive Netherlands."

75. See the anonymous play *A Larum for London* (London, 1602). Cunningham defines Walloons as people who "came from Artois, Hainault, part of Flanders and Brabant, Namur and Luxemburg, and spoke a dialect of French" (*Alien Immigrants*, 155).

76. Scouloudi, *Returns of Strangers*, 223–31.

77. Owen Felltham, *A brief character of the Low-Countries under the states being three weeks observation of the vices and vertues of the inhabitants* (London, 1652), 1–5. Conversely,

Schama hears in these lines an emphasis on the Netherlands' distinctiveness from "the reassuringly cliff-girt insularity of Albion" (*Embarrassment of Riches*, 265).

78. On the composition date, political context, and literary influences on Marvell's poem, see Marvell, "The Character of Holland," in *The Poems of Andrew Marvell*, ed. Nigel Smith, rev. ed. (London: Pearson Longman, 2007), 246–56; all citations are from this edition. See also John Kerrigan *Archipelagic English: Literature, History, and Politics, 1603–1707* (Oxford: Oxford University Press, 2008), 238–43.

79. Years later, Marvell would once again posit the Netherlands as England's frontier: "the *Spanish Nether-land,* which had alwayes been considered as the natural Frontier of *England*" (*An Account of the Growth of Popery, and Arbitrary Government in England* [London, 1677], 17–18).

80. Felltham, *Brief character*, 41; and Marvell, *Character of Holland*. On the frog as a "stock type of Hollandophobic caricature," see Schama, *Embarrassment of Riches*, 263–64.

81. Against critical dismissal of Marvell's poem as merely "jingoistic," Richard Todd demonstrates the nuanced "distinctive balance" operative in Marvell's characterization of Hollanders ("Equilibrium and National Stereotyping in 'The Character of Holland,'" in *On the Celebrated and Neglected Poems of Andrew Marvell*, ed. Claude J. Summers and Ted-Larry Pebworth [Columbia: University of Missouri Press, 1992], 169–91).

82. Personal communication.

83. On representations of the Dutch in early modern drama, see Andrew Fleck, "Marking Difference and National Identity in Dekker's *The Shoemaker's Holiday*," *Studies in English Literature* 46.2 (2006): 349–70, and "'Ick Verstaw You Niet': Performing Foreign Tongues on the Early Modern English Stage," *Medieval and Renaissance Drama in England* 20 (2007): 204–21, and also his manuscript "The Dutch Device." For a more comprehensive survey of "foreigners," including the Dutch, on the English stage, see A. J. Hoenselaars, *Images of Englishmen and Foreigners in the Drama of Shakespeare and His Contemporaries: A Study of Stage Characters and National Identity in English Renaissance Drama, 1558–1642* (London: Associated University Presses, 1992).

84. Linda Colley, "Britishness and Otherness: An Argument," *Journal of British Studies* 31.4 (1992): 316. This article offers a condensed articulation of the argument Colley advances in *Britons: Forging the Nation, 1707–1837* (New Haven, Conn.: Yale University Press, 1992). For a persuasive critique of how Colley's argument depends on eliding and estranging the figure of the Catholic, the familiar religious Other residing within Protestant England, see Frances E. Dolan, *Whores of Babylon: Catholicism, Gender, and Seventeenth-Century Print Culture* (Ithaca, N.Y.: Cornell University Press, 1999), esp. 43.

85. In *Renaissance Self-Fashioning*, Stephen Greenblatt argues for England's national self-fashioning as a process "achieved in relation to something perceived as alien, strange or hostile . . . [something that] must be discovered or invented in order to be attacked or destroyed" (*Renaissance Self-Fashioning: From More to Shakespeare* [Chicago: University of Chicago Press, 1980], 9). Emily Bartels offers a trenchant diachronic review of critical approaches to the topic of representation of "Others" in "Shakespeare's 'Other' Worlds: The Critical Trek," *Literature Compass* 5.6 (2008): 1111–38.

86. Michael Neill, "Broken English and Broken Irish: Nation, Language, and the Optic of Power in Shakespeare's Histories," *Shakespeare Quarterly* 45.1 (1994): 14.

87. Janette Dillon, *Language and Stage in Medieval and Renaissance England* (Cambridge: Cambridge University Press, 1998), 164.

88. Hoenselaars, *Images of Englishmen*, 25.

89. Duffy, *Englishman*, 13. Though Duffy identifies xenophobia as the sentiment driving much of satirical printmaking in England, he finds that "xenophobia was in fact sufficiently diverse in its origins to give considerable flexibility to the portrayal of the foreigner in the prints either as entertainment or as propaganda. . . . The prints therefore do not only show the English image of different foreigners, they also show how that image was manipulated for other purposes" (44).

90. Ibid. Two recent books offer a revision to this thesis: Griffin, *English Renaissance Drama*; and Fuchs, *Exotic Nation*.

91. Jean Howard, "An English Lass amid the Moors: Gender, Race, Sexuality, and National Identity in Heywood's *The Fair Maid of the West*," in *Women, "Race," and Writing in the Early Modern Period,* ed. Margo Hendricks and Patricia Parker (London: Routledge, 1994), 111.

92. Ibid, 111–12.

93. James Shapiro, *Shakespeare and the Jews* (New York: Columbia University Press, 1996), 5. Lindsay Kaplan nuances this argument significantly, demonstrating a correspondence between medieval and early modern constructions of Jewishness in England: "Jessica's Mother: Medieval Constructions of Jewish Race and Gender in *The Merchant of Venice*," *Shakespeare Quarterly* 58.1 (2007): 1–30.

94. Shapiro, *Shakespeare and the Jews*, 170. For an illuminating reading of the tropes that give rise to these and other questions in literary representations of the Jew, see Janet Adelman, "Her Father's Blood: Race, Conversion, and Nation in *The Merchant of Venice*," *Representations* 81 (Winter 2003): 4–30.

95. Ania Loomba, *Shakespeare, Race, and Colonialism* (Oxford: Oxford University Press, 2002), 105.

96. Ibid. On English representation of Anglo-Islamic relations, see Daniel J. Vitkus, *Turning Turk: English Theater and the Multicultural Mediterranean, 1570–1630* (New York: Palgrave Macmillan, 2003); Nabil Matar, *Turks, Moors, and Englishmen in the Age of Discovery* (New York: Columbia University Press, 1999); and Nabil Matar and Gerald MacLean, *Britain and the Islamic World, 1558–1713* (Oxford: Oxford University Press, 2011), which provides a robust bibliography on the topic.

97. Emily Bartels, *Spectacles of Strangeness: Imperialism, Alienation, and Marlowe* (Philadelphia: University of Pennsylvania Press, 1993), xv.

98. Neill, "Broken English," 3–4. Andrew Murphy emphasizes instead how representations of Anglo-Irish proximity reveal the English confronting their own self-fragmentation (*But the Irish Sea Betwixt Us: Ireland, Colonialism, and Renaissance Literature* [Lexington: University Press of Kentucky, 1999]). Other historians concur, arguing that Ireland is the proximate Other whose relations with England provided "both a mirror and a hammer—reflecting and fragmenting images of England" (Brendan Bradshaw,

Andrew Hadfield, and Willy Maley, eds., *Representing Ireland: Literature and the Origins of Conflict 1534–1660* [Cambridge: Cambridge University Press, 1993], 15).

99. Ann Rosalind Jones, "Italians and Others: *The White Devil* (1612)," in *Staging the Renaissance: Reinterpretations of Elizabethan and Jacobean Drama*, ed. David Scott Kastan and Peter Stallybrass (New York: Routledge, 1991), 260.

100. Homi Bhabha, *The Location of Culture* (London: Routledge, 1994), 44.

101. Lynda Boose, "'The Getting of a Lawful Race': Racial Discourse in Early Modern England and the Unrepresentable Black Woman," in *Women, "Race," and Writing in the Early Modern Period,* ed. Margo Hendricks and Patricia Parker (London: Routledge, 1994), 38.

102. These and other scholars working on the history of sexuality and gender constitute important exceptions to my general observation. Jonathan Dollimore articulates constructive skepticism regarding what he characterizes as a critical "fetishization of difference" in *Sexual Dissidence: Augustine to Wilde, Freud to Foucault* (Oxford: Clarendon Press, 1991), especially 63. On how representations of erotic sameness came to underpin "the naturalness of heterosexual monogamy," see Valerie Traub, "Mapping the Global Body," in *Early Modern Visual Culture: Representation, Race, and Empire in Renaissance England,* ed. Peter Erickson and Clark Hulse (Philadelphia: University of Pennsylvania Press, 2000), 44–97, and *The Renaissance of Lesbianism in Early Modern England* (Cambridge: Cambridge University Press, 2002). Kathryn Schwarz has demonstrated that Amazons, figures that would seem to function as the quintessential exotic Other, were dangerous not for their difference but because of how they were like men, mothers, wives, and queens and therefore reveal "the perversity of the inside" (*Tough Love: Amazon Encounters in the English Renaissance* [Durham, N.C.: Duke University Press, 2000], 9). Jean Feerick has shown how the early modern category of race "describe[s] differences *internal* to a polity," and so was understood as "a category proximate to that of rank," and argues for the importance of attending to the clustering of race, blood, and lineage in the period (*Strangers in Blood: Relocating Race in the Renaissance* [Toronto: University of Toronto Press, 2010], 8–9). Scholars working on the history of friendship have also focused attention on early modern ideas about "likeness" and similitude. Laurie Shannon has uncovered the early modern "politics of likeness" in *Sovereign Amity: Figures of Friendship in Shakespearean Contexts* (Chicago: University of Chicago Press, 2002). For the ways in which collaboration and friendship disrupt paradigms of difference, see Jeffrey Masten, *Textual Intercourse: Collaboration, Authorship and Sexualities in Renaissance Drama* (Cambridge: Cambridge University Press, 1997). Even religious difference, that most vexed and divisive of categories in Reformation England, raised pressing questions about similarity. In *Whores of Babylon*, Frances Dolan illuminates the ways in which "familiarity, similarity, and proximity were not a comfort" when it came to the topic of Catholicism in early modern England. Instead, Catholics prove "troubling figures precisely because they represented the foreign or strange from inside geographical and conceptual boundaries of Englishness" (43). Further afield, historians working on European–Native American encounters in the eighteenth century have emphasized the interplay of difference and sameness in constructing ideas of race in colonial America; see Nancy Shoemaker, *A*

Strange Likeness: Becoming Red and White in Eighteenth Century North America (Oxford: Oxford University Press, 2004).

103. Dollimore, *Sexual Dissidence*, 52.

104. Murphy, *But the Irish Sea Betwixt Us*, 32.

105. Emily Bartels, *Speaking of the Moor: From Alcazar to Othello* (Philadelphia: University of Pennsylvania Press, 2008).

106. Dollimore, *Sexual Dissidence*, 33.

107. "*Aliens and Englishness* sees Elizabethans' reflections on English identity as increasingly a process of finding and absorbing alien aspects around them and less the simple phenomenon of frictionally and uncooperatively rubbing up 'against non-Englishness.'" Lloyd Edward Kermode, *Aliens and Englishness in Elizabethan Drama* (Cambridge: Cambridge University Press, 2009), 9.

108. Ibid., 15–16.

109. Ibid., 16.

110. Robert Young, *The Idea of English Ethnicity* (Malden, Mass.: Blackwell, 2008), 19–20.

111. In his recent study of sexual types, Mario DiGangi resists collapsing type and identity by reading for how sexual types in early modern drama are "symptoms of ideological conflicts that extend beyond sexuality" (*Sexual Types: Embodiment, Agency, and Dramatic Character from Shakespeare to Shirley* [Philadelphia: University of Pennsylvania Press, 2011], 6). In this way, DiGangi's study proposes a different way through some of the problems of the relation of identity to character, figure, and type that my emphasis on the semiotics of Dutchness also seeks to address.

112. Kermode, *Aliens and Englishness*, 4.

113. Archer's *Citizen Shakespeare* also resists reading drama in terms of representation of "types" to explore instead the "historical semantics" of citizenship in Shakespeare's works.

114. Book-length monographs on early modern epistemologies of race in the English context, which I do not address at length elsewhere, include: Eldred Jones, *Othello's Countrymen: The African in English Renaissance Drama* (London: Oxford University Press, 1965), and *The Elizabethan Image of Africa* (Charlottesville: University Press of Virginia, 1971); Winthrop D. Jordan, *White over Black: American Attitudes Toward the Negro, 1550–1812* (Chapel Hill: University of North Carolina Press, 1968); Anthony Gerard Barthelemy, *Black Face, Maligned Race: The Representation of Blacks in English Drama from Shakespeare to Southerne* (Baton Rouge: Louisiana State University Press, 1987); Jack D'Amico, *The Moor in English Renaissance Drama* (Tampa: University of South Florida Press, 1991); John Gillies, *Shakespeare and the Geography of Difference* (Cambridge: Cambridge University Press, 1994); Kim Hall, *Things of Darkness: Economies of Race and Gender in Early Modern England* (Ithaca: Cornell University Press, 1995); Shapiro, *Shakespeare and the Jews*; Matar, *Turks, Moors, and Englishmen*; Dympna Callaghan, *Shakespeare Without Women: Representing Gender and Race on the Renaissance Stage* (New York: Routledge, 2000); Loomba, *Shakespeare, Race, and Colonialism*; Mary Floyd-Wilson, *English Ethnicity and Race in Early Modern Drama* (Cambridge: Cambridge University Press, 2003); Joyce

Green MacDonald, *Women and Race in Early Modern Texts* (Cambridge: Cambridge University Press, 2002); Sujata Iyengar, *Shades of Difference: Mythologies of Skin Color in Early Modern England* (Philadelphia: University of Pennsylvania Press, 2005); Virginia Mason Vaughan, *Performing Blackness on English Stages, 1500–1800* (Cambridge: Cambridge University Press, 2005); Robert Markley, *The Far East and the English Imagination, 1600–1730* (Cambridge: Cambridge University Press, 2006); Lara Bovilsky, *Barbarous Play: Race on the English Renaissance Stage* (Minneapolis: University of Minnesota Press, 2008); Bartels, *Speaking of the Moor*; Ian Smith, *Race and Rhetoric in the Renaissance: Barbarian Errors* (New York: Palgrave Macmillan, 2009); and Feerick, *Strangers in Blood*. Often cited critical collections include: Hendricks and Parker, *Women, "Race," and Writing*; Ania Loomba and Martin Orkin, eds., *Post-Colonial Shakespeares* (New York: Routledge, 1988); Joyce Green MacDonald, ed., *Race, Ethnicity, and Power in the Renaissance* (Madison: Associated University Presses, 1997); Erickson and Hulse, *Early Modern Visual Culture*; Catherine M. S. Alexander and Stanley Wells, eds., *Shakespeare and Race* (New York: Cambridge University Press, 2000); and Philip D. Beidler and Gary Taylor, eds., *Writing Race Across the Atlantic World* (New York: Palgrave Macmillan, 2005). The best introduction to the topic is Ania Loomba and Jonathan Burton, eds., *Race in Early Modern England: A Documentary Companion* (Basingstoke, England: Palgrave Macmillan, 2007).

115. Feminist scholars as well as scholars working in the field of sexuality studies have demonstrated the importance of understanding the coevolution of ideas shaping notions of race, ethnicity, gender, sexuality, embodiment, and rank. Thus, much work attentive to the category of gender has also been instrumental in demonstrating how variously and fully coarticulated these categories have been historically. Many of the works cited in the note above also obtain here. While the field of scholarship is too vast to site comprehensively, some influential book-length monographs that address sexuality or embodiment together with the period's gender (and sometimes also race) categories, include: Alan Bray, *Homosexuality in Renaissance England* (New York: Columbia University Press, 1995); Lisa Jardine, *Still Harping on Daughters: Women and Drama in the Age of Shakespeare* (Brighton: Harvester, 1983); Wendy Wall, *The Imprint of Gender: Authorship and Publication in the English Renaissance* (Ithaca, N.Y.: Cornell University Press, 1993); Gail Kern Paster, *The Body Embarrassed: Drama and the Disciplines of Shame in Early Modern England* (Ithaca, N.Y.: Cornell University Press, 1993); Kathleen M. Brown, *Good Wives, Nasty Wenches and Anxious Patriarchs: Gender, Race, and Power in Colonial Virginia* (Chapel Hill: University of North Carolina Press, 1996); Stephen Orgel, *Impersonations: The Performance of Gender in Shakespeare's England* (Cambridge: Cambridge University Press, 1996); Laura Gowing, *Domestic Dangers: Women, Words, and Sex in Early Modern London* (Oxford: Clarendon Press, 1996); Jean Howard and Phyllis Rackin, *Engendering a Nation: A Feminist Account of Shakespeare's English Histories* (New York: Routledge, 1997); Masten, *Textual Intercourse*; Michael Schoenfeldt, *Bodies and Selves in Early Modern England: Physiology and Inwardness in Spenser, Shakespeare, Herbert, and Milton* (Cambridge: Cambridge University Press, 1999); Traub, *Renaissance of Lesbianism*; Phyllis Rackin, *Shakespeare and Women* (Oxford: Oxford University Press, 2005); Will Fisher, *Materializing Gender in Early Modern English Literature and Culture* (Cambridge: Cambridge University

Press, 2006); Gina Bloom, *Voice in Motion: Staging Gender, Shaping Sound in Early Modern England* (Philadelphia: University of Pennsylvania Press, 2007); and DiGangi, *Sexual Types*. Often cited collections include: Margaret W. Ferguson, Maureen Quilligan, and Nancy J. Vickers, eds., *Rewriting the Renaissance: The Discourses of Sexual Difference in Early Modern England* (Chicago: University of Chicago Press, 1986); Susan Zimmerman, ed., *Erotic Politics: Desire on the Renaissance Stage* (New York: Routledge, 1992); Valerie Traub, M. Lindsay Kaplan, and Dympna Callaghan, eds., *Feminist Readings of Early Modern Culture* (Cambridge: Cambridge University Press, 1996); Louise Olga Fradenburg and Carla Freccero, eds., *Premodern Sexualities* (New York: Routledge, 1996); Dympna Callaghan, ed., *A Feminist Companion to Shakespeare* (Oxford: Blackwell, 2000); and Madhavi Menon, ed., *Shakesqueer: A Queer Companion to the Complete Works of Shakespeare* (Durham, N.C.: Duke University Press, 2011).

116. See especially Keith Wrightson, *Earthly Necessities: Economic Lives in Early Modern Britain* (New Haven, Conn.: Yale University Press, 2000).

117. Pierre Bourdieu, *Distinction: A Social Critique of the Judgment of Taste* (Cambridge, Mass.: Harvard University Press, 1984), 479.

118. Floyd-Wilson, *English Ethnicity*, 12.

119. Ibid., 2.

120. Floyd-Wilson's careful sifting through literary, philosophical, medical, and travel literature reveals that the sixteenth- and early seventeenth-century English were revising classical ethnographies (structured through the binaries of inner/outer and body/environment) in order to denaturalize long-standing connections between humoral and climate theories that rendered them intemperate and marginalized their geographic, cultural, and humoral status (ibid.).

121. Ibid., 48.

122. Ibid., 54.

123. It has been often noted that the word "ethnic" as it has come to be understood today is anachronistic to early modern usage (see Raymond Williams, *Keywords: A Vocabulary of Culture and Society* [New York: Oxford University Press, 1976], 119). Only as recently as 1953 did sociologists begin employing the word "ethnicity" to characterize their object of study (see Thomas Hylland Eriksen, *Ethnicity and Nationalism: Anthropological Perspectives*, 2nd ed. [London: Pluto Press, 2002], 4).

124. Colin Kidd, "Identity Before Identities: Ethnicity, Nationalism and the Historian," in *History and Nation*, ed. Julia Rudolph (Lewisburg, Pa.: Bucknell University Press, 2006), 25.

125. Ibid., 21.

126. Peter Stallybrass offers a strikingly parallel analysis of the word "individual" in William Shakespeare's corpus, arguing that "in the 'Shakespearean' context, 'individual,' whatever its range of possible meanings, suggests a *relation* (of part to whole, of part to part, of member to body, of body to body) not a separate entity" ("Shakespeare, the Individual, and the Text," in *Critical Studies*, ed. Lawrence Grossberg, Cary Nelson, and Paula Treichler [New York: Routledge, 1992], 606). Unlike our current commonplace

usage, for writers including Shakespeare and John Milton, individual meant, quite liter-ally, *indivisible*. When Kidd writes that "identity" has come to mean "individuality," he has momentarily forgotten the early modern sense of "individual," which aligns closely with the early modern sense of "identity." Both the literary critic and historian concur, by way of different evidence, that concepts of "identity" and the "individual" have under-gone significant transformations since the Renaissance.

127. Diana Fuss, *Identification Papers* (New York: Routledge, 1995), 2, 10.

128. Ibid.

129. Judith Butler, *Bodies That Matter* (London: Routledge, 1993), 105.

130. Robert Bartlett, "Medieval and Modern Concepts of Race and Ethnicity," *Journal of Medieval and Early Modern Studies* 31.1 (2001): 40.

131. Floyd-Wilson, *English Ethnicity*, 54.

132. Rogers Brubaker, *Ethnicity Without Groups* (Cambridge, Mass.: Harvard University Press, 2004).

133. Eriksen, *Ethnicity and Nationalism*, 12, 12n2. The shift I characterize was cata-lyzed by the influential work of Fredrik Barth, who in *Ethnic Groups and Boundaries: The Social Organization of Cultural Difference* (Boston: Little, Brown, 1969) argued that the critical focus of ethnic studies should be "the ethnic *boundary* that defines the group, not the cultural stuff that it encloses" (15). For a concise overview of the influence of Barth's work on the study of ethnicity, see Eriksen, *Ethnicity and Nationalism*, 36–40.

134. John Comaroff and Jean Comaroff, *Ethnography and the Historical Imagination* (Boulder, Colo: Westview, 1992), 54.

135. This formulation is indebted to Eve Sedgwick's claim that "to identify *as* must always include multiple processes of identification *with*" (*Epistemology of the Closet* [Berke-ley: University of California Press, 1990], 61).

136. This line of reasoning raises the question of *who* is the agent of this identifica-tion. My thinking on this question aligns most closely with Brubaker (*Ethnicity Without Groups*), who, influenced by Stuart Hall's work, contends that "identification does not *require* a specifiable 'identifier'; it can be pervasive and influential without being accom-plished by discrete, specified persons or institutions. Identification can be carried more or less anonymously by discourse or public narratives" (43). See also Stuart Hall, "Introduc-tion: Who Needs 'Identity'?," in *Questions of Cultural Identity*, ed. Paul Du Gay and Stuart Hall (London: Sage Publications, 1996), 1–17.

137. I have been influenced in this regard by Dollimore's argument pertaining to gender and cross-dressing that "a difference of degree can be as real as a difference of kind but in a different way. . . . [T]he same becomes more different than difference itself. But never utterly—i.e. securely—*other*" (*Sexual Dissidence*, 251–52). Valerie Traub emphasizes the importance of attending to how differences of degree were constructed, demonstrating that the "logic of the grid" in early cartographic representations of people and place enabled "degrees of difference to function as the literal coordinates by which the world's diverse peoples were identified and differentiated, labeled and categorized, classified and compared" ("The Nature of Norms in Early Modern England: Anatomy, Cartography, *King Lear*," *South Central Review* 26.1–2 [2009]: 59).

138. This question is raised by Kerrigan, whose *Archipelagic English* offers a nuanced analysis of the complexities of "ethnicity" across England, Scotland, Ireland, and Wales.

139. On the complex relation of ethnicity to nationhood, see especially Kidd, "Identity Before Identities"; Young, *Idea of English Ethnicity*; and Kerrigan, *Archipelagic English*.

140. Richard Helgerson, *Forms of Nationhood: The Elizabethan Writing of England* (Chicago: University of Chicago Press, 1992), 22.

141. Richard Helgerson, "Before National Literary History," *Modern Language Quarterly* 64 (2003): 171.

142. Helgerson goes on to stress the importance of likeness to the forms and formation of English nationhood: "for all the differences and all the qualifications of those differences, national literary history, wherever it occurs, remains an exercise in generic mimicry, an attempt to put homegrown flesh on a skeleton that once lived elsewhere" (ibid., 179). Claire McEachern concurs: while "difference, and borders, and insularity are all key features of this England . . . so are resemblance, passage, and permeability" (*The Poetics of English Nationhood, 1590–1612* [Cambridge: Cambridge University Press, 1996], 30).

143. Recent historiography situating England in the Atlantic context suggests that this shift is under way. See the introduction to Kerrigan, *Archipelagic English*; and John R. Chávez, *Beyond Nations: Evolving Homelands in the North Atlantic World, 1400–2000* (New York: Cambridge University Press, 2009).

144. Patricia Parker, *Shakespeare from the Margins: Language, Culture, Context* (Chicago: University of Chicago Press, 1996), 13.

145. Thomas Scott, *Belgicke Pismire* (London [i.e., Holland], 1622), 49.

146. Peter Burke, *Languages and Communities in Early Modern Europe* (Cambridge: Cambridge University Press, 2004), 38.

147. Dillon, *Language and Stage*; Kermode, *Aliens and Englishness*.

148. John Considine, *Dictionaries in Early Modern Europe: Lexicography and the Making of Heritage* (Cambridge: Cambridge University Press, 2008).

CHAPTER 1. GOING DUTCH IN LONDON CITY COMEDY

1. Notable full-length studies of Tudor and Stuart city comedy include Brian Gibbons, *Jacobean City Comedy: A Study of Satiric Plays by Jonson, Marston and Middleton* (1968; Cambridge, Mass.: Harvard University Press, 1980); Alexander Leggatt, *Citizen Comedy in the Age of Shakespeare* (Toronto: University of Toronto Press, 1973); Theodore B. Leinwand, *The City Staged: Jacobean City Comedy, 1603–1613* (Madison: University of Wisconsin Press, 1986); Jean E. Howard, *Theater of a City: The Places of London Comedy, 1598–1642* (Philadelphia: University of Pennsylvania Press, 2007); and Heather Easterling, *Parsing the City: Jonson, Middleton, Dekker, and City Comedy's London as Language* (New York: Routledge, 2007). Following Adam Zucker, I find useful a broad definition of the city comedy: "to denote a play obviously set in London that relies predominately on comic narrative elements (i.e., romance, intrigue, the 'untying of the knot of all the error')

to produce and make sense of the complexities of an urban setting" ("The Social Logic of Ben Jonson's *Epicoene*," *Renaissance Drama* 33 [2004]: 60n25).

2. For Anglo-Dutch working relations, see Laura Hunt Yungblut, *Strangers Settled Here Amongst Us: Policies, Perceptions and the Presence of Aliens in Elizabethan England* (London: Routledge, 1996); and Ian Archer, *The Pursuit of Stability: Social Relations in Elizabethan London* (Cambridge: Cambridge University Press, 1991), 131–40. On the Dutch Church in London, see Andrew Pettegree, *Foreign Protestant Communities in Sixteenth-Century London* (Oxford: Clarendon Press, 1986).

3. John Marston, *The Dutch Courtesan* (London, 1605); Henry Glapthorne, *The Hollander* (London,1640); and Shackerley Marmyon, *Hollands Leaguer* (London, 1632). All citations are from *The Dutch Courtesan*, ed. David Crane (London: A & C Black, 1997).

4. Laura Hunt Yungblut, "Straungers and Aliaunts: The 'Un-English' Among the English in Elizabethan England," in *Crossing Boundaries: Issues of Cultural and Individual Identity in the Middle Ages and the Renaissance*, ed. Sally McKee (Turnhout: Brepols, 1999), 273.

5. E.g., Leinwand, *City Staged*, 3–20; see also A. J. Hoenselaars, *Images of Englishmen and Foreigners in the Drama of Shakespeare and His Contemporaries: A Study of Stage Characters and National Identity in English Renaissance Drama, 1558–1642* (London: Associated University Presses, 1992). John Michael Archer (*Citizen Shakespeare: Freemen and Aliens in the Language of the Plays* [New York: Palgrave Macmillan, 2005]) offers an important critique of the scholarly tradition that has emphasized "representation rather than language" in city comedies (18–20).

6. Leinwand, *City Staged*, 13.

7. Ibid., 12.

8. Important recent exceptions include Nigel Goose, " 'Xenophobia' in Elizabethan and Early Stuart England: An Epithet Too Far?" in *Immigrants in Tudor and Early Stuart England*, ed. Nigel Goose and Lien Luu (Brighton: Sussex Academic Press, 2005), 110–35; and Christian M. Billing, "The Dutch Diaspora in English City Comedy: 1598–1618," in *Transnational Exchange in Early Modern Theater,* ed. Robert Henke and Erick Nicholson (Burlington: Ashgate, 2008), 119–39.

9. Leinwand, *City Staged*, 13. Though she does not attend primarily to constructions of ethnicity in *Parsing the City*, Easterling also emphasizes the "language consciousness" of city comedy, particularly the ways in which ideas about the vernacular were thematized and interrogated.

10. I borrow this phrase from Mary Floyd-Wilson, *English Ethnicity and Race in Early Modern Drama* (Cambridge: Cambridge University Press, 2003), 48.

11. Garrett A. Sullivan Jr. argues that in this passage "brothels function in two ways: on one level, they help preserve the chastity of the wife by giving potential unmarried male adulterers a sexual outlet; on another, they provide that same outlet for philandering husbands" (" 'All Things Come into Commerce': Women, Household Labor, and the Spaces of Marston's *The Dutch Courtesan*," *Renaissance Drama* 27 [1996]: 27–28). This logic extends back into medieval social justifications for prostitution. Ruth Mazo Karras finds that in the medieval period "one justification given for establishing official brothels,

or for tolerating private ones, was the 'lesser evil' argument. Masculine sexuality, particularly that of unmarried men (whether workers and apprentices, who could not afford to marry, or priests, who were not allowed to), was seen as an irrepressible force that needed some sort of outlet. If there were no prostitutes—already fallen women—to provide this outlet, these men would corrupt and cause the fall of 'honest' women" (*Common Women: Prostitution and Sexuality in Medieval England* [Oxford: Oxford University Press, 1996], 133. This medieval logic apparently informs Freevill's defense of prostitution.

12. Jean E. Howard observes, "seen from Freevill's starkly Anglocentric point of view, the Dutch are not fellow allies in a Protestant cause so much as inhabitants of a convenient buffer zone keeping Spanish troops from attacking England" ("Mastering Difference in *The Dutch Courtesan,*" *Shakespeare Studies* 24 [1996]: 108).

13. See Yungblut, *Strangers Settled Here*; Bernard Cottret, *The Huguenots in England: Immigration and Settlement c. 1550–1700* (Cambridge: Cambridge University Press, 1991); and Goose and Luu, *Immigrants in Tudor and Early Stuart England.*

14. In *Locating Privacy in Tudor London,* Lena Cowen Orlin explores a wealth of historical and material evidence that challenges attempts to draw too firm a line between conceptions of public and private space in the period and emphasizes the ways privacy "inspired an uneasy mixture of desire and distrust" and was often an "unanticipated effect of spaces built for other purposes" (Oxford: Oxford University Press, 2007), 8–10. Freevill's failed efforts to divide house and home from common public space, though a conventional trope in city comedy, nonetheless bears witness to the complexities of ideas about privacy beyond the Tudor period.

15. For a full-length study of the Family of Love, see Christopher Marsh, *The Family of Love in English Society, 1550–1630* (Cambridge: Cambridge University Press, 1994).

16. Sullivan reminds us, "given the failure in the period to draw a sharp distinction between the domestic and economic, a reading that sees the partitioning of space as separating the commercial from the 'private' or familial is problematic" ("'All Things Come into Commerce,'" 24). Because the stage directions do not distinguish between the Mulligrubs' home and their tavern, I assume that there is a fluid boundary between where the Mulligrubs reside and where they do business.

17. 2.1.84, 2.1. 91, 2.1.92, 2.1.155, 2.1.155, 3.1.225, 3.1.259, 4.2.17, 4.3.1 (Crane glosses "cacafuego" as "spitfire" [Lat. *cacare* = to shit; Sp. *fuego* = fire]), 4.3.8, 4.3.15.

18. Howard emphasizes the mixedness of Franceschina: "her entry into the internationalized marketplace has left her a linguistic monster, called a Dutch courtesan, textually coded as an Italian, and speaking a one-woman Babylonian dialect, as if all the tongues of Pentecost had visited her at once" ("Mastering Difference," 115).

19. Qtd. in E. J. Burford, *Bawds and Lodgings: A History of London Bankside Brothels c. 100–1675* (London: Owen, 1976), 77–78.

20. Ibid., 79.

21. Karras, *Common Women,* 56.

22. Ibid., 57.

23. Sir William Brereton, *Travels in Holland, the United Provinces, England, Scotland, and Ireland, 1634–1635* (London: Chetham Society, 1844), 55.

24. Martin L. Wine ed., *The Dutch Courtesan*, Regents Renaissance Drama series. (Lincoln: University of Nebraska Press, 1965), xixn.15. See also Howard, "Mastering Difference," 115.

25. The play text is, of course, silent as to how the actor speaking Franceschina's lines pronounced "Ick sal." In performance, an actor may have amplified or minimized the foreignness of sound in stage Dutch speech.

26. On stage Dutch, see Andrew Fleck, "'Ick Verstaw You Niet': Performing Foreign Tongues on the Early Modern English Stage," *Medieval and Renaissance Drama in England* 20 (2007): 204–21.

27. Thomas Dekker, *The Shoemaker's Holiday or The Gentle Craft*, in *The Roaring Girl and Other City Comedies*, ed. James Knowles (Oxford: Oxford University Press, 2001), 1–65. Knowles glosses the exchange thus:

"1–5 *Ik . . . Hans?* 'I shall tell you what to say, Hans; this ship that comes from Candy [Crete], is all full, by God's sacrament, of sugar, civet, almonds, cambric, and all things—a thousand, thousand things. Take it, Hans, take it for your master. There are the bills of lading [inventories]. Your master Simon Eyre shall have a good bargain. What say you, Hans?'

"6 *Wat . . . slopen.* Firk's mockery of the Skipper.

"9 *Mine . . . Hodge:* 'My dear brother Firk, bring Master Eyre to the Sign of the Swan [a tavern]. There you will find this skipper and me. What say you, brother Firk? Do it, Hodge.'" (311–33)

28. William Haughton, *William Haughton's Englishmen for My Money; or, a Woman Will Have Her Will*, ed. Albert Croll Baugh (Philadelphia: [s.n.], 1917).

29. Thomas Dekker and John Webster, *Northward Ho* (1607), in *The Dramatic Works of Thomas Dekker*, ed. Fredson Bowers, vol. 2 (Cambridge: Cambridge University Press, 1955), 410–90. I discuss this exchange at greater length in chapter four.

30. Sir Philip Sidney, *The Defence of Poesy*, in *Sir Philip Sidney: A Critical Edition of the Major Works*, ed. Katherine Duncan-Jones (Oxford: Oxford University Press, 1989), 248.

31. This term of endearment is one Franceschina repeats throughout the play. Each time the word appears differently on the page. She calls Freevill her "aderliver love" (1.2.81) and later declares "mine aderlievest affection!" (2.2.50–51). She will refer to Malheureux as "O mynheer man, aderliver love," which appears in the 1605 quarto as "a dere liver" (5.1.18). Had the actor delivered *aderliver* as "a dear liver"—thus transferring to the liver Franceschina's heart's desire—further mockery of her desire would have been enabled in performance.

32. See William C. Johnson, "The Family of Love in Stuart Literature: A Chronology of Name-Crossed Lovers," *Journal of Medieval and Renaissance Studies* 7 (1977): 95–112; and Richard Levin, "The Family of Lust and *The Family of Love*," *Studies in English Literature* 6.2 (1966): 309–22.

33. Cited in Charles Cathcart, "Lodge, Marston, and the Family of Love," *Notes and Queries* 50.1 (2003): 70.

34. Ibid.

35. Jean Dietz Moss, "The Family of Love and English Critics," *Sixteenth Century Journal* 6.1 (1975): 50–51.

36. Not only were Familists notoriously close-mouthed about their faith, according to Marsh, they seemed to have held only the most clandestine of meetings (*Family of Love*). On the critical debate regarding both the authorship and dating of *Family of Love*, see Gary Taylor, Paul Mulholland, and MacDonald P. Jackson, "Thomas Middleton, Lording Barry, and *The Family of Love*," *Papers of the Bibliographical Society of America* 93.2 (1999): 213–41. Taylor et al. argue that the play "seems to have been completed no earlier than the second half of May 1605" (224), and argue for Lording Barry as the play's author.

37. Qtd. in Michael Srigley, "The Influence of Continental Familism in England After 1570," *Cultural Exchange Between European Nations during the Renaissance*, spec. issue of *Acta Universitatis Upsaliensis, Studia Anglistica Upsaliensia* 86 (1994): 100. See also Jean Dietz Moss, "Godded with God: Hendrik Niclaes and His Family of Love," *Transactions of the American Philosophical Society* 71.8 (1981): 1–89. I follow Moss in her spelling of Hendrik Niclaes.

38. Srigley, "Influence of Continental Familism," 100.

39. Moss ("Godded with God" 27) cites John Rogers, *Displaying* (1579), fol. E8.

40. Moss summarizes Van Haemstede's story in "Godded with God," 22–23.

41. For the ways in which this conflation in James's *Basilikon Doron* might have provoked the Familists' *Supplication*, see Marsh, *Family of Love*, 200–205.

42. My use of the phrase "cultural fantasy" has been informed by Wendy Wall's definition of fantasy in *Staging Domesticity: Household Work and English Identity in Early Modern Drama* (Cambridge: Cambridge University Press, 2002). Wall defines fantasy "not simply as the wish of an individual (the *object* of desire) but instead as the cultural setting or syntax for desire" (12). The cultural fantasy that I suggest is developing in the religious-political context of mid-sixteenth-century sectarianism links stranger communities in London to faith "imported" from abroad and does so, at times, by conflating "radical" sects with one another in order to amplify their difference from the Anglican church. That the Dutch Church must respond to charges of its minister's Familist (or Anabaptist) sympathies suggests that, at the highest clerical levels within the stranger community, those marked as "strangers" were working to jettison this association from their community.

43. Srigley avers that in the seventeenth century Familism was "absorbed into Quakerism" ("Influence of Continental Familism," 97); Keith Thomas argues that Familists "were a powerful influence upon the Quakers, and barely distinguishable from some of the Ranters" (*Religion and the Decline of Magic* [Oxford: Oxford University Press, 1997], 376). Moss discusses a tract by Henry Hallywell entitled *An Account of Familism as it is Practiced by the Quakers* (1673), which lends textual weight to the perception of ideological affiliation between Familism and Quakerism ("Godded with God," 67–68). But in her final analysis, Moss argues that "there are no names that furnish final proof, no lists of Quakers who admitted to having been Familists" (68).

44. Srigley, "Influence of Continental Familism," 100.

45. Ibid., 98.

46. Keith Thomas explains: "The Familists, who held that Christ was 'a Type, and but a Type,' believed that it was possible for man 'totally to be inhabited by Christ'. That is to say, they were perfectionists, envisaging that men could attain a holy state in this existence" (*Religion and the Decline*, 375–76).

47. Srigley, "Influence of Continental Familism," 98.

48. See Proclamation 652, "Ordering Prosecution of the Family of Love," in Paul L. Hughes and James F. Larkin, eds., *Tudor Royal Proclamations*, vol. 2 (New Haven, Conn.: Yale University Press, 1969), 474–75. Hughes and Larkin note: "the Privy Council had already been active in efforts to suppress this group in orders of 25 May 1579 . . . and 12 April earlier in the present year [1580]" (2: 474n1). Nevertheless, Marsh argues, the Family of Love was "established at the court of Elizabeth and James I to a degree that has never previously been realized" (*Family of Love*, 16).

49. Hughes and Larkin, *Tudor Royal Proclamations*, 474.

50. *A supplication of the Family of Love . . . for grace and favour Examined, and found to be derogatorie in an hie degree, unto the glorie of God, the honour of our King, and the religion in this realme both soundly professed & firmly established* (London, 1606), 3. The *Supplication* is introduced by the anonymous "Examiner," who quotes from James's *Basilikon Doron* to presume the Familists' "foule . . . and fantasicall opinions" (1).

51. In the *Supplication,* the Familists declare that they "utterly disclaime and detest . . . the disobedient, and erroneous Sectes of the Anabaptistes, Browne, Penrie, Puritanes, and all other proude-minded Sectes" (*Supplication*, 2–3) and attempt to persuade the throne that their beliefs are not heretical. According to the text, James responded by demanding that the Familists "professe the same religion with him . . . and laye aside all *H.N.* his erroneous and detestable writinges; if they will approve the *Service* of the Church of *England* . . . they neede feare no persecution, or trouble" (*Supplication*, 56). For a discussion of James's negative opinions regarding Familism when he was on the Scottish throne, see Janet Halley, "Heresy, Orthodoxy, and the Politics of Religious Discourse: The Case of the English Family of Love," *Representations* 15 (1986): 110.

52. Marsh, *Family of Love*, 203.

53. For discussion of the sexualizing of the Catholic, for example, see Frances E. Dolan, *Whores of Babylon: Catholicism, Gender, and Seventeenth-Century Print Culture* (Ithaca, N.Y.: Cornell University Press, 1999).

54. Jean E. Howard, "Women, Foreigners, and the Regulation of Urban Space in *Westward Ho*," in *Material London Ca. 1600*, ed. Lena Cowen Orlin (Philadelphia: University of Pennsylvania Press, 2000), 159; and Valerie Traub, *Desire and Anxiety: Circulations of Sexuality in Shakespearean Drama* (New York: Routledge, 1992), 71–87.

55. For the conventionality of such gulling in city comedy, see Leinwand, *City Staged*, 53.

56. Samuel Rowley, *The noble souldier. Or, A contract broken, justly reveng'd. A tragedy* (London, 1634), F4v.

57. *Oxford English Dictionary*, s.v. "Mulligrub" (n. 1. b).

58. Ibid., n. 2. The word could also mean "a state or fit of depression: low spirits. Also: a bad temper or mood" (n. 1. a).

59. Wall, *Staging Domesticity*, 6.

60. Ibid.

61. Patricia Fumerton, introduction to Patricia Fumerton and Simon Hunt, eds., *Renaissance Culture and the Everyday* (Philadelphia: University of Pennsylvania Press, 1999), 6.

62. F. D., *The Dutch-Mens Pedigree, or a Relation, Shewing How They Were First Bred, and Descended from a Horse-Turd, Which Was Enclosed in a Butter-Box* (London, 1653), Thomason Tracts 246:669.F.16[81].

63. Glapthorne, *The Hollander*, 3.1.

64. Crane, in Marston, *The Dutch Courtesan*, 45n10.

65. Gordon Williams asserts that "women who made or sold butter were proverbially fractious. . . . They might also be wanton" (*A Dictionary of Sexual Language and Imagery in Shakespearean and Stuart Literature*, vol. 1 [London: Athlone Press, 1994], 181).

66. For a discussion of the allusions to Revelation in this passage, see Mark Thronton Burnett, "Calling 'Things by Their Right Names': Troping Prostitution, Politics and *The Dutch Courtesan*," in *Renaissance Configurations: Voices/Bodies/Spaces, 1580–1690*, ed. Gordon McMullan (New York: St. Martin's Press, 1998), 179–80.

67. Howard, "Women, Foreigners," 154.

CHAPTER 2. "BY COMMON LANGUAGE RESEMBLED"

1. Thomas Scott, *Belgicke Pismire* (London [i.e., Holland], 1622), 49. When date or place of publication is false on the imprint, I have entered the corrected information in brackets as it appears in the English Short Title Catalogue (hereafter, STC).

2. The United Provinces included Holland, Zeeland, Utrecht, Gelderland, Overijssel, Groningen, Friesland (as well as Drenth, which later became a separate province). Scott's political argument pertains to the United Provinces rather than all of the Low Countries' seventeen provinces. Scott's use of the term "Hollanders" for people from all seven of the United Provinces was a common misnomer of the period, an effect of Holland's commercial and cultural centrality.

3. *Declaration of the Causes Mooving the Queene of England. . . .* (London, 1585), rpt. in *A Collection of Scarce and Valuable Tracts*, ed. John Somers and Walter Scott, vol. 1 (London: Cadell and Davies, 1809), 413.

4. Graham Parry, *The Trophies of Time: English Antiquarians of the Seventeenth Century* (Oxford: Oxford University Press, 1995), 2.

5. In exploring the ways in which the philological debates informed and were informed by notions of racial heritage, we will be considering notions of race as kinship, ideas that were informed far more by Mosaic history than by the premodern (particularly seventeenth-century) and Enlightenment epistemologies that linked race to skin color. On the Mosaic paradigm, see Benjamin Braude, "Sons of Noah and the Construction of Ethnic and Geographical Identities in the Medieval and Early Modern Periods," *William*

and Mary Quarterly 54.1 (1997): 103–42; and Colin Kidd, *British Identities Before Nationalism: Ethnicity and Nationhood in the Atlantic World, 1600–1800* (Cambridge: Cambridge University Press, 1999), 9–33.

6. Richard Mulcaster, *Mulcaster's Elementarie*, ed. E. T. Campagnac (Oxford: Clarendon Press, 1925), 172. All references are to this edition.

7. Richard Foster Jones contends: "the suddenness with which writers began to recognize the eloquent nature of the mother tongue enables us to date the turning point not earlier than 1575 nor later than 1580" (*The Triumph of the English Language: A Survey of Opinions Concerning the Vernacular from the Introduction of Printing to the Restoration* [Stanford: Stanford University Press, 1953], 211). Charles Barber characterizes this ideological transition: "For the most part . . . the attitude to English in the early Tudor period was apologetic. . . . [B]y the end of the sixteenth century, uncomplimentary comparisons of English with other languages have largely disappeared. In the seventeenth century, writers are more likely to go to the other extreme, and boast of the superiority of English to other languages" (*Early Modern English* [London: André Deutsch, 1976], 76). For a deeper consideration of English "eloquence," see Carla Mazzio, *The Inarticulate Renaissance: Language Trouble in an Age of Eloquence* (Philadelphia: University of Pennsylvania Press, 2009).

8. Richard Bailey, *Images of English: A Cultural History of the Language* (Ann Arbor: University of Michigan Press, 1991), 53.

9. George Gascoigne, "Certayne Notes of Instruction," in *The Posies* (1575), ed. John W. Cunliffe (1907; Cambridge: Cambridge University Press, 1969), 468.

10. Thomas Wilson, *The arte of rhetorique, for the use of all such as are studious of eloquence, set forth in English* (London, 1553), folio 86.

11. William Haughton, *William Haughton's Englishmen for My Money; or, a Woman Will Have Her Will*, ed. Albert Croll Baugh (Philadelphia: [s.n.], 1917), line 338.

12. Thomas Dekker and John Webster, *Westward Ho* (1607), in *The Dramatic Works of Thomas Dekker*, ed. Fredson Bowers, vol. 2 (Cambridge: Cambridge University Press, 1955), 311–403.

13. Wilson, *Arte of rhetorique*, folio 86.

14. William A. Oram et al., eds., *The Yale Edition of the Shorter Poems of Edmund Spenser* (New Haven, Conn.: Yale University Press, 1989), 16.

15. George Puttenham, *The Arte of English Poesie*, ed. Gladys Doidge Willcock and Alice Walker (Cambridge: Cambridge University Press, 1936), 252.

16. William Camden, *Remaines of a greater worke, concerning Britaine* (London, 1605), 20. Hereafter, *Remaines*.

17. On the process and statistics regarding denization in England, see the Introduction.

18. Mulcaster, *Mulcaster's Elementarie*, 90–91.

19. On the economic and legal metaphors in early modern accounts of language, see Paula Blank, *Broken English: Dialects and the Politics of Language in Renaissance Writings* (New York: Routledge, 1996), 33–68.

20. Mulcaster, *Mulcaster's Elementarie*, 173–74.

21. The *Oxford English Dictionary* defines the adjectival use of the word "mere": "pure, unmixed, unalloyed; undiluted, unadulterated" (1a).

22. Jean E. Howard, *Theater of a City: The Places of London Comedy, 1598–1642* (Philadelphia: University of Pennsylvania Press, 2007), 10.

23. Focusing on the question of how the language debates of the period figure "by synecdoche the debates about the establishment and recognition of Englishness itself," Emma Smith contends that *Mulcaster's Elementarie* "imagines word borrowing as a strategic mutually beneficial alliance with a friendly country whose citizens might be denizened" ("'Signes of a Stranger': The English Language and the English Nation in the Late Sixteenth Century," in *Archipelagic Identities: Literature and Identity in the Atlantic Archipelago, 1550–1800*, ed. Philip Schwyzer and Simon Mealor [Burlington: Ashgate, 2004], 169–79, quote on 173). Smith contends that, for Mulcaster, the denizen words of the English language never "shake off their intrinsic foreignness" (178). Cast in this light, Mulcaster's denizen is a figure indelibly marked by its own alterity. I am arguing, conversely, that the denizen is a figure mobilized to signify a state of transition. Though originally a stranger whose difference required incorporation, Mulcaster's denizen emerges in my reading as a potentially deconstructive agent of linguistic change.

24. Camden, *Remaines*, 20.

25. Camden explicitly links linguistic transculturation and national assimilation, as this quote suggests. R. D. Dunn, editor of *Remaines*, explains: "In the *Britannia* Camden was interested in languages as the 'surest evidence of the original of a nation.' . . . This preoccupation with national identity has given way [in *Remaines*] to a relaxed consideration of languages in general, their characteristics and development" (*Remains Concerning Britain*, ed. R. D. Dunn (Toronto: University of Toronto Press, 1984), xxii).

26. Samuel Daniel, *A Panegyrike Congratulatorie . . . Also Certaine Epistles, with a Defence of Ryme* (London, 1603), unpaginated (final recto of text).

27. William Camden, *Britain; or, A chorographicall description of the most flourishing kingdomes, England, Scotland, and Ireland, and the ilands adjoyning, out of the depth of antiquitie* (London, 1610), 16.

28. Jones, *Triumph*, 214.

29. On the Teutonic thesis, see: Barber, *Early Modern English*; Jones, *Triumph*; Kidd, *British Identities*, esp. 75–98; Hugh A. MacDougall, *Racial Myth in English History: Trojans, Teutons, and Anglo-Saxons* (Montreal: Harvest House, 1982); Mary Floyd-Wilson, *English Ethnicity and Race in Early Modern Drama* (Cambridge: Cambridge University Press, 2003), esp. 161–83.

30. Jones, *Triumph*, 214–15. Apropos of Jones, Dunn refers to this movement as a "Nordic craze" (*Remains*, 374). I refer to this critical interest in Teutonic origins as the Teutonic thesis, rather than "mania" or "craze," for as Kidd has demonstrated (*British Identities*), the influence of the Teutonic thesis reaches, with important historical variation, well into the nineteenth century, a legacy the word "craze" risks obscuring.

31. Camden and Verstegan propose that while first the Gauls and then the Romans invaded Britain, only the Anglo-Saxons made a full conquest—a conquest never fully undone by the subsequent invasions of Danes and Normans. On Camden and Verstegan's

influence on ideas of English nationhood, see MacDougall. *Racial Myth*, 45–50; Floyd-Wilson, *English Ethnicity*, 161–83; and Kidd, *British Identities*, 86–87, 216–19.

32. Floyd-Wilson, *English Ethnicity*, 17.

33. Kidd, *British Identities*, 30.

34. Blank, *Broken English*, 128.

35. Ibid., 126–68.

36. Kidd, *British Identities*, 216. This is a point Kidd nuances significantly by arguing that while English Gothicists relied on Tacitean ideas to bolster an ethnic idea of Englishness, "which implied the Saxon beginnings of the 'English' constitution in customs transplanted from the woods of Germany," they were also compelled by "a territorial identity in which the same broad contours of the institutions of 'England' could be discerned in the British past long before the arrival of Germanic customs" (87).

37. Ibid., 214–15.

38. For a detailed history of the fifteenth-century "rediscovery" and influence of Tacitus, see *Tacitus Germania*, trans. and introduction by J. B. Rives (Oxford: Clarendon Press, 1999), 70–74. MacDougall places Camden among a broad network of contemporaries invested in the work of Tacitus (*Racial Myth*, 45).

39. Camden, *Britain*, 16.

40. Kidd rightly argues that "whatever the logic of Gothicism, this ethnic story of Germanic transplants never, over the course of the seventeenth and eighteenth centuries, fully occluded the idea of the immemorial constitution or the relevance of the ancient Britons" (*British Identities*, 81).

41. Camden *Remaines* (1605) 13.

42. Camden, *Remaines, concerning Britaine but especially England, and the inhabitants thereof.* (London, 1614), 20–21.

43. Ibid., 21.

44. Ibid. 22, 30. Camden distinguishes English from "the British tongue or Welsh (as we now call it)," which he posits "was in use onely [*sic*] in this Island, having great affinitie with the olde *Gallique* of *Gaule*, now *France*, from whence the first inhabitants in all probability came hither" (19).

45. Ibid., 30.

46. Gerhard Mercator, *Atlas; or, A geographicke description of the regions, countries and kingdomes of the world, through Europe, Asia, Africa, and America, represented by new & exact maps* (Amsterdam, 1636), 53, Huntington Library 32890. Hereafter, I cite Huntington Library copies with the abbreviation HEH.

47. Quoted in Jones, *Triumph*, 220, 220. There is uncertainty about the precise date of this publication. The STC suggests the early 1580s while Jones posits the year 1603.

48. Barber, *Early Modern English*, 129–30.

49. MacDougall, *Racial Myth*, 47.

50. The grandson of a refugee from Gelderland, Verstegan enrolled at Oxford as "Richard Rowlands," left before taking his degree to avoid oaths of allegiance to the Anglican church, and became a freeman of the Goldsmiths' Company in London. Scholars have suggested that it was "as a result of his enthusiasm for the Germanic background

of English [that] he assumed his grandfather's Dutch surname on leaving the University" (MacDougall, *Racial Myth*, 47; Bailey, *Images*, 38). From March 1587 Verstegan resided in Antwerp, where he "worked as a publishing and intelligence agent" overseeing the "printing of numerous English Catholic works" (*Dictionary of National Biography*, s.v. Richard Verstegan). His ties to Antwerp developed further when in 1610 he married his second wife, Catherina de Sauchy of Antwerp. *Restitution* was penned at least in part from Antwerp, where he signed his prefatory *Epistle to our* [English] *Nation.* The text was printed in Antwerp by Robert Bruney to be sold in London.

51. Richard Verstegan, "Epistle to our Nation," in *A Restitution of Decayed Intelligence* (Antwerp, 1605), n.pag.

52. Ibid. n.pag.

53. Verstegan, *Restitution*, 42.

54. Ibid., 42–43. This passage had widespread influence on readers of the day, as is evidenced in the case of one reader who penned it into the margins of the Huntington copy of John Speed's "Description of Germany," in *A Prospect of the Most Famous Parts of the World* (London, 1631), 15, HEH 330658.

55. Unless otherwise noted, all citations of Tacitus are drawn from the HEH copy (601575): Cornelius Tacitus, *The description of Germanie* (London, 1604 [i.e., 1605]), 259.

56. Kidd, *British Identities*, 211.

57. Verstegan, *Restitution*, 83.

58. Ibid., 147.

59. Cited in George J. Metcalf, "Abraham Mylius on Historical Linguistics," *PMLA* 68.3 (1953): 546.

60. Verstegan, *Restitution*, 121–22.

61. This description is part of the *Parergon*, an appendix of historical maps and descriptions added to the *Theatrum*. Abraham Ortelius, *Theatrum Orbis Terrarum.* . . . (London,1606 [i.e., 1608?]), section 9, HEH 62823. Regarding the variety of names used for the Low Countries on sixteenth- and seventeenth-century maps, see Cornelis Koeman and Marco van Egmond, "Surveying and Official Mapping in the Low Countries, 1500–ca. 1670," in *The History of Cartography: Cartography in the Renaissance*, ed. David Woodward, vol. 3, pt. 2 (Chicago: University of Chicago Press, 2007), 1246–95.

62. Ortelius, *Theatrum*, xiiij. For Ortelius the proximity of London and Antwerp was personal, as well as geographic, as his sister, with whom he corresponded, resided in London and his friend James Cole also resided in London on Lime Street among a cadre of Continental refugees, merchants, and intellectuals. On Ortelius's connections to London, see Deborah Harkness, *The Jewel House: Elizabethan London and the Scientific Revolution* (New Haven, Conn.: Yale University Press, 2007), 24–25.

63. See the Introduction for my discussion of this passage.

64. Gerhard Mercator, *Atlas sive cosmographicae, meditationes de fabrica mundi et fabricati figura* (Duisburg, 1595), HEH 238463. The same enjambment of names along the coastlines appears in the 1632 edition.

65. Robert Devereux, Earl of Essex, *An Apologie of the Earle of Essex . . . 1598* (London, 1603), D3r.

66. For a survey of the production of Leo Belgicus maps, see H. A. M. van der Heijden, *Leo Belgicus: An Illustrated and Annotated Carto-Bibliography* (Alphen aan den Rijn: Canaletto, 1990). England continues to be tucked into the frame of this map into the eighteenth century.

67. Barbara Fuchs, *Exotic Nation: Maurophilia and the Construction of Early Modern Spain* (Philadelphia: University of Pennsylvania Press, 2009).

68. Verstegan, *Restitution*, 196.

69. Ibid., 196.

70. Ibid., 198.

71. Ibid., 198–99. On the use of black letter to represent English and Dutch speech in this period, see Chapter 4.

72. Ibid., 199.

73. A century later, John Farrington would assert an even closer relation between English and Dutch: "I think there is very considerable agreement in a great many of their words, especially their monosyllables as house, hose, smith, way, rain and all which are pronounced just as we do" (*An account of a journey through Holland, Frizeland, Westphalia . . . in severall letters to Mr. N.H., Aug.–Dec. 1710,* qtd. in C. D. van Strien, *British Travellers in Holland During the Stuart Period: Edward Browne and John Locke as Tourists in the United Provinces* [Leiden: E. J. Brill, 1993], 230n88). Where Verstegan finds "neernes," Farrington hears phonetic sameness.

74. Richard Carew, "The Excellency of the English Tongue," appears in Camden's *Remaines*, 40. The date of composition of Carew's essay is unknown. Editors have suggested a range from 1595 to 1614. Dunn (in Camden, *Remains*, 376–77) notes that its first publication was in the 1614 edition of *Remaines*.

75. "Our ancient English-Saxon language is to bee accompted [considered] the Teutonic toung" (Verstegan, *Restitution*, 188).

76. The idea that the Dutch language, "more than any" other, preserved old Teutonic was repeated by English authors throughout the seventeenth century. As late as 1689, for example, Edward Richardson in the introduction to his *Anglo-Belcica, the English and Netherdutch Academy. . . .* (Amsterdam, 1689) writes: "Touching the *Nether-dutch,* I find it upon severall gronds preferred by Authors, at le[a]st so far as it hath affinity with the old *Teutonick,* before many other." He then prophesies that "this *Belgick* is likely to be yet far more esteemed of, and usefull then it's Neighbour-Languages" (6). At the turn of the eighteenth century, John Northleigh considered Dutch "a kind of a dialect of the old Teutonic, modelled into many monosyllables and pronounced with a more tart and voluble fineness" (*Topographical Descriptions with Historico-Political and Medico-Physical Observations, Made in Two Several Voyages through Most Parts of Europe* [1702], qtd. in Van Strien, *British Travellers,* 212). For Verstegan, Carew, and Richardson alike, old Teutonic was a kind of parent language from which German, Nether-Dutch (or Low Dutch), and English derived. For all three authors, contemporary Dutch was thought to retain a closer linguistic affiliation to old Teutonic than did English.

77. *Origines Antwerpianae* (Antwerp, 1569), qtd. in Jones, *Triumph,* 216. For examples of French, Swiss, Welsh, and Slavic authors making a similar case for their native

language, see Peter Burke, *Languages and Communities in Early Modern Europe* (Cambridge: Cambridge University Press, 2004), 21, 69. Becanus hinged his case on the assertion that the Cimbri, the direct descendants of Japhet and ancestors of the Flemish people, had not been present at Babel; therefore Becanus's contemporary Flemish dialect, spoken in Antwerp, wholly preserved the language of the Garden of Eden. Abraham van der Myl (1563–1637) differed with Becanus, finding instead that Hebrew was the most ancient of languages. He concurred with Becanus, however, that the "purity" of old Teutonic could be found in the contemporary idiom of Belgian (Metcalf, "Abraham Mylius," 541).

78. Qtd. in Metcalf, "Abraham Mylius," 550. Not surprisingly, Van der Myl concludes that it was Belgian, "which had originated with Gomer, son of Japheth[,] . . . that it was the heart, so to speak, of a language family" that spread "widely over the Old World and the New" (554).

79. Qtd. and trans. in Herman. Scherpbier, *Milton in Holland: A Study in the Literary Relations of England and Holland Before 1730* (Amsterdam: H. J. Press, 1933), 93. Scherpbier quotes the 1663 folio on 244.

80. James Howell, "Divers Centuries of New Sayings," in *Paroimiographia* (London, 1659), 9, HEH 18915.

81. Simon Stevin, *The Principal Works of Simon Stevin*, ed. Ernst Crone et al., vol. 1 (Amsterdam: C. V. Swets & Zeitlinger, 1955), 59–93.

82. Ibid., 63.

83. Ibid.

84. Stevin goes further than his contemporaries on this point, compiling a table more than ten pages in length that lists all Dutch, Latin, and Greek monosyllabic nouns, adjectives, and other words (ibid., 67–79). For an overview of how monosyllabic words were considered an "authentic characteristic of the native [English] tongue," see Jones, *Triumph*, 199; and Bailey, *Images*, 39–42.

85. Additionally, Dutch authors praised Dutch for its ease in creating compound words: "Hendrik Spieghel of Amsterdam argued that Netherlanders should take pride in their language following the example of the Italians, the French and the English and agreed with Stevin about the wealth of Dutch and its propensity to create compounds such as *handschoen* for gloves ('hand-shoes') or *woordboek* for dictionary ('word-book')" (Burke, *Languages and Communities*, 66–67).

CHAPTER 3. DOUBLE DUTCH TONGUES

Note to epigraph: *Sir Philip Sidney: A Critical Edition of the Major Works*, ed. Katherine Duncan-Jones (Oxford: Oxford University Press, 1989), 245.

1. Wilson Clough, "The Broken English of Foreign Characters on the Elizabethan Stage," *Philological Quarterly* 12.3 (1933): 255–68; and A. J. Hoenselaars, *Images of Englishmen and Foreigners in the Drama of Shakespeare and His Contemporaries: A Study of Stage*

Characters and National Identity in English Renaissance Drama, 1558–1642 (London: Associated University Presses, 1992), 26–76. For a reading that associates the performance of linguistic differences with English xenophobia, see Janette Dillon, *Language and Stage in Medieval and Renaissance England* (Cambridge: Cambridge University Press, 1998), 162–87.

2. Peter Burke, *Languages and Communities in Early Modern Europe* (Cambridge: Cambridge University Press, 2004), 11.

3. Ibid., 38.

4. Ibid., 29–32.

5. William Haughton, *William Haughton's Englishmen for My Money; or, a Woman Will Have Her Will*, ed. Albert Croll Baugh (Philadelphia: [s.n.], 1917), lines 179–84.

6. Jill L. Levenson, ed., *A Critical Edition of the Anonymous Elizabethan Play "The Weakest Goeth to the Wall"* (New York: Garland, 1980), 4.66–75. The editor glosses 4.70–72: "Listen to me for a moment. I have a small shop, a little stall, near the door of my house. You shall have that as a place of business."

7. Thomas Dekker, *The Shoemaker's Holiday or The Gentle Craft,* in *The Roaring Girl and Other City Comedies*, ed. James Knowles (Oxford: Oxford University Press, 2001), 4.45, 4.76–85. All references are to this edition.

8. Henry Glapthorne, *The Hollander* (London, 1640), D2 verso.

9. Thomas Dekker and John Webster, *"Westward Ho* (1607)" in *The Dramatic Works of Thomas Dekker*, ed. Fredson Bowers, vol. 2 (Cambridge: Cambridge University Press, 1955), 311–403.

10. Thomas Dekker, *The Gulls Horn-Book* (1609), in *Thomas Dekker: The Wonderful Year, the Gull's Horn-Book, Penny-Wise, Pound Foolish, English Villainies Discovered by Lantern and Candlelight and Selected Writings*, ed. E. D. Pendry, vol. 4 (Cambridge, Mass.: Harvard University Press, 1968), 107.

11. Ole Peter Grell, "The French and Dutch Congregations in London in the Early Seventeenth Century," *Proceedings of the Huguenot Society* 24.5 (1987): 368. On the stricter English notion of sabbatarianism, see K. H. D. Haley, *The British and the Dutch: Political and Cultural Relations Through the Ages* (London: George Phillip, 1988), 70.

12. John Taylor catalogues the names and locations of London's taverns in *Taylors Travels. . . .* (London, 1636). I am grateful to Laura Williamson Ambrose for directing me to this text.

13. Irene Scouloudi, "Notes on Strangers in the Precinct of St. Katherine-by-the-Tower, c. 1500–1687, and on the 'Flemish Cemetery,'" *Proceedings of the Huguenot Society* 25.1 (1989): 79; Ben Jonson, *The Devil Is an Ass*, ed. Peter Happé (Manchester: Manchester University Press, 1996), 1.1.61–63.

14. R. E. G. Kirk and Ernest F. Kirk, *Returns of Aliens Dwelling in the City and Suburbs in London from the Reign of Henry VIII to That of James I*, 4 vols. (Aberdeen: University Press, 1900–1908), 10.1.443, 10.2.94.

15. Raymond Fagel, "Immigrant Roots: The Geographical Origins of Newcomers from the Low Countries in Tudor England," in *Immigrants in Tudor and Early Stuart*

England, ed. Nigel Goose and Lien Luu (Brighton: Sussex Academic Press, 2005), 52. On the linguistic influence of Dutch on East Anglian English, see Peter Trudgill, "Third-Person Singular Zero," in *East Anglian English*, ed. Jacek Fisiak and Peter Trudgill (Cambridge: D. S. Brewer, 2001), 179–86.

16. The population survey of 1593 records that of the 2,357 people employed by 7,113 strangers living in the City and Liberties, 1,671 were English: "This figure of 1671 English persons employed comprised 950 men and boys labouring in the strangers' homes as well as 457 women and girls. . . . What is of special note is that, although a small figure, 264 English persons were 'set on work' but not actually living in strangers' homes" (Irene Scouloudi, ed., *Returns of Strangers in the Metropolis 1593, 1627, 1635, 1639: A Study of an Active Minority* (London: Huguenot Society, 1985). Quarto Ser. 57, 137, 81). The percentage of English apprentices to stranger tradesmen is in fact higher than this statistic would suggest since 686 of the 7,113 reported strangers living in London were themselves servants of strangers. Thus the total number of strangers who might potentially employ English people was 6,427 (less still if we account for children). Lien Bich Luu summarizes: "over half of those listed in the 1593 Return employed no workers at all, a quarter had *only* English employees, and a smaller proportion both English and stranger workers" ("Assimilation or Segregation: Colonies of Alien Craftsmen in Elizabethan London," *Proceedings of the Huguenot Society* 26.2 [1995]: 166). Incidentally, these figures suggest that one reason for the perception of strangers' mercantile success may have been the large number of English persons employed by strangers in the 1590s.

17. Scouloudi, *Returns of Strangers*, 85. The educated elite would have also been schooled in Latin and may have known Italian and Spanish as well; see Maria A. Schenkeveld, *Dutch Literature in the Age of Rembrandt: Themes and Ideas* (Amsterdam: John Benjamins, 1991), 137–42.

18. Scouloudi, *Returns of Strangers*, 219n1140.

19. Ibid., 213n1060.

20. Ibid., 184n603.

21. Charles Barber, *Early Modern English* (London: André Deutsch, 1976), 182. Unless otherwise noted, the following list of words and their date of entry into English are drawn from Barber.

22. From Middle Dutch *pant*, early modern Dutch *pand*, "a gallery, colonnade, or covered walk; *esp.* one in a bazaar, market, exchange, etc., within which traders display their goods for sale" (*OED Online*, s.v. "pawn" n.4). The word enters English in connection with the Royal Exchange.

23. Seventeenth-century Anglo-Dutch dictionaries and grammars included: Marten Le Mayre, *The Dutch Schoole Master wherein is shewed the true and perfect way to learne the Dutch tongue, to the furtherance of all those which would gladlie learne it* (London, 1606); *Den grooten vocabulaer Engels ende Duyts . . . The great vocabuler, in English and Dutch* (Rotterdam, 1639) (subsequent edition in 1644, an anonymous vocabulary, attributed to Willem de Groot, based on Noël de Berlemont's Flemish-French colloquies and dictionary [Antwerp, 1539]); *The English Schole-master or certaine rules and helpes whereby the natives of the Netherlandes, may bee, in a short time, taught to read, understand, and speake,*

the English tongue . . . *Den Engelschen School-Meester* (Amsterdam, 1646) (subsequent editions in 1658 and 1663); Henry Hexham, *Het Groot Woorden-Boeck* . . . *A Copious English and Netherduytch Dictionarie* (otherwise entitled *A Large Netherdutch and English Dictionarie*) (Rotterdam, 1647–48) (subsequent editions in 1658 and 1660 and a "new edition" in 1675); *The Dutch-tutor or, a new-book of Dutch and English* (London, 1660); (subsequent edition in 1669); J. G. van Heldoren, *An English and Nether-dutch dictionary composed out of the best English authors* . . . *Een Engels en Nederduits Woortboek* (Amsterdam, 1675); Francois Hillenius, *Den Engelschen ende Ne'erduitschen onderrichter* . . . *The English, and Low-dutch Instructer* (Rotterdam, 1664) (subsequent editions in 1671, 1677, 1678 and 1686); Edward Richardson, *Anglo-Belgica, the English and Netherdutch Academy in three parts* (Amsterdam, 1677) (subsequently published as *Anglo-Belcica* by the widow of Steven Swart in 1689 and 1698); William Sewel, *A new dictionary English and Dutch* . . . *Nieuw woordenboek der Engelsche en Nederduytsche* (Amsterdam, 1691).

In his study of English and Dutch dictionaries, N. E. Osselton includes a text I have not been able to consult: *Dictionarium, Ofte Woorden-Boeck, Begrijpende de Schat der Nederlandtsche Talke, met de Engelsche Uytlegginge* (Rotterdam, 1672 subsequent edition in 1678). See *The Dumb Linguists: A Study of the Earliest English and Dutch Dictionaries* (Leiden: University Press, 1973).

24. This information is printed on the book's title page. Little else is known about the author.

25. Le Mayre, *Dutch Schoole Master*, A3 verso.

26. Ibid.

27. George Metcalf, "Abraham Mylius on Historical Linguistics," *PMLA* 68.3 (1953): 537.

28. Thomas Middleton, *"No Wit, [No] Help Like a Woman's,"* ed. John Jowett, in *Thomas Middleton: The Collected Works*, ed. Gary Taylor and John Lavagnino (Clarendon Press: Oxford, 2007): 779–832, here 1.3.98–101. All citations are from this edition with the exception of passages in stage Dutch. Jowett regularizes and modernizes Middleton's stage Dutch while Middleton appears instead to have transliterated Dutch into roughly intelligible stage Dutch. Jowett finds that except for Savourwit's inauthentic stage Dutch, Middleton aimed to provide "simple and roughly correct Dutch" in the text (on Jowett's editorial methods, see Gary Taylor and John Lavagnino, eds., *Thomas Middleton and Early Modern Textual Culture: A Companion to the Collected Works* [Oxford: Clarendon Press, 2007]: 1149–51). Middleton's transliterations, as they appear in the 1657 edition, fall short of the "real" Dutch speech of Jowett's modernization. I have thus transcribed all lines that appear in stage Dutch from the Huntington Library 1657 edition (shelfmark 146896) and have interwoven them with Jowett's edition. Jowett's line numbers are retained.

29. Hoenselaars, *Images of Englishmen*, 40.

30. *An Enterlude of Welth, and Helth* (London, ca.1565), C recto. Brackets within the passage indicate letters that are illegible in the text.

31. Dekker, *Shoemaker's Holiday*, 4.36–41, 316n41.

32. Clough argues instead that Vandalle's Dutch would have been "certainly unintelligible to one who knows next to no Dutch" ("Broken English," 261).

33. Ben Jonson, *Timber or Discoveries Made upon Men and Matter*, ed. Felix E. Schelling (Boston: Ginn, 1892), 64.

34. Samuel Daniel, *A Panegyrike . . . Defence of Ryme* (London, 1603), n. pag.

35. Marianne Montgomery argues persuasively that the translation scene in this play establishes the Dutch merchant as a double emissary, a figure from the Continent who brings news to the English and a "metaphorical emissary to the playhouse audience, making audible Dutch commercial culture by letting playgoers hear and understand Dutch speech" ("Listening to the Emissary in Middleton's *No Wit, No Help like a Woman's*," in *Emissaries in Early Modern Literature and Culture: Mediation, Transmission, Traffic, 1550–1700*, ed. Brinda Charry and Gitanjali Shahani [Burlington: Ashgate, 2009], 194). While Montgomery similarly stresses the "implicitly metatheatrical" nature of Savourwit's inauthentic Dutch, her argument diverges from my own by emphasizing that Savourwit's performance "suggests how stage Dutch was heard by English audiences" (201), a point that I contend may have applied to Marian drama, but no longer applies in seventeenth-century city comedies. I contend that from start to finish what is funny about Savourwit is how unlike a Dutchman he sounds. More, Montgomery understands the Dutch merchant's bilingualism as a trait that initially "call[s] his credibility into question" (194), while I find little evidence of suspicion of the Dutch merchant in Sir Oliver's response. If Sir Oliver is skeptical of the news the Dutch merchant brings to his home, it is not because he does not trust the bilingual Dutchman, but instead because his own monolingualism renders him unable to clarify the matter once Savourwit begins his "false translation" scene. The audience, in on the ruse, has little reason to be suspicious of the bilingual Dutchman.

36. On the perception of inherent danger within kinship relations, see Frances E. Dolan*, Dangerous Familiars: Representations of Domestic Crime in England, 1550–1700* (Ithaca, N.Y.: Cornell University Press, 1994).

37. Jowett edition, 793: "*Ick weet niet wat hij zegt—Ik en verstaan U niet*. ('I don't know what he says—I understand you not')."

38. Jowett ed., 793: "*Waar is je nijgen en je dank-je?* ('Where is your bow and your thank-you?')."

39. Jowett ed., 793: "*Ik dank je voor Uw Edelman vriendelijkheid.* ('I thank you for your kindness')" *Edelman* is literally "nobleman"; this deferential form of address was antiquated.

40. Jowett ed., 793: *Ik antwoord nooit geen klappende hik. Ik denk uit zijn zinnen.* ('I never answer beating hiccups [i.e., nonsense]. I think [he is] out of his mind.')

41. *OED Online*, s.v. "goose, n." Jowett suggests that the phrase *gull the goose* was "slang for 'cheat the idiot,' or *guilder-goose*, from the Dutch coin guilder, 'fool with his money'." See Taylor and Lavagnino, *Thomas Middleton*, 794n191.

42. Simon Stevin, *The Principal Works of Simon Stevin*, ed. Ernst Crone et al., vol. 1 (Amsterdam: C. V. Swets & Zeitlinger, 1955), 65. On the use of Dutch vernacular for humanist pursuits, see Peter Burke, *Towards a Social History of Early Modern Dutch* (Amsterdam: Amsterdam University Press, 2005), 16.

43. Burke demonstrates that arguments for the perfection of European vernaculars (French, Polish, German, etc.) were commonplace in the period (*Languages and Communities*, 68–69).

44. Metcalf, "Abraham Mylius," 540n16. On *Origines*, see John Considine, *Dictionaries in Early Modern Europe: Lexicography and the Making of Heritage* (Cambridge: Cambridge University Press, 2008), 141–42.

45. Richard Verstegan, *A Restitution of Decayed Intelligence: In Antiquities. Concerning the Most Noble and Renowmed [sic] English Nation. By the Studie and Travaile of R.V. Dedicated Unto the Kings Most Excellent Maiestie* (Antwerp, 1605), 190.

46. Ben Jonson, *The Alchemist*, ed. Gordon Campbell (Oxford: Oxford University Press, 1995), 2.1.80–85.

47. Metcalf, "Abraham Mylius," 544.

48. Verstegan argues that like early modern Dutch, Teutonic "consisted moste at the first of woords of monosillable, each having his own proper signification, as by instinct of God and nature they first were receaved and understood" (*Restitution*, 189). Old Teutonic was not the original language of Eden, according to Verstegan, but was among the seventy-two languages created in the wake of the destruction of the Tower of Babel (71).

49. For a comprehensive survey of Elizabethan discussions regarding monosyllables, see Richard Foster Jones, *The Triumph of the English Language: A Survey of Opinions Concerning the Vernacular from the Introduction of Printing to the Restoration* (Stanford, Calif.: Stanford University Press, 1953), 199–200.

50. A butter firkin was a container for storing and shipping butter.

51. Jowett ed., 795: "DUTCH MERCHANT: How, how's this?—*Zeg, jongen, ik ben gekweld met een dolligheid, een ontijd van de maan, en koeterwalend?* ('Tell me, boy, I, am I tortured with a madness, a bad time of the moon, and raving?')

"DUTCH BOY: *Wee ik! Hij liegt in zijn bakkes die't zegt.* ('Woe is me! He lies in his face that says it')."

52. Shakespeare's history plays make much of this representational strategy for depicting foreigners; see Paula Blank, *Broken English: Dialects and the Politics of Language in Renaissance Writings* (London: Routledge, 1996); Michael Neill, "Broken English and Broken Irish: Nation, Language, and the Optic of Power in Shakespeare's Histories," *Shakespeare Quarterly* 45.1 (1994): 1–32; and Dillon, *Language and Stage*, esp. 162–87. On the various shifts in ideas about language from the later sixteenth century to the seventeenth century and the representation of those attitudes on stage, see Patricia Fumerton, "Homely Accents: Ben Jonson Speaking Low," in *Renaissance Culture and the Everyday*, ed. Patricia Fumerton and Simon Hunt (Philadelphia: University of Pennsylvania Press, 1999), 92–111, who contends that the influential arguments made by Stephen Greenblatt in "Invisible Bullets" and Steven Mullaney in "The Rehearsal of Cultures," both of whom emphasize a sixteenth-century story whereby "the vernacular produced, reveled in, and then suppressed alien discourses—foreign and native languages as well as dialects—in order to emerge as pure" (98), do not pertain to the seventeenth century "with its increased sense of language's instability and variation"; concurring with R. F. Jones's study on the history of English, Fumerton stresses that the seventeenth century's "influx of new

and foreign terms sparked the beginnings of an antiquarian interest . . . that furthered the sense of language's instability" (94). Regarding city comedy, see Emma Smith, " 'So Much English by the Mother': Gender, Foreigners, and the Mother Tongue in William Haughton's *Englishman for My Money*," *Medieval and Renaissance Drama in England* 13 (2000): 165–81.

53. Dillon argues that the theater forges a link between foreign speech and duplicity: "Political, religious and economic discourses of the period all offer potential perspectives for collapsing foreignness into duplicity, constructing English in the position of strength, firmly allied with plainness and transparency" (*Language and Stage*. 164). I contend that Middleton, along with other dramatists of the period, poses a significant challenge to Dillon's emphasis on the duplicity of foreign speech.

54. The phrase is borrowed from Pierre Bourdieu's discussion of the linguistic marketplace in *Language and Symbolic Power* (Cambridge, Mass.: Harvard University Press, 1991), 57. I am suggesting that rather than an education system having a monopoly on creating producers of linguistic competence, the early modern theater was exploring the bounds of what constituted linguistic competence in London's linguistically expanding marketplace.

CHAPTER 4. DUTCH IMPRESSIONS

Epigraph: Ben Jonson, *Timber or Discoveries Made upon Men and Matter,* ed. Felix E. Schelling (Boston: Ginn, 1892), 64.

Throughout, I abbreviate the *English Short Title Catalogue* (STC), the Huntington Library shelf mark (HEH), and *Early English Books Online* (*EEBO*).

1. Thomas Dekker and John Webster, "*Northward Ho* (1607)," in *The Dramatic Works of Thomas Dekker*, ed. Fredson Bowers, vol. 2 (Cambridge: Cambridge University Press, 1955), 2.1.60–62. All references are to this edition; instances of typographic arrangement in the playbook are drawn from the Huntington Library's copy of the 1607 quarto edition.

2. Early instances include "Hance bere pot" (Hans Beerpot) in the anonymous *Enterlude of Welth, and Helth* (London, ca. 1565); and Haunce of Ulpian Fullwell's *A pleasant enterlude . . . Like will to like* (London, 1568); contemporary with *Northward Hoe* and from Dekker's own corpus is Hans of *The sho[e]maker's holiday. . . .* (London, 1600) and Hans of *Westward Hoe* (London, 1607).

3. Then as now, Augsburg was not a city of the Low Countries. Despite Hans's claim that his father lives in "Ausburgh," the play associates Hans with the Netherlands, first before his arrival on stage, when Doll claims that from his "trampling" steps she can identify "my Flemish Hoy" (2.1.59), and then upon his departure from the scene, when Doll exclaims, "father lanch out this hollander" (2.1.117). The interchangeability of Flanders and Holland, even "Ausburgh," makes Hans an example of the indifference to geographic specificity regarding the Low Countries that is symptomatic of how English city comedies imagined the category "Dutch."

4. "Fucker" is not a headword in Florio's *Worlde of Wordes* (London, 1598), but an English definition for the Italian word Fottitore (fucker) and Fottitrice *(woman fucker).* The online *Lexicons of Early Modern English* provides a detailed analysis of the word's emergence into English (http://leme.library.utoronto.ca/).

5. Gordon Williams cites Hans's unwitting use of the word "fucker" in *Northward Hoe* as the first instance of its dramatic usage on the English stage. See *A Dictionary of Sexual Language and Imagery in Shakespearean and Stuart Literature*, vol. 1 (London: Athlone Press, 1994), 563–64.

6. Only proper and place names, interspersed throughout Hans's speech, appear in italic. The convention in drama of the period was to set such names in italic, thus visually distinguishing them from the rest of the speech.

7. Jennifer Richards and Fred Schurink, eds., "Introduction" to Special Issue: The Textuality and Materiality of Reading in Early Modern England, *Huntington Library Quarterly* 73.2 (2010): 345.

8. D. F. McKenzie, *Bibliography and the Sociology of Texts* (London: British Library, 1986), 26. Throughout his seminal series of Panizzi Lectures in the mid-1980s, McKenzie argued that the work of bibliographers is the study of the sociology of texts, thus radically revising the far more restricted, influential definition of bibliography that Sir Walter Greg proposed in 1966: "what the bibliographer is concerned with is pieces of paper or parchment covered with certain written or printed signs. With these signs he is concerned merely as arbitrary marks; their meaning is no business of his" (10). In reconsidering how "forms affect meaning," the field of New Textualism that followed in McKenzie's wake has increasingly drawn attention to "the symbolic function of typographic signs as an interpretive system" (9). For McKenzie, critical exclusion of the typographic sign had been an effect of "Saussure's insistence upon the primacy of speech," which shifted critical attention away from the nonverbal sign systems of texts (26). Margreta de Grazia and Peter Stallybrass coined the term "New Textualism" in their article "The Materiality of the Shakespearean Text," *Shakespeare Quarterly* 44.3 (1993): 255–83. For a review of the field of New Textualism, see Alan B. Farmer, "Shakespeare and the New Textualism," in *The Shakespearean International Yearbook*, vol. 2 (Burlington: Ashgate, 2002), 158–79.

9. Charles Mish, "Black Letter as Social Discriminant in the Seventeenth Century," *PMLA* 68.3 (1953): 627–31. See also John King, "Foxe's *Book of Martyrs* and the History of the Book." *Explorations in Renaissance Culture* 30.2 (2004): 176–96. For trenchant critiques of Mish's argument, see Lori Humphrey Newcomb, *Reading Popular Romance in Early Modern England* (New York: Columbia University Press, 2002), 140; and Zachary Lesser, "Typographic Nostalgia: Play-Reading, Popularity, and the Meanings of Black Letter," in *The Book of the Play: Playwrights, Stationers, and Readers in Early Modern England,* ed. Marta Straznicky (Amherst: University of Massachusetts Press, 2006), 99–126.

10. Julie Stone Peters contends, "in drama, as in other genres, printers continued to experiment throughout the sixteenth and early seventeenth centuries with page space, lettering types, and colour to differentiate various kinds of material, relating information spatially on the page. . . . By the later sixteenth century, however, conventions had begun

to harden. At least as important, printers seem to have come to rely on a readership familiar with both the theatre and the typographic conventions of the drama. They seem to have come to rely on the *mise en page*—the visual semiotics of the dramatic text—to explain through visual form what narrative descriptions might do at greater length. . . . The typographic-visual distinction of the drama from other kinds of writing during the sixteenth century played a crucial role in the representation of drama as a distinct genre" (*Theatre of the Book, 1480–1880: Print, Text, and Performance in Europe* [Oxford: Oxford University Press, 2003], 24).

11. W. W. Greg developed a distinction between the "substantive" and "accidental" aspects of a text in which "spelling, punctuation, word division, and the like [those aspects] affecting mainly [a text's] formal presentation" were considered accidents or "accidentals" ("The Rationale of Copy-Text," in *Collected Papers,* ed. J. C. Maxwell [Oxford: Clarendon Press, 1966], 376). For an important critique of Greg's distinction, see D. F. McKenzie, "Typography and Meaning: The Case of William Congreve," in *Making Meaning: "Printers of the Mind" and Other Essays,* ed. Peter D. McDonald and Michael F. Suarez (Amherst: University of Massachusetts Press, 2002), 198–236.

12. Renewed attention to the marginal spaces of playbooks has attuned critics to the theatricality of the playbook page. For a particularly sensitive account of the role of "spectacular typography" in rendering "print as a medium for performance," see Holger Schott Syme, "Unediting the Margin: Jonson, Marston, and the Theatrical Page," *English Literary Renaissance* 38.1 (2008): 142–71.

13. See de Grazia and Stallybrass, "Materiality of the Shakespearean Text."

14. Historians of print culture will understandably wish for a more nuanced analysis of *kinds* of black letter. The *textura* typeface of the Gutenberg Bible (1455) and later the King James Bible (1611) differs in provenance from *schwabacher,* which appears first in 1492 and is based on bastarda scripts; these differ also from *fraktur,* which derived from sixteenth-century German courts chancery scripts. This history is explored in Peter Bain and Paul Shaw, eds., *Blackletter: Type and National Identity* (New York: Princeton Architectural Press, 1998). See also Harry G. Carter, *A View of Early Typography up to About 1600* (Oxford: Clarendon Press, 1969); Alexander Lawson, *Anatomy of a Typeface* (Boston: Godine, 1990); and Sabrina Alcorn Baron, "Red Ink and Black Letter: Reading Early Modern Authority," in *The Reader Revealed,* ed. Sabrina Alcorn Baron, Elizabeth Walsh, and Susan Scola (Washington, D.C.: Folger Shakespeare Library, 2001), 19–30. Given my focus on playbooks, I do not suspect that printers were experimenting with more nuanced differences among kinds of black letter—instead, the typographic difference between black letter and roman created the semiotic distinctions that mattered.

15. On the introduction of roman in English texts, Mark Bland finds that "the earliest surviving use of roman in an English printed book dates from 8 September 1509, and the earliest extant use of roman in an English non-Latin publication [is] 1555" ("The Appearance of Text in Early Modern England," *TEXT* 11 [1998]: 93). Italic first appears in England in a polyglot text, Wynken de Wordes's edition of Robert Wakefield's *Oratio de laudibus & utilitate trium linguarum Arabicae Chaldaicae & Hebraicae,* published in 1528.

On italic, see Joseph F. Loewenstein, "*Idem:* Italics and the Genetics of Authorship," *Journal of Medieval and Renaissance Studies* 20.2 (1990): 205–24.

16. Lesser, "Typographic Nostalgia," 114. Peter Blayney arrives at similar figures in "The Publication of Playbooks," in *A New History of Early English Drama*, ed. John D. Cox and David Scott Kastan (New York: Columbia University Press, 1997), 415. For slightly different figures, which include calculations for court pageants, see Bland, "Appearance of Text," 105. As Lesser and others have been careful to qualify, black letter did not ever fully disappear in English printing; see also Adrian Weiss, "Casting Compositors, Foul Cases, and Skeletons: Printing in Middleton's Age," in *Thomas Middleton and Early Modern Textual Culture*, ed. Gary Taylor and John Lavagnino (Oxford: Oxford University Press, 2007), 195–225.

17. I consulted the following editions through the *Early English Books Online* database: *The Weakest Goeth to the Wall* (London, 1600), STC (2nd ed.) 25144 (London, 1618), STC (2nd ed.) 25145; Dekker and Webster, *Westward Hoe* (London, 1607), STC (2nd ed.) 6540; John Marston, *The Dutch Courtesan* (London, 1605), STC (2nd ed.) 17475; *The Workes of Mr. John Marston, being tragedies and comedies collected into one volume* (London, 1633), STC (2nd ed.) 17471; John Ford, *The Ladies Triall* (London, 1639), STC (2nd ed.) 11161; Henry Glapthorne, *The Hollander* (London, 1640), STC (2nd ed.) 11909; Thomas Middleton, *No Wit, [No] Help Like a Woman's* (London, 1657), Wing/M195.

18. *Northward Hoe* was printed in London by G. Eld. *The Roaring Girl* was printed in London by Nicholas Okes. The *English Short Title Catalogue* does not provide a full name for the printer of Jonson's masque.

19. *Northward Hoe* was acted by the Children of Pauls. *The Roaring Girl* was performed by The Prince His Players at the Fortune Theater. The *Masque of Augures* was performed twice at court, 6 January and 5 or 6 May 1622. Little else is known about the performance of Jonson's *Augures*; it is not, for instance, among the masques discussed by Stephen Orgel in *The Jonsonian Masque* (Cambridge, Mass.: Harvard University Press, 1965).

20. See Thomas Middleton and Thomas Dekker, *The Roaring Girl*, ed. Paul A. Mulholland (Manchester: Manchester University Press, 1987), 4; and Dekker and Webster, *Northward Hoe*, 407–8.

21. Thomas Dekker coauthored *Northward Hoe* and *The Roaring Girl* with John Webster and Thomas Middleton respectively. This might suggest Dekker's hand in designing the look of stage Dutch on his playbook pages. However, my review of Dekker's corpus of plays containing Dutch characters reveals no consistent pattern of black letter typeface for stage Dutch. Dekker and Webster's *Westward Hoe* (1607) provides the most promising source for suggesting whether Dekker was indicating to printers how certain aspects of his playbooks should look, a practice that would have been highly unusual in the period. Like *Northward Hoe*, *Westward Hoe* was performed by the Children's company and printed in the same year, and it too features a character named Hans who speaks stage Dutch. But in *Westward Hoe* Hans's stage Dutch is printed, like the rest of the play, in roman, and there is no use of black letter at all (I have consulted the British Library copy [1607]: STC 6540). Conversely, Dekker's *The Shoemaker's Holiday*, which features

the Englishman Lacy playing a Dutch shoemaker named Hans, is printed entirely in black letter throughout its seventeenth-century print history. Though it diverges from the seventeenth-century trend of printing English playbooks in roman typeface, no typographic distinction is given to Hans's stage Dutch, insofar as his black letter speech looks like that of all other characters on the playbook page. Though it is striking that Dekker, whose patronymic suggests Dutch heritage, is a common denominator in two of three cases, a close look at Dekker's dramatic works does not lead to any definitive conclusions about whether he might have given printers a historically unconventional direction pertaining to the setting of stage Dutch in these two plays.

22. Joseph Moxon, *Mechanick Exercises: On the Whole Art of Printing, 1683–4*, ed. Herbert Davis and Harry Carter (London: Oxford University Press, 1958), 218.

23. Yvonne Schwemer-Scheddin, "Broken Images: Blackletter Between Faith and Mysticism," in Bain and Shaw, *Blackletter*, 50. For a historically situated consideration of the visual representation of speech in print, particularly in the form of speech scrolls in theatrical frontispieces, see Holger Schott Syme, "The Look of Speech," *Textual Cultures* 2.2 (2007): 34–60.

24. Stephen Orgel, "What Is an Editor?" *Shakespeare Studies* 24 (1996): 23.

25. David Scott Kastan, *Shakespeare and the Book* (Cambridge: Cambridge University Press, 2001), 7–8.

26. Marta Straznicky, "Introduction: Plays, Books, and the Public Sphere," in Straznicky, *Book of the Play*, 4.

27. Straznicky, "Introduction," 6. On the relation of print and performance, see William Worthen, "Prefixing the Author: Print, Plays, and Performance," in *A Companion to Shakespeare and Performance*, ed. Barbara Hodgdon and W. B. Worthen (Malden: Blackwell, 2005), 212–30.

28. Mish, "Black Letter as Social Discriminant," 630.

29. Baron, "Red Ink," 25.

30. Ibid., 25–26.

31. Ibid., 24. Peter Blayney qualifies this history, noting that the first edition of the King James Bible was printed in blackletter, "as were all subsequent large folios and more than half the quartos. The smaller folios, octavos, and duodecimos were all in roman" ("Publication of Playbooks," 422n66).

32. Baron, "Red Ink," 24.

33. Ibid., 26.

34. Keith Thomas, "The Meaning of Literacy in Early Modern England," in *The Written Word: Literacy in Transition*, ed. Gerd Baumann (Oxford: Clarendon Press, 1986), 99.

35. King, "Foxe's *Book of Martyrs*," 177.

36. Lesser, "Typographic Nostalgia," 107.

37. Lesser (ibid.) does not argue for the *inability* of typography to serve as a transmitter for the voice of authority or as a stable material index to a class of readers, but instead for its instability, thus keeping alive the possibility that black letter functioned also—but not exclusively—as a social discriminant.

38. For an important critique of the notion of "popular culture" in relation to texts and interpretive communities, see Roger Chartier, "Texts, Printing, Readings," in *The New Cultural History*, ed. Aletta Biersack and Lynn Avery Hunt (Berkeley: University of California Press, 1989), 154–75, esp. 169–70.

39. Lesser contends that "a large part of what scholars are discovering when they see 'popular culture' in black letter is the construction of this nostalgia in the very texts they are reading" ("Typographic Nostalgia," 107).

40. Richard Verstegan, *A Restitution of Decayed Intelligence: In Antiquities. Concerning the Most Noble and Renowmed [sic] English Nation. By the Studie and Travaile of R.V. Dedicated Unto the Kings Most Excellent Maiestie* (Antwerp, 1605), 199.

41. Italic was used to mark other kinds of distinctions in nondramatic texts of the period. Talbot Baines Reed and A. F. Johnson summarize: "The italic was at first intended and used for the entire text of a classical work. Subsequently, as it became more general, it was used to distinguish portions of a book not properly belonging to the work, such as introductions, prefaces, indexes, and notes; the text itself being in Roman. Later, it was used in the text for quotations; and finally served the double part of emphasizing certain words in some works, and in others, chiefly the translations of the Bible, of marking words not rightly forming a part of the text" (*A History of the Old English Letter Foundries: With Notes Historical and Bibliographical on the Rise and Progress of English Typography* [London: Faber and Faber, 1952], 46). Moxon notes that "*English* obsolete words" are also set in "*English* Character," or black letter (*Mechanick Exercises*, 218). On the use of italic to indicate a different voice in a single text, especially in dialogues such as William Cunningham's *The Cosmographical Glasse* (1559), and to "convey the orality of the text," see Bland, "Appearance of Text," 99–100. Peter Stallybrass and Zachary Lesser have shown how italic typeface was also used to indicate commonplacing in early modern playbooks ("The First Literary Hamlet and the Commonplacing of Professional Plays," *Shakespeare Quarterly* 59.4 [2008]: 371–420).

42. The 1598 quarto does not survive, according to Albert Croll Baugh, editor of *William Haughton's Englishmen for My Money; or, a Woman Will Have Her Will* (Philadelphia: [s.n.], 1917). All citations and reproductions of typographic arrangement are drawn from the 1616 quarto (STC 12931).

43. The speech of the play's foreigners is primarily printed in roman throughout the play because the foreigners speak broken English more often than they do their native tongues. I have examined the Huntington Library copy of the 1616 edition (call number 61322) as well as the 1616 British Museum edition (available through *Early English Books Online* (*EEBO*), STC 12931) and the 1626 Folger Shakespeare Library edition (available through *EEBO*, STC 12932) and Huntington Library copy (call number 61324), and the 1631 Yale Library edition (available through *EEBO*, STC 12933) and the Huntington Library copy (call number 60682). The typographic pattern I describe is consistent across these three editions.

44. The introduction of roman font in the 1530s was also a moment when typography displayed its powers of differentiation and depended on comparison with the then predominant use of black letter to make that difference matter. Tom Conley argues that

"roman font of the 1530s constituted an unsolicited effect of difference. It recalled what it had just replaced, the fake effect of the manuscript in the *lettre bâtarde* or *lettre de forme*. While eliciting comparison with Gothic typography, the Roman letter was endowed with a sense of its transformative agency, thus begging its readers to take note of the figural history it was developing" (*The Graphic Unconscious in Early Modern French Writing* [Cambridge: Cambridge University Press, 1992], 6, Cambridge Studies in French). I share with Conley the conviction that the semiotics of type depends significantly on the dynamic context of the mise en page. Black letter, roman, and italic do not signify *in and of themselves* so much as they signify in relation to one another as they appear across the page.

45. The nuance of the semiotics of type in *Englishmen for My Money* comes further to light when we compare it to the typographic organization of dialogues in nondramatic texts from the same period. Catechisms commonly featured speakers in dialogue by setting forth the lines of each speaker in a different type font. Edward Vaughan's *A plaine and perfect Method, for the easie understanding of the whole Bible* (London, 1617) is illustrative of the typographic arrangement of many such early modern catechisms. In it, the Parishioner's discourses are set in roman type and the Pastor's in black letter. In terms of staging a dialogue on the page, the typographic variation of the catechism helps the reader track who is speaking and, as D. F. McKenzie and Sabrina Alcorn Baron have suggested, may also have imparted the "authority" of the speaker's voice insofar as the Pastor's speech, printed in black letter, mirrors the typography of so many of the authorized Bibles of the period. A similar effect of typographic variation underscoring different "speakers" on a page appears in pamphlet debates, in which an author-speaker's questions may appear printed in italic, followed by answers printed in black letter, and a retort or commentary printed in roman. In both catechisms and pamphlet debates, the difference type makes pertains to the subject position of the speaker, and less to the *relation* of the speakers' speech to one another. On the relation of speech to print in early modern catechisms, see D. F. McKenzie, "Speech—Manuscript—Print," in *Making Meaning: "Printers of the Mind" and Other Essays*, ed. Peter D. McDonald and Michael F. Suarez (Amherst: University of Massachusetts Press, 2002), 237–58; and Baron "Red Ink."

46. I am grateful to Scott Schofield and Piers Brown for their helpful insights into this passage.

47. Margreta de Grazia, "Homonyms Before and After Lexical Standardization," *Deutsche Shakespeare-Gesellschaft West: Jahrbuch* (1990): 153.

48. Middleton and Dekker, *The Roaring Girl*, ed. Mulholland. All line numbers are from this edition. Images of typographic arrangement are drawn from the quarto edition, STC (2nd ed.) 17908.

49. Mulholland glosses "jobbering" as "jabbering": speech rendered unintelligible to listeners (Middleton and Dekker, *The Roaring Girl*, 215).

50. Ben Jonson, *The Masque of Augures* (London, 1621), STC (2nd ed.) 14777. I have compared this edition to the 1631 edition of *The Masque of Augures*, which appears in the folio of *The Workes of Benjamin Jonson*, vol. 2 (London, 1640), HEH 606593a. There is some variation in the spelling and word order of Van Goose's speech between the two

editions. However, both editions set Van Goose's speech in black letter and his is the *only* incidence of black letter being used to mark the speech of a particular character in all of Jonson's *Workes* (1640). There are, however, a few instances of the appearance of black letter type in Jonson's corpus of dramatic works; cf. *The Alchemist* (London, [1680?]), 26, 32, 35, Wing J1007. No black letter appears in the earlier 1612 edition of the *Alchemist*; see HEH 62097.

51. Irene Scouloudi, "Notes on Strangers in the Precinct of St. Katherine-by-the-Tower, c. 1500–1687, and on the 'Flemish Cemetery,' " *Proceedings of the Huguenot Society* 25.1 (1989): 75–82.

52. Thomas Wilson, *The art of rhetorique* . . . (London, 1553), folio 86.

53. Cited in Sigmund Freud, "Group Psychology and the Analysis of the Ego," in *The Standard Edition of the Complete Psychological Works of Sigmund Freud*, trans. James Strachey, vol. 18 (London: Hogarth Press, 1973), 101n.1. Freud first discusses the narcissism of minor difference in his 1917 essay: "The Taboo of Virginity" in *Standard Edition*, vol. 11, 199.

54. Freud, "Group Psychology," 101.

55. Sigmund Freud, *Civilization and Its Discontents* (Garden City, N.Y.: Doubleday, 1958): 64–65.

56. Anton Blok, *Honour and Violence* (Malden, Mass.: Blackwell, 2001), 123, 119. My discussion of Freud's narcissism of minor difference is deeply indebted to Blok's reflections on how Freud's insight sheds light on the triggers of ethnic violence and ethnic "cleansing" in twentieth century contexts; see especially 115–35.

57. Cited in Blok, *Honour and Violence*, 115. Girard runs the logic of Freud's insight the other way around as he begins by assuming distinction between groups and argues that its loss leads to the threat of sameness, which leads to a dis-ease expressed in the eruption of violence between groups. Thus, while Freud begins with a presumption of group identification (across a "company of porcupines" or "South Germans") and Girard begins with distinction, the tension between identity (as an assertion of difference) and identification (as an assertion of bonds) emerges as what characterizes group psychology. In forging social identity within conditions of proximate relations, sustaining the tension between distinction and conflation, difference and sameness, is key to fostering and maintaining group identity for both Girard and Freud.

58. John Considine, *Dictionaries in Early Modern Europe: Lexicography and the Making of Heritage* (Cambridge: Cambridge University Press, 2008), 109.

59. Zachary Lesser advances the notion of typographic inevitability in his discussion of continuous printing in playbooks but misidentifies black letter stage Dutch as another instance of it: "Walter Burre and the Knight of the Burning Pestle," *English Literary Renaissance* 29.1 (1999): 31.

60. A study of the typographic arrangement of all early modern wordbooks is needed if we are to understand more fully the work of typography in forging relations across the various languages of early modern wordbooks. This scholarship would contribute significantly to work already compiled by the contributors to the electronic database *DEEP* (http://deep.sas.upenn.edu/index.html).

61. Considine, *Dictionaries*, 289.

62. On Berlaimont's *Colloquia et Dictionariolum* see ibid.

63. N. E. Osselton, *The Dumb Linguists: A Study of the Earliest English and Dutch Dictionaries* (Leiden: University Press, 1973), 14.

64. Unless otherwise noted, all following citations refer to the second edition of the STC. All except the first were published without identifying the author. The Berlaimont editions are: Noël de Berlemont, *Colloques ou Dialogues, avec un Dictionaire en quatre langues. Flamen, Anglois, Francois, & Latin* (Leiden, 1585), HEH 15140; *Colloquia dictionariolum septem linguarum* (Antwerp, 1586), Bodleian Library, STC 1431.9; *Colloques ou dialogues septem linguarum* (Liège, 1589), HEH 335113; *Colloquia et dictionariolum septem linguarum* (Padua, 1592), University of Illinois, STC 1431.12 (Leiden, 1593), British Library, STC 1431.13 (Liège, 1595), Folger Shakespeare Library, STC 1431.14 (Liège, 1597), British Library, STC 1431.15; (Liège, 1600), University of Illinois, STC 1431.17 (Venice, 1606), Folger Shakespeare Library, STC 1431.19 (Liège, 1610), Harvard University, STC 1431.20 (Antwerp, 1616), Folger Shakespeare Library, STC 1431.25; *Colloquia et dictionariolum octo linguarum* (Delft, 1598), University of Illinois, STC 1431.16 (Delft, 1613), Harvard University, STC 1431.22 (Flushing, 1613), Cambridge Library, STC 1431.23 (Hague, 1613), University of Illinois, STC 1431.24 (Amsterdam, 1622), British Library, STC 1431.27 (Amsterdam, 1623), University of Illinois, STC 1431.28 (Venice, 1627), Cambridge University, STC 1431.29 (Antwerp, 1630), Harvard University, STC 1431.30 (*EEBO* mistakenly locates STC 1431.30 at the Huntington Library) (Amsterdam, 1631), Cambridge University, STC 1431.31 (Middleburg, 1631), Cambridge University, STC 1431.32 (Delft, 1631), Harvard University, STC 1431.33; *Colloquia et dictionariolum sex linguarum* (Geneva, 1608), University of Chicago, STC 1431.19a; *The English, Latine, French, Dutch Schole-master* (London, 1637), Cambridge University, STC 1432.5; and *New Dialogues or Colloquies, and A Little Dictionary of eight Languages* (London, 1639), British Library, STC 1432.

65. Leiden 1593, STC (2nd ed.) 1431.13.

66. Of course, this argument extends to the ways typography forges other relations on the page as well, the much-needed study of which lies beyond the scope of this book.

67. The German language appears in black letter in many other wordbooks of the period. On German "dictionaries" from this period, see Considine, *Dictionaries*, 101–55. While a thorough survey of the typography of the 858 German bilingual and polyglot wordbooks from the period 1467–1600 and 1,150 more from the seventeenth century lies beyond the scope of my study, four German wordbooks in the special collections of the University of California, Los Angeles, print German in black letter type and Latin in roman, without exception, in cases where black letter is used: Robert Estienne and Johannes Frisius, *Lexicon Trilingue* (Strasbourg, 1587), shelf mark PA 2364 E79l; Johannes Frisius, *Dictionarium Latinogermanicum* (Zurich, 1568), shelf mark PA 2365 G5 F9 1568; Hadrianus Junius, Adam Siber, and Rodolphus Agricola, *Adami Siberi Gemma Gemmarum, Sev Nomenclatoris Had. Junii Epitome* (Leipzig, 1579), shelf mark PA2365.G3 J9; and Jonas Petri, *Dictionarium. Latino-Sveco-Germanicum* (Linkoping, 1640), shelf mark PA 2364 P44d 1640. In early sixteenth-century polyglot wordbooks, such as *A Lytell Treatyse*

for to Lerne Englysshe and Frensshe (Antwerp, ca. 1530), English, French, and Dutch all appear in black letter (HEH 131401:9).

68. These include Delft, 1613; Flushing, 1613; Hague, 1613; and Antwerp, 1616. In Amsterdam, 1622 (STC [2nd ed.] 1431.27), Amsterdam, 1623 (STC [2nd ed.] 1431.28), and Venice, 1627 (STC [2nd ed.] 1431.29), black letter is not used.

69. In the survey I have conducted it is notable that both Venice editions, 1606 (STC [2nd ed.] 1431.19) and 1627 (STC [2nd ed.] 1431.29), are printed entirely in roman font. No italic or black letter is used. What I refer to as a typographic "pattern" in the rotation of fonts, column by column, pertains to all editions printed in northern Europe from 1585 to 1639, the historical scope of my study.

70. Unless otherwise noted, shelf marks (below) refer to the University of Michigan rare book collections: *Sex linguarum Latinae, Gallicae, Hispanicae, Italicae, Anglicae & Teutonic[a]e* (Zurich, 1579), HEH 379000; John Barret, *An Alvearie or triple dictionarie, in Englishe, Latin, and French* (London, 1574), HEH 45909, and *An Alvearie or Quadruple Dictionarie* (London, 1580), shelf mark PA 2364.B3; Thomas Cokayne, *A Greek English Lexicon* (London, 1658), shelf mark PA 881.C68; Randal Cotgrave, *A dictionarie of French and English tongues* (London, 1598), shelf mark PC2640.A2.C84 (London 1571), HEH 59062; John Florio, *A Worlde of Wordes* (London, 1598), shelf mark PR 3072.F64, and *Queen Anna's New World of Words* (London, 1611), shelf mark PC 1640 .F64 1611; James Howell, *Lexicon tetraglotton, an English-French-Italian-Spanish dictionary* (London, 1660), HEH 140922; Guy Miege, *A New Dictionary French and English, with another English and French* (London, 1679), HEH 441874; Richard Perceval, *A dictionary in Spanish and English* (London, 1623), shelf mark PC 4640.P43.1623; John Rider, *Dictionarie . . . Latin, French, and other languages* (London, 1640), shelf mark PE 1620.R54.1640; Robert Sherwood, *Dictionaire anglois et francois* (London, 1632), shelf mark PC2640.A2.C84.1632; William Somner, *Dictionarium Saxonico-Latino-Anglicum voces* (London, 1659), HEH 226542; and Giovanni Torriano, *The Italian Tutor* (London, 1640), shelf mark PC1109.T68.

71. E.g., Barret, *Alvearie or triple dictionarie* and *Alvearie or Quadruple Dictionarie*; Perceval, *Dictionary*; Sherwood, *Dictionaire*; and Somner, *Dictionarium*. Occasionally, as in Perceval's 1623 Spanish-English and English-Spanish dictionary, English appears in italic in the Spanish half of the dictionary, but in the second half of the dictionary, when English provides the headwords, it appears in black letter.

72. André Madoet, *Thesaurus theutonicae linguae / Schat der Nederduytscher spraken* (Antwerp, 1573), HEH 375140. Considine points out, though as modern readers we "regard *Teutonic* as meaning 'Germanic'," the word *teutonicus* "could be used to mean 'Dutch' in the sixteenth-century Low Countries, as opposed to *germanicus* 'German'" (*Dictionaries*, 146).

73. So too the resources various printers had at hand in their print shops would have determined some of these typographic choices. Here, however, the printer evidently had access to black letter and roman type, but elected to print the English in black letter.

74. Considine, *Dictionaries*, 29. Ambrogio Calepino, *Ambrosii Calepini Dictionarium undecim linguarum* (Basel, 1598), HEH 355056. Though I have not been able to

examine all editions of Calepino's *Dictionarium*, in the 1598 edition both "Germanica" and "Belgica" are set in black letter, "Anglica" in italic.

75. John Minsheu, *Hēgemōn eis tas glōssas* (London, 1617), HEH 357181.

76. My dramatic archive includes sixteen plays, which I have consulted in their various editions whenever possible (all published in London): *An Enterlude of Welth, and Helth* (ca. 1565); Haunce of Ulpian Fullwell, *A pleasant enterlude . . . Like will to like* (1568, 1587); Wapull, *The tyde taryeth no man A moste pleasant and merry commody, right pythie and full of delight* (1576); *The Life and Death of Jack Straw* (1594, 1604); Dekker, *Sho[e]-makers holiday* (1600); *The Weakest Goeth to the Wall* (1600); *A Larum for London* (1602); *The London prodigall* (1605); Marston, *The Dutch Courtesan* (1605); Dekker and Webster, *Westward Hoe* (1607); *Northward Hoe* (1607); Middleton and Dekker, *Roaring Girle* (1611); William Haughton, *Englishmen for my Money* (1616, 1626, 1631); Ford, *The Ladies Triall* (1639); Glapthorne, *The Hollander* (1640); and Middleton, *No wit, [no] help like a woman's* (1657).

77. The first English dictionaries, grammars, and hard-word books used roman, black letter, and italic type. In Robert Cawdrey's *A Table Alphabetical* (1604), English words appear in roman type and their definitions are set in black letter, a typographic arrangement that continues in the three subsequent editions: original, London, 1604, STC (2nd ed.) 4884; subsequent, London, 1609, STC (2nd ed.) 4884.5, London, 1613, STC (2nd ed.) 4885, and London, 1617, STC (2nd ed.) 4886.

In John Bullokar's *An English Expositor* (1616), the hard-word list is printed entirely in italic and roman fonts, a typographic arrangement that continues throughout the manifold editions of its seventeenth-century life. See London editions: 1641, Harvard Library, Wing B5429; 1654, National Library of Wales, Wing (2nd ed.) B5429A; 1656, HEH 113428; 1663, National Library of Wales, Wing (2nd ed.) B5430A; 1695, British Library, Wing B5435A; 1698, and British Library, Wing B5436. See also, Cambridge editions: 1667, Cambridge University Library, Wing B5431; 1671, Cambridge University Library, Wing (2nd ed., 1994) B5431A; 1676, HEH 446719; 1680, University of Illinois, Wing (2nd ed., 1994) B5433; 1684, National Library of Wales, Wing (2nd ed., 1994) B5434; and 1688, Harvard University, Wing B5435.

So too in Henry Cockeram's *The English Dictionary* (1623), English words are set in italic and their definitions in roman type; *The English Dictionary* (London, 1623), Folger Shakespeare Library, STC (2nd ed.) 5461.2. I have consulted the following Huntington Library copies (all published in London), which are also printed in roman and italic only: 1626, 306965; 1631, 18897; and 1637, 13630.

78. *The Dutch-tutor; or, A new-book of Dutch and English*: London, 1660, Wing (2nd ed.) D2907, and London, 1669, Wing (2nd ed.) D2907A.

79. On Henry Hexham's lifelong engagements in Anglo-Dutch politics and religion, which made him a particularly qualified candidate for the production of his monumental dictionary, see G. Scheurweghs, "English Grammars in Dutch and Dutch Grammars in English in the Netherlands Before 1800," *English Studies: A Journal of English Letters and Philology* 41.3 (1960): 129–67.

80. Osselton emphasizes the uniqueness of this venture, "To give an idea of what this means we may compare the present-day *Concise Oxford Dictionary*, which has rather less than 40,000 entries. No English dictionary in the seventeenth century approaches this number: the most substantial was Edward Phillips's *New World of English Words*, which had 11,000 entries when it first appeared in 1658, and grew to 17,000 by the time of the 1696 edition" (*Dumb Linguists*, 35n5). We do not know why Hexham's dictionary did not continue the typographic pattern of earlier Anglo-Dutch grammars, phrasebooks, and vocabularies. Indeed there are many issues relating to the availability of type that might have been determining factors in publishing such a lengthy text. Perhaps Hexham and his printer were influenced by the typographic arrangement of the source text to which Hexham was heavily indebted for the English-Dutch half of his dictionary, John Rider's English-Latin dictionary, *Bibliotheca scholastica* (1589), as revised by Francis Holyoke (1640). Both editions were printed using exclusively roman and italic type (*Bibliotheca scholastica. A double dictionarie* [Oxford, 1589], STC [2nd ed.] 21031.5, and *Riders dictionarie . . . Now newly corrected and much augmented by Francis Holy-oke* [London, 1640], HEH 20742; also, STC [2nd ed.] 21036a.7, available on *EEBO*). For the Dutch-English half of his dictionary Hexham borrowed not from Rider but instead from the popular Dutch-French dictionary *Le Grand dictionaire françois flamen* (1618), which enjoyed eleven editions over the course of the century. On Hexham's indebtedness to earlier dictionary sources, see Osselton, *Dumb Linguists*, 34–57.

81. I consulted the following editions on *EEBO* and, when possible, in the original: Henry Hexham, *Het Groot Woorden-Boeck . . . A Copious English and Netherduytch Dictionarie* (otherwise entitled *A Large Netherdutch and English Dictionarie*), all published in Rotterdam: 1647, Wing (2nd ed.) H1648; 1648, Wing H1649 and 1648, Wing (2nd ed.) H1653; 1658, Wing (2nd ed.) H1653A and HEH 434409; 1660, Wing H1650 and HEH 287052; 1672, HEH 287052a; and 1675, Wing H1651.

I thank Carol Sommer, head of reader services at the University of California, Los Angeles, William Andrews Clark Memorial Library, for confirming the typographic arrangement of the 1675 edition of the dictionary. I have not been able to consult this edition; however, according to Scheurweghs, "this edition is the same as that of 1672; the original title-page has been cut off and a new leaf has been pasted on the remaining edge of paper" ("English Grammars," 146).

82. J. G. van Heldoren, *An English and Nether-dutch dictionary composed out of the best English authors . . . Een Engels en Nederduits Woortboek* (Amsterdam, 1675), HEH 449438, *A New and Easy English grammar* (Amsterdam, 1675), HEH 449437, and *A New and Easie English Grammar* (London, 1690), Wing (2nd ed.) H1372C. Van Heldoren's *English and Nether-dutch dictionary*, is not, strictly speaking, a dictionary, but "belong[s] instead] to the nomenclator tradition" (Osselton, *Dumb Linguists*, 33).

83. William Sewel, *A new dictionary English and Dutch . . . Nieuw woordenboek der Engelsche en Nederduytsche* (Amsterdam, 1691), and *Nieuw woordenboek der Nederduytsche en Engelsche taale . . . A new dictionary Dutch and English* (Amsterdam, 1691), HEH 478634. These texts are bound together but have separate dated title pages, registers and

pagination. The former is English-Dutch and the latter is Dutch-English. For brief biographies of the authors of Anglo-Dutch dictionaries from the period, all of whose lives were shaped at the crossroads of Anglo-Dutch relations, see Scheurweghs, "English Grammars," 132–42.

CHAPTER 5. LONDON AS PALIMPSEST

Epigraph: Mark Rakatansky, "Why Architecture Is Neither Here nor There," in *Drifting: Architecture and Migrancy*, ed. Stephen Cairns (New York: Routledge, 2004), 99.

1. British Airways London Eye, http://www.londoneye.com/ (accessed on 26 September 2005).

2. On the history of the Royal Exchange, see Ann Saunders, ed., *The Royal Exchange* (London: London Topographical Society, 1997), hereafter abbreviated *RE*.

3. Quoted in John William Burgon, *The Life and Times of Sir Thomas Gresham, Knt. Founder of the Royal Exchange*, 2 vols. (London: Effingham Wilson, 1839), vol. 2, 505.

4. For the Exchange as a site of rumor, see Thomas Heywood's *Fair Mayde of the Exchange* (*A Critical Edition of "The Faire Maide of the Exchange,"* ed. Karl E. Snyder [New York: Garland, 1980], 3.2.19–21).

5. Quoted in Charles Welch, *Illustrated Account of the Royal Exchange and the Pictures Therein* (London: Johnson, Riddle, 1913), 23.

6. Welch, *Illustrated Account*, 24.

7. *Royal Exchange Inquest-book*, quoted in Welch, *Illustrated Account*, 24–25. Orange-selling women were also regularly spotted at the theaters where they "operated as intermediaries negotiating discreet acquaintances between male admirers and actresses and prostitutes" (John L. McMullan, *The Canting Crew: London's Criminal Underworld, 1550–1700* [New Brunswick, N.J.: Rutgers University Press, 1984], 137).

8. Ole Peter Grell, "The French and Dutch Congregations in London in the Early Seventeenth Century," *Proceedings of the Huguenot Society* 24.5 (1987): 368.

9. Michel de Certeau defines "poetic geography" as that which is "on top of the geography of the literal, forbidden or permitted meaning" (*The Practice of Everyday Life* [Berkeley: University of California Press, 1984], 105). Recovering the poetic geography of London's Exchange depends on attending to its material history and its textual representations as well as recovering the spatial practices of the Dutch stranger community residing in London.

10. Stephen Cairns, Introduction to *Drifting: Architecture and Migrancy*, ed. Stephen Cairns (New York: Routledge, 2004), 1–16.

11. Stephen Cairns, "Drifting: Architecture/Migrancy," in Cairns, *Drifting*, 18.

12. Ibid.

13. De Certeau, *Practice of Everyday Life*, 118.

14. Ibid., 117.

15. Ibid.

16. Ann Saunders, "The Building of the Exchange," in *RE*, 39n17.

17. Burgon, *Life and Times*; and Ian Blanchard, "Sir Thomas Gresham c. 1518–1579," in *RE*, 11–19.

18. Guido Marnef characterizes the Antwerp Beurs as the "commercial and financial nerve-center of Antwerp" in *Antwerp in the Age of Reformation: Underground Protestantism in a Commercial Metropolis, 1550–1577* (Baltimore: Johns Hopkins University Press, 1996), 186. On the economic trends that shaped Antwerp's important role in the early modern European and global economy, see Michael Limberger, "No Town in the World Provides More Advantages: Economies of Agglomeration and the Golden Age of Antwerp," in *Urban Achievement in Early Modern Europe: Golden Ages in Antwerp, Amsterdam and London*, ed. Patrick O'Brien, Derek Keene, Marjolein 't Hart, and Herman van der Wee (Cambridge: Cambridge University Press, 2001), 39–62. On Antwerp's Beurs as a site generative of cosmopolitanism, see Margaret Jacob, *Strangers Nowhere in the World: The Rise of Cosmopolitanism in Early Modern Europe* (Philadelphia: University of Pennsylvania Press, 2006), 66–94.

19. Saunders, "Building," 36.

20. Burgon, *Life and Times*, 1.409.

21. For Gresham's negotiations with the city, see Saunders, "Building," 36–39; see also *A Booke Concernynge the Newe Burse* (1566), reprinted in *RE*, 416–26.

22. On Anglo-Dutch commercial relations, see David Ormrod, *The Rise of Commercial Empires: England and the Netherlands in the Age of Mercantilism, 1650–1770* (Cambridge: Cambridge University Press, 2003).

23. Welch, *Illustrated Account*, 19.

24. Ibid.

25. Saunders, "Building," 39.

26. I have searched for such references in the archives of the Mercers' Company (London) and in the collection of the Guardian of the Royal Exchange (London).

27. This cultural fantasy is nascent insofar as the commercial realities of London's position in the larger networks of global trade at this time might more accurately be characterized as "marginal." See David Baker, "'The Allegory of a China Shop': Jonson's *Entertainment at Britain's Burse*," *ELH* 72 (2005): 159–80.

28. According to the *Oxford English Dictionary*, the word "pawn" (gallery, colonnade, or covered walk) derives from early modern Dutch *pandt* (cloister). The Royal Exchange not only introduces Dutch-identified architecture into London, it also brings with it Dutch vocabulary.

29. Quoted in Saunders, "Building," 44.

30. John Stow, *A Survey of London*, ed. Charles Lethbridge Kingsford, vol. 1 (1908; Oxford: Clarendon Press, 2000), 193.

31. Thomas Heywood, *If You Know Not Me You Know Nobody, Part II* (Oxford University Press: Malone Society Reprints, 1934), lines 2100–2110; Theophilus Philalethes, *Great Britains Glory; or, A brief Description of the Present State, Splendor, and Magnificence*

of the Royal Exchange (London, 1672), 5–7. For how the site figured in the drama of the period, see Jean Howard, "Staging Commercial London: The Royal Exchange," in *Theater of a City: The Places of London Comedy, 1598–1642* (Philadelphia: University of Pennsylvania Press, 2007), 29–67.

32. See Christopher Eimer, "Medals of the Royal Exchange," in *RE*, 349; Ingrid Roscoe, "'The Statues of the Sovereigns of England': Sculpture for the Second Building, 1695–1831," in *RE*, 184; Clare A. P. Willsdon, "The Mural Decoration at the Royal Exchange," in *RE*, plate x (b).

33. The *Oxford English Dictionary* posits that the word "burse" arose either at Bruges "from the sign of a purse, or three purses, on the front of the house which the merchants there bought to meet in" or at Antwerp.

34. Volume 2 of the *Repertories*, housed in the Mercers' Company, runs from 1629 to 1669 and records the committee's negotiations following the building's destruction in the Great Fire.

35. See Heywood, *If You Know Not Me*, in which Gresham consistently refers to his building as "my burse" while the queen calls it the "Royal Exchange"; see also Thomas Middleton, *Chaste Maid in Cheapside*, ed. Richard Dutton (Oxford: Oxford University Press, 1999), 1.2.31–34; and Thomas Dekker, *The Gulls Horn-Book* (1609), in *Thomas Dekker: The Wonderful Year, the Gull's Horn-Book, Penny-Wise, Pound Foolish, English Villainies Discovered by Lantern and Candlelight and Selected Writings*, ed. E. D. Pendry, vol. 4, Stratford-Upon-Avon Library 4 (Cambridge, Mass.: Harvard University Press, 1968).

36. For the "complementary relationship" between London and Antwerp markets in the sixteenth century, see Derek Keene, "Material London in Time and Space," in *Material London ca. 1600*, ed. Lena Cowen Orlin (Philadelphia: University of Pennsylvania Press, 2000), 55–74.

37. Quoted in Jean Imray, "Origins of the Exchange," in *RE*, 27.

38. Thomas Platter, reprinted in Lawrence Manley, ed., *London in the Age of Shakespeare: An Anthology* (University Park: Pennsylvania State University Press, 1986), 39.

39. Howard explores this shift in the play's focus from Antwerp to the Levant in *Theater of a City*, 29–67.

40. I borrow this characterization from Peter Burke, *Antwerp: A Metropolis in Comparative Perspective* (Ghent: Snoeck-Ducaju & Zoon, 1993).

41. On this era, see Jonathan Israel, *The Dutch Republic: Its Rise, Greatness, and Fall, 1477–1806* (Oxford: Clarendon Press, 1995).

42. On the New Exchange, see Thomas N. Brushfield, "Britain's Burse, or the New Exchange," *Journal of British Archaeological Society* 9 (1903): 33–48, 81–94; Lawrence Stone, "Inigo Jones and the New Exchange," *Archaeological Journal* 114 (1957): 105–21; and Ann Saunders, "The Second Exchange," *RE*, 121–35. James Knowles has recently discovered and published Jonson's *Entertainment at Britain's Burse*, a performance for King James upon the opening of the New Exchange ("Jonson's *Entertainment at Britain's Burse*," in *Re-presenting Ben Jonson: Text, History, Performance*, ed. Martin Butler [New York: St. Martin's Press, 1999], 114–51). This includes both an edited text and Knowles's commentary on it. See also James Grantham Turner, "'News from the New Exchange':

Commodity, Erotic Fantasy, and the Female Entrepreneur," in *The Consumption of Culture, 1600–1800: Image, Object, Text*, ed. Ann Bermingham and Jon Brewer (London: Routledge 1995), 419–33; Janette Dillon, "Court Meets City: The Royal Entertainment at the New Exchange," *Research Opportunities in Renaissance Drama* 38 (1999): 1–21; Baker, "Allegory."

43. Donald Lupton, *London and the Countrey Carbonadoed and Quartered into Severall Characters* (London, 1632), 22–23.

44. An event of this magnitude drew on the finances of London's guilds and its stranger communities and on the talents of some of its finest authors, architects, and artisans. For authorial collaboration between Thomas Dekker, Thomas Middleton, and Ben Jonson on James's "Magnificent Entertainment," see Fredson Bowers's textual introduction to Thomas Dekker, "The Magnificent Entertainment: Given to King James (1604)," in *The Dramatic Works of Thomas Dekker,* vol. 2 (Cambridge: Cambridge University Press, 1955), 231–52; and Robert Withington, *English Pageantry: An Historical Outline*, vol. 1 (Cambridge, Mass.: Harvard University Press, 1918), 222–26. Dekker reports that Stephen Harrison, "Joyner[,] was appointed chiefe; who was the sole Inventor of the Architecture, and from whom all directions, for so much as belonged to Carving, Joyning, Molding, and all other worke in those five Pageants of the Citie (Paynting excepted) were set downe" ("Magnificent Entertainment," 303). In a historically unprecedented move, Harrison authors his own version of the pageant, a folio entitled *The Arch's of Triumph Erected in Honor of the High and Mighty Prince James* (London, 1604), which provides description and engravings of the seven pageant arches. Regarding Harrison's folio, see David Bergeron, *Practicing Renaissance Scholarship: Plays and Pageants, Patrons and Politics* (Pittsburgh: Duquesne University Press, 2000), 174–79, and "Harrison, Jonson, and Dekker: *The Magnificent Entertainment of King James* (1604)," *Journal of the Warburg and Courtald Institute* 31 (1968): 445–48. Five of the pageant's seven arches were paid for by funds levied against the city's companies; "the other two *Arch's* erected by Merchant-Strangers (viz the *Italians* and *Dutchmen*) were only their owne particular charge" (Harrison, *Arch's*, K). On a contemporary Dutch account of the Dutch arch and pageant, entitled *Beschryvivghe vande herlycke Arcus Triumphal . . . ter eeren . . . Coninck Iacobo* (Middleburg, 1604–5), see Gervase Hood, "A Netherlandic Triumphal Arch for James I," in *Across the Narrow Seas: Studies in the History and Bibliography of Britain and the Low Countries. Presented to Anna E. C. Simoni,* ed. Susan Roach (London: British Library, 1991), 67–82; and Ole Peter Grell, *Calvinist Exiles in Tudor and Stuart England* (Brookfield, Vt.: Scolar Press, 1996), 163–90.

45. For London as a "ceremonial city," see Steven Mullaney, *The Place of the Stage: License, Play, and Power in Renaissance England* (1988; Chicago: University of Chicago Press, 2000), 10. Lawrence Manley explores the "ceremonial syntax" of London pageantry in *Literature and Culture in Early Modern London* (Cambridge: Cambridge University Press, 1995), 223.

46. David Bergeron's *English Civic Pageantry, 1558–1642*, rev. ed. (Tempe: Arizona State University Press, 2003), exemplifies trenchant scholarship of this kind. See also Withington, *English Pageantry*; John Nicols, *The Progresses, Processions, and Magnificent*

Festivities of King James the First, 4 vols. (New York: B. Franklin, 1964); Gordon Kipling, "Triumphal Drama: Form in English Civic Pageantry," *Renaissance Drama* 8 (1977): 37–56; and Glynne Wickham, *Early English Stages 1300–1660*, vol. 1 (New York: Columbia University Press, 1980), 51–111.

47. Manley, *Literature and Culture*, 223.

48. For an "idealized" version of the "Entertainment," one that blends the accounts of Thomas Dekker, Ben Jonson, Stephen Harrison, and other printed and manuscript sources into one edition, see Gary Taylor and John Lavagnino, eds., *Thomas Middleton: The Collected Works* (Oxford: Clarendon Press, 2007), 219–79.

49. For a comparative perspective on the progresses of Queen Mary and Elizabeth I, see Anne Lancashire, "Dekker's Accession Pageant for King James I," *Early Theatre* 12.1 (2009): 39–50.

50. Regarding Queen Elizabeth's royal entry, see Bergeron, *Practicing Renaissance Scholarship*, 17–65.

51. This was not the first royal progress in which the Dutch "strangers" of London performed, however. On the "Dutch" acrobat whose nimble antics captured London's attention during Mary Tudor's royal entry in 1553, see Scott Oldenburg, "Toward a Multicultural Mid-Tudor England: The Queen's Royal Entry Circa 1553, the Interlude of Wealth and Health, and the Question of Strangers in the Reign of Mary I," *ELH* 76.1 (2009): 99–129.

52. Bergeron, *English Civic Pageantry*, 76. For a thorough description of each arch, see 67–109.

53. The arch was "designed by Christopher de Steur and Assuerus Regemorterus[,] . . . the architect was Coenraet Janszoon, and the chief decorators or painters were Daniel de Vos and Pauwel van Overbeke" (William John Charles Moens, ed., *The Marriage, Baptismal, and Burial Registers, 1571–1874, and Monumental Inscriptions, of the Dutch Reformed Church, Austin Friars, London* [Lymington: King and sons, 1884], xxviii).

54. Hood reconstructs the biography of Coenraet Janszoon in "Netherlandic Triumphal Arch," 73.

55. Ibid.

56. That James was represented as a "stranger" is less surprising given that "we still find forty-nine scotchmen individually listed in the returns of strangers made during the reign of his son, Charles I, King of England" (Irene Scouloudi, "The Stranger Community in London 1558–1640," *Proceedings of the Huguenot Society* 24.5 [1987]: 436).

57. Irene Scouloudi, ed., *Returns of Strangers in the Metropolis 1593, 1627, 1635, 1639: A Study of an Active Minority*, Quarto Ser. 57 (London: Huguenot Society, 1985), 57–66.

58. Scouloudi, *Returns of Strangers*, 85.

59. The four accounts are Stow's *Survey*, Harrison's *Arch's*, Dekker's "Magnificent Entertainment," and Gilbert Dugdale's account of the king's visit to the Royal Exchange just days before the pageant (*The Time Triumphant* [London, 1604]).

60. While I have not found any records that answer definitively why the Dutch community selected Cornhill "by the Exchange" for the site of their pageant, what we do know about the placement of the Dutch arch is twofold. First, the Royal Exchange was

located alongside the conduit at Cornhill where, before the erection of the building, pageants were conventionally staged. Thus, while the Royal Exchange was a new site along the city's ceremonial route, it occupied familiar ceremonial terrain. Second, the decisions made regarding the artistic design of the Dutch arch reveal the Dutch community's investment in highlighting Dutch commercial prosperity as something alive and well both abroad and in London.

61. In emphasizing the Dutch Beurs in his narrative account, Dekker chose to emphasize a detail that went unrecorded in the Dutch account, or was not in fact a detail on the back side of the Dutch arch. Neither Hood ("Netherlandic Triumphal Arch") nor Grell (*Calvinist Exiles*) note the "Exchange" as a feature described or depicted in *Beschryvivghe vande herlycke Arcus Triumphal*. While the Dutch engravings do not appear to include the image of the Antwerp Beurs on the backside of the arch, the *Beschryvivghe vande herlycke Arcus Triumphal* does share with Dekker's account a pictorial and narrative emphasis on the industry and productivity of London's denizen Dutch community.

62. Crystal Bartolovich, "'Baseless Fabric': London as 'World City,'" in *The Tempest and Its Travels*, ed. Peter Hulme and William Sherman (London: Reaktion, 2000), 13–26.

63. In reading temporary spatial practices as potential political acts, I concur with Elizabeth Grosz, who echoes de Certeau in arguing that the city is "both a mode for the regulation and administration of subjects but also an urban space in turn re-inscribed by the particularities of its occupation and use" ("Bodies-Cities," in *Space, Time, and Perversion* [New York: Routledge, 1995], 109).

64. Roland Barthes, "Semiology and the Urban," in *Rethinking Architecture: A Reader in Cultural Theory*, ed. Neil Leach (1997; London: Routledge, 2003), 172.

65. Throughout my discussion of Munday's *Triumphes* I distinguish the ship the *Royall Exchange* from London's marketplace by retaining Munday's spelling (Royall Exchange) and placing the name of the ship in italics. For a critical edition of this text, see David Bergeron, *Pageants and Entertainments of Anthony Munday: A Critical Edition* (New York: Garland, 1985), 1–23. I cite Bergeron's edition throughout. See also Tracey Hill, *Anthony Munday and Civic Culture: Theatre, History and Power in Early Modern London, 1580–1633* (Manchester: Manchester University Press, 2004).

66. Bergeron, *Pageants and Entertainments*, 7. The little critical interest Munday's pageant has received has tended to focus on the conceit of the Brutus-Troy myth, e.g., Hill, *Anthony Munday*, 149–52; and Bergeron, *English Civic Pageantry*, 145. In her most recent work, *Pageantry and Power: A Cultural History of the Early Modern Lord Mayor's Show, 1585–1639* (Manchester: Manchester University Press, 2010), Tracey Hill underscores the ways in which the Mayoral Shows tended to "provide an overview of the new Lord Mayor's career and notable roles," and that this "trend within the Shows began quite early in the period [with the performance of Munday's *Triumphs of re-united Britania*] and accelerated from then on," 289.

67. This venture was a *commercial* success. Regarding lives lost on this first venture, see Anthony Farrington, *Trading Places: The East India Company and Asia, 1600–1834* (London: British Library, 2002).

68. For the effects of the 1603 shipments on London's market, see K. N. Chaudhuri, *The English East India Company: The Study of an Early Joint-Stock Company, 1600–1640* (London: Frank Cass, 1965), 153–56.

69. Chaudhuri explains: since both the English and Dutch domestic markets were restricted in terms of how much spice their markets could absorb, "the profits of the pepper trade depended almost entirely on its re-export to the Continent" (ibid., 141).

70. See Manley, *Literature and Culture*, 261; and Daryl W. Palmer, *Hospitable Performances: Dramatic Genre and Cultural Practices in Early Modern England* (West Lafayette: Purdue University Press, 1992), 119–55.

71. Chaudhuri, *English East India Company*, 167, 169–70.

72. The suspicion that the Dutch would create a monopoly was sparked in 1599 when news arrived in London that six ships of the Dutch East Indies company, De Vereenigde Oost-Indische Compagnie, laden with pepper and spices, had returned to Holland from the East Indies. Had the Dutch company secured a monopoly, the English would have been unable to compete, especially if the Dutch engaged in price-cutting wars. Even when the English established factories in the East Indies, they suffered "chronic fear that 'the Flemings might fill the market abroad' or if there was a shortage in the London market bring it into England and sell at a high price" (ibid., 145).

73. Ibid., 226–34.

CHAPTER 6. DOPPELGÄNGER DILEMMAS

1. The Spice Islands, or "Spiceries," is a way of referring to the "profusion of islands which lie scattered in the seas south of the Philippines, east of Borneo and Java, north of Australia, and west of New Guinea" (Donald F. Lach and Edwin J. Van Kley, eds., *Asia in the Making of Europe*, vol. 1, part 2 [Chicago: University of Chicago Press, 1965], 592). Though I use the term when referring to this collections of islands, experts on Southeast Asia caution that the term casts a seeming coherence across what was and remains a diverse collection of cultures in the Indonesian archipelago; see Anthony Reid, introduction to *Southeast Asia in the Early Modern Era: Trade, Power, and Belief*, ed. Anthony Reid (Ithaca, N.Y.: Cornell University Press, 1993); and Leonard Y. Andaya, "Cultural State Formation in Eastern Indonesia," in Reid, *Southeast Asia*, 23–41, and *Leaves of the Same Tree: Trade and Ethnicity in the Straits of Melaka* (Honolulu: University of Hawaii Press, 2008).

2. John Dryden, *Amboyna; or, The Cruelties of the Dutch to the English Merchants*, in *The Works of John Dryden*, ed. Vinton A. Dearing, vol. 12 (Berkeley: University of California Press, 1994), 2.1.14–20. All references are to this edition.

3. This agreement applied to all the spices of the East Indies except for the pepper trade of Java, which was to be distributed evenly between the Dutch and English. For more on the "Treaty of Defense" (July 1619), see Kenneth R. Andrews, *Trade, Plunder and Settlement: Maritime Enterprise and the Genesis of the British Empire, 1480–1630* (Cambridge: Cambridge University Press, 1984), 268–69.

4. The English East India Company frames its interest in the East as an investment in "fair and free commerce" in the letter to the reader that prefaces *A True Relation, of the Unjust, Cruell and Barbarous Proceedings against the English at Amboyna* (London, 1624), A3r. For a discussion of the factors that determined the signing of the 1619 treaty, see Vincent C. Loth, "Armed Incidents and Unpaid Bills: Anglo-Dutch Rivalry in the Banda Islands in the Seventeenth Century," *Modern Asian Studies* 29.4 (1995): 705–40, esp. 717–22.

5. Shankar Raman, *Framing "India": The Colonial Imaginary in Early Modern Culture* (Stanford, Calif.: Stanford University Press, 2001), 234.

6. Robert Markley, "Violence and Profits on the Restoration Stage: Trade, Nationalism, and Insecurity in Dryden's *Amboyna*," *Eighteenth-Century Life* 22 (1998): 9; a lightly reworked version of this essay appears in Markley's monograph *The Far East and the English Imagination, 1600–1730* (Cambridge: Cambridge University Press, 2006), 143–76. I refer to Markley, "Violence and Profits," throughout.

7. Markely, "Violence and Profits," 9.

8. See Cynthia Lowenthal, *Performing Identities on the Restoration Stage* (Carbondale: Southern Illinois University Press, 2003), 35–75.

9. This characterization has prevailed from George Edmundson's *Anglo-Dutch Rivalry During the First Half of the Seventeenth Century* (Oxford: Clarendon Press, 1911) through recent work, including Nicolas Tarling, ed., *The Cambridge History of Southeast Asia*, vol. 1, part 2 (Cambridge: Cambridge University Press, 1999). For an important critique of the economic thesis driving most notions of Anglo-Dutch rivalry, see Steven Pincus, *Protestantism and Patriotism: Ideologies and the Making of English Foreign Policy, 1650–1668* (Cambridge: Cambridge University Press, 1996), and "From Butterboxes to Wooden Shoes: The Shift in English Popular Sentiment from Anti-Dutch to Anti-French in the 1670s," *Historical Journal* 38.2 (1995): 333–61.

10. Louis Montrose, "The Work of Gender in the Discourse of Discovery," *Representations* 33 (1991): 17–18.

11. Eric J. Griffin, *English Renaissance Drama and the Specter of Spain: Ethnopoetics and Empire* (Philadelphia: University of Pennsylvania Press, 2009).

12. See my discussion of Richard Verstegan's *A Restitution* in Chapter 2.

13. Alison Games, "Anglo-Dutch Connections and Overseas Enterprises: A Global Perspective on Lion Gardiner's World," *Early American Studies* 9.2 (2011): 458.

14. Michael Neill, "Putting History to the Question: An Episode of Torture at Bantam in Java, 1604," in *Putting History to the Question: Power, Politics, and Society in English Renaissance Drama* (New York: Columbia University Press, 2000), 290. Though I do not discuss Neill's essay or the "episode" addressed in it, his essay offers an important corollary to the history and discourse discussed in this chapter. For a concise overview of the first twenty years of EIC engagements with Dutch and other foreign powers in the Indonesian archipelago, see Andrews, *Trade, Plunder*, 256–79.

15. Anthony Farrington, *Trading Places: The East India Company and Asia, 1600–1834* (London: British Library, 2002), 39.

16. The first English account of an East India Company voyage, *A true and large discourse of the voyage.* . . . , published in London in 1603 without a preface, introduction, or dedication, was written by one of the crew of the *Ascension* on the first East India Company voyage. Thirty-four pages in length, the journal is primarily concerned with navigation and trade, though occasionally portraits of cultural encounters with the people and rulers of Bantam emerge. Scott's *Exact Discourse* and the anonymous *Last East-Indian voyage,* both accounts of the second voyage, were published in London in 1606, following the return of the second East India Company fleet. For a complete bibliography of early works relating to the East India Company ventures, see Lach and Van Kley, *Asia in the Making of Europe,* vol. 3, part 1, 547–69; see also John Parker, *Books to Build an Empire: A Bibliographical History of English Overseas Interests to 1620* (Amsterdam: N. Israel, 1965), 173–91.

17. The dates of the first decade of EIC outward-bound ventures were 1601, 1604, 1607, 1608, 1609, and 1610. For a complete list of EIC ventures, the ships that sailed, their destinations, and return dates, see K. N. Chaudhuri, *The English East India Company: The Study of an Early Joint-Stock Company, 1600–1640* (London: Frank Cass, 1965), 226–32.

18. Edmund Scott, *An exact discourse* (London, 1606), B2v.

19. In order to avoid confusion about the people to whom Scott refers in his text, I will use the early modern terminology "Javan" rather than "Javanese" for the people of Bantam. Neill notes that "Javanese is technically inaccurate since the people of Bantam were properly speaking Sundanese" ("Putting History to the Question," 479n9). For a trenchant study of the ethnic diversity of the Spice Islands in this period, see Andaya, *Leaves of the Same Tree.*

20. On the pervasiveness of the "Dutch friend" in English accounts of overseas ventures in the Americas as well as East Indies, see Games, "Anglo-Dutch Connections," here 441.

21. Scott, *Exact Discourse,* A4v.

22. On the European encounter with this region in the period from native perspectives, see Leonard Y. Andaya, *The World of Maluku: Eastern Indonesia in the Early Modern Period* (Honolulu: University of Hawaii Press, 1993).

23. *The Last East-Indian voyage* is often attributed to Middleton.

24. Rui Manuel Loureiro, "Early Portuguese Perceptions of the 'Dutch Threat' in Asia," in *Rivalry and Conflict: European Traders and Asian Trading Networks in the 16th and 17th Centuries,* ed. Ernst Van Veen and Leonard Blussé (Leiden: CNWS Publications, 2005), 170.

25. The I series, Records Relating to Other Europeans in India, 1475–1824, in the Asia, Pacific, and African Collections of the British Library is a rich manuscript resource of Dutch accounts regarding their relations in the Spice Islands and Asia. In the late 1900s, Frederick Charles Danvers, then registrar and superintendent of the records of the India Office, examined and drew up a report of the Dutch records regarding activities in the East. The I series, housed in the British Library, was translated from Dutch into English. I/3 are manuscript translations of the Dutch and Portuguese records. Volumes 1–106 are organized chronologically; I/3/86 is the manuscript index of the I series. I have

read volumes 2, 4, 6, 8, 10, 12, and 14, relating to Dutch activities in the East spanning the years 1602–26. In citing the manuscript volumes, I refer to the series (I/3), volume number (2–14), and the number that Danvers assigned to each letter, which he penciled at the top of each letter in roman numerals. Because all of my citations are from I/3, my in-text citations refer only to the volume and letter number.

26. Scott was not alone in comprehending the dangers of this "usurpation." As Michael Neill was first to alert us, when the *Exact Discourse* was reproduced in an abbreviated form and published in *Hakluytus Posthumus* (1625), Samuel Purchas entitled Scott's narrative "*Differences* [i.e., quarrels] betwixt the Hollanders (styling themselves English), the Javans, and other things remarkable" ("'Mulattos,' 'Blacks,' and "Indian Moors': *Othello* and Early Modern Constructions of Human Difference," in *Putting History to the Question*, 278).

27. William Shakespeare, *The Norton Shakespeare,* ed. Stephen Greenblatt, Walter Cohen, Jean E. Howard, and Katharine Eisaman Maus (New York: W.W. Norton, 1997).

28. Of course, what is also interesting about this crisis is the possibility that "Englishmen" *is* functioning just as the people on Bantam want it to. Scott is unable to consider the possibility that intra-European differences might not matter to those on Bantam.

29. Evidence of the company's interest in Malay is evident even in *A true and large discourse,* which lists fifty-two Malay words and phrases. In 1614, *Dialogues in the English and Malaiane Languages* was printed in London. See Farrington, *Trading Places,* 36.

30. Farrington, *Trading Places,* 39.

31. Quoted in Mary Floyd-Wilson, *English Ethnicity and Race in Early Modern Drama* (Cambridge: Cambridge University Press, 2003), 55–56.

32. Farrington, *Trading Places,* 48–54.

33. On Southeast Asian exchange with Europeans, see Tarling, *Cambridge History of Southeast Asia*. On the Dutch VOC and English EIC engagements in the Moluccas, see Lach and Van Kley. *Asia in the Making of Europe,* vol. 3, part 1, 40–88. See also TANAP .net (*Toward a New Age of Partnership in Dutch East India Company Archives and Research*), which offers access to VOC archives from around the world.

34. *A True Relation* was printed twice in 1624 and reprinted under slightly altered titles in 1632, 1651, 1665, and 1672.

35. Karen Chancey, "The Amboyna Massacre in English Politics, 1624–1632," *Albion* 30.4 (1999): 588.

36. For an insightful reading of the relation of the Amboyna massacre pamphlets and the making of an early modern public sphere, see Andrew Fleck, "Deep Designs of Empire: English Representations of the Dutch from the Armada to the Glorious Revolution," diss., Claremont Graduate University, 2000, 190–243. Frances E. Dolan explores the complex interrelation of ideas of evidence and seventeenth century "reports" of this kind in *True Relations: Reading, Literature, and Evidence in Seventeenth-Century England* (Philadelphia: University of Pennsylvania Press, 2013).

37. *News out of East India*, a ballad summarizing the pamphlets of 1624, was circulated that same year (reprinted in *A Pepysian Garland: Black-Letter Broadside Ballads of the*

Years 1595–1639, ed. Hyder E. Rollins [Cambridge, Mass.: Harvard University Press, 1971], 200–206). The ballad's frontispiece is identical to that of *A True Relation*. Walter Mountfort's manuscript play *The Launching of the Mary; or, The Seaman's Honest Wife*, which deals with the massacre, was prepared for the stage in 1625 but suppressed by the Privy Council (London: Malone Society and Oxford University Press, 1933). A Dutch apologia entitled *A True Declaration of the News Concerning a Conspiracy Discovered in the Island of Amboyna and the Punishment that followed thereof* appeared in London in English in 1628. It was reprinted and refuted in *A Remonstrance of the Directors of the Netherlands East-India Company . . . and the Reply of the English East India Company to the Said Remonstrance and Defence* (London, 1632). English pamphlets describing the massacre appear in 1651, 1653, 1665, and 1672: *Bloody News of the East-Indies, being a Relation and Perfect Abstract of the Barbarous Proceedings of the Dutch against the English at Amboyna* (London, 1651); *A Memento for Holland; or, A True and Exact History of the Cruelties used on the English Merchants Residing in Amboyna* (London, 1653); Abraham Woofe, *The Tyranny of the Dutch against the English* (London, 1653); [John Darrell], *A True and Compendious Narration; or, Second Part of Amboyna* (London, 1665); and John Beaumont, *The emblem of ingratitude: a true relation of the unjust, cruel, and barbarous proceedings against the English at Amboyna in the East-Indies, by the Netherlandish governour & council there: also, a farther account of the deceit, cruelty, and tyranny of the Dutch against the English, and several others; from their first to their present estate: with remarks upon the whole matter. faithfully collected from antient* [sic] *and modern records* (London, 1672). Montague Summers, the editor of Dryden's plays, concludes that John Dryden "doubtless had perused the narrative 'Cruelty of the Dutch in Amboyna' which is given at some length (576–78) in Sir William Sanderson's 'A Compleat History Of the Lives and Reigns Of Mary Queen of Scotland, And her Son and Successor, James . . . ,' folio, 1656. Most of Dryden's details, however, are directly derived from *A True Relation* . . . 1624 [and] *A True and Compendious Narration; Or (Second Part of Amboyna)* . . . 1665" (*Dryden: The Dramatic Works* [New York: Gordian Press, 1968], 3.345).

Visual imagery of the massacre was splashed as frontispieces across many of these pamphlets, beginning with the 1624 *True Relation*. The identical image appears on the ballad published that same year. An anonymous engraving dating to 1649 depicts the murder of the British at Amboyna using the familiar iconography of the woodcut (*Allegory concerning the murder of the British at Ambon*, Rijksmuseum, Amsterdam, inventory no. RP-P-OB-75–328); this image can be viewed on the Atlas of Mutual Heritage website, available through the Nationaal Archief at http://www.atlasofmutualheritage.nl/detail .aspx?page = dafb⟨ eqen&id = 206 5#tab2 (accessed 1 July 2013).

38. Robert Wilkinson, *The Stripping of Joseph; or, The Crueltie of Brethren to a Brother* (London, 1625).

39. Quoted from Beaumont's 1672 *Emblem of ingratitude*; the text is a copy of the 1624 letter to the reader in *A True Relation*.

40. The Dutch had reason to be concerned that any one of the many trading nations on Amboyna might turn against them. They recognized that their own success in capturing the Portuguese fort at Amboyna had depended on the indigenous population turning

against the Portuguese. For a discussion of the "psychological impact" of the Dutch usurpation of the Portuguese fort at Amboyna, see Loureiro, "Early Portuguese Perceptions," 178.

41. The Dutch believed that the Japanese, who worked within the Dutch castle, aided the English in a plot to seize the castle and oust the Dutch from the island. On the impracticability of the supposed plot, see D. K. Bassett, "The Amboyna Massacre of 1623," *Journal of Southeast Asian History* 1 (1960): 1–19. Incidentally, many of Bassett's conclusions are drawn from ideas advanced by the English in *The Answer unto the Dutch Pamphlet. . . .* (London, 1624).

42. On the Anglo-Dutch wars, see J. R. Jones, *The Anglo-Dutch Wars of the Seventeenth Century* (London: Longman, 1996); Jonathan Israel, *The Dutch Republic: Its Rise, Greatness, and Fall 1477–1806* (Oxford: Clarendon Press, 1995), 713–22, 766–74, 785, 796–97, 812–13; D. R. Hainsworth and Christine Churches, *The Anglo-Dutch Naval Wars, 1652–1674* (Stroud: Sutton, 1998); Pincus, *Protestantism and Patriotism*. On the relation of the Dutch wars and English ideas regarding British identity, see Peter Furtado, "National Pride in Seventeenth-Century England," in *Patriotism: The Making and Unmaking of British National Identity*, ed. Raphael Samuel, vol. 1 (London: Routledge, 1989), 44–56.

43. Beaumont, *Emblem of ingratitude*. On the twin topoi of Dutch tyranny and innocence in the American context of Dutch colonialism, see Benjamin Schmidt, *Innocence Abroad: The Dutch Imagination and the New World, 1570–1670* (Cambridge: Cambridge University Press, 2001); on how the Amboyna massacre was deployed also in the Americas, see esp. 295–97. On the trope of Dutch ingratitude as it circulated in the early American context, see Carla Gardina Pestana, "Cruelty and Religious Justifications for Conquest in the Mid-Seventeenth-Century English Atlantic," in *Empires of God: Religious Encounters in the Early Modern Atlantic,* ed. Linda Gregerson and Susan Juster (Philadelphia: University of Pennsylvania Press, 2011), 37–57.

44. Summers notes that the play is entered into the stationer's books 26 June 1673 and that "it is probably correct to assign the original performance of this tragedy to a date no later than the first week of the preceding May" (*Dryden*, 347).

45. See Dryden's "Dedication to the Right Honourable Lord Clifford of Chudleigh," at the opening of *Amboyna*. Regarding the play's scholarly reception, Summers writes, "it has been called 'unworthy'; I should prefer to term it 'official' " (*Dryden*, 347). Louis I. Bredvold finds that "no one cares to urge that *Amboyna* has literary merit" ("Political Aspects of Dryden's *Amboyna* and *The Spanish Fryar*," reprinted in *Essential Articles for the Study of John Dryden*, ed. H. T. Swedenberg [Hamden, Conn.: Archon Books, 1966], 300). More recently, the play has been characterized as a "hack work" (Derek Hughes, *English Drama, 1660–1700* [Oxford: Clarendon Press, 1996], 91).

46. *Amboyna* would have been a somewhat shocking spectacle of horror for audiences in the early 1670s, as "the real glut of stage horror made its appearance after 1678" (Jean I. Marsden, "Spectacle, Horror, and Pathos," in *The Cambridge Companion to English Restoration Theatre*, ed. Deborah Payne Fisk [Cambridge: Cambridge University Press, 2000], 179).

47. On Dryden's sources, see Summers, *Dryden*, 345.

48. Colin Visser suggests that Dryden derived the name "Ysabinda" from a misreading of the name "Tsabinda"—a Japanese man arrested at Amboyna—whose name appears in Beaumont's *Emblem of ingratitude* ("John Dryden's *Amboyna* at Lincoln's Inn Fields, 1673," *Restoration and 18th Century Theater Research* 15.1 [1976]: 1–11). More recently, Bindu Malieckal has discovered the historical origins of the figure of Ysabinda ("Mariam Khan and the Legacy of Mughal Women in Early Modern Literature of India," in *Early Modern England and Islamic Worlds*, ed. Bernadette Diane Andrea and Linda McJannet [New York: Palgrave Macmillan, 2011], 97–122).

49. With such a focus, critical readings of Dryden's *Amboyna* support Bridget Orr's assessment that Restoration drama demonstrates a "strong tendency to figure English colonial activity indirectly and in the context of a comparison by which another European empire suffers" and that a "repeated pattern of disavowal in the representation of colonization is symptomatic of the ambivalence, indeed contradictions, which . . . riddle[d] English imperial ideology" (*Empire on the English Stage, 1660–1714* [Cambridge: Cambridge University Press, 2001], 280).

50. Markley, "Violence and Profits," 9. Markley develops this binary by demonstrating how English class antagonism, particularly the vilification of the upstart merchant who was seen as draining the nation's resources in risky EIC ventures, is displaced onto Dutch boors (14). Similarly, for Raman, the struggle between Towerson and Harman for Ysabinda aims "first, to make explicit the qualitative difference between their respective desires, and, second, to establish the ethical superiority of the English position. . . . [T]he brutality and illegality [of the crime against Ysabinda] represent the logical culmination of a Dutch mercantilism governed solely by the category of self-interest" (*Framing "India,"* 212–13).

51. Raman, *Framing "India,"* 210.

52. Ibid., 203.

53. Ibid., 212.

54. Ibid., 230, 235.

55. As described in n. 51, Markley argues that this national distinction allows class antagonisms *within* England to be displaced onto Dutch boors ("Violence and Profits," 14).

56. Ibid., 3, 8.

57. The VOC was, in fact, interested in controlling Amboyna's clove trade at the time of the Amboyna massacre: "Met by Iberian, English, and local Asian resistance, the Dutch painfully and slowly enforced an effective control over the Banda Islands, Amboina, Ceram, and the Moluccas. The Bandas, completely conquered by the Dutch in 1621, had long supplied nutmeg and mace in exchange for foodstuffs and textiles. Once they were taken over by the Dutch colonists the Company possessed complete control over nutmeg and mace production. In the meantime the Company sought to concentrate clove production by limiting it to the villages of Amboina and by destroying the trees on the nearby and much larger island of Ceram. This decision was based on the conviction that Amboina could produce enough by itself to meet the combined demand of Europe

and Asia, and that by limiting cultivation to Amboina the Company could easily monopolize the trade and set the purchase and sale prices of the cloves" (Lach and Van Kley, *Asia in the Making of Europe*, vol. 3, part 1, 68).

58. Ibid., 64.

59. Chaudhuri, *English East India Company*, 140–72.

60. Ibid., 167–68.

61. *Calendar of State Papers, East Indies, 1622–1624*, quoted in Chaudhuri, *English East India Company*, 170.

62. Historians contend that the Amboyna massacre did not cause the English withdrawal from Amboyna but marked the end of a complex set of events in which they were driven out: "It should not be assumed, however, that the English withdrawal in 1623 from the Spiceries, Japan, and Siam resulted from the 'Massacre'; it was rather the Company's earlier disillusionment with the unwillingness of the Dutch to abide by the Accord in the Indonesian region that prompted the directors in London to order the abandonment of factories unable to operate at profit" (Lach and Van Kley, *Asia in the Making of Europe*, vol. 3, part 1, 77). Even so, the massacre was long represented in the pamphlet literature as a cause of England's failed colonial enterprises in the Spice Islands.

63. Montrose, "Work of Gender."

64. The play blurs meaningful historical distinctions between Spanish and Portuguese colonial engagement in Amboyna. Historically speaking, the Portuguese were the initial European rivals to the Dutch in the region. Even so, Julia's "Spanish" identity is meant to identify her as a part of the Portuguese and, broadly speaking, Iberian history at Amboyna.

65. On geohumoralism, see Floyd-Wilson, *English Ethnicity and Race*. Following this exchange, Julia invites the Dutchman and the Englishman to express their thoughts about one another's nations, an exchange that predictably catalyzes equally negative characterizations of Dutch and English people. In both cases, the English and Dutch *as merchants* becomes the focus of the national portrait. Unlike their mutual characterization of the Spaniard, Anglo-Dutch antipathy is not expressed as a racial difference.

66. Here, I propose a very different reading than Raman advances in *Framing "India,"* wherein the "invisibility" of Ysabinda's rape is understood to suppress "the violence of colonial domination": "In distinguishing the two nations, Dryden opposes the extralegal and uncivilized act of Dutch rape to English marriage, the socially sanctioned form of colonial intercourse. But as a form of violence that the Dutch and the English both participate in, the rape has to be subordinated to what really matters: the production of an intra-European difference. That we do not see the rape effects just such a subordination. . . . The invisibility of the rape ensures that the violence of colonial domination remains concealed, unable to interfere with or detract from the spectacle of national humiliation [that follows]" (235).

67. This line is spoken by an unnamed "English woman" who is the third female character invented by Dryden. She makes only a brief appearance during the torture scene.

68. Orr, *Empire*, 280.

69. Montrose, "Work of Gender," 17.

CODA

1. Geoffrey Parker, *The Dutch Revolt* (Ithaca, N.Y.: Cornell University Press, 1977), 178. The history of this event is far more complex than I have space to recount here. Behind the Spanish Fury is the story of a mutiny of the unpaid Spanish troops. The Spanish and Dutch armies were far from homogeneously constituted, so drawing clear distinctions of ethnicity between these warring factions would risk effacing the ethnic diversity of these troops. Even so, in English publications regarding the Fury, also known as the "siege of Antwerp," the Spaniard emerges as the vilified figure of political aggression. See, for instance, the anonymous English play *A Larum for London* (London, 1602); and Anne L. Mackenzie, "A Study in Dramatic Contrasts: The Siege of Antwerp in *A Larum for London* and *El saco de Amberes*," *Bulletin of Hispanic Studies* 59 (1982): 283–300.

2. George Gascoigne, *The Spoyle of Antwerpe. Faithfully reported, by a true Englishman, who was present at the same* (London, 1576), A3v. On early modern Antwerp, see Guido Marnef, *Antwerp in the Age of Reformation: Underground Protestantism in a Commercial Metropolis, 1550–1577* (Baltimore: Johns Hopkins University Press, 1996); and Peter Burke, *Antwerp: A Metropolis in Comparative Perspective* (Ghent: Snoeck-Ducaju & Zoon, 1993). On the literature of "alarm" and the association of Antwerp with London, see S. M. Pratt, "Antwerp and the Elizabethan Mind," *Modern Language Quarterly* 24 (1963): 53–60.

3. Frances E. Dolan, *True Relations: Reading, Literature, and Evidence in Seventeenth-Century England* (Philadelphia: University of Pennsylvania Press, 2013), 7. While Dolan focuses on the seventeenth century, a period in which hundreds of title pages identify their works as "true relations," she notes that sixteenth- and eighteenth-century texts also participate in "thinking about truth in and as relation" (2). What interests me here is less the question of whether Gascoigne's *Spoyle of Antwerpe* is a precursor to the "true relation" than that his narrative strategies seem designed to produce in the reader what Dolan characterizes as "imaginative reenactment" (7).

4. Indeed, Gascoigne reports, Englishmen were victims of the Spanish Fury at Antwerp. Some were killed in the streets, others were slain even within the walls of the English House.

5. Edmund Scott, *An exact discourse. . . .* (London, 1606), B2v.

BIBLIOGRAPHY

PRIMARY SOURCES

Barret, John. *An Alvearie or Quadruple Dictionarie.* London, 1580.

———. *An Alvearie or triple dictionarie, in Englishe, Latin, and French.* London, 1574.

Beaumont, John. *The emblem of ingratitude: a true relation of the unjust, cruel, and barbarous proceedings against the English at Amboyna in the East-Indies, by the Netherlandish governour & council there: also, a farther account of the deceit, cruelty, and tyranny of the Dutch against the English, and several others; from their first to their present estate: with remarks upon the whole matter. faithfully collected from antient* [sic] *and modern records.* London, 1672.

Berlaimont, Noël de, *Colloquia et dictionariolum octo linguarum.* Delft, 1598, 1613; Flushing, 1613; Hague, 1613; Amsterdam, 1622, 1623, 1631; Venice, 1627; Antwerp, 1630; Middleburg, 1631; Delft, 1631.

———. *Colloquia et dictionariolum septem linguarum.* Antwerp, 1586, 1616; Padua, 1592; Leiden, 1593; Liège, 1595, 1597, 1600, 1610; Venice, 1606.

———. *Colloquia et dictionariolum sex linguarum.* Geneva, 1608.

———[as Berlemont, Noël de]. *Colloques ou Dialogues, avec un Dictionaire en quatre langues. Flamen, Anglois, Francois, & Latin.* Leiden, 1585.

———. *Colloques ou dialogues septem linguarum.* Liège, 1589.

Beyer, Guillaume. *La vraye instruction des trois langues la Francoise, l'Angloise, & la Flamende . . . Right instruction of three languages French, English and Dutch.* Dordrecht, 1661.

Bloody News of the East-Indies, being a Relation and Perfect Abstract of the Barbarous Proceedings of the Dutch against the English at Amboyna. London, 1651.

A Booke Concernynge the Newe Burse. London, 1566. Rpt. in *The Royal Exchange.* Ed. Ann Saunders. London: London Topographical Society, 1997. 416–26.

Brereton, Sir William. *Travels in Holland, the United Provinces, England, Scotland, and Ireland, 1634–1635.* London: Chetham Society, 1844.

Bullokar, John. *An English Expositor.* London, 1616, 1641, 1654, 1656, 1663, 1695, 1698.

———. *An English Expositor.* Cambridge, 1667, 1671, 1676, 1680, 1684, 1688.

Calepino, Ambrogio. *Ambrosii Calepini Dictionarium undecim linguarum.* Basel, 1598.

Camden, William. *Britain; or, A chorographicall description of the most flourishing king-domes, England, Scotland, and Ireland, and the ilands adjoyning, out of the depth of antiquitie.* London, 1610.

———. *Remaines of a greater worke, concerning Britaine.* London, 1605.

———. *Remaines, concerning Britaine but especially England, and the inhabitants thereof.* London, 1614.

———. *Remains Concerning Britain.* Ed. R. D. Dunn. Toronto: University of Toronto Press, 1984.

Carew, Richard. "The Excellency of the English Tongue." William Camden, *Remaines, concerning Britaine.* London, 1614.

Cawdrey, Robert. *A Table Alphabetical.* London, 1604, 1609, 1613, 1617.

Cockeram, Henry. *The English Dictionary.* London, 1623, 1626, 1631, 1637.

Cokayne, Thomas. *A Greek English Lexicon.* London, 1658.

Cotgrave, Randal. *A dictionarie of French and English tongues.* London, 1571, 1598.

Cunningham, William. *The cosmographical glasse conteinyng the pleasant principles of cosmo-graphie, geographie, hydrographie, or nauigation.* London, 1559.

Daniel, Samuel. *A Panegyrike Congratulatorie . . . Also Certaine Epistles, with a Defence of Ryme.* London, 1603.

[Darrell, John]. *A True and Compendious Narration; or, Second Part of Amboyna.* London, 1665.

Declaration of the Causes Mooving the Queene of England to give aide to the Defence of the People afflicted and oppressed in the Lowe Countries. London, 1585. Rpt. in *A Collection of Scarce and Valuable Tracts.* Ed. John Somers and Walter Scott. Vol. 1. London: Cadell and Davies, 1809. 410–19.

Dekker, Thomas. "The Magnificent Entertainment: Given to King James (1604)." *The Dramatic Works of Thomas Dekker.* Ed. Fredson Bowers. Vol. 2. Cambridge: Cambridge University Press, 1955. 230–303.

———. *The Shoemaker's Holiday or The Gentle Craft. The Roaring Girl and Other City Comedies.* Ed. James Knowles. Oxford: Oxford University Press, 2001. 1–65.

———. *The sho[e]makers holiday; or, The gentle craft.* [London], 1600, 1610, 1618, 1631, 1657.

———. *Thomas Dekker: The Wonderful Year, the Gull's Horn-Book, Penny-Wise, Pound Foolish, English Villainies Discovered by Lantern and Candlelight and Selected Writings.* Ed. E. D. Pendry. Cambridge, Mass.: Harvard University Press, 1968.

Dekker, Thomas, and John Webster. *Northward Ho* (1607). *The Dramatic Works of Thomas Dekker.* Ed. Fredson Bowers. Vol. 2. Cambridge: Cambridge University Press, 1955. 410–90.

———. *Northward Hoe.* London, 1607.

———. *Westward Ho* (1607). *The Dramatic Works of Thomas Dekker.* Ed. Fredson Bowers. Vol. 2. Cambridge: Cambridge University Press, 1955. 311–403.

Den grooten vocabulaer Engels ende Duyts . . . The great vocabuler, in English and Dutch. Rotterdam, 1639.

Dictionarium, Ofte Woorden-Boeck, Begrijpende de Schat der Nederlandtsche Talke, met de Engelsche Uytlegginge. Rotterdam, 1672, 1678.

Dryden, John. *Amboyna; or, The Cruelties of the Dutch to the English Merchants. The Works of John Dryden.* Ed. Vinton A. Dearing. Vol. 12. Berkeley: University of California Press, 1994.

———. "Dedication to the Right Honourable Lord Clifford of Chudleigh." *The Works of John Dryden.* Ed. Vinton A. Dearing. Vol. 12. Berkeley: University of California Press, 1994.

Dugdale, Gilbert. *The Time Triumphant.* London, 1604.

The Dutch-tutor; or, A new-book of Dutch and English. London, 1660, 1669.

The English, Latine, French, Dutch Schole-master. London, 1637.

The English Schole-master or certaine rules and helpes whereby the natives of the Netherlandes, may bee, in a short time, taught to read, understand, and speake, the English tongue . . . Den Engelschen School-Meester. Amsterdam, 1646, 1658, 1663.

An Enterlude of Welth, and Helth. London, ca.1565.

Essex, Robert Devereux, Earl of. *An Apologie of the Earle of Essex . . . Penned by himselfe in anno 1598.* London, 1603.

Estienne, Robert, and Johannes Frisius. *Lexicon Trilingue.* Strasbourg, 1587.

F.D. *The Dutch-Mens Pedigree, or a Relation, Shewing How They Were First Bred, and Descended from a Horse-Turd, Which Was Enclosed in a Butter-Box.* London, 1653.

Felltham, Owen. *A brief character of the Low-Countries under the states being three weeks observation of the vices and vertues of the inhabitants.* London, 1652.

Florio, John. *A Worlde of Wordes, or Most copious, and exact dictionarie in Italian and English.* London, 1598.

———. *Queen Anna's New World of Words, or Dictionarie of the Italian and English tongues.* London, 1611.

Ford, John. *The Ladies Triall.* London, 1639.

Frisius, Johannes. *Dictionarium Latinogermanicum.* Zurich, 1568.

Fullwell, Haunce of Ulpian. *A pleasant enterlude, intituled, Like will to like.* London, 1568, 1587.

Gascoigne, George. "Certayne notes of Instruction." *The Posies.* Ed. John W. Cunliffe. 1907. Cambridge: Cambridge University Press, 1969. 465–73.

———. *The Spoyle of Antwerpe. Faithfully reported, by a true Englishman, who was present at the same.* London, 1576.

Glapthorne, Henry. *The Hollander.* London, 1640.

Harrison, Stephen. *The Arch's of Triumph Erected in Honor of the High and Mighty Prince James.* London, 1604.

Haughton, William. *English-men for My Money.* 1598. London, 1616, 1626, 1631.

———. *William Haughton's Englishmen for My Money; or, a Woman Will Have Her Will.* Ed. Albert Croll Baugh. Philadelphia, 1917.

Heldoren, J. G. van. *An English and Nether-dutch dictionary composed out of the best English authors . . . Een Engels en Nederduits Woortboek.* Amsterdam, 1675.

———. *A new and easy English grammar, containing brief fundamental rules, usual phrases pleasant and choise [sic] dialogues concerning the present state and court of England. Whereunto is added a nomenclature, English and Dutch.* Amsterdam, 1675; London, 1690.

Hexham, Henry. *Het Groot Woorden-boeck . . . A Copious English and Netherduytch Dictionarie* [alternatively entitled *A large Netherdutch and English Dictionarie*]. Rotterdam, 1647, 1648, 1658, 1660, 1672, 1675, 1678.

Heywood, Thomas. *A Critical Edition of "The Faire Maide of the Exchange."* Ed. Karl E. Snyder. New York: Garland, 1980.

———. *If You Know Not Me You Know Nobody, Part II.* Oxford: Malone Society Reprints and Oxford University Press, 1934.

Hillenius, François. *Den Engelschen ende Ne'erduitschen onderrichter . . . The English, and Low-dutch Instructer.* Rotterdam, 1664, 1671, 1677, 1678, 1686.

Howell, James. "Divers Centuries of New Sayings." *Paroimiographia.* London, 1659.

———. *Lexicon tetraglotton, an English-French-Italian-Spanish dictionary.* London, 1660.

Jonson, Ben. *The Alchemist.* Ed. Gordon Campbell. Oxford: Oxford University Press, 1995.

———. *The Alchemist.* London, 1612; [1680?].

———. *The Devil Is an Ass.* Ed. Peter Happé. Manchester: Manchester University Press, 1996.

———. *The Masque of Augures.* London, 1621.

———. *The Masque of Augures.* 1631. Rpt. in *The Workes of Benjamin Jonson.* Vol. 2. London, 1640.

———. *Timber or Discoveries Made upon Men and Matter.* Ed. Felix E. Schelling. Boston: Ginn, 1892.

———. *The Workes of Benjamin Jonson.* London, 1640.

Junius, Hadrianus, Adam Siber, and Rodolphus Agricola. *Adami Siberi Gemma Gemmarum, Sev Nomenclatoris Had. Junii Epitome.* Leipzig, 1579.

A Larum for London. London, 1602.

The last East-Indian voyage Containing much varietie of the state of the severall kingdomes where they have traded: with the letters of three severall Kings to the Kings Majestie of England, begun by one of the voyage: since continued out of the faithfull observations of them that are come home. London, 1606.

Le Grand dictionaire françois flamen. Rotterdam, 1618.

Le Mayre, Marten. *The Dutch Schoole Master wherein is shewed the true and perfect way to learne the Dutch tongue, to the furtherance of all those which would gladlie learne it.* London, 1606.

Le Petit, Jean François. *A Generall Historie of the Netherlands . . . by Ed. Grimeston.* London, 1608.

The Life and Death of Jacke Straw, a notable rebell in England: who was kild in Smithfield by the Lord Mayor of London. London, 1593 [i.e., 1594].

The life and death of Jacke Straw, a notable rebell in England: who was killed in Smithfield, by the Lord Mayor of London. London, 1604.

The London prodigall. As it was plaide by the Kings Maiesties servants. London, 1605.

Lupton, Donald. *London and the Countrey Carbonadoed and Quartered into Severall Characters.* London, 1632.

A Lytell Treatyse for to Lerne Englysshe and Frensshe. Antwerp, ca. 1530.

Madoet, André. *Thesaurus theutonicae linguae. Schat der Neder-duytscher spraken.* Antwerp, 1573.

Marmion, Shackerley. "Holland's Leaguer (Critical Edition)." *The Dramatic Works of Shackerley Marmion.* Ed. James Maidment and William Hugh Logan. Edinburgh, W. Paterson, 1875.

Marmyon, Shackerley. *Hollands Leaguer.* London, 1632.

Marston, John. *The Dutch Courtesan.* London, 1605.

———. *The Dutch Courtesan.* Ed. David Crane. London: A & C Black, 1997.

———. *The Workes of Mr. John Marston, tragedies and comedies collected into one volume.* London, 1633.

Marvell, Andrew. *An Account of the Growth of Popery, and Arbitrary Government in England.* London, 1677.

———. *The Character of Holland.* London, 1665.

———. "The Character of Holland." *The Poems of Andrew Marvell.* Ed. Nigel Smith. Rev. ed. London: Pearson Longman, 2007. 246–56.

A Memento for Holland; or, A True and Exact History of the Cruelties used on the English Merchants Residing in Amboyna. London, 1653.

Mercator, Gerhard. *Atlas; or, A geographicke description of the regions, countries and kingdomes of the world, through Europe, Asia, Africa, and America, represented by new & exact maps.* Amsterdam, 1636.

———. *Atlas sive cosmographicae, meditationes de fabrica mundi et fabricati figura.* Duisburg, 1595; Amsterdam, 1623.

Mercers' Company Archives. *Gresham Repertories.* Vol. 2. London, 1629–69.

Middleton, Thomas. *Chaste Maid in Cheapside.* Ed. Richard Dutton. Oxford: Oxford University Press, 1999.

———. *No wit, [no] help like a womans.* London, 1657.

———. *No Wit, [No] Help like A Woman's.* Ed. John Jowett. *Thomas Middleton: The Collected Works.* Ed. Gary Taylor and John Lavagnino. Oxford: Clarendon Press, 2007. 779–832.

Middleton, Thomas, and Thomas Dekker. *The Roaring Girle.* London, 1611.

———. *The Roaring Girl.* Ed. Paul A. Mulholland. Manchester: Manchester University Press, 1987.

Miege, Guy. *A New Dictionary French and English, with another English and French.* London, 1679.

Minsheu, John. *Hēgemōn eis tas glōssas id est, Ductor in linguas, The guide into tongues.* London, 1617.

Mountfort, Walter. *The Launching of the Mary; or, The Seaman's Honest Wife.* London: Malone Society and Oxford University Press, 1933.

Moxon, Joseph. *Mechanick Exercises: On the Whole Art of Printing, 1683–4.* Ed. Herbert Davis and Harry Carter. London: Oxford University Press, 1958.

———. *Regulae Trium Ordinum Literarum Typographicarum, or, the Rules of the Three Orders of Print Letters Viz. The Roman, Italick, English Capitals and Small.* London, 1676.

Mulcaster, Richard. *The First Part of the Elementarie Which Entreateth Chefelie of the Right Writing of Our English Tung, Set Furth by Richard Mulcaster.* London, 1582.

———. *Mulcaster's Elementarie.* Ed. E. T. Campagnac. Oxford: Clarendon Press, 1925.

New Dialogues or Colloquies, and A Little Dictionary of eight Languages. London, 1639.

News out of East India. 1624.

Ortelius, Abraham. *Theatrum Orbis Terrarum . . . The Theatre of the Whole World: Set Forth by That Excellent Geographer.* London, 1606 [i.e., 1608].

———. *Theatrum Orbis Terrarum.* Antwerp, 1570.

A Pepysian Garland: Black-Letter Broadside Ballads of the Years 1595–1639. Ed. Hyder E. Rollins. Cambridge, Mass.: Harvard University Press, 1971.

Perceval, Richard. *A dictionary in Spanish and English.* London, 1623.

Petri, Jonas. *Dictionarium. Latino-Sveco-Germanicum.* Linkoping, 1640.

Philalethes, Theophilus. *Great Britains Glory; or, A brief Description of the present State, Splendor, and Magnificence of the Royal Exchange.* London, 1672.

Phillips, Edward. *New World of English Words.* London, 1658.

Puttenham, George. *The Arte of English Poesie.* Ed. Gladys Doidge Willcock and Alice Walker. Cambridge: Cambridge University Press, 1936.

Records Relating to Other Europeans in India. 1475–1824. India Office Records and Private Papers (IOR)/I. British Library.

A Remonstrance of the Directors of the Netherlands East-India Company . . . and the Reply of the English East India Company to the Said Remonstrance and Defence. London, 1632.

Richardson, Edward. *Anglo-Belgica, the English and Netherdutch Academy in three parts.* Amsterdam, 1677.

———. *Anglo-Belcica* [sic], *the English and Netherdutch Academy in three parts.* Amsterdam, 1689, 1698.

Rider, John. *Bibliotheca scholastica. A double dictionarie.* Oxford, 1589.

———. *Dictionarie . . . Latin, French, and other languages.* London, 1640.

———. *Riders dictionarie . . . Now newly corrected and much augmented by Francis Holyoke.* London, 1640.

Rowley, Samuel. *The noble souldier. Or, A contract broken, justly reveng'd. A tragedy.* London, 1634.

Scott, Edmund. *An exact discourse of the subtilties, fashishions* [sic], *pollicies, religion, and ceremonies of the East Indians as well Chyneses as Javans, there abyding and dweling. Together with the manner of trading with those people, as well by us English, as by the Hollanders: as also what hath happened to the English nation at Bantan in the East Indies, since the 2. of February 1602. until the 6. of October 1605. Whereunto is added a briefe discription of Java Major. Written by Edmund Scott, resident there, and in other places neere adioyng* [sic]*, the space of three yeeres and a halfe.* London, 1606.

Scott, Thomas. *Belgicke Pismire.* London [i.e., Holland], 1622.

Sewel, William. *A new dictionary English and Dutch . . . Nieuw woordenboek der Engelsche en Nederduytsche.* Amsterdam, 1691.

———. *Nieuw woordenboek der Nederduytsche en Engelsche taale . . . A new dictionary Dutch and English.* Amsterdam, 1691.

Sex linguarum Latinae, Gallicae, Hispanicae, Italicae, Anglicae & Teutonic[a]e. Zurich, 1579.

Shakespeare, William. *The Norton Shakespeare.* Ed. Stephen Greenblatt, Walter Cohen, Jean E. Howard, and Katharine Eisaman Maus. New York: W.W. Norton, 1997.

Sherwood, Robert. *Dictionaire anglois et francois.* London, 1632.

Sidney, Philip. *The Defence of Poesy. Sir Philip Sidney: A Critical Edition of the Major Works.* Ed. Katherine Duncan-Jones. 1989. Oxford: Oxford University Press, 2002. 212–50.

Somner, William. *Dictionarium Saxonico-Latino-Anglicum voces.* London, 1659.

Speed, John. *A Prospect of the Most Famous Parts of the World.* London, 1631.

———. *The Theatre of the Empire of Great Britaine.* London, 1611, 1632.

Spenser, Edmund. Epistle to *The Shepheardes Calendar. The Yale Edition of the Shorter Poems of Edmund Spenser.* Ed. William A. Oram, et al. New Haven, Conn.: Yale University Press, 1989.

Stevin, Simon. *The Principal Works of Simon Stevin.* Trans. C. Dikshoorn. Ed. Ernst Crone et al. Vol. 1. Amsterdam: C. V. Swets and Zeitlinger, 1955.

Stow, John. *A Survey of London.* Ed. Charles Lethbridge Kingsford. Vol. 1. 1908. Oxford: Clarendon Press, 2000.

A supplication of the Family of Love (said to be presented into the Kings royall hands, knowen to be dispersed among his loyall subjectes) for grace and favour Examined, and found to be derogatorie in an hie degree, unto the glorie of God, the honour of our King, and the religion in this realme both soundly professed & firmly established. London, 1606.

Tacitus, Cornelius. *The description of Germanie.* London, 1604 [i.e., 1605].

———. *Tacitus Germania.* Trans. J. B. Rives. Oxford: Clarendon Press, 1999.

Taylor, John. *Taylors Travels and Circular Perambulations through, and by more then thirty times twelve signs of the Zodiack, of the Famous Cities of London and Westminster.* London, 1636.

Torriano, Giovanni. *The Italian Tutor.* London, 1640.

A true and large discourse of the voyage of the whole fleete of ships set forth the 20. of Aprill 1601. by the Governours and assistants of the East Indian marchants in London, to the East Indies Wherein is set downe the order and manner of their trafficke, the discription of the countries, the nature of the people and their language, with the names of all the men dead in the voyage. London, 1603.

A True Declaration of the News Concerning a Conspiracy Discovered in the Island of Amboyna and the Punishment that followed thereof. London, 1628.

A True Relation, of the Unjust, Cruell and Barbarous Proceedings against the English at Amboyna in the East-Indies, by the Neatherlandish gouernour and councel there Also the copie of a pamphlet, set forth first in Dutch and then in English, by some Neatherlander; falsly entituled, A true declaration of the newes that came out of the East-Indies, with the pinace called the Hare, which arriued at Texel in Iune, 1624. Together with an answer to the same pamphlet. London, 1624.

A true relation of the unjust, cruell, and barbarous proceedings against the English at Amboyna. London, 1632.

Vaughan, Edward. *A plaine and perfect Method, for the easie understanding of the whole Bible.* London, 1617.

Verstegan, Richard. *Newes from the low-countreyes; or, The anatomy of Calvinisticall calumnyes, manifested in a dialogue betweene a Brabander, and a Hollander.* Saint-Omer, 1622.

————. *A Restitution of Decayed Intelligence: In Antiquities. Concerning the Most Noble and Renowmed [sic] English Nation. By the Studie and Travaile of R.V. Dedicated Unto the Kings Most Excellent Majestie.* Antwerp, 1605.

————. *A Restitution of Decayed Intelligence.* Ed. D. M. Rogers. London: Scolar Press, 1976.

Wakefield, Robert. *Oratio de laudibus & utilitate trium linguarum Arabicae Chaldaicae & Hebraicae.* London, 1528.

Wapull, George. *The tyde taryeth no man A moste pleasant and merry commody, right pythie and full of delight.* London, 1576.

The Weakest Goeth to the Wall. London, 1600, 1618.

Wilkinson, Robert. *The Stripping of Joseph; or, The Crueltie of Brethren to a Brother.* London, 1625.

Wilson, Thomas. *The arte of rhetorique, for the use of all such as are studious of eloquence, set forth in English.* London, 1553.

Woofe, Abraham. *The Tyranny of the Dutch against the English.* London, 1653.

SECONDARY SOURCES

Adelman, Janet. "Her Father's Blood: Race, Conversion, and Nation in *The Merchant of Venice*." *Representations* 81 (Winter 2003): 4–30.

Alexander, Catherine M. S., and Stanley Wells, eds. *Shakespeare and Race.* New York: Cambridge University Press, 2000.

Andaya, Leonard Y. "Cultural State Formation in Eastern Indonesia." In *Southeast Asia in the Early Modern Era: Trade, Power, and Belief.* Ed. Anthony Reid. Ithaca, N.Y.: Cornell University Press, 1993. 23–41.

————. *Leaves of the Same Tree: Trade and Ethnicity in the Straits of Melaka.* Honolulu: University of Hawaii Press, 2008.

————. *The World of Maluku: Eastern Indonesia in the Early Modern Period.* Honolulu: University of Hawaii Press, 1993.

Andrews, Kenneth R. *Trade, Plunder and Settlement: Maritime Enterprise and the Genesis of the British Empire, 1480–1630.* Cambridge: Cambridge University Press, 1984.

Archer, Ian. *The Pursuit of Stability: Social Relations in Elizabethan London.* Cambridge: Cambridge University Press, 1991.

Archer, John Michael. *Citizen Shakespeare: Freemen and Aliens in the Language of the Plays.* New York: Palgrave Macmillan, 2005.

Armstrong, C. A. J. "The Language Question in the Low Countries: The Use of French and Dutch by the Dukes of Burgundy and Their Administration." In *Europe in the Late Middle Ages.* Ed. J. R. Hale, J. R. L. Highfield, and Beryl Smalley. Evanston, Ill.: Northwestern University Press, 1965. 386–409.

Bailey, Richard. *Images of English: A Cultural History of the Language.* Ann Arbor: University of Michigan Press, 1991.

Bain, Peter, and Paul Shaw, eds. *Blackletter: Type and National Identity.* New York: Princeton Architectural Press, 1998.

Baker, David. "'The Allegory of a China Shop': Jonson's *Entertainment at Britain's Burse.*" *English Literary History* 72 (2005): 159–80.

Barber, Charles. *Early Modern English.* London: André Deutsch, 1976.

Baron, Sabrina Alcorn. "Red Ink and Black Letter: Reading Early Modern Authority." In *The Reader Revealed.* Ed. Sabrina Alcorn Baron, Elizabeth Walsh, and Susan Scola. Washington, D.C.: Folger Shakespeare Library, 2001. 19–30.

Bartels, Emily Carroll. "Shakespeare's 'Other' Worlds: The Critical Trek." *Literature Compass* 5.6 (2008): 1111–38.

———. *Speaking of the Moor: From Alcazar to Othello.* Philadelphia: University of Pennsylvania Press, 2008.

———. *Spectacles of Strangeness: Imperialism, Alienation, and Marlowe.* Philadelphia: University of Pennsylvania Press, 1993.

Barth, Fredrik. *Ethnic Groups and Boundaries: The Social Organization of Cultural Difference.* Boston: Little, Brown, 1969.

Barthelemy, Anthony Gerard. *Black Face, Maligned Race: The Representation of Blacks in English Drama from Shakespeare to Southerne.* Baton Rouge: Louisiana State University Press, 1987.

Barthes, Roland. "Semiology and the Urban." In *Rethinking Architecture: A Reader in Cultural Theory.* Ed. Neil Leach. 1997. London: Routledge, 2003. 166–71.

———. *S/Z: An Essay.* Trans. Richard Miller. New York: Hill & Wang, 1974.

Bartlett, Robert. "Medieval and Modern Concepts of Race and Ethnicity." *Journal of Medieval and Early Modern Studies* 31.1 (2001): 39–56.

Bartolovich, Crystal. "'Baseless Fabric': London as 'World City'." In *The Tempest and Its Travels.* Ed. Peter Hulme and William Sherman. London: Reaktion, 2000. 13–26.

Bassett, D. K. "The Amboyna Massacre of 1623." *Journal of Southeast Asian History* 1 (1960): 1–19.

Beidler, Philip D., and Gary Taylor, eds. *Writing Race Across the Atlantic World.* New York: Palgrave Macmillan, 2005.

Bense, J. F. *Anglo-Dutch Relations from the Earliest Times to the Death of William the Third.* The Hague: Martinus Nijhoff, 1925.

Bergeron, David. *English Civic Pageantry, 1558–1642.* Rev. ed. Tempe: Arizona State University, 2003.

————. "Harrison, Jonson, and Dekker: *The Magnificent Entertainment of King James* (1604)." *Journal of the Warburg and Courtald Institute* 31 (1968): 445–48.

————. *Pageants and Entertainments of Anthony Munday: A Critical Edition.* New York: Garland, 1985.

————. *Practicing Renaissance Scholarship: Plays and Pageants, Patrons and Politics.* Pittsburgh: Duquesne University Press, 2000.

Bhabha, Homi. *The Location of Culture.* London: Routledge, 1994.

Billing, Christian M. "The Dutch Diaspora in English City Comedy: 1598–1618." In *Transnational Exchange in Early Modern Theater.* Ed. Robert Henke and Erick Nicholson. Burlington, Vt.: Ashgate, 2008. 119–39.

Blanchard, Ian. "Sir Thomas Gresham c. 1518–1579." In Saunders, *The Royal Exchange,* 11–19.

Bland, Mark. "The Appearance of Text in Early Modern England." *TEXT* 11 (1998): 91–154.

Blank, Paula. *Broken English: Dialects and the Politics of Language in Renaissance Writings.* New York: Routledge, 1996.

Blayney, Peter. "The Publication of Playbooks." In *A New History of Early English Drama.* Ed. John D. Cox and David Scott Kastan. New York: Columbia University Press, 1997. 383–422.

Blok, Anton. *Honour and Violence.* Malden, Mass.: Blackwell, 2001.

Bloom, Gina. *Voice in Motion: Staging Gender, Shaping Sound in Early Modern England.* Philadelphia: University of Pennsylvania Press, 2007.

Boose, Lynda. "'The Getting of a Lawful Race': Racial Discourse in Early Modern England and the Unrepresentable Black Woman." In Hendricks and Parker, *Women, "Race," and Writing,* 35–54.

Bourdieu, Pierre. *Distinction: A Social Critique of the Judgement of Taste.* Cambridge, Mass.: Harvard University Press, 1984.

————. *Language and Symbolic Power.* Ed. John B. Thompson. Trans. Gino Raymond and Matthew Adamson. Cambridge, Mass.: Harvard University Press, 1991.

Bovilsky, Lara. *Barbarous Play: Race on the English Renaissance Stage.* Minneapolis: University of Minnesota Press, 2008.

Bowers, Fredson, ed. *The Dramatic Works of Thomas Dekker.* Vol. 2. Cambridge: Cambridge University Press, 1955.

Bradshaw, Brendan, Andrew Hadfield, and Willy Maley, eds. *Representing Ireland: Literature and the Origins of Conflict, 1534–1660.* Cambridge: Cambridge University Press, 1993.

Braude, Benjamin. "Sons of Noah and the Construction of Ethnic and Geographical Identities in the Medieval and Early Modern Periods." *William and Mary Quarterly* 54.1 (1997): 103–42.

Bray, Alan. *Homosexuality in Renaissance England.* New York: Columbia University Press, 1995.

Bredvold, Louis I. "Political Aspects of Dryden's *Amboyna* and *The Spanish Fryar.*" Rpt. in *Essential Articles for the Study of John Dryden.* Ed. H. T. Swedenberg. Hamden, Conn.: Archon Books, 1966. 300–13.

Brown, Kathleen M. *Good Wives, Nasty Wenches, and Anxious Patriarchs: Gender, Race, and Power in Colonial Virginia.* Chapel Hill: University of North Carolina Press, 1996.

Brubaker, Rogers. *Ethnicity Without Groups.* Cambridge, Mass.: Harvard University Press, 2004.

Brushfield, Thomas N. "Britain's Burse, or the New Exchange." *Journal of the British Archaeological Society* 9 (1903): 33–48, 81–94.

Burford, E. J. *Bawds and Lodgings: A History of London Bankside Brothels c. 100–1675.* London: Owen, 1976.

Burgon, John William. *The Life and Times of Sir Thomas Gresham, Knt. Founder of the Royal Exchange.* 2 vols. London: Effingham Wilson, 1839.

Burke, Peter. *Antwerp: A Metropolis in Comparative Perspective.* Ghent: Snoeck-Ducaju and Zoon, 1993.

———. *Languages and Communities in Early Modern Europe.* Cambridge: Cambridge University Press, 2004.

———. *Towards a Social History of Early Modern Dutch.* Amsterdam: Amsterdam University Press, 2005.

Burnett, Mark Thronton. "Calling 'Things by Their Right Names': Troping Prostitution, Politics and *The Dutch Courtesan.*" In *Renaissance Configurations: Voices/Bodies/ Spaces, 1580–1690.* Ed. Gordon McMullan. New York: St. Martin's Press, 1998. 171–90.

Butler, Judith. *Bodies That Matter.* London: Routledge, 1993.

Cairns, Stephen, ed. *Drifting: Architecture and Migrancy.* New York: Routledge, 2004.

———. Introduction. In Cairns, *Drifting,* 1–16.

Callaghan, Dympna, ed. *A Feminist Companion to Shakespeare.* Oxford: Blackwell, 2000.

———. *Shakespeare Without Women: Representing Gender and Race on the Renaissance Stage.* New York: Routledge, 2000.

Carter, Harry G. *A View of Early Typography up to About 1600.* Oxford: Clarendon Press, 1969.

Cathcart, Charles. "Lodge, Marston, and the Family of Love." *Notes and Queries* 50.1 (2003): 68–70.

Chancey, Karen. "The Amboyna Massacre in English Politics, 1624–1632." *Albion* 30.4 (1999): 583–98.

Chartier, Roger. "Texts, Printing, Readings." In *The New Cultural History.* Ed. Aletta Biersack and Lynn Avery Hunt. Berkeley: University of California Press, 1989. 154–75.

Chaudhuri, K. N. *The English East India Company: The Study of an Early Joint-Stock Company, 1600–1640.* London: Frank Cass, 1965.

Chávez, John R. *Beyond Nations: Evolving Homelands in the North Atlantic World, 1400– 2000.* New York: Cambridge University Press, 2009.

Clough, Wilson. "The Broken English of Foreign Characters on the Elizabethan Stage." *Philological Quarterly* 12.3 (1933): 255–68.

Colley, Linda. "Britishness and Otherness: An Argument." *Journal of British Studies* 31.4 (1992): 309–329.

———. *Britons: Forging the Nation, 1707–1837*. New Haven, Conn.: Yale University Press, 1992.

Collinson, Patrick. "Europe in Britain: Protestant Strangers and the English Reformation." In Vigne and Littleton, *From Strangers to Citizens*, 57–67.

Comaroff, John, and Jean Comaroff. *Ethnography and the Historical Imagination*. Boulder, Colo.: Westview, 1992.

Conley, Tom. *The Graphic Unconscious in Early Modern French Writing*. Cambridge: Cambridge University Press, 1992.

Considine, John. *Dictionaries in Early Modern Europe: Lexicography and the Making of Heritage*. Cambridge: Cambridge University Press, 2008.

Cottret, Bernard. *The Huguenots in England: Immigration and Settlement c. 1550–1700*. Trans. Peregrine and Adriana Stevenson. Cambridge: Cambridge University Press, 1991.

Cunningham, William. *Alien Immigrants to England*. 1897. 2nd ed. New York: Augustus M. Kelly, 1969.

D'Amico, Jack. *The Moor in English Renaissance Drama*. Tampa: University of South Florida Press, 1991.

Dearing, Vinton A., ed. *The Works of John Dryden*. Vol. 12. Berkeley: University of California Press, 1994.

de Certeau, Michel. *The Practice of Everyday Life*. Trans. Steven Rendall. Berkeley: University of California Press, 1984.

de Grazia, Margreta. "Homonyms Before and After Lexical Standardization." *Deutsche Shakespeare-Gesellschaft West: Jahrbuch* (1990): 143–56.

de Grazia, Margreta, and Peter Stallybrass. "The Materiality of the Shakespearean Text." *Shakespeare Quarterly* 44.3 (1993): 255–83.

DiGangi, Mario. *Sexual Types: Embodiment, Agency, and Dramatic Character from Shakespeare to Shirley*. Philadelphia: University of Pennsylvania Press, 2011.

Dillon, Janette. "Court Meets City: The Royal Entertainment at the New Exchange." *Research Opportunities in Renaissance Drama* 38 (1999): 1–21.

———. *Language and Stage in Medieval and Renaissance England*. Cambridge: Cambridge University Press, 1998.

Dolan, Frances E. *Dangerous Familiars: Representations of Domestic Crime in England, 1550–1700*. Ithaca, N.Y.: Cornell University Press, 1994.

———. *True Relations: Reading, Literature, and Evidence in Seventeenth-Century England*. Philadelphia: University of Pennsylvania Press, 2013.

———. *Whores of Babylon: Catholicism, Gender, and Seventeenth-Century Print Culture*. Ithaca, N.Y.: Cornell University Press, 1999.

Dollimore, Jonathan. *Sexual Dissidence: Augustine to Wilde, Freud to Foucault*. Oxford: Clarendon Press, 1991.

Dorsten, J. A. van, J. van den Berg, and Alastair Hamilton, eds. *The Anglo-Dutch Renaissance: Seven Essays*. Leiden: E. J. Brill, 1988.

Duffy, Michael. *The Englishman and the Foreigner: The English Satirical Print, 1600–1832*. Cambridge: Chadwyck-Healey, 1986.

Duke, Alastair. "The Elusive Netherlands: The Question of National Identity in the Early Modern Low Countries on the Eve of the Revolt." In *Dissident Identities in the Early Modern Low Countries*. Ed. Judith Pollmann and Andrew Spicer. Burlington, Vt.: Ashgate, 2009. 9–56.

Duncan-Jones, Katherine, ed. *Sir Philip Sidney: A Critical Edition of the Major Works*. Oxford: Oxford University Press, 1989.

Easterling, Heather. *Parsing the City: Jonson, Middleton, Dekker, and City Comedy's London as Language*. New York: Routledge, 2007.

Eastman, Max. *Enjoyment of Laughter*. London: Hamish Hamilton, 1937.

Edmundson, George. *Anglo-Dutch Rivalry During the First Half of the Seventeenth Century*. Oxford: Clarendon Press, 1911.

Eimer, Christopher. "Medals of the Royal Exchange." In Saunders, *The Royal Exchange*, 349–65.

Erickson, Peter, and Clark Hulse, eds. *Early Modern Visual Culture: Representation, Race, and Empire in Renaissance England*. Philadelphia: University of Pennsylvania Press, 2000.

Eriksen, Thomas Hylland. *Ethnicity and Nationalism: Anthropological Perspectives*. 2nd ed. London: Pluto Press, 2002.

Evers, M. "Religionis et Libertatis Ergo: Dutch Refugees in England and English Exiles in the Netherlands." In *Refugees and Emigrants in the Dutch Republic and England: Papers of the Annual Symposium, Held on 22 November 1985*. Leiden: Sir Thomas Brown Institute, 1986. 7–27.

Fagel, Raymond. "Immigrant Roots: The Geographical Origins of Newcomers from the Low Countries in Tudor England." In Goose and Luu, *Immigrants in Tudor and Early Stuart England*, 41–56.

———. "The Netherlandish Presence in England Before the Coming of the Stranger Churches, 1480–1560." In Vigne and Littleton, *From Strangers to Citizens*, 7–16.

Farmer, Alan B. "Shakespeare and the New Textualism." In *The Shakespearean International Yearbook*. Vol. 2. Burlington, Vt.: Ashgate, 2002. 158–79.

Farrington, Anthony. *Trading Places: The East India Company and Asia, 1600–1834*. London: British Library, 2002.

Feerick, Jean E. *Strangers in Blood: Relocating Race in the Renaissance*. Toronto: University of Toronto Press, 2010.

Ferguson, Margaret W., Maureen Quilligan, and Nancy J. Vickers, eds. *Rewriting the Renaissance: The Discourses of Sexual Difference in Early Modern England*. Chicago: University of Chicago Press, 1986.

Fisher, Will. *Materializing Gender in Early Modern English Literature and Culture*. Cambridge: Cambridge University Press, 2006.

Fleck, Andrew. "Deep Designs of Empire: English Representations of the Dutch from the Armada to the Glorious Revolution." Diss., Claremont Graduate University, 2000.

———. "'Ick Verstaw You Niet': Performing Foreign Tongues on the Early Modern English Stage." *Medieval and Renaissance Drama in England* 20 (2007): 204–21.

———. "Marking Difference and National Identity in Dekker's *The Shoemaker's Holiday*." *Studies in English Literature* 46.2 (2006): 349–70.

Floyd-Wilson, Mary. *English Ethnicity and Race in Early Modern Drama*. Cambridge: Cambridge University Press, 2003.

Fradenburg, Louise Olga, and Carla Freccero, eds. *Premodern Sexualities*. New York: Routledge, 1996.

Freud, Sigmund. *Civilization and Its Discontents*. Trans. Joan Riviere. Garden City, N.Y.: Doubleday, 1958.

———. "Group Psychology and the Analysis of the Ego." In *The Standard Edition of the Complete Psychological Works of Sigmund Freud*. Trans. James Strachey. Vol. 18. London: Hogarth Press, 1973. 65–143.

———. "The Taboo of Virginity." In *The Standard Edition of the Complete Psychological Works of Sigmund Freud*. Trans. James Strachey. Vol. 11. London: Hogarth Press, 1973. 191–208.

Fuchs, Barbara. *Exotic Nation: Maurophilia and the Construction of Early Modern Spain*. Philadelphia: University of Pennsylvania Press, 2009.

Fumerton, Patricia. "Homely Accents: Ben Jonson Speaking Low." In Fumerton and Hunt, *Renaissance Culture and the Everyday*, . 92–111.

Fumerton, Patricia, and Simon Hunt, eds. *Renaissance Culture and the Everyday*. Philadelphia: University of Pennsylvania Press, 1999.

Furtado, Peter. "National Pride in Seventeenth-Century England." In *Patriotism: The Making and Unmaking of British National Identity*. Vol. 1. Ed. Raphael Samuel. London: Routledge, 1989. 44–56.

Fuss, Diana. *Identification Papers*. New York: Routledge, 1995.

Games, Alison. "Anglo-Dutch Connections and Overseas Enterprises: A Global Perspective on Lion Gardiner's World." *Early American Studies* 9.2 (2011): 435–61.

Gibbons, Brian. *Jacobean City Comedy: A Study of Satiric Plays by Jonson, Marston and Middleton*. 1968. Cambridge, Mass.: Harvard University Press, 1980.

Gillies, John. *Shakespeare and the Geography of Difference*. Cambridge: Cambridge University Press, 1994.

Goose, Nigel. "Immigrants in Tudor and Early Stuart England." In Goose and Luu, *Immigrants in Tudor and Early Stuart England*, 1–40.

———. "'Xenophobia' in Elizabethan and Early Stuart England: An Epithet Too Far?" In Goose and Luu, *Immigrants in Tudor and Early Stuart England*, 110–35.

Goose, Nigel, and Lien Luu, eds. *Immigrants in Tudor and Early Stuart England*. Brighton: Sussex Academic Press, 2005.

Gowing, Laura. *Domestic Dangers: Women, Words, and Sex in Early Modern London*. Oxford: Clarendon Press, 1996.

Greenblatt, Stephen. *Renaissance Self-Fashioning: From More to Shakespeare*. Chicago: University of Chicago Press, 1980.

Greg, W. W. "The Rationale of Copy-Text." In *Collected Papers*. Ed. J. C. Maxwell. Oxford: Clarendon Press, 1966. 374–391.

Grell, Ole Peter. *Calvinist Exiles in Tudor and Stuart England*. Brookfield, Vt.: Scolar Press, 1996.

———. *Dutch Calvinists in Early Stuart London: The Dutch Church in Austin Friars, 1603–1642*. Leiden: E. J. Brill, 1989.

———. "The French and Dutch Congregations in London in the Early Seventeenth Century." *Proceedings of the Huguenot Society* 24.5 (1987): 362–77.

Griffin, Eric J. *English Renaissance Drama and the Specter of Spain: Ethnopoetics and Empire*. Philadelphia: University of Pennsylvania Press, 2009.

Groenveld, Simon, and Michael Wintle, eds. *The Exchange of Ideas: Religion, Scholarship and Art in Anglo-Dutch Relations in the Seventeenth Century*. Zutphen: Walburg Instituut, 1994.

Grosz, Elizabeth. "Bodies-Cities." In *Space, Time, and Perversion*. New York: Routledge, 1995. 103–10.

Haigh, Christopher. *English Reformations: Religion, Politics, and Society Under the Tudors*. Oxford: Clarendon Press, 1993.

Hainsworth, D. R., and Christine Churches. *The Anglo-Dutch Naval Wars, 1652–1674*. Stroud: Sutton, 1998.

Haley, Kenneth Harold Dobson. *The British and the Dutch: Political and Cultural Relations Through the Ages*. London: George Phillip, 1988.

Hall, Kim. *Things of Darkness: Economies of Race and Gender in Early Modern England*. Ithaca, N.Y.: Cornell University Press, 1995.

Hall, Stuart. "Introduction: Who Needs 'Identity'?" In *Questions of Cultural Identity*. Ed. Paul Du Gay and Stuart Hall. London: Sage Publications, 1996. 1–17.

Halley, Janet. "Heresy, Orthodoxy, and the Politics of Religious Discourse: The Case of the English Family of Love." *Representations* 15 (1986): 98–120.

Harkness, Deborah. *The Jewel House: Elizabethan London and the Scientific Revolution*. New Haven, Conn.: Yale University Press, 2007.

Heijden, H. A. M. van der. *Leo Belgicus: An Illustrated and Annotated Carto-Bibliography*. Alphen aan den Rijn: Canaletto, 1990.

Helgerson, Richard. "Before National Literary History." *Modern Language Quarterly* 64 (2003): 169–79.

———. *Forms of Nationhood: The Elizabethan Writing of England*. Chicago: University of Chicago Press, 1992.

Hendricks, Margo, and Patricia Parker, eds. *Women, "Race," and Writing in the Early Modern Period*. New York: Routledge, 1994.

Hill, Tracey. *Anthony Munday and Civic Culture: Theatre, History and Power in Early Modern London, 1580–1633*. Manchester: Manchester University Press, 2004.

———. *Pageantry and Power: A Cultural History of the Early Modern Lord Mayor's Show, 1585–1639*. Manchester: Manchester University Press, 2010.

Hoenselaars, A. J. *Images of Englishmen and Foreigners in the Drama of Shakespeare and His Contemporaries: A Study of Stage Characters and National Identity in English Renaissance Drama, 1558–1642*. London: Associated University Presses, 1992.

Hoenselaars, Ton, and Holger Klein, eds. Shakespeare and the Low Countries. Lewiston, N.Y.: Edwin Mellen Press, 2005. Shakespeare Yearbook 15.

Hood, Gervase. "A Netherlandic Triumphal Arch for James I." In Roach, *Across the Narrow Seas*, 67–82.

Howard, Jean E. "An English Lass amid the Moors: Gender, Race, Sexuality, and National Identity in Heywood's *The Fair Maid of the West*." In Hendricks and Parker, *Women, "Race," and Writing*, 101–17.

———. "Mastering Difference in *The Dutch Courtesan*." *Shakespeare Studies* 24 (1996): 105–17.

———. *Theater of a City: The Places of London Comedy, 1598–1642*. Philadelphia: University of Pennsylvania Press, 2007.

———. "Women, Foreigners, and the Regulation of Urban Space in *Westward Ho*." In *Material London Ca. 1600*. Ed. Lena Cowen Orlin. Philadelphia: University of Pennsylvania Press, 2000. 150–68.

Howard, Jean E., and Phyllis Rackin. *Engendering a Nation: A Feminist Account of Shakespeare's English Histories*. New York: Routledge, 1997.

Hughes, Derek. *English Drama, 1660–1700*. Oxford: Clarendon Press, 1996.

Hughes, Paul L. and James. F. Larkin, eds. *Tudor Royal Proclamations*. 3 vols. New Haven, Conn.: Yale University Press, 1969.

Imray, Jean. "Origins of the Exchange." In Saunders, *The Royal Exchange*, 20–35.

Israel, Jonathan. *The Dutch Republic, Its Rise, Greatness, and Fall, 1477–1806*. Oxford: Clarendon Press, 1995.

Iyengar, Sujata. *Shades of Difference: Mythologies of Skin Color in Early Modern England*. Philadelphia: University of Pennsylvania Press, 2005.

Jacob, Margaret. *Strangers Nowhere in the World: The Rise of Cosmopolitanism in Early Modern Europe*. Philadelphia: University of Pennsylvania Press, 2006.

Jardine, Lisa. *Going Dutch: How England Plundered Holland's Glory*. London: Harper Press, 2008.

———. *Still Harping on Daughters: Women and Drama in the Age of Shakespeare*. Brighton: Harvester, 1983.

Johnson, William C. "The Family of Love in Stuart Literature: A Chronology of Name-Crossed Lovers." *Journal of Medieval and Renaissance Studies* 7 (1977): 95–112.

Jones, Ann Rosalind. "Italians and Others: *The White Devil* (1612)." In *Staging the Renaissance: Reinterpretations of Elizabethan and Jacobean Drama*. Ed. David Scott Kastan and Peter Stallybrass. New York: Routledge, 1991. 251–62.

Jones, Eldred. *The Elizabethan Image of Africa*. Charlottesville: University Press of Virginia, 1971.

———. *Othello's Countrymen: The African in English Renaissance Drama*. London: Oxford University Press, 1965.

Jones, J. R. *The Anglo-Dutch Wars of the Seventeenth Century*. London: Longman, 1996.

Jones, Richard Foster. *The Triumph of the English Language: A Survey of Opinions Concerning the Vernacular from the Introduction of Printing to the Restoration.* Stanford, Calif.: Stanford University Press, 1953.

Jordan, Winthrop D. *White over Black: American Attitudes Toward the Negro, 1550–1812.* Chapel Hill: University of North Carolina Press, 1968.

Kaplan, Benjamin. *Divided by Faith: Religious Conflict and the Practice of Toleration in Early Modern Europe.* Cambridge, Mass.: Belknap Press of Harvard University Press, 2007.

Kaplan, Lindsay. "Jessica's Mother: Medieval Constructions of Jewish Race and Gender in *The Merchant of Venice.*" *Shakespeare Quarterly* 58.1 (2007): 1–30.

Karras, Ruth Mazo. *Common Women: Prostitution and Sexuality in Medieval England.* Oxford: Oxford University Press, 1996.

Kastan, David Scott. *Shakespeare and the Book.* Cambridge: Cambridge University Press, 2001.

Keene, Derek. "Material London in Time and Space." In *Material London Ca. 1600.* Ed. Lena Cowen Orlin. Philadelphia: University of Pennsylvania Press, 2000. 55–74.

Kermode, Lloyd Edward. *Aliens and Englishness in Elizabethan Drama.* Cambridge: Cambridge University Press, 2009.

Kerrigan, John. *Archipelagic English: Literature, History, and Politics, 1603–1707.* Oxford: Oxford University Press, 2008.

Kidd, Colin. *British Identities Before Nationalism: Ethnicity and Nationhood in the Atlantic World, 1600–1800.* Cambridge: Cambridge University Press, 1999.

———. "Identity Before Identities: Ethnicity, Nationalism and the Historian." In *History and Nation.* Ed. Julia Rudolph. Lewisburg, Pa.: Bucknell University Press, 2006. 9–44.

King, John. "Foxe's *Book of Martyrs* and the History of the Book." *Explorations in Renaissance Culture* 30.2 (2004): 176–96.

Kipling, Gordon. "Triumphal Drama: Form in English Civic Pageantry." *Renaissance Drama* 8 (1977): 37–56.

Kirk, R. E. G., and Ernest F. Kirk. *Returns of Aliens Dwelling in the City and Suburbs in London from the Reign of Henry VIII to That of James I.* 4 vols. Aberdeen: University Press, 1900–1908. Publications of the Huguenot Society of London 10.

Knowles, James. "Jonson's *Entertainment at Britain's Burse.*" In *Re-presenting Ben Jonson: Text, History, Performance.* Ed. Martin Butler. New York: St. Martin's Press, 1999. 114–51.

Koeman, Cornelis, and Marco van Egmond. "Surveying and Official Mapping in the Low Countries, 1500–ca. 1670." In *The History of Cartography: Cartography in the Renaissance.* Ed. David Woodward. Vol. 3, pt. 2. Chicago: University of Chicago Press, 2007. 1246–95.

Lach, Donald F., and Edwin J. Van Kley, eds. *Asia in the Making of Europe.* 3 vols. Chicago: University of Chicago Press, 1965–93.

Lancashire, Anne. "Dekker's Accession Pageant for King James I." *Early Theatre* 12.1 (2009): 39–50.

Lawson, Alexander. *Anatomy of a Typeface*. Boston: Godine, 1990.

Leggatt, Alexander. *Citizen Comedy in the Age of Shakespeare*. Toronto: University of Toronto Press, 1973.

Leinwand, Theodore B. *The City Staged: Jacobean City Comedy, 1603–1613*. Madison: University of Wisconsin Press, 1986.

Lesser, Zachary. "Typographic Nostalgia: Play-Reading, Popularity, and the Meanings of Black Letter." In *The Book of the Play: Playwrights, Stationers, and Readers in Early Modern England*. Ed. Marta Straznicky. Amherst: University of Massachusetts Press, 2006. 99–126.

———. "Walter Burre and the Knight of the Burning Pestle." *English Literary Renaissance* 29.1 (1999): 22–43.

Levenson, Jill L. *A Critical Edition of the Anonymous Elizabethan Play "The Weakest Goeth to the Wall."* New York: Garland, 1980.

Levin, Richard. "The Family of Lust and *The Family of Love*." *Studies in English Literature* 6.2 (1966): 309–22.

Limberger, Michael. "'No Town in the World Provides More Advantages': Economies of Agglomeration and the Golden Age of Antwerp." In *Urban Achievement in Early Modern Europe: Golden Ages in Antwerp, Amsterdam and London*. Ed. Patrick O'Brien, Derek Keene, Marjolein 't Hart, and Herman van der Wee. Cambridge: Cambridge University Press, 2001. 39–62.

Littleton, Charles. "Social Interactions of Aliens in Late Elizabethan London: Evidence from the 1593 Return and the French Church Consistory Actes." *Proceedings of the Huguenot Society* 26.2 (1995): 147–59.

———. "The Strangers, Their Churches and the Continent: Continuing and Changing Connexions." In Goose and Luu, *Immigrants in Tudor and Early Stuart England*, 177–91.

Loewenstein, Joseph F. "*Idem*: Italics and the Genetics of Authorship." *Journal of Medieval and Renaissance Studies* 20.2 (1990): 205–24.

Loomba, Ania. *Shakespeare, Race, and Colonialism*. Oxford: Oxford University Press, 2002.

Loomba, Ania, and Jonathan Burton, eds. *Race in Early Modern England: A Documentary Companion*. Basingstoke, England: Palgrave Macmillan, 2007.

Loomba, Ania, and Martin Orkin, eds. *Post-Colonial Shakespeares*. New York: Routledge, 1988.

Loth, Vincent C. "Armed Incidents and Unpaid Bills: Anglo-Dutch Rivalry in the Banda Islands in the Seventeenth Century." *Modern Asian Studies* 29.4 (1995): 705–40.

Loureiro, Rui Manuel. "Early Portuguese Perceptions of the 'Dutch Threat' in Asia." In *Rivalry and Conflict: European Traders and Asian Trading Networks in the 16th and 17th Centuries*. Ed. Ernst Van Veen and Leonard Blussé. Leiden: CNWS Publications, 2005. 166–87.

Lowenthal, Cynthia. *Performing Identities on the Restoration Stage*. Carbondale: Southern Illinois University Press, 2003.

Luu, Lien Bich. "Assimilation or Segregation: Colonies of Alien Craftsmen in Elizabethan London." *Proceedings of the Huguenot Society* 26.2 (1995): 160–72.

———. "Natural-Born Versus Stranger-Born Subjects: Aliens and Their Status in Elizabethan London." In Goose and Luu, *Immigrants in Tudor and Early Stuart England*, 57–75.

———. "'Taking the Bread out of Our Mouths': Xenophobia in Early Modern London." *Immigrants and Minorities* 19 (2000): 1–22.

MacDonald, Joyce Green, ed. *Race, Ethnicity, and Power in the Renaissance*. Madison: Associated University Presses, 1997.

———. *Women and Race in Early Modern Texts*. Cambridge: Cambridge University Press, 2002.

MacDougall, Hugh A. *Racial Myth in English History: Trojans, Teutons, and Anglo-Saxons*. Montreal: Harvest House, 1982.

Mackenzie, Anne L. "A Study in Dramatic Contrasts: The Siege of Antwerp in *A Larum for London* and *El saco de Amberes*." *Bulletin of Hispanic Studies* 59 (1982): 283–300.

Malieckal, Bindu. "Mariam Khan and the Legacy of Mughal Women in Early Modern Literature of India." In *Early Modern England and Islamic Worlds*. Ed. Bernadette Diane Andrea and Linda McJannet. New York: Palgrave Macmillan, 2011. 97–122.

Manley, Lawrence. *Literature and Culture in Early Modern London*. Cambridge: Cambridge University Press, 1995.

———, ed. *London in the Age of Shakespeare: An Anthology*. University Park: Pennsylvania State University Press, 1986.

Markley, Robert. *The Far East and the English Imagination, 1600–1730*. Cambridge: Cambridge University Press, 2006.

———. "Violence and Profits on the Restoration Stage: Trade, Nationalism, and Insecurity in Dryden's *Amboyna*." *Eighteenth-Century Life* 22 (1998): 2–17.

Marnef, Guido. *Antwerp in the Age of Reformation: Underground Protestantism in a Commercial Metropolis, 1550–1577*. Trans. J. C. Grayson. Baltimore: Johns Hopkins University Press, 1996.

Marsden, Jean I. "Spectacle, Horror, and Pathos." In *The Cambridge Companion to English Restoration Theatre*. Ed. Deborah Payne Fisk. Cambridge: Cambridge University Press, 2000. 174–90.

Marsh, Christopher. *The Family of Love in English Society, 1550–1630*. Cambridge: Cambridge University Press, 1994.

Masten, Jeffrey. *Textual Intercourse: Collaboration, Authorship and Sexualities in Renaissance Drama*. Cambridge: Cambridge University Press, 1997.

Matar, Nabil. *Turks, Moors, and Englishmen in the Age of Discovery*. New York: Columbia University Press, 1999.

Matar, Nabil, and Gerald MacLean. *Britain and the Islamic World, 1558–1713*. Oxford: Oxford University Press, 2011.

Mazzio, Carla. *The Inarticulate Renaissance: Language Trouble in an Age of Eloquence*. Philadelphia: University of Pennsylvania Press, 2009.

McEachern, Claire Elizabeth. *The Poetics of English Nationhood, 1590–1612.* Cambridge: Cambridge University Press, 1996.

McKenzie, D. F. *Bibliography and the Sociology of Texts.* London: British Library, 1986.

———. "Speech—Manuscript—Print." In *Making Meaning: "Printers of the Mind" and Other Essays.* Ed. Peter D. McDonald and Michael F. Suarez. Amherst: University of Massachusetts Press, 2002. 237–58.

———. "Typography and Meaning: The Case of William Congreve." In *Making Meaning: "Printers of the Mind" and Other Essays.* Ed. Peter D. McDonald and Michael F. Suarez. Amherst: University of Massachusetts Press, 2002. 198–236.

McMullan, John L. *The Canting Crew: London's Criminal Underworld, 1550–1700.* New Brunswick, N.J.: Rutgers University Press, 1984.

Menon, Madhavi, ed. *Shakesqueer: A Queer Companion to the Complete Works of Shakespeare.* Durham, N.C.: Duke University Press, 2011.

Metcalf, George J. "Abraham Mylius on Historical Linguistics." *PMLA* 68.3 (1953): 535–54.

Mish, Charles. "Black Letter as Social Discriminant in the Seventeenth Century." *PMLA* 68.3 (1953): 627–31.

Moens, William John Charles, ed. *The Marriage, Baptismal, and Burial Registers, 1571–1874, and Monumental Inscriptions, of the Dutch Reformed Church, Austin Friars, London.* Lymington: King and sons, 1884.

Montgomery, Marianne. "Listening to the Emissary in Middleton's *No Wit, No Help like a Woman's.*" In *Emissaries in Early Modern Literature and Culture: Mediation, Transmission, Traffic, 1550–1700.* Ed. Brinda Charry and Gitanjali Shahani. Burlington, Vt.: Ashgate, 2009. 193–203.

Montrose, Louis. "The Work of Gender in the Discourse of Discovery." *Representations* 33 (1991): 1–41.

Moss, Jean Dietz. "The Family of Love and English Critics." *Sixteenth Century Journal* 6.1 (1975): 35–52.

———. "Godded with God: Hendrik Niclaes and His Family of Love." *Transactions of the American Philosophical Society* 71.8 (1981): 1–89.

Mullaney, Steven. *The Place of the Stage: License, Play, and Power in Renaissance England.* 1988. Chicago: University of Chicago Press, 2000.

Murphy, Andrew. *But the Irish Sea Betwixt Us: Ireland, Colonialism, and Renaissance Literature.* Lexington: University Press of Kentucky, 1999.

Murray, John J. "The Cultural Impact of the Flemish Low Countries on Sixteenth- and Seventeenth-Century England." *American Historical Review* 62.4 (1957): 837–85.

Neill, Michael. "Broken English and Broken Irish: Nation, Language, and the Optic of Power in Shakespeare's Histories." *Shakespeare Quarterly* 45.1 (1994): 1–32.

———. *Putting History to the Question: Power, Politics, and Society in English Renaissance Drama.* New York: Columbia University Press, 2000.

Newcomb, Lori Humphrey. *Reading Popular Romance in Early Modern England.* New York: Columbia University Press, 2002.

Nicols, John. *The Progresses, Processions, and Magnificent Festivities of King James the First.* 4 vols. New York: B. Franklin, 1964.

Oldenburg, Scott. "Toward a Multicultural Mid-Tudor England: The Queen's Royal Entry Circa 1553, the Interlude of Wealth and Health, and the Question of Strangers in the Reign of Mary I." *ELH* 76.1 (2009): 99–129.

Orgel, Stephen. *Impersonations: The Performance of Gender in Shakespeare's England.* Cambridge: Cambridge University Press, 1996.

———. *The Jonsonian Masque.* Cambridge, Mass.: Harvard University Press, 1965.

———. "What Is an Editor?" *Shakespeare Studies* 24 (1996): 23–29.

Orlin, Lena Cowen. *Locating Privacy in Tudor London.* Oxford: Oxford University Press, 2007.

Ormrod, David. *The Rise of Commercial Empires: England and the Netherlands in the Age of Mercantilism, 1650–1770.* Cambridge: Cambridge University Press, 2003.

Orr, Bridgett. *Empire on the English Stage, 1660–1714.* Cambridge: Cambridge University Press, 2001.

Osselton, N. E. *The Dumb Linguists: A Study of the Earliest English and Dutch Dictionaries.* Leiden: University Press, 1973.

Palmer, Daryl W. *Hospitable Performances: Dramatic Genre and Cultural Practices in Early Modern England.* West Lafayette, Ind.: Purdue University Press, 1992.

Parker, Geoffrey. *The Dutch Revolt.* Ithaca, N.Y.: Cornell University Press, 1977.

Parker, John. *Books to Build an Empire: A Bibliographical History of English Overseas Interests to 1620.* Amsterdam: N. Israel, 1965.

Parker, Patricia. *Shakespeare from the Margins: Language, Culture, Context.* Chicago: University of Chicago Press, 1996.

Parry, Graham. *The Trophies of Time: English Antiquarians of the Seventeenth Century.* Oxford: Oxford University Press, 1995.

Paster, Gail Kern. *The Body Embarrassed: Drama and the Disciplines of Shame in Early Modern England.* Ithaca, N.Y.: Cornell University Press, 1993.

Pestana, Carla Gardina. "Cruelty and Religious Justifications for Conquest in the Mid-Seventeenth-Century English Atlantic." In *Empires of God: Religious Encounters in the Early Modern Atlantic.* Ed. Linda Gregerson and Susan Juster. Philadelphia: University of Pennsylvania Press, 2011. 37–57.

Peters, Julie Stone. *Theatre of the Book, 1480–1880: Print, Text, and Performance in Europe.* Oxford: Oxford University Press, 2003.

Pettegree, Andrew. *Foreign Protestant Communities in Sixteenth-Century London.* Oxford: Clarendon Press, 1986.

Pincus, Steven. "From Butterboxes to Wooden Shoes: The Shift in English Popular Sentiment from Anti-Dutch to Anti-French in the 1670s." *Historical Journal* 38.2 (1995): 333–61.

———. *Protestantism and Patriotism: Ideologies and the Making of English Foreign Policy, 1650–1668.* Cambridge: Cambridge University Press, 1996.

Pollmann, Judith, and Andrew Spicer, eds. *Public Opinion and Changing Identities in the Early Modern Netherlands: Essays in Honour of Alastair Duke.* London: Brill, 2007.

Prak, Maarten. *The Dutch Republic in the Seventeenth Century: The Golden Age.* Trans. Diane Webb. Cambridge: Cambridge University Press, 2005.

Pratt, S. M. "Antwerp and the Elizabethan Mind." *Modern Language Quarterly* 24 (1963): 53–60.

Rackin, Phyllis. *Shakespeare and Women.* Oxford: Oxford University Press, 2005.

Rakatansky, Mark. "Why Architecture Is Neither Here nor There." In Cairns, *Drifting*, 99–115.

Raman, Shankar. *Framing "India": The Colonial Imaginary in Early Modern Culture.* Stanford, Calif.: Stanford University Press, 2001.

Reed, Talbot Baines, and A. F. Johnson. *A History of the Old English Letter Foundries: With Notes Historical and Bibliographical on the Rise and Progress of English Typography.* London: Faber and Faber, 1952.

Reid, Anthony, ed. *Southeast Asia in the Early Modern Era: Trade, Power, and Belief.* Ithaca, N.Y.: Cornell University Press, 1993. Richards, Jennifer, and Fred Schurink, eds. "Introduction" Special Issue: The Textuality and Materiality of Reading in Early Modern England. *Huntington Library Quarterly* 73.2 (2010): 345–61.

Rickwood, Douglas. "The Norwich Strangers, 1565–1643: A Problem of Control." *Proceedings of the Huguenot Society* 24.2 (1984): 119–28.

Roach, Susan, ed. *Across the Narrow Seas: Studies in the History and Bibliography of Britain and the Low Countries: Presented to Anna E. C. Simoni.* London: British Library, 1991.

Roscoe, Ingrid. "'The Statues of the Sovereigns of England': Sculpture for the Second Building, 1695–1831." In Saunders, *The Royal Exchange*, 174–87.

Saunders, Ann. "The Building of the Exchange." In Saunders, *The Royal Exchange*, 36–47.

———, ed. *The Royal Exchange.* London: London Topographical Society, 1997.

———. "The Second Exchange." In Saunders, *The Royal Exchange*, 121–35.

Schama, Simon. *The Embarrassment of Riches: An Interpretation of Dutch Culture in the Golden Age.* New York: Knopf, 1987.

Schenkeveld, Maria A. *Dutch Literature in the Age of Rembrandt: Themes and Ideas.* Amsterdam: John Benjamins, 1991.

Scherpbier, Herman. *Milton in Holland: A Study in the Literary Relations of England and Holland Before 1730.* Amsterdam: H. J. Press, 1933.

Scheurweghs, G. "English Grammars in Dutch and Dutch Grammars in English in the Netherlands Before 1800." *English Studies: A Journal of English Letters and Philology* 41.3 (1960): 129–67.

Schmidt, Benjamin. *Innocence Abroad: The Dutch Imagination and the New World, 1570–1670.* Cambridge: Cambridge University Press, 2001.

Schoenfeldt, Michael. *Bodies and Selves in Early Modern England: Physiology and Inwardness in Spenser, Shakespeare, Herbert, and Milton.* Cambridge: Cambridge University Press, 1999.

Schoenveld, Cornelis W. *Intertraffic of the Mind: Studies in Seventeenth-Century Anglo-Dutch Translation.* Leiden: E. J. Brill, 1983.

Schwarz, Kathryn. *Tough Love: Amazon Encounters in the English Renaissance.* Durham, N.C.: Duke University Press, 2000.

Schwemer-Scheddin, Yvonne. "Broken Images: Blackletter Between Faith and Mysticism." In Bain and Shaw, *Blackletter,* 50–67.

Scouloudi, Irene. "Notes on Strangers in the Precinct of St. Katherine-by-the-Tower, C. 1500–1687, and on the 'Flemish Cemetery.'" *Proceedings of the Huguenot Society* 25.1 (1989): 75–82.

———, ed. *Returns of Strangers in the Metropolis 1593, 1627, 1635, 1639: A Study of an Active Minority.* London: Huguenot Society, 1985. Quarto Ser. 57.

———. "The Stranger Community in London 1558–1640." *Proceedings of the Huguenot Society* 24.5 (1987): 434–41.

Sedgwick, Eve. *Epistemology of the Closet.* Berkeley: University of California Press, 1990.

Selwood, Jacob. *Diversity and Difference in Early Modern London.* Burlington, Vt.: Ashgate, 2010.

Shannon, Laurie. *Sovereign Amity: Figures of Friendship in Shakespearean Contexts.* Chicago: University of Chicago Press, 2002.

Shapiro, James. *Shakespeare and the Jews.* New York: Columbia University Press, 1996.

Shetter, William Z., and Inge van der Cruysse-Van Antwerpen. *Dutch: An Essential Grammar.* New York: Routledge, 2002.

Shoemaker, Nancy. *A Strange Likeness: Becoming Red and White in Eighteenth Century North America.* Oxford: Oxford University Press, 2004.

Smith, Emma. "'Signes of a Stranger': The English Language and the English Nation in the Late Sixteenth Century." In *Archipelagic Identities: Literature and Identity in the Atlantic Archipelago, 1550–1800.* Ed. Philip Schwyzer and Simon Mealor. Burlington, Vt.: Ashgate, 2004. 169–79.

———. "'So Much English by the Mother': Gender, Foreigners, and the Mother Tongue in William Haughton's *Englishman for My Money.*" *Medieval and Renaissance Drama in England* 13 (2000): 165–81.

Smith, Ian. *Race and Rhetoric in the Renaissance: Barbarian Errors.* New York: Palgrave Macmillan, 2009.

Smith, Nigel, ed. *The Poems of Andrew Marvell.* Rev. ed. London: Pearson Longman, 2007.

Somers, John, and Walter Scott, eds. *A Collection of Scarce and Valuable Tracts.* London: Cadell and Davies, 1809–15.

Spicer, Andrew. "'A Place of Refuge and Sanctuary of a Holy Temple': Exile Communities and the Stranger Churches." In Goose and Luu, *Immigrants in Tudor and Early Stuart England,* 91–109.

Srigley, Michael. "The Influence of Continental Familism in England After 1570." *Cultural Exchange Between European Nations during the Renaissance.* Spec. issue of *Acta Universitatis Upsaliensis, Studia Anglistica Upsaliensia* 86 (1994): 97–110.

Stallybrass, Peter. "Shakespeare, the Individual, and the Text." In *Critical Studies.* Ed. Lawrence Grossberg, Cary Nelson, and Paula Treichler. New York: Routledge, 1992. 593–612.

Stallybrass, Peter, and Zachary Lesser. "The First Literary Hamlet and the Commonplacing of Professional Plays." *Shakespeare Quarterly* 59.4 (2008): 371–420.

Statt, Daniel. "The Birthright of an Englishman: The Practice of Naturalization and Denization of Immigrants Under the Later Stuarts and Early Hanoverians." *Proceedings of the Huguenot Society* 25.1 (1989): 61–74.

Stewart, Alan. " 'Every Soyle to Mee is Naturall': Figuring Denization in William Haughton's *Englishmen for My Money*." *Renaissance Drama* 35 (2006): 55–81.

Stone, Lawrence. "Inigo Jones and the New Exchange." *Archaeological Journal* 114 (1957): 105–21.

Straznicky, Marta. "Introduction: Plays, Books, and the Public Sphere." In *The Book of the Play: Playwrights, Stationers, and Readers in Early Modern England*. Ed. Marta Straznicky. Amherst: University of Massachusetts Press, 2006. 1–22.

Strien, C. D. van. *British Travellers in Holland During the Stuart Period: Edward Browne and John Locke as Tourists in the United Provinces*. Leiden: E. J. Brill, 1993.

Strong, Roy, and J. A. van Dorsten. *Leicester's Triumph*. Leiden: Sir Thomas Brown Institute and University Press, 1964.

Sullivan, Garrett A., Jr. " 'All Things Come into Commerce': Women, Household Labor, and the Spaces of Marston's *The Dutch Courtesan*." *Renaissance Drama* 27 (1996): 19–46.

Summers, Montague, ed. *Dryden: The Dramatic Works*. New York: Gordian Press, 1968.

Syme, Holger Schott. "The Look of Speech." *Textual Cultures* 2.2 (2007): 34–60.

———. "Unediting the Margin: Jonson, Marston, and the Theatrical Page." *English Literary Renaissance* 38.1 (2008): 142–71.Tarling, Nicolas, ed. *The Cambridge History of Southeast Asia*. Vol. 1, part 2. Cambridge: Cambridge University Press, 1999.

Taylor, Gary, and John Lavagnino, eds. *Thomas Middleton and Early Modern Textual Culture: A Companion to the Collected Works*. Oxford: Clarendon Press, 2007.

———, eds. *Thomas Middleton: The Collected Works*. Oxford: Clarendon Press, 2007.

Taylor, Gary, Paul Mulholland, and MacDonald P. Jackson. "Thomas Middleton, Lording Barry, and *The Family of Love*." *Papers of the Bibliographical Society of America* 93.2 (1999): 213–41.

Thomas, Keith. "The Meaning of Literacy in Early Modern England." In *The Written Word: Literacy in Transition*. Ed. Gerd Baumann. Oxford: Clarendon Press, 1986. 97–131.

———. *Religion and the Decline of Magic*. Oxford: Oxford University Press, 1997.

Todd, Richard. "Equilibrium and National Stereotyping in 'The Character of Holland.' " In *On the Celebrated and Neglected Poems of Andrew Marvell*. Ed. Claude J. Summers and Ted-Larry Pebworth. Columbia: University of Missouri Press, 1992. 169–91.

Traub, Valerie. *Desire and Anxiety: Circulations of Sexuality in Shakespearean Drama*. New York: Routledge, 1992.

———. "Mapping the Global Body." In Erickson and Hulse, *Early Modern Visual Culture*, 44–97.

———. "The Nature of Norms in Early Modern England: Anatomy, Cartography, *King Lear*." *South Central Review* 26.1–2 (2009): 41–81.

———. *The Renaissance of Lesbianism in Early Modern England.* Cambridge: Cambridge University Press, 2002.

Traub, Valerie, M. Lindsay Kaplan, and Dympna Callaghan, eds. *Feminist Readings of Early Modern Culture.* Cambridge: Cambridge University Press, 1996.

Trudgill, Peter. "Third-Person Singular Zero." In *East Anglian English.* Ed. Jacek Fisiak and Peter Trudgill. Cambridge: D. S. Brewer, 2001. 179–86.

Turner, James Grantham. "'News from the New Exchange': Commodity, Erotic Fantasy, and the Female Entrepreneur." In *The Consumption of Culture, 1600–1800: Image, Object, Text.* Ed. Ann Bermingham and Jon Brewer. London: Routledge 1995. 419–33.

Vaughan, Virginia Mason. *Performing Blackness on English Stages, 1500–1800.* Cambridge: Cambridge University Press, 2005.

Vigne, Randolph, and Charles Littleton, eds. *From Strangers to Citizens: The Integration of Immigrant Communities in Britain, Ireland, and Colonial America, 1550–1750.* Brighton: Sussex Academic Press, 2001.

Visser, Colin. "John Dryden's *Amboyna* at Lincoln's Inn Fields, 1673." *Restoration and 18th Century Theater Research* 15.1 (1976): 1–11.

Vitkus, Daniel J. *Turning Turk: English Theater and the Multicultural Mediterranean, 1570–1630.* New York: Palgrave Macmillan, 2003.

Wall, Wendy. *The Imprint of Gender: Authorship and Publication in the English Renaissance.* Ithaca, N.Y.: Cornell University Press, 1993.

———. *Staging Domesticity: Household Work and English Identity in Early Modern Drama.* Cambridge: Cambridge University Press, 2002.

Ward, Joseph. "Fictitious Shoemakers, Agitated Weavers and the Limits of Popular Xenophobia in Elizabethan London." In Vigne and Littleton, *From Strangers to Citizens,* 80–87.

Weiss, Adrian. "Casting Compositors, Foul Cases, and Skeletons: Printing in Middleton's Age." *Thomas Middleton and Early Modern Textual Culture.* Ed. Gary Taylor and John Lavagnino. Oxford: Oxford University Press, 2007. 195–225.

Welch, Charles. *Illustrated Account of the Royal Exchange and the Pictures Therein.* London: Johnson, Riddle, 1913.

Wickham, Glynne. *Early English Stages, 1300–1660.* Vol. 1. New York: Columbia University Press, 1980.

Williams, Gordon. *A Dictionary of Sexual Language and Imagery in Shakespearean and Stuart Literature.* 3 vols. London: Athlone Press, 1994.

Williams, Raymond. *Keywords: A Vocabulary of Culture and Society.* New York: Oxford University Press, 1976.

Willsdon, Clare A. P. "The Mural Decoration at the Royal Exchange." In Saunders, *The Royal Exchange,* 311–35.

Wine, Martin L. ed., *The Dutch Courtesan,* Regents Renaissance Drama series. Lincoln: University of Nebraska Press, 1965.

Withington, Robert. *English Pageantry: An Historical Outline.* Vol. 1. Cambridge, Mass.: Harvard University Press, 1918.

Worthen, William. "Prefixing the Author: Print, Plays, and Performance." In *A Companion to Shakespeare and Performance*. Ed. Barbara Hodgdon and W. B. Worthen. Malden, Mass.: Blackwell, 2005. 212–30.

Wrightson, Keith. *Earthly Necessities: Economic Lives in Early Modern Britain*. New Haven, Conn.: Yale University Press, 2000.

Young, Robert. *The Idea of English Ethnicity*. Malden, Mass.: Blackwell, 2008.

Yungblut, Laura Hunt. *Strangers Settled Here Amongst Us: Policies, Perceptions, and the Presence of Aliens in Elizabethan England*. London: Routledge, 1996.

———. "Straungers and Aliaunts: The 'Un-English' Among the English in Elizabethan England." In *Crossing Boundaries: Issues of Cultural and Individual Identity in the Middle Ages and the Renaissance*. Ed. Sally McKee. Turnhout: Brepols, 1999. 263–76.

Zimmerman, Susan, ed. *Erotic Politics: Desire on the Renaissance Stage*. New York: Routledge, 1992.

Zucker, Adam. "The Social Logic of Ben Jonson's *Epicoene*." *Renaissance Drama* 33 (2004): 37–62.

INDEX

Languages and Communities in Early Modern Europe (Burke), 89
Larum for London, A (anonymous), 118
Last East-Indian Voyage, The (anonymous), 198–200, 207
Latin language, 59, 93, 104, 149, 150
Leinwand, Theodore, 39
Le Mayre, Marten, 94, 140–42, 270n23
"Leo Belgicus" (Belgian Lion) maps, 78, 80, *81*
Lesser, Zachary, 116, 121–22, 277n16, 278n37, 281n59
lexicography, early modern, 35, 141, 152. *See also* dictionaries
Life and Death and Jack Straw (anonymous), 118
Like will to Like (Fulwell), 118, 274n2
likeness, 22, 28, 31–32, 183, 192, 238, 251n102, 256n142; typography and, 125; mise-en-page and, 149. *See also* approximation; similitude
Lingua Belgica (van der Myl), 73, 105
literature, national, 32
London, city of, 1, 11, 164; alien population, 12; Broadstreet Ward, 12; commercial and sexual traffic with Antwerp, 99, 172; cosmopolitanism, 12; Dutch residents/refugees in, 2–3, 7, 13, 38, 168; Dutch sex workers in, 43; Dutch speech on streets of, 102; East India Company and, 186; Great Fire (1666), 164, 171, 286n9; Mercer's Company, 172; Old Exchange (Gresham's Burse), 170–72, 174–75, 184, 236; poetic geography of, 167, 286n9; population surveys, 92–93, 270n16; sexual geographies of, 2, 3. *See also* Royal Exchange
London and the Country Carbonadoed and Quartered into Several Characters (Lupton), 174
London Prodigal, The (anonymous), 117, 119
Loomba, Ania, 21
Loureiro, Rui Manuel, 198
Low Countries, as place, 8, 12, 16, 104, 152, 262n2; battles with Spain, 2, 10, 176; black letter printing in, 156; English love for, 40–42; Family of Love and, 42, 47; languages of, 14–15, 93; maps of, 74–76, *75–81*, 80, 83; as sexual pun, 1–3, 41, 55; paradoxical representation of, 17–18; Spanish oppression in, 7, 38. *See also* Netherlands

Lupton, Donald, 174
Luson, Sir Richard, 196
Luu, Lien Bich, 270n16

Madoet, André, 154
"Magnificent Entertainment Given to King James" (Dekker), 176, 177, 179–83
Magnificent Entertainment of King James, The (Dekker), 36, 167
Malay language, 205, 295n29
Manley, Lawrence, 175
Margaret of Parma, 7
Marian drama, 23, 34, 272n35
Markley, Robert, 216–17, 298n50
Marlowe, Christopher, 21
marriage: Anglo-Dutch marriages in London, 9, 11, 38, 177, 244n29; Anglo-Dutch rivalry in Dryden's *Amboyna* and, 228–29, 299n66; intra-European, 60
Marston, John, 32, 33, 46, 117
martyrology, 49
Marvell, Andrew, 17–19, 76, 80, 249n81
Masque of Augures (Jonson), 280–81n50; black letter type in, 117, 119, 136, 137, 281n50; performance of, 277n19; typography and typology in, 135–37
McKenzie, D. F., 113, 275n8, 280n45
Mechanick Exercises on the Whole Art of Printing (Moxon), 117
Mennonites, 49
Mercator, Gerhard, 34, 69, 78. *See also Atlas sive*
Metcalf, George, 94
Meteren, Emanuel van, 86–87
Middleton, Sir Henry, 198, 199
Middleton, Thomas, 1, 19, 32, 34; black letter type and, 117; on Familists, 48; on language and identity, 94–95. *See also Any Thing for a Quiet Life; Father Hubburds Tales; No Wit; Roaring Girl*
Milton, John, 255n16
Minsheu, John, 157
Mish, Charles, 121
Molière, 89
Moluccas (Malukan Islands), 198, 207, 208, 226, 298n57
monolingualism, 108, 109
Monsieur Thomas (Fletcher), 52
Montgomery, Marianne, 272n35
Montrose, Louis, 192, 233–34
Moors/Moorish culture, representation of, 23, 83, 227

ACKNOWLEDGMENTS

This project began at the University of Michigan among a fellowship of colleagues and friends who gave rise to many of my greatest inspirations and debts. Members of the Early Modern Colloquium encouraged and enriched this project with generosity of conversation, rigorous and encouraging feedback, and good-spirited celebration of the finish lines along the way. Laura Williamson-Ambrose, Amy Rodgers, Ari Friedlander, and Stephen Spiess read chapters in progress and offered invaluable insights, for which I will always be grateful. For their generosity of conversation and intellectual conviviality, I thank Kentston Bauman, Gina Bloom, Holly Dugan, Jennie Evenson, Gavin Hollis, William Ingram, Michael MacDonald, Steven Mullaney, Patricia Simons, and Doug Trevor. For his enthusiastic support of this project from the start and for his wonderful questions, I thank Michael Schoenfeldt. Anne Herrmann and Celeste Brusati are encouraging interlocutors and models for how to offer brilliant advice that illuminates the way forward. Most of all, I am indebted to Valerie Traub, who has shaped this project and my path in the profession in the most inspiring ways. She divines in the fault lines of my work the questions that most deeply motivate me, and emboldens me to pursue them. I never feel more alive to the world of ideas, or more delighted by the pursuit of the paradoxes therein, than in my conversations with Valerie.

Research for this project was completed at the British Library, the Mercers' Company of London, the Cambridge University Library, the University of Michigan Special Collections Library, the Folger Shakespeare Library, the Newberry Library, the Thomas Fisher Rare Book Library, and the Huntington Library. I thank the librarians and staff at these institutions for their expert and generous assistance. For their many kindnesses and patience with requests large and small, I thank the Huntington Library's Reader Services Department, especially Christopher Adde, Guan Gomez, Kadin Henningsen,

Jaeda Snow, Laura Stalker, and Catherine Wehrey. A world always in bloom with an abundance of rare books, generous colleagues, and warm camaraderie, the Huntington has been a home away from home. For generously responding to drafts in progress, while also serving up great meals and spirited good laughs, I am grateful to my Los Angeles reading group: Will Fisher, Rebecca Lemon, Heidi Brayman Hackel, and Carla Mazzio. For conversations that have shaped how I have pursued this project and my professional development, I am grateful to Frances Dolan. For trenchant and encouraging responses to my manuscript, I thank Emma Smith and an anonymous reader for the University of Pennsylvania Press. For generously sharing their scholarship with me before its appearance in print, I am grateful to Jean Howard and Andy Fleck. Kim Hall's Folger Shakespeare Library seminar provided me with a timely opportunity to develop the ideas that would take shape in the final chapter of this book. Alison Hobgood, whom I had the good fortune to meet there, has been a generous interlocutor, reader, and friend ever since. The Newberry Library generously supported a one-day symposium on Anglo-Dutch relations in a global context. I am grateful to Kristina Bross for co-organizing that symposium with me, to Carla Zecher and Karen Christianson for orchestrating a seamless event, and to the participants and audience who offered such rich insights. Finally, I want to thank the participants in my Shakespeare Association of America seminar on "Likeness" for venturing so creatively and broadly across the terrain of that topic with me.

This book has been supported by a number of grants and fellowships. I want to thank the Departments of English and Women's Studies and the Center for European Studies at the University of Michigan for grants that supported travel to rare book libraries. An Andrew W. Mellon foundation fellowship, granted by the University of Warwick and Newberry Library, enabled me to spend a remarkable summer researching in England and participating in an interdisciplinary seminar on the built environment. The model for cross-disciplinary conversation that was made manifest over the course of that summer continues to inform my research and teaching. I am especially grateful to Steve Hindle, who extended such warm hospitality and orchestrated a truly challenging and successful series of discussions among social historians, art historians, and literary critics that summer. Finally, I am grateful to the Connaught Foundation for a new researcher award, which allowed me to complete my research and writing, and to the Department of English at the University of Toronto for granting me a semester research leave.

For their generous responses to my work over the years, I am grateful to my colleagues at the University of Toronto: Peter Blayney, David Galbraith, Elizabeth Harvey, Katie Larson, Jeremy Lopez, Stephen Johnson, Lynne Magnusson, Randy McLeod, Mary Nyquist, Holger Schott Syme, Paul Stevens, Leslie Thompson, and Chris Warley. Nicholas Terpstra deserves special thanks for joining me, with his characteristic enthusiasm and intellectual rigor, in bridging the gap between the Departments of English and History to co-organize a series of workshops, graduate course offerings, and a conference wherein I refined many of the ideas that appear on these pages. The Jackman Humanities Institute provided funding and a welcome space for our cross-disciplinary dialogues. Christine Bolus-Reichert and Alan Bewell are remarkable chairs, both of whom have supported the balance and integration of my research and teaching life. Malcolm Campbell, Vice-Principal of Research, has also offered invaluable institutional support for this project. For sharing his unrivaled knowledge of the Thomas Fisher Rare Book library with me, I thank Scott Schofield. For his meticulous work preparing the manuscript for press, I am grateful beyond measure to Noam Lior. I also thank Sarah Ash Georgi and David Adkins for their editorial assistance.

I could not have hoped for a more insightful, gracious and supportive editor than Jerome Singerman. It has been a true pleasure working with him. At the University of Pennsylvania Press, I am also grateful to Robert Milks for his copyediting. Caroline Hayes, Noreen O'Connor-Abel, and Caroline Winschel were also instrumental in preparing this book for press. Two of the chapters have appeared in earlier forms. Chapter 1 first appeared in *English Literary Renaissance* Winter 40.1 (2010): 88–112. I am grateful to the editor, Arthur Kinney, for permission to reprint it here. Chapter 5 first appeared as "An Urban Palimpsest: Migrancy, Architecture, and the Making of an Anglo-Dutch Royal Exchange," in *Dutch Crossing: A Journal of Low Countries Studies* 33.1. (April 2009): 23–43. While it has been revised and expanded since, I am grateful to Manely Publishers for permission to reprint significant portions of it here.

Since this study is about proximate relations, it perhaps goes without saying that an especially important role was played by those closest to me. For the joys of friendship and for knowing just when (not) to ask about the book, I thank Laura Williamson-Ambrose, Stephanie Heck, Elspeth Healey, Monique Hyman, Mary Davis, and Linda Rubright. Marc Amodio, John Miles Foley, and William Kerwin have been extraordinary teachers and friends. For their celebratory welcome whenever I walk through their doors,

I thank my beloved aunts, Ginny Dimpfl and Glenn Rubright. And finally, I wish to thank my parents. They have always encouraged my intellectual curiosities, supported my love of language and literature, and indulged my digressions over word choice during debates at the dinner table. For their faith in me, I am delighted to have this opportunity to say thank you.